AMERICAN
GOVERNMENT

This brief textbook highlights the tension between constitutional democracy and populism in American government, focusing on questions of constitutionalism. In this well-written book, Cal Jillson gets students to ask key questions regarding the dynamic, complicated relationship between contemporary populism and government institutions in an interesting and well-executed departure from his usual American political development focus.

Mark C. Miller, *Clark University*

This timely text is a fantastic resource for students and professors, focusing on the most pressing issue facing America today: the functioning of our constitutional democracy amid increasing partisanship, polarization, and populism. The book is well-written, well-organized, and well-focused on the concepts, theories, and history that will allow students to engage the big questions of the modern day.

Morgan Hazelton, *Saint Louis University*

Cal Jillson's new brief textbook is outstanding. With a well-researched, comprehensive set of historical analyses and effective writing style that is clear and flows well, it will be easy for American Government students to follow. I will surely use it in the future, and highly recommend it!

Benjamin J. Kassow, *University of North Dakota*

In *American Government: Constitutional Democracy Under Pressure*, Cal Jillson provides an accessible and engaging treatment of the U.S. federal government. Understanding the formal and practical features of the Republic has arguably never been more important than in the midst of these challenging times. Constitutionally designed to lean into the winds of change, the structure and flows of the Republic are wonderfully elucidated and explained by Jillson in this text.

John W. Patty, *University of Chicago*

AMERICAN

GOVERNMENT

Constitutional Democracy Under Pressure

CAL JILLSON

Southern Methodist University

Routledge
Taylor & Francis Group

NEW YORK AND LONDON

Published 2018
by Routledge
711 Third Avenue, New York, NY 10017

and by Routledge
2 Park Square, Milton Park, Abingdon, Oxon, OX14 4RN

Routledge is an imprint of the Taylor & Francis Group, an informa business

Visit the eResources: https://www.routledge.com/9780815375753

Library of Congress Cataloging in Publication Data
Names: Jillson, Calvin C., 1949- author.
Title: American government : constitutional democracy under pressure /
    Cal Jillson, Southern Methodist University.
Description: New York, NY : Routledge, 2019. | Includes bibliographical
    references and index.
Identifiers: LCCN 2018001479| ISBN 9780815375746 (hbk) |
    ISBN 9780815375753 (pbk) | ISBN 9781351239226 (ebk)
Subjects: LCSH: United States—Politics and government. |
    Democracy—United States. | Political culture—United States. |
    Polarization (Social sciences)—Political aspects—United States.
Classification: LCC JK275 .J55 2019 | DDC 320.473—dc23
LC record available at https://lccn.loc.gov/2018001479

ISBN: 9780815375746 (hbk)
ISBN: 9780815375753 (pbk)
ISBN: 9781351239226 (ebk)

Typeset in ITC Giovanni
by Swales & Willis Ltd, Exeter, Devon, UK

TO JANE

"In framing a government which is to be administered by men over men, the great difficulty lies in this: you must first enable the government to control the governed; and in the next place to oblige it to control itself."

James Madison, *Federalist* No. 51, 1788

CONTENTS

SPECIAL FEATURES ix

PREFACE xiii

ACKNOWLEDGMENTS xix

THE AUTHOR xxi

Chapter 1 THE REVOLUTION AND THE CONSTITUTION 1

Chapter 2 FEDERALISM AND THE AMERICAN CONSTITUTIONAL ORDER 35

Chapter 3 CIVIL LIBERTIES: DEMOCRACY AND THE EXPANSION OF LIBERTY'S REALM 63

Chapter 4 CIVIL RIGHTS: WHERE LIBERTY AND EQUALITY COLLIDE 92

Chapter 5 SHAPING AMERICANS: POLITICAL SOCIALIZATION, PUBLIC OPINION, AND THE MEDIA 122

Chapter 6 FACTIONS TODAY: INTEREST GROUPS AND POLITICAL PARTIES 152

Chapter 7 DEMOCRACY'S MOMENT: VOTING, CAMPAIGNS, AND ELECTIONS 184

Chapter 8 CONGRESS: PARTISANSHIP, POLARIZATION, AND GRIDLOCK 217

Chapter 9 THE EXECUTIVE BRANCH: THE PRESIDENT, THE BUREAUCRACY, AND EXECUTIVE POWER 251

Chapter 10 THE FEDERAL COURTS: ORIGINALISM VERSUS LIVING CONSTITUTIONALISM 285

Appendix A THE DECLARATION OF INDEPENDENCE A-1

Appendix B CONSTITUTION OF THE UNITED STATES B-1

Appendix C FEDERALIST NUMBERS 10, 51, AND 78 C-1

INDEX I-1

SPECIAL FEATURES

THE CONSTITUTION TODAY

CHAPTER 1   The Founders and the People   2
CHAPTER 2   If Marijuana Is Illegal, Why Are They Selling It in California?   36
CHAPTER 3   The Second Amendment and Gun Rights in America   64
CHAPTER 4   Sexual Privacy, the Ninth Amendment, and Unenumerated Rights   93
CHAPTER 5   What Explains the U.S. Commitment to the Death Penalty?   123
CHAPTER 6   The First Amendment Rights to Assemble and Petition, and Their Limits   153
CHAPTER 7   Is the Electoral College Outdated?   185
CHAPTER 8   The Census, Reapportionment, and Gerrymandering   218
CHAPTER 9   The Unitary Executive Theory of Presidential Authority   252
CHAPTER 10   Does the Constitution Envision Judicial Review?   286

PRO & CON BOXES

CHAPTER 1   Do We Need a Bill of Rights?   28
CHAPTER 2   The Continuing Relevance of States' Rights   50
CHAPTER 3   Defending the USA Patriot Act (2001–Present)   82
CHAPTER 4   Recognizing Gay Marriage   96
CHAPTER 5   Is the Media Biased?   132
CHAPTER 6   Black Commitment to the Democratic Party   173
CHAPTER 7   Is the Supreme Court Right to See Money as Speech   210
CHAPTER 8   Should Representatives Represent Their Consciences or Their Constituents?   226
CHAPTER 9   Must Presidents Have the Initiative in War-Making?   263
CHAPTER 10   Does the U.S. Political System Need Judicial Activism to Work?   310

TABLES

1.1 The Virginia and New Jersey Plans 20

1.2 State Ratification of the Proposed Constitution 26

2.1 Strengths and Weaknesses of Federalism 37

2.2 The Evolution of American Federalism 58

3.1 The Incorporation Doctrine: A Timeline 68

6.1 Political Parties in Democratic Politics 167

6.2 Party Identification in the Electorate, 1952–2016 (Seven-Point Scale) 169

6.3 Party Identification in the Electorate, 1952–2016 (Three-Point Scale) 171

7.1 Voting Turnout by Population Characteristics, 1972–2016 189

8.1 Differences between the House and the Senate 226

8.2 Major Committees in the Contemporary Congress 234

8.3 Senate Action on Cloture Motions, 1950–Present 239

8.4 Major Steps in Preparation of the Fiscal Year 2018 Budget 244

9.1 Treaties and Executive Agreements, 1789–2017 265

9.2 Presidential Vetoes and Overrides, 1933–2016 268

9.3 Demographic Characteristics of the Federal Bureaucracy 271

9.4 Cabinet Departments of the U.S. Government 272

9.5 Membership, Terms, and Partisan Balance of Major Federal Regulatory Agencies 273

10.1 Number of Federal Statutes Held Unconstitutional by the Supreme Court, 1790–2014 292

10.2 Number of State Laws and Local Ordinances Held Unconstitutional by the Supreme Court, 1790–2014 293

10.3 Demographic Characteristics of Federal Judicial Appointments, Presidents Johnson through Obama 300

FIGURES

1.1 Two Methods of Amending the Constitution 25

2.1 Percent of Government Expenditures by Level of Government, 1902–2016 51

3.1 The U.S. Incarceration Rate, 1930–2015 86

4.1 Family Income by Race, 1947–2014 110

4.2 Median Income by Gender, 1947–2015 117

5.1 How Do Americans Feel about Their Government? 142

5.2 Distribution of Ideological Identification 144

5.3 A Two-Dimensional View of Political Ideology in America 145

6.1 Presidential Support in Congress 175

6.2 Party Unity Scores in the House and Senate 177

7.1 Electoral College Map for 2016 204

7.2 Spending by Presidential Campaigns, 1976–2016 208

8.1 Number of Women and Minorities in Congress, 1953–2017 223

8.2 Percent of U.S. House and Senate Members Standing for Reelection Who Are Reelected, 1946–2016 225

8.3 Leadership Structures in the U.S. House and Senate 229

8.4 The Traditional Legislative Process: How a Bill Becomes a Law 235

8.5 Public Disapproval of Congress, 1974–2016 245

9.1 Ranking the Performance of U.S. Presidents 259

9.2 Presidential Approval: Presidential Job Performance Ratings, 1937–Present 266

9.3 Executive Office of the President 277

10.1 Boundaries for Circuit Courts of Appeals 296

10.2 How a Case Gets to the Supreme Court 297

PREFACE

American Government: Constitutional Democracy Under Pressure is a modestly foreboding title. But few, certainly not American government teachers and their students, have watched the struggles of the Trump administration without being aware of the tension between the structure of our political institutions and the ideological, partisan, and populist politics of our time. Still, it takes just a moment's thought to recall that President Obama was stymied during the last six years of his administration, both Bushes left office in disappointment, and Bill Clinton was impeached though not convicted during his presidency. Our constitutional democracy has been under pressure for some time, but fears for its fate have deepened in just the past few years. This new book offers to help American Government teachers lead their students to a nuanced theoretical and practical understanding of Constitutional Democracy and of what is happening in and to ours.

Constitutional democracy is democracy constrained. The Founders believed that a written constitution, with limited and separated powers, checks and balances, federalism, a bill of rights, and an empowered people and press would authorize and protect both government and liberty. The U.S. Constitution was designed to make governing slow and deliberate, but it was not designed to make it impossible or even unsteady. Nevertheless, we must acknowledge that our modern politics have become increasingly partisan, polarized, and populist and our political institutions have struggled to govern in ways that citizens accept as valid and see as effective.

How concerned should we be about the state of our politics. After all, the Founders designed the Constitution both to frustrate populist insurgencies and to require compromise, even of passionate majorities. Presidents arriving in Washington flushed with victory and with partisan majorities in Congress, whether Barack Obama with the adulation of Grant Park still fresh in his mind or Donald Trump with a blue collar uprising pushing him to unexpected victory, feel entitled to enact their agenda and are disappointed when opposition soon arises to check their momentum. However, Obama was a former constitutional law professor, so he understood and respected, even if he struggled against, the constraints that the Constitution placed on his powers and options. Trump, a real estate tycoon and reality television star, become an insurgent populist candidate for the Republican presidential nomination and then a somewhat populist president is—shall we say—less predictable. How Donald Trump will respond to the frustration of our Constitutional Democracy is the question of the moment.

What makes American politics feel especially uncertain today is that populism directly challenges constitutionalism. We are familiar with partisanship, Democrats versus Republicans, and ideology, conservatives versus liberals, but populism is different. Populism is more a perspective on politics than it is a partisan or ideological commitment. That is why we see populist insurgencies on the left and the right. A few years ago, both the Occupy Wall Street movement and the Tea Party movement were described as populist and in 2016 both Bernie Sanders and Donald Trump were so described. Though these movements and candidates differed in many ways, they all shared a distinctly populist conviction that politics is "us against them," the people against an entrenched and corrupt elite intent on serving their own purposes and interests. The Founders mistrusted populist insurgencies so they built our constitutional democracy to check, at least for a time, just the kinds of populist passions that we see at large in our nation today.

American Government: Constitutional Democracy Under Pressure highlights the necessary tension between our constitutional principles and institutions and the populist heat that sometimes roils our national politics. We assume that our political institutions will limit and contain contemporary populism, just as the Founders intended and as these institutions have in the past, but will they? An increasingly polarized electorate, urging their representatives to fight and never compromise, will put our *Constitutional Democracy Under Pressure*, and ultimately, perhaps, under threat, just as the subtitle of this new book suggests.

I have chosen to write the brief American government text that you have before you rather than a book three times its size, because faculty know too much that is fascinating and students have too many interesting questions for any book to try to anticipate and address them all. What I have tried to do is to describe how the American political system works, why it seems to struggle in so many ways, and what the general range of possibilities, both for continuity and for change, seem to be. Where the conversation goes from there is up to students and their teachers, as it should be.

To students, I hope to say more than that politics is important, that it will affect your lives, time and again, continuously, and in important ways. I hope to provide a sense of how politics works so that when an issue arises about which you care deeply you will not feel helpless. Politics is not just a spectator sport. Rather, it is a sport in which all who turn out make the team and all who come to practice get to start—not always with the varsity, to be sure, but politics is a game that we are all entitled to play. To faculty teaching American government, I hope to help you communicate to your students both what we know as political scientists and how much fun we had in being part of the process of discovering it and teaching about it.

FEATURES

This new brief *American Government* text contains several important learning and engagement features.

The Constitution Today

"The Constitution Today" opens each chapter with a vignette that highlights the continuing relevance, even centrality, of the Constitution to our most critical modern political debates and controversies. The United States is very unusual in this regard. The Founders invented the idea of a written constitution resting on the foundation of popular sovereignty. Many nations now have written constitutions, but no nation reveres its constitution the way Americans do theirs. Moreover, no nation gives its constitution the central role that Americans do in shaping the outcome of important substantive political debates and battles. But few today would deny that our Constitution is under great stress from a populist polarization that roils our politics—deepening partisan divisions among our people and deadlock among our governing institutions. This book explores the sources of these dangerous pressures and how they might be relieved.

In each chapter we highlight the relevance of key provisions of the Constitution to our most important contemporary political battles. The first chapter of this book deals with the origins of American political principles and how those principles informed and shaped the Declaration of Independence and the Constitution. We open the chapter with an exploration of what the Founders meant by the Constitution's opening phrase, "We the People." This feature, "The Constitution Today," spotlights the way that the provisions of the Constitution shape and structure our fights over issues like gay marriage, gun control, campaign contributions and free speech, states rights, congressional redistricting, health care reform, domestic surveillance, war powers, and much more. These vignettes bring to life provisions of the Constitution by highlighting the critical issues that they decide. They are identified in the text by the following symbol:

The Constitution TODAY

Focus Questions

Each chapter opens with a set of focus questions that prepare the student for the major points made in the chapter. The questions later appear in the margin where the text addresses that particular question, allowing students to easily scan the chapter for a quick review after they have completed their reading.

Pro & Con Boxes

"Pro & Con" features offer opposing viewpoints on controversial issues currently in the news. For example, what are the arguments, Pro & Con, for the continuing relevance of states' rights, seeing money as speech, judicial activism, and federal resistance to marijuana sales in the states.

Struggling Toward Democracy Boxes

In each chapter, "Struggling Toward Democracy" boxes will feature several brief references to striking people, events, and facts that highlight the ongoing struggle to realize and refine our democracy.

What Do You Think?

We include a feature called "What Do You Think?" Throughout the book, where an important and interesting question has been discussed, we pose a couple of questions designed to make students stop and think. These are also an invitation to teachers to pause the lecture and engage the class in a discussion of an important issue.

End-of-Chapter Features

Each chapter closes with a summary, a list of key terms, and suggestions for additional reading. Finally, students also are directed to the Internet for more information on topics discussed in the text. At the end of each chapter are URLs that direct students to further information on issues, institutions, groups, and data discussed in the book.

Online Instructor Resources

A full Test Bank for all chapters, with multiple choice, true-false, and open ended questions, is available to professors as a password-protected Word document on the eResource tab on the Web page for the book.

PLAN OF THE BOOK

American Government: Constitutional Democracy Under Pressure is divided into ten chapters. Each chapter begins with a vignette and several focus questions designed to introduce and display the main themes of the chapter. The subject matter of each chapter is presented in five or six major sections, with each major section divided internally into subsections, in explicit outline form, so that it is easy for students to understand and study.

Chapters 1 through 4 present the political principles and constitutional foundations of American politics. Chapter 1 describes the social, economic, and political institutions that were in place in the American colonies as the Revolution approached. The historical and practical knowledge of the revolutionary generation provided the menu of institutional possibilities from which they chose as they designed their state governments, the Articles of Confederation, and later the U.S. Constitution. Chapter 2 describes changes in the broad structure of American federalism as the nation evolved from agriculture, to industrial powerhouse, to global superpower. Chapters 3 and 4 link the changing scope and character of our civil liberties and civil rights to the evolving character of our society.

Chapters 5 through 7 describe how Americans learn about politics, organize their thinking about politics, and come together in interest groups and political parties to affect the course of politics. Chapter 5 describes how Americans get their political information, what the distribution of partisan and political opinion among Americans looks like, and the role that the media play in determining which political issues and what political information comes to our collective attention. Chapter 6 describes how Americans come together in interest groups and political parties to press their ideas, interests, and demands for change on government. Chapter 7 describes how citizens, variously informed and organized, use the process of campaigns, elections, and voting to select their political leaders and, much more broadly, the policies that their leaders will implement.

Chapters 8 through 10 describe the major institutions of the national government and how they relate to each other and to the problems and issues that confront them. Chapter 8 describes the structure of the Congress and the legislative process through which it seeks to represent and respond to the ideas, needs, and interests at large in the country. Chapter 9 describes the range of responsibilities and expectations that confront the American president and the American presidency. Chapter 10 presents the structure of the federal judiciary and the ongoing controversy over whether its role should be one of judicial activism or of judicial restraint.

ACKNOWLEDGMENTS

Many debts were incurred in the writing and production of this book. My greatest debt remains to all the authors who went before and upon whom I had the good fortune to draw. Completion of this brief edition of *American Government* leaves me with a renewed sense of pleasure and pride in our collective enterprise—political science.

Much of this sense of pleasure and pride comes from remembering how many fine people contributed to the conception, development, and completion of this book, particularly the Routledge team and the reviewers. Jennifer Knerr, acquisitions editor, was unwavering in support of this enterprise. The team that she assembled eased my way tremendously. Ze'ev Sudry, Anna Dolan and Colin Morgan pulled all of the pieces together in the end and actually made a book of the raw materials that I provided them. Thanks also to John Pottenger for his work on the Test Bank.

I owe special thanks to the wonderful support staff of the Political Science Department and the John Tower Center for Political Studies at Southern Methodist University. Several colleagues, including Dennis Ippolito, the late Dennis Simon, Joe Kobylka, Brad Carter, Matthew Wilson, and Jim Hollifield came to my aid more frequently than either they or I would like to remember.

Finally, the expertise and patience of friends and colleagues around the country were shamelessly exploited. Among the reviewers, whose invaluable and constructive feedback I've incorporated throughout the book, were Morgan L.W. Hazelton, Saint Louis University; Benjamin Kassow, University of North Dakota; Mark C. Miller, Clark University; Michael G. Miller, Barnard College; Glenn W. Richardson Jr., Kutztown University of Pennsylvania; and Steven White, Lafayette College.

Credits for the Chapter opener images are as follows:

Chapter 1: AP Photo/J. David Ake
Chapter 2: AP Photo/Eric Risberg
Chapter 3: AP Photo/SIPPL Sipa USA/Erik McGregor
Chapter 4: AP Photo/SIPPL Sipa USA/Alex Milan Tracy
Chapter 5: AP Photo/Rex Features/Paul Sancya

Chapter 6: AP Photo/Todd Kirkland
Chapter 7: AP Photo/Elaine Thompson
Chapter 8: AP Photo/Manuel Balce Ceneta
Chapter 9: AP Photo/Alex Brandon
Chapter 10: AP Photo/Human Rights Campaign/Kevin Wolf

THE AUTHOR

Cal Jillson earned a PhD from the University of Maryland and has taught at Louisiana State University and the University of Colorado, where he chaired the Department of Political Science from 1989 to 1993. He joined the faculty of Southern Methodist University in 1995 as professor and chair of the Department of Political Science (1995–2001). He is a member of the American Political Science Association and several regional political science associations. Professor Jillson has written a number of books dealing with the origins of the American political culture and the health and performance of contemporary American politics and political institutions. His recent books were *American Government: Political Development and Institutional Change*, 9th ed., 2018; *Lone Star Tarnished: A Critical Look at Texas Politics and Public Policy*, 3rd ed., 2018; *Texas Politics: Governing the Lone Star State*, 6th ed., 2017; and *The American Dream in History, Politics, and Fiction*, 2017.

Chapter 1

THE REVOLUTION
AND THE CONSTITUTION

Focus Questions: from reading to thinking

Q1 What circumstances led Europeans to leave their homelands to settle in America?

Q2 What are the decisive events and arguments that produced the American Revolution?

Q3 What changes in institutional design and allocation of powers were reflected in the first state constitutions?

Q4 How did the Virginia and New Jersey Plans differ about the kind of national government that each envisioned?

Q5 What role did the debate over a bill of rights play in the adoption of the U.S. Constitution?

The Constitution TODAY

THE FOUNDERS AND THE PEOPLE

Preamble to the Constitution (in part): "We the People of the United States, in Order to form a more perfect Union, . . . do ordain and establish this Constitution for the United States of America."

Article IV, section 4 (in part): "The United States will guarantee to every State in this Union a Republican Form of Government."

Most of the Founders, though not all, respected the common people even if they did not fully trust them. Because they were ambivalent about the political capacities of the common people, the Founders set out to build a republican form of government—not a democracy. Sorting out how the Founders felt about "the People" will help us understand why they favored republics and feared democracies.

The Founders believed that stable government rested on the consent of the governed, but most did not believe that the people could or should govern directly. The Constitutional Convention of 1787, which drafted the U.S. Constitution, debated the strengths and weaknesses of the people and the roles that they might play in government. One of the delegates most skeptical of the people was Alexander Hamilton of New York. On June 18, relatively early in the convention, Hamilton made a long speech in which he declared; "The people are turbulent and changing; they seldom judge or determine right." Hamilton was not alone. John Dickinson of Pennsylvania and Delaware, in an extended debate on voter qualification on August 7, declared that, "the freeholders of the Country . . . [were] the best guardians of liberty; And . . . a necessary defence agst. the dangerous influence of those multitudes without property & without principle."

Others took a more generous view of the people's rights and abilities. In the same August 7 debate mentioned above, Benjamin Franklin favored a broad suffrage and "expressed his dislike of every thing that tended to debase the spirit of the common people." Virginia's George Mason put the whole question of voting rights in a more modern framework, warning that, "We all feel too strongly the remains of ancient prejudices, . . . A Freehold is the qualification in England, & hence it is imagined to be the only proper one. The true idea . . . was that every man having evidence of attachment to & permanent common interest with the Society ought to share in all its rights and privileges."

James Madison, as he so often did, sought the middle ground. The people, Madison thought, should have the responsibility for selecting local officials, state legislators, and members of the lower house of Congress; but then, in his famous phrase, the people's choices should be subject to "successive filtrations" in search of the best men to serve in higher offices. Madison advocated popular election of members of the lower house of Congress, but no more. State legislatures would select U.S. senators, the Electoral College would select the president, and the president, with the advice and consent of the Senate, would select high officials of the executive branch, judges, ambassadors, and military officers.

An ancient prejudice even stronger than that in favor of freehold suffrage was that opposed to democracy. Since Plato and Aristotle in ancient Athens, democracy had been defined narrowly to mean direct democracy—government immediately by the people themselves. Madison stated the distinction between democracy and republic in *Federalist* No. 14; writing that, "in a democracy, the people meet and exercise the government in person; in a republic they assemble and administer it by their representatives and agents. [Elected representatives] refine and enlarge the public views, by passing them through the medium of a chosen body of citizens, whose wisdom may best discern the true interest of their country." Everyone understood that the new nation was too large to be a direct democracy, but they worried that the democratic elements of the new government, limited though they might be, could produce tumult.

Over the course of the Constitutional Convention, James Madison and others came to believe that a written constitution allowed institutions to be carefully constructed to limit and separate power, to allow officeholders to watch and check each other, and to define and secure the liberty of citizens. In this chapter, we see the Founders move tentatively toward independence, and then, after a period of instability, confront the complexity of building their republican form of government—what today, after 230 years and several critical constitutional amendments, we call a constitutional democracy.

The Founders were an educated, accomplished, confident elite wrestling with questions and problems that they knew were unprecedented. A few, like John Adams, James Madison, and Thomas Jefferson, were deeply read in ancient and contemporary European history and politics and most were broadly familiar with these topics. All knew that human history was the story of chiefs and warlords, kings and tyrants, ruling the mass of common people in their own interest and for their own benefit. Ancient chieftains won and held dominance by raw force. Sometimes, as with the Roman Republic in the centuries before the birth of Christ, law would seem for a time to control force, only to fall again as Julius Caesar or his kind swept to power.

As late as the seventeenth century, European monarchs claimed to hold their thrones by "divine right," by the will and gift of God. These powerful claims left common people with a fearsome choice: obey or resist and, in resisting, risk the wrath of the king and of God. Most chose obedience until oppression forced another choice: fight or flee. Those who fought always looked for arguments to justify and explain their resistance and those who fled often gained the space to think anew. The English colonies in North America provided such space in abundance.

In this chapter, we survey the European history and colonial political experience upon which the Founders drew in thinking about what kinds of political institutions would well serve their newly independent nation. We describe their initial fumblings with state constitutions and the Articles of Confederation before turning to a more detailed consideration of the preparations for and struggles in the Constitutional Convention of 1787. To resolve populist concerns that this more powerful national government posed threats to the people's liberties, the first Congress added a Bill of Rights. The U.S. Constitution has

Thomas Hobbes thought that only a sovereign, an absolute monarch, could constrain self-interest and secure social peace and order.

individualism The idea that the people are the legitimate sources of political authority and that they have rights that government must respect.

more than weathered the tests of time; it has been tested throughout our history and is again being tested today.

THE ROOTS OF AMERICAN POLITICS

During the sixteenth and seventeenth centuries, traditionalists argued that social order required hierarchy and privilege while new voices proclaimed choice and opportunity for more, if never all, people. The steady rise of **individualism**, first in religious thought, then in politics, and later in economics, was the solvent that weakened and ultimately dissolved privileges and hierarchy as the dominant ways of thinking about social organization. Francis Bacon (1561–1626), Thomas Hobbes (1588–1679), John Locke (1632–1704), and Charles Secondat, the Baron de Montesquieu (1689–1755), represented the growing commitment to freedom and progress that would come to dominate thinking in Europe and America. Once the battle was won, this period became known as the Age of Reason. The idea that freedom has an order and structure of its own found its brightest moment in the era of the American Revolution.[1]

Francis Bacon believed that science, discovery, and invention work to the eternal benefit of human society. The sense that progress might characterize the future was a dramatic departure from both ancient and medieval views. Human history need not always collapse back into tyranny and barbarism. Christians need not merely suffer through life in this world in order to earn salvation in the next. Rather, social, economic, and political progress—perhaps interrupted now and again by backsliding and slippage, but always tending toward discovery and improvement—could be the new future of humanity in the world. Two centuries later, Bacon's optimism endeared him to Americans like Benjamin Franklin and Thomas Jefferson.

Unfortunately, English politics in the half-century following Bacon's death in 1626 seemed to mock this vision of peace and progress. England's rising middle class and its representatives in Parliament challenged the monarchy and landed aristocracy for the right to guide the nation's future. England's ruling elites fought back and the nation suffered the misery and violence of civil war.

For many, including Thomas Hobbes, the constant political conflict and frequent violence inspired such fear that absolute monarchy seemed the only way out. Hobbes' classic work, *Leviathan* (1651), argued that individual self-interest, unconstrained by political force, would produce a war of all against all in which life would be, in his memorable phrase, "solitary, poor, nasty, brutish, and short."[2] Only after an all-powerful monarch had established and assured peace was it even reasonable to think about social and economic progress. Hobbes thought that individualism without hierarchy would result in chaos. He was wrong. After nearly fifty years of political conflict and civil war, Parliament and England's new commercial middle class finally triumphed in the Glorious Revolution of 1688.

John Locke thought that the Glorious Revolution offered the opportunity of peace and security based on freedom and equality. In the second of his famous *Two Treaties of Government* (1689), Locke rejected divine right monarchy and, instead, reasoned that "Men being by Nature, all free, equal, and independent, no man can be subjected to the Political Power of another, without his own Consent, by agreeing with other Men to join and unite into a Community, for their comfortable, safe, and peaceable living one amongst another."[3] Clearly, free men, thinking about what kind of government would be most useful to them, would choose a limited, moderate, constitutional regime to protect rather than to threaten them. Locke's **social contract theory,** which held that only the consent of the governed can produce political legitimacy, peace, and prosperity, and Montesquieu's description of separation of powers as a means to limit and control government authority, underlay the political thinking of the American eighteenth century.[4]

North Wind Picture Archives

John Locke thought that the rule of law and limited government could produce peace and order.

Montesquieu made two points that shaped the thinking of the American Founders. The first was that a nation's institutions and laws must fit its people and their circumstances. Poverty and ignorance might require the strong hand of a monarch, but freedom and equality made moderate government, a government of laws and not of men, possible. The second was that political power was limited most effectively if the government's power was distributed across executive and legislative offices and institutions—separation of powers.

social contract theory
Argument identified with Hobbes and Locke that the legitimate origin of government is in the agreement of a free people.

Within less than a century, Adam Smith (1723–1790) had applied the ideas of free choice and consent to the economic realm, arguing that commerce and markets, when not regulated by the state, have a natural order too.[5] The implication was that hierarchy and compulsion were not required to assure peace and order in religious, political, and economic life. Peace and order were compatible with—in fact, they might require—freedom and choice as opposed to hierarchy and compulsion.

These ideas had to struggle for recognition in the societies of Europe, with their titled nobilities, state-supported churches, and managed economies. In America, on the other hand, questions about what kinds of political and economic institutions men would create if their society had none—questions that seemed merely academic in Europe—were of immediate and even urgent importance. Over time, as these new ideas influenced law and policy, Americans evolved from subjects to citizens.

01 What circumstances led Europeans to leave their homelands to settle in America?

Immigrants in a New Land

The English civil wars and similar disturbances in other European lands drove tens of thousands of settlers to America during the seventeenth century. Throughout the colonial period, individuals and groups fled religious persecution in their own countries to settle in America. Others fled poverty, starvation, and a seemingly permanent lack of economic opportunity. Still others fled from political oppression. Many of these early settlers sought to guarantee their new liberties by oppressing others, but they soon found that vast open spaces, cheap land, and a diverse population made freedom and toleration too difficult to deny. Ideas that were radical in Europe—individualism, freedom, liberty, and equality—seemed invited by the vast openness of America to fulfill themselves, at least for some.

Religious Persecution. Over the course of American colonial history, wave after wave of European immigrants were driven to American shores by a desire to worship God in a way denied them by authorities at home. The English Pilgrims and Puritans came first and they were followed by rising tides of English Quakers, French Huguenots, German Pietists, and many others.

English Pilgrims and Puritans came generally from among the middling merchants, artisans, yeomen, and husbandmen, usually free and often successful, but barred on the basis of their religious beliefs from advancing through the social and political hierarchies of the day. Puritan religious and secular leaders worked with Puritan parliamentary leaders to open up English society. Not surprisingly, the king, the established Anglican Church, and economic elites benefiting from royal favor opposed with force Puritan demands for religious freedom. Twenty-one thousand English Puritans led by John Winthrop and John Cotton departed for New England between 1620 and 1640. They were willing to sever ties to the place of their birth in exchange for the opportunity to build what they intended to be a more godly society in America.

Others facing religious oppression in their homelands made similar decisions. In 1682, the first English Quakers left for Pennsylvania to pursue William Penn's "holy experiment" in peace. Only three years later, Louis XIV's revocation of the Edict of Nantes, the century-old promise of toleration to Protestant French Huguenots, led fifteen thousand of them to flee to America. Several colonies, including Pennsylvania, Delaware, and Maryland, were established as safe havens for the oppressed of one or all of these religious groups.

Denial of Social and Economic Opportunity. Although religious motivations were strong, defeat in the social and economic struggles that swirled around the religious conflicts in England and the rest of Europe also helped to people America. For example, when Oliver Cromwell and Parliament rose up against Charles I and Archbishop Laud, defeat of the royalists in 1642 and again in 1651 led thousands to flee to the new settlements in Virginia. Even after Charles II was restored to the throne in 1660, the exodus to Virginia of land-hungry second and third sons and cousins of English country lords continued.

Longing for economic betterment that seemed impossible within the constrained social systems of Europe drove many to America. For most European men below the propertied classes, feudal restrictions made the prospect of

AP Photo/North Wind Picture Archives

Representation of the *Mayflower's* arrival in Plymouth Harbor with the first Pilgrims in 1620.

obtaining one's own land almost inconceivable. Visions of immense opportunity, of free or cheap land in a society that had no entrenched and oppressive hereditary aristocracy, energized the poor and even the middle classes to consider removal to America.

Nonetheless, few colonists came to America willing to live and let live. Most whites came, as the Puritans did, to establish societies in a particular form and for particular purposes. America, however, was simply too spacious, too open and bountiful, to permit elites to hold common men to patterns and purposes that were not their own. Throughout the colonial period, it was possible to go just down the road or just over the next hill to organize one's religious, political, or economic life just as one wished. Open space and a diverse population corroded hierarchy in colonial America.

As a result, when Roger Williams ran afoul of the orthodoxy of John Winthrop and John Cotton in Massachusetts, they could simply banish him, as they did, and he could simply flee south with his followers into what is now Rhode Island, which he did. Similarly, when Anne Hutchinson and her followers became too troublesome, they too were banished and made their way to Rhode Island.

Similarly, the arrival of the Scotch-Irish in Quaker Philadelphia beginning around 1720 was deeply troubling to the Quakers. The Quakers considered the Scotch-Irish to be dirty, ignorant, quarrelsome, violent, and given to heavy drink. The Quaker response was to hurry them through Philadelphia to the frontier. The Scotch-Irish, drawn forward by the promise of cheap land, filled the inland hills and valleys of Pennsylvania, Virginia, and the Carolinas.

Economic Opportunity and Social Fluidity. The social and economic openness of the British colonies in North America to white men during the eighteenth century was distinctive in the world. The populations of all of the colonies were overwhelmingly rural and agrarian. Even as late as 1765, only five American cities—Boston, New York, Newport, Philadelphia, and Charleston—could claim more than eight thousand inhabitants. These cities contained only 5 percent of the population, and fully eight in ten Americans drew their livings directly from the land. Throughout the colonial period, as William Penn noted, America was "a good poor Man's country." Although "land was easier to acquire, keep, work, sell, and will in the colonies than in any other place in the Atlantic world," it was the special combination of "cheap land, high wages, short supply, and increasing social mobility [that] permitted the worker to shift for himself with some hope of success."[6] Although great wealth was rare, sufficiency was available to the hardworking, and movement into the ranks of the gentry was open to the smart and the fortunate.

Still, to be entirely true to our early history, we must always keep clearly in mind that these lofty ideals applied only to propertied white men.[7] While we often describe freedom, liberty, and opportunity in colonial and founding America in general terms, they applied to white women through their fathers and husbands, and they applied to Indians and slaves not at all. American history has been and remains a slow and as yet incomplete unfolding of equal rights for all.

BACKGROUND TO THE REVOLUTION

Revolutions are inherently tumultuous affairs. Among the great revolutions of modern history—the American (1774–1781), the French (1787–1800), the Russian (1917–1921), and the Chinese (1911–1949)—most American historians have judged our revolution to have been less thoroughgoing, bloody, and socially divisive than the others. This reading promoted a smooth storyline from America wronged, to a just and moderate revolution, and the founding of the world's first popular, if not quite yet democratic, government. Contemporary historians, led by German-born, British-educated, University of Pittsburgh historian, Holger Hoock, author of *Scars of Independence: America's Violent Birth*, increasingly describe a violent national birth that left social and political traumas that never fully healed.[8]

The Colonial Political Environment

British rule rested lightly on the colonists in America. For the most part, although the opportunity to direct and control was always there, imperial administrators in London chose not to involve themselves deeply in the political and economic affairs of the colonies.

Political Control in Colonial America. The basic structures of the colonial governments varied little. Familiar ideas drawn from Locke and Montesquieu, popular sovereignty, separation of powers, checks and balances, representation, and bicameralism were present from the beginning.[9] Each colonial government was headed by a governor. Generally, governors were empowered to call and dismiss legislatures, collect taxes and propose expenditures, enforce imperial and colonial laws, command troops, and appoint officers of the executive branch. Behind each governor stood the power and majesty of the British king and Parliament.

There were, however, important limitations on the powers of the governors, and these limitations became tighter over time. Each governor faced a legislature composed primarily, if not exclusively, of colonials. Most of these colonial legislatures had an upper house selected by the governor and a lower house elected by the people. The upper house, often referred to as the Governor's Council, represented the interests of the governor and the empire to the lower house and to the people of the colony. The lower house, frequently called the House of Representatives, the House of Burgesses, or simply the Assembly, used the "power of the purse" to control and limit the independence of colonial governors. In almost every colony, the people's representatives gained the upper hand over the governor and his council.

The rights and responsibilities of citizenship also varied by colony. In all of the colonies there were limitations on who could vote. Most commonly, the limitations involved race, gender, and property holding. Moreover, most of the colonies had restrictions on office holding. These restrictions often increased with the prestige of the office or required that service in a less prestigious office precede service in a more prestigious office.[10] Nonetheless, the average white man in colonial America wielded an economic and political influence enjoyed by the mass of men in no other place on earth because most had access to property.

Adding Economic Muscle.   In the seventy-five years preceding the American Revolution, the people and economy of the British colonies in North America became self-sustaining. Between the year 1700 and independence, the population of the colonies doubled approximately every twenty years, rising from 250,000 to 2,500,000. As population grew, the domestic economy became more important and the burden of imperial regulations less obviously beneficial.[11]

Q2 What are the decisive events and arguments that produced the American Revolution?

Removal of the French Threat.   The political implications of the social and economic growth of the colonies were masked for a time by the presence of the French in Canada. This was particularly true while the massed forces of the British and French empires clashed worldwide between the mid-1750s and 1763 in the Seven Years War. In North America, this conflict was known as the French and Indian War. British victory in the Seven Years War made Canada a British colony, thereby removing the threat that hostile French troops had posed. Dangers still lurked all around, Indians on the frontier, the Spanish to the south and west, but the greatest threat of the past century had, it seemed, been removed.

The Assertion of British Imperial Authority.   The Seven Years War left England with a national debt twice what it had been before the war. In the view of the British government, because an important part of the war had been fought in North America, it seemed reasonable that the colonists would help address some of the debt. The American colonists took a different view. They regarded imposition of a tax designed to raise revenue in America to fill British coffers in London as a dramatic change of imperial relations.

Passage in Parliament of the Sugar Act late in 1764 and the Stamp Act early in 1765 brought protests and threats of boycott from individual colonial legislatures and from an intercolonial meeting called the **Stamp Act Congress**. Howls from London merchants that their valuable colonial trade was being harmed (what we would call interest group activity today) led Parliament in February 1766 to rescind the Stamp Act and to modify the Sugar Act.

To cover its retreat on the Stamp Act, Parliament passed the **Declaratory Act**, which restated its right to make laws binding on the American colonies "in all cases whatsoever." Relations remained strained between Parliament and the American colonies, erupting most strikingly in the **Boston Massacre** on March 5, 1770, and the **Boston Tea Party** on December 16, 1773. The Boston Tea Party was an act of civil disobedience in which the Boston Sons of Liberty, disguised as Indians, dumped three ship loads of tea into Boston Harbor rather than pay the taxes levied on it.

Parliament's reaction to continued colonial resistance was broad, firm, and inflammatory. Collectively, Parliament's actions have come to be known as the **Intolerable Acts**. First, General Thomas Gage, commander of the British troops in Boston, was appointed governor of Massachusetts. Second, citizens were required to house his troops in their homes. Third, the port of Boston was closed to commerce. Fourth, town meetings were suspended, and the right to appoint the Governor's Council was removed from the Assembly and transferred to the king. And fifth, colonists were informed that Crown officials accused of committing crimes while pursuing their official duties were to be tried not in Boston but in Nova Scotia or London.

A young Thomas Jefferson spoke for many Americans when he declared that "single acts of tyranny may be ascribed to the accidental opinion of a day, [but] a series of oppressions pursued unalterably plainly prove a deliberate and systematic plan of reducing us to slavery." Jefferson's conclusion seemed equally obvious: "when tyranny is abroad, submission is a crime."[12] Few Americans chose to submit, but fewer still had any idea of how far resistance would take them.

First Steps toward Independence

After Americans decided to resist, and the authorities in London decided to meet their resistance with force, the impulses that led to Lexington, Concord, Bunker Hill, and independence took over. Misinterpretation of motives, overreaction on both sides, and the difficulties of transatlantic communication led first to heated rhetoric and then to a spiral of threats and violence that neither side knew how to stop.[13]

The First Continental Congress. The publication of the Intolerable Acts in America in May 1774 brought calls for an intercolonial conference to develop a coordinated response. Every state but Georgia appointed delegates to meet in

---

Stamp Act Congress
Delegates from nine colonies met in New York City in October 1765 to coordinate their resistance to Parliament's attempt to tax the colonies directly. They argued that only colonial legislatures could levy taxes in the colonies.

Declaratory Act An act passed in Parliament in March 1766 declaring that the British king and Parliament had the right to pass laws binding on the colonies in America "in all cases whatsoever."

Boston Massacre A clash on March 5, 1770 between British troops and a Boston mob that left five colonists dead and eight wounded.

Boston Tea Party Boston patriots oppose British attempts to tax the colonies by dumping tea into Boston Harbor rather than pay the required taxes.

Intolerable Acts Acts passed in Parliament during the spring of 1774, in response to the Boston Tea Party and similar events, to strengthen British administration of the colonies.

Tensions between British troops and colonists erupted in the Boston Massacre on March 5, 1770. Five colonists were killed immediately, and eight others were wounded. Two of the wounded died later.

the first **Continental Congress**. The Congress met in Philadelphia and began its deliberations on September 5, 1774.

Independence was not on the agenda. Most of the delegates hoped to heal the rift that had developed between the colonies and England. Therefore, the Congress appointed two committees. The first was to compose a petition stating grievances and seeking redress, and the second was to state the rights of trade and manufacture due the colonies and to identify the grounds upon which these rights rested. The petitions that resulted from the work of these committees were adopted by the Congress and forwarded to the king and Parliament in London. The delegates to the first Continental Congress adjourned on October 26, 1774, after agreeing that if necessary they would hold a second Congress in the spring.

Continental Congress Met in September 1774 and from May 1775 forward to coordinate protests against British policy and then revolution. The Continental Congress was superseded by the Confederation Congress when the Articles of Confederation went into effect on March 1, 1781.

Revolutionary Action. British authorities took the mere fact that a Continental Congress had met in America to be defiance. The American petitions were rejected summarily, and talk in Parliament quickly turned to the use of force. Parliament ordered reinforcements to Boston, extended the trade sanctions then in place against Boston to all of New England, and ordered General Gage to seize arms and military stores that might be used by colonial rebels. Benjamin Franklin, then in London as agent for several of the colonies, sent word to Congress that "three regiments of foot, one of dragoons, seven hundred marines, six sloops of war, and two frigates are now under orders for America."[14]

Preparation and posturing on both sides erupted into violence early on the morning of April 19, 1775. A column of British troops dispatched from Boston to seize weapons clashed with colonial militia at Lexington and Concord. Finding no military stores in either place, the troops sought to withdraw to Boston. The militia harassed the redcoats from cover all along the line of march, inflicting heavy casualties. When the column finally reached Boston, the militia took up defensive positions on the hills surrounding the city to block further incursions into the countryside.

Blood had been shed on both sides, but many colonists still hoped for reconciliation. It was not to be. Into this volatile situation stepped a recent Irish immigrant named Thomas Paine. Paine captured the emotion of the moment in an incendiary pamphlet called *Common Sense*. Paine denounced King George as the "royal brute," called for immediate independence, and declared that "the cause of America is in a great measure the cause of all mankind." *Common Sense* sold 120,000 copies in the first three months of 1776 and shifted the tone of public discussion toward confrontation.

The Second Continental Congress. New England delegates returning to Philadelphia for the second Continental Congress in early May 1775 traveled roads clogged with militia moving to reinforce the patriots encamped on the hills around Boston. Delegates arriving from the southern colonies pledged their firm support. By May 10, 1775, forty-nine delegates, virtually all of them veterans of the first Congress, were present and the Congress was gavelled into session.

The second Congress agreed to organize a Continental Army (really to adopt the troops around Boston). Colonel George Washington, a delegate from Virginia, was selected to take command of this new army. Congress also authorized signing contracts with and soliciting loans from foreign governments, particularly the French. The French could be expected to support anyone willing to give their British enemies a difficult time.

The Declaration of Independence

On May 15, 1776, the Virginia House of Burgesses voted to instruct its delegates in Congress to propose independence. On June 7, 1776, Virginia's Richard

Henry Lee introduced the following resolution: "These United Colonies are, and of right ought to be, free and independent States, that they are absolved from all allegiance to the British Crown, and that all political connection between them and the State of Great Britain is, and ought to be, totally dissolved." Lee's resolution was set aside in order to give each member time to consider its implications.

On June 10, 1776, Congress elected a committee of its leading members—Thomas Jefferson, John Adams, Benjamin Franklin, Roger Sherman, and Robert R. Livingston—to prepare an explanation and justification of Lee's motion. Jefferson's reputation as a literary craftsman led the committee to assign him the task of producing a draft. Jefferson's draft declaration was lightly revised, mostly by Franklin and Adams, and submitted to the full Congress. The work of this committee, debated and amended in Congress in early July and adopted on July 4, is the document that we call the **Declaration of Independence**. In fact, the actual declaration, Lee's resolution, had been passed two days earlier.

The imprint of John Locke's social contract theory is especially heavy on the Declaration of Independence (the Declaration is Appendix A in the back of this book). Jefferson put human rights, the right of individuals to security, respect, and self-development, at the core of the American promise. The justly famous second paragraph of the Declaration reads, "We hold these truths to be self-evident, that all men are created equal, that they are endowed by their Creator with certain unalienable Rights, that among these are Life, Liberty, and the pursuit of Happiness.—That to secure these rights, Governments are instituted among Men, deriving their just powers from the consent of the governed,—That whenever any Form of Government becomes destructive of these ends, it is the Right of the People to alter or to abolish it, and to institute new Government, laying its foundation on such principles and organizing its powers in such form, as to them shall seem most likely to effect their safety and Happiness."

The opening sentence of that paragraph makes two key points. First, it defines as "self-evident," meaning beyond dispute, that "certain unalienable rights," "among" which are "Life, Liberty, and the pursuit of Happiness" belong to all men. The idea of self-evidence is a striking way of saying, despite all of the evidence of difference and inequality that you see around you, a free society must treat people as fundamentally equal. Moreover, the simple phrase "among these" suggests that there may be, and probably are, inalienable rights in addition to life, liberty, and the pursuit of happiness.

Second, John Locke's identification of life, liberty, and property as fundamental rights was significantly softened, broadened, and enriched by Jefferson's substitution of "pursuit of Happiness" for property. Life and liberty remain fundamental for Jefferson, as for Locke, and there is no doubt that Jefferson valued property, but "pursuit of Happiness" is an open promise while property is defensive and exclusionary.

The Declaration argues that free men create governments, through a process of social contract, to create order and security and if government fails to do so, they can redesign or replace it. But it did more than that. Thomas Jefferson's declaration defined the goals of American public life—the promise of Life, Liberty, and the pursuit of Happiness—in positive and expansive language that has thrilled and challenged every subsequent generation of Americans.

Declaration of Independence The document adopted in the Continental Congress on July 4, 1776, to explain and justify the decision of the American colonies to declare their independence from Britain.

Thomas Jefferson and his colleagues prepare the Declaration of Independence. The declaration was meant to provide the reasons justifying American independence from Great Britain.

GOVERNANCE DURING THE REVOLUTIONARY PERIOD

In May 1776, the Continental Congress advised states that had not already done so to discard institutions based on ties to Britain and to establish governments grounded on their own authority. This was a more complicated instruction than might first appear. No nation in the world, including Great Britain, had a written constitution. The colonies had written charters, but these assumed the superior authority of British laws and institutions. Ten new or revised state constitutions were produced in 1776 alone. Between 1776 and 1787 all thirteen states produced at least one new constitution.

In the American experience, constitutions are written documents that describe and define the structure and powers of government. They usually begin with a preamble describing the goals and purposes of government and contain a bill of rights designed to prohibit government from imposing on the freedom and liberty of citizens. The bulk of the document, usually in a series of numbered articles or sections, describe the structure of the government, how the parts relate to each other, their respective powers, and how one achieves election or appointment to these offices. Constitutions frame and legitimate politics; they are prior to and superior to regular laws and other decisions of government, so they must be approved by popular vote and can only be amended or changed by popular vote.[15]

Q3 What changes in institutional design and allocation of powers were reflected in the first state constitutions?

Independence Sparks Constitutional Change

The call to armed resistance and ultimately to revolution, based as it was on the rhetoric of liberty, equality, and popular sovereignty, sparked extensive political change. Political institutions were redesigned to remove powers from their more elitist elements and add powers to their more popular elements. Despite the rousing rhetoric of the Revolution, few white men imagined and even fewer argued that rights and liberties should be expanded to groups—women, slaves, Indians—that had not previously enjoyed them.

The State Constitutions. Most of the new state constitutions retained the basic structure of a legislature with an upper and a lower house and an executive branch headed by a governor, although the distribution of power within and among the institutions shifted dramatically. In all of the constitutions of 1776, most power was lodged in the lower house of the legislature. The upper house and the governor, suggesting the monarchical and aristocratic elements of the old regime, were reduced in influence. Governors frequently lost the veto power, appointment power, and control over the budget. Popular involvement was usually assured through an expanded suffrage and through annual, or at most biannual, elections.

The new state constitutions were careful to expand and make more explicit the protection of individual rights and liberties traditionally enjoyed by white men including trial by jury, free speech, press, and assembly, and protections against unreasonable searches and standing armies in peacetime. These rights and others like them were widely seen as part of the fundamental law that controlled and limited the power of government over society and citizens.

The Articles of Confederation. The Confederation Congress produced a "league" of states, not a nation of citizens. Each state delegation had a single vote, and the presidency of the Congress rotated among the states. There was no executive, no judiciary, no separation of powers, and no checks and balances. The Revolution created an increased sense of unity among Americans, but not yet a sense of nationhood.

The **Articles of Confederation** granted the **Confederation Congress** authority over foreign policy, including sending and receiving ambassadors, negotiating treaties and alliances, and making decisions of war and peace. Congress was empowered to regulate its own coinage, fix the standards for weights and measures, establish a postal system, regulate trade with Indians living outside the individual states, and appoint the senior officers of army and navy units serving under the control of the Congress. Congress was authorized to borrow money and to requisition the states for money, men, and materials needed to fight the war and support Congress's other activities.

On the other hand, certain critical powers were denied to Congress altogether. Congress had no power to regulate trade and commerce between the states or to tax the citizens of the individual states. Congress's only domestic source of revenue was requisitions on the states. Finally, amendments to the Articles required the unanimous approval of the thirteen state legislatures. No amendment ever passed because at least one state always opposed, no matter how critical the need seemed to the others. Despite the powers granted to the Congress by the Articles, the reality was that the states remained almost completely sovereign, obeying the Congress only when they saw fit.

In a nation fighting its way to independence, the flaws and weaknesses of the Articles were frustrating to many and infuriating to some—including General Washington. The root of the problem was that while Congress could requisition from the states the men and supplies needed to fight the war, it was the hard-pressed states that decided whether to comply in full, in part, or not at all. Even after the war ended in victory, Congress's inability to resolve commercial disputes, or even consistently to keep a quorum, deepened pessimism about the new nation's future.

Articles of Confederation
Written in the Continental Congress in 1776 and 1777, the Articles outlining America's first national government were finally adopted on March 1, 1781. The Articles were replaced by the U.S. Constitution on March 4, 1789.

Confederation Congress
The Congress served under the Articles of Confederation from its adoption on March 1, 1781, until it was superseded by the new Federal Congress when the U.S. Constitution went into effect on March 4, 1789.

Political Instability during "The Critical Period"

Volatile state legislatures and a weak and impoverished Congress created a sense of instability and drift in the new nation. Many Americans came to believe that the weakening of the executives and the upper houses of the state legislatures and their total elimination at the national level had left American governments unable to ensure social stability and foster economic growth. State governments sought to address this instability through constitutional reform. By 1780 both New York and Massachusetts had adopted new constitutions that reempowered their governors and upper houses.

Other states, especially Rhode Island, but Pennsylvania, North Carolina, and Georgia as well, seemed to drift toward a dangerous populism. The right to vote had been expanded and new men, sometimes poor farmers and debtors, challenged traditional elites for places in town councils and state legislatures. Wartime inflation threatened the value of property and state legislatures frequently sided with poor debtors. Men of property and wealth concluded that

North Wind Picture Archives

Massachusetts farmers led by Daniel Shays rose up against high taxes and oppressive government during the winter of 1786–1787. The movement—a scene from which is shown here—came to be called Shays's Rebellion.

a national government capable of restraining the too democratic state governments was necessary to restore order, security, and prosperity.

The Annapolis Convention. In 1786, Virginia proposed an interstate conference to discuss commercial regulation. Although disputes between Maryland and Virginia concerning trade on the Chesapeake provided the focus, other states were invited in the hope that a general set of commercial recommendations might be crafted. The **Annapolis Convention** met on September 11, agreed that trade issues were part of a larger set of federal issues that needed to be dealt with together, and adjourned on September 14. Its report, sent to Congress and the states, called for a general convention to meet in Philadelphia in May 1787 "to render the constitution of the Federal Government adequate to the exigencies of the Union." Events conspired to suggest that the Philadelphia meeting would be of the utmost importance.

Annapolis Convention Held in Annapolis, Maryland, in September 1786 to discuss problems arising from state restriction on interstate commerce, it was a precursor to the Constitutional Convention.

Shays's Rebellion An uprising of Massachusetts farmers during the winter of 1786–1787 that convinced many Americans that political instability in the states required a stronger national government.

Shays's Rebellion. Although a modest conflict by any realistic measure, **Shays's Rebellion** was taken by many to be a warning of worse to come. The conservative administration of Massachusetts Governor James Bowdoin had increased taxes on land. This bore heavily on the small farmers of central and western Massachusetts who frequently found their farms seized for back taxes. In August 1786 and throughout the subsequent winter, farmers under the leadership of Daniel Shays, a Revolutionary War veteran and local officeholder, closed courts, opposed foreclosures by force of arms, and clashed with local militia called out to restore order.[16] By February 1787, troops of the state militia, paid with $20,000 in private money raised mostly among the merchants and tradesmen of Boston, put the rebels to flight in a series of skirmishes. Nonetheless, the threats that social instability posed to persons and property worried conservatives.

THE CONSTITUTIONAL CONVENTION

Failure of the Annapolis Convention and concern over Shays's Rebellion focused great attention on the **Constitutional Convention** (also called the Federal Convention) held in Philadelphia from May to September 1787. Virginia, the largest and most prominent state, sent a delegation that included George Washington, Governor Edmund Randolph, James Madison, and George Mason. Other states also sent their leading citizens.

History and experience offered the delegates several pieces to the still-unsolved puzzle of democratic constitutionalism—limited government, separation of powers, checks and balances, bicameralism, and federalism—but no persuasive description of how the pieces fit together to produce justice, strength, and stability over time. Most delegates shared a sense that the central government had to be strengthened and that, at minimum, this meant that authority to control commerce and collect taxes had to be lodged with the Congress. This suggested, however, that the central government would need executive agencies to enforce

Struggling Toward Democracy

In the wake of Shays's Rebellion, 4,000 rebels confessed to taking part and received pardons. Eighteen leaders were tried and sentenced to death, though only two, John Bly and Charles Rose, were actually hanged. The rest were eventually pardoned. Shays escaped, hid out until tensions died down, and eventually was pardoned too.

What do you think?

- In a democracy, should public protest, even if it slides toward violence, be lightly punished or not?
- Would you be willing to engage in protest over something you felt strongly about, even if it became violent?

Constitutional Convention
Met in Philadelphia between May 25 and September 17, 1787, and produced the U.S. Constitution. It is sometimes referred to as the Federal Convention or Philadelphia Convention.

its laws and judicial agencies to resolve disputes. Nonetheless, it was unclear whether the necessary reforms, whatever they turned out to be, would add up to a truly national government or merely to a series of amendments to the existing Articles of Confederation.[17]

The Convention Debates

Fifty-five delegates from twelve states (Rhode Island refused to send delegates) attended and took some part in the proceedings of the Federal Convention. Thirty-nine delegates remained to the end and signed the final document. The delegates were often relatively young, generally well educated, and usually well placed within their state's social, economic, and political elite.[18]

Most of the delegates had already seen extensive public service. Twenty-four had served in the Continental Congress between 1774 and 1781, and thirty-nine had served in the Confederation Congress between 1781 and 1787. Twenty-one had fought in the Revolutionary War, seven had served as governors of their states, and fully forty-six had served in their state legislature. They knew firsthand the problems that faced the new nation, and they knew how to pursue solutions in a political setting.[19]

Although the delegates making their way toward Philadelphia shared a broad commitment to the ideas of limited and representative government, federalism, separation of powers, bicameralism, and checks and balances, it was not at all clear where these commitments would lead once the discussions began. The northern states had interests that the southern states did not share, and large states hoped that their greater numbers and wealth would be reflected in greater influence over the national councils. Political principles and practical political interests clashed loudly and repeatedly at the convention. Finally, most delegates thought the new nation's fate depended upon creating a more powerful national government. Delegates and delegations willing to threaten the convention's success were likely to be accommodated—if only grudgingly.[20]

Virginia's James Madison had thought long and hard about what benefits might flow from a more powerful national government.[21] He laid out his ideas in letters to Washington, Jefferson, and Virginia Governor Edmund Randolph in March and April of 1787. Madison's boldest ideas were communicated only to Washington, who responded warmly. Confident that Washington's influence in the convention would be great, Madison modeled his ideas into a draft constitution to be laid before the upcoming convention.

The Federal Convention began on May 25, 1787. Its first act, to no one's surprise, was to elect Washington to preside. On the first day of the convention, and on every day thereafter, Madison took a position in the front of the room, facing the members, to record the debates and decisions of the body. Most of what we know about how the convention worked and how the Constitution actually took shape during the debates we owe to James Madison. Keenly aware of the delicate task before them, the delegates adopted brief rules of procedure, closed the windows and doors, swore one another to secrecy, and set to work.

George Washington presided over the Federal Convention that met from May 25 through September 17, 1787. Having led the American Revolutionary armies to victory, Washington was the most trusted man in America. His calm and serious presence as presiding officer kept the members of the convention focused on the task at hand.

The Virginia Plan.   The **Virginia Plan** was written by Madison, endorsed by Washington and by most of the delegates from the large states, and introduced on May 29 by Governor Edmund Randolph, leader of the Virginia delegation. The Virginia Plan envisioned a powerful national government. The legislature was to be the dominant branch. It would consist of two houses, the first elected by the people, the second elected by the first from among nominees put forward by the state legislatures. The numbers in each house were to be proportional to state population. The proposed Congress was to have authority to legislate in all cases where it might judge the individual states to be "incompetent" or in which it conceived that their individual legislation would disrupt the "harmony" of the new nation.

Both the executive and the judiciary would derive their appointments from the legislature. The executive would be chosen by the national legislature for a single term of seven years. A national judiciary, to consist of one supreme court, would be appointed by the Senate, with lower courts to be created by the national legislature. The new Constitution was to be ratified by popularly elected state conventions rather than by the state legislatures.[22] Most of the major provisions of the Virginia Plan were adopted by the convention during the first two weeks of debate.

The New Jersey Plan.   On June 14, the New Jersey delegation asked that time be given to allow delegates who had been developing a "purely federal" plan

Virginia Plan Outline of a strong national government, written by Virginia's James Madison and supported by most of the delegates from the large states, that guided early discussion in the Constitutional Convention.

Q4 How did the Virginia and New Jersey Plans differ about the kind of national government that each envisioned?

The Granger Collection, New York

New Jersey Plan A plan to add a limited number of new powers to the Articles, supported by most of the delegates from the small states, introduced into the Constitutional Convention as an alternative to the Virginia Plan.

to complete their work. The **New Jersey Plan**, presented to the convention on June 15, represented a more limited national government. Absence of powers to tax and regulate commerce were widely seen as the key deficiencies in the confederation government. The New Jersey Plan would add these powers to the existing Congress, but even here, it would hedge them in with state powers and discretion.

The national executive and judicial powers envisioned by the New Jersey Plan, while new, were limited. The Congress would elect a federal executive who would be ineligible for a second term and removable by Congress upon petition of a majority of the state executives. The national judiciary was even more constrained. Virtually all original jurisdiction over American citizens was to be exercised by the state courts. Following three full days of debate over the merits and deficiencies of the two plans, the convention voted 7–3, with one delegation deadlocked, to approve the Virginia Plan as amended instead of the New Jersey Plan. Though defeated in this first major encounter, the supporters of the New Jersey Plan continued to press their demands. Before moving on, ask yourself how the federal government might look today if the New Jersey Plan, rather than the Virginia Plan, had been selected as the basis for the new constitution (see Table 1.1).

The Great Compromise on Representation. After delegates determined that the Virginia Plan would provide the general outline for the convention's work, it was clear to all that the next major stumbling block was the issue of representation. Large states wanted seats in both the House and the Senate to be distributed according to population (commonly referred to as proportional representation). The small states wanted each state to have one vote in each house. The southern states wanted their slaves to be counted for representation; the northern states opposed unless their property was counted too.

As early as June 11, delegates from Connecticut proposed a compromise in which the states would be represented on the basis of population in the House and each state would be represented equally in the Senate. The convention

TABLE 1.1 The Virginia and New Jersey Plans	
Virginia Plan	**New Jersey Plan**
Based on popular sovereignty	Based on state sovereignty
Bicameral legislature	Unicameral legislature
Congressional seats allocated according to state population or contributions	Equal votes for states in Congress
Broad powers to legislate where the "harmony" of the U.S. requires it	Authority of the old Congress plus limited powers over taxation and commerce
"A National Executive" chosen and removable by Congress	Multiple executives chosen by Congress and removable upon petition of the states
Federal court system with broad powers	Supreme tribunal with narrow powers
Ratification by the people	Ratification by the states

took five more weeks of intense debate to move grudgingly toward the middle ground that the Connecticut delegation had identified.[23] Finally, on July 12, the northern states agreed to count each slave as three-fifths of a person for purposes of representation if the southern states agreed to apply this proportion to taxes as well. They so agreed. On July 16, the convention narrowly adopted proportional representation in the House, as the large states wished, and equal votes in the Senate, as the small states demanded.

The Commerce and Slave Trade Compromise.   Once the issue of representation was settled, new regional differences over commerce and slavery rose to threaten the convention. Delegates representing northern commercial interests were little concerned with slavery, although a few did speak stirringly against it, but they were quite determined to control national commercial and trade policy. Delegates representing southern interests sought to limit northern control of southern exports, slavery, and the slave trade. In the face of southern threats to abandon the convention, the delegates agreed to acknowledge northern control of commerce and southern control over slavery, although limits on importation of new slaves after 1808 were permitted.

The Compromises on Voting and Presidential Selection.   The members of the Constitutional Convention were, at best, reluctant democrats. Some of the northern states allowed male citizens over 21 the right to vote, but some southern states had high wealth and property qualifications for voting. Rather than trying to battle their way to a constitutional rule for suffrage, they agreed to allow each state to set the rules for voting and conducting elections.

Not surprisingly, as the convention approached the completion of its business, the contentious topic of presidential selection remained unresolved. Delegates advocating a powerful national government wanted an independent executive strong enough to check a volatile legislature, whereas those who opposed great power at the national level wanted an executive dependent upon, even selected by, the legislature. But legislative selection of the executive seemed too obvious a violation of separation of powers.

As they had with other difficult issues, the convention voted to turn the issue of executive selection over to a committee composed of one member from each state. This committee, known as the Brearley Committee, crafted a solution that many believed balanced the interests of the large and small states. The Brearley Committee proposed an electoral college in which the number of electors assigned to a state was equal to the number of House and Senate seats assigned to that state. However, many delegates were convinced that electors voting in their separate states could not coordinate their votes to elect a president on the first round and that candidates from the larger states would likely receive the most votes. If no candidate received a majority, the Senate, where the small states had equal votes, would select the president from among the top five candidates.

Floor debate on the Brearley Committee proposal raised the troublesome issue of whether the power to select the president from a list of five candidates, in addition to the Senate's other powers, might make the Senate a dangerous aristocracy. Connecticut's Roger Sherman proposed that the final selection be made by the House of Representatives, voting by states. This solution left the advantage over final choice among candidates to the small states, but removed the objection that the Senate was too powerful. With this last major deadlock broken, the Federal Convention moved rapidly to conclude its work.

The Constitution as Finally Adopted

After nearly four months of debate broken only by a brief respite to observe the Fourth of July, thirty-nine delegates signed the Constitution on September 17, 1787 (the Constitution is Appendix B in the back of this book). How did the principles and interests that the delegates brought to the convention show up in the final document?

The Preamble: A Statement of Our Goals. The Preamble declared the Constitution to be an act of the sovereign people of the United States to secure the public purposes that they held most dear. The Articles of Confederation had been an agreement among the states, whereas the Constitution was an act of the people. The Preamble reads: "We the people of the United States, in Order to form a more perfect Union, establish Justice, insure domestic Tranquility, provide for the common defence, promote the general Welfare, and secure the Blessings of Liberty to ourselves and our Posterity, do ordain and establish this Constitution of the United States of America." These goals—like the self-evident truths enumerated by Thomas Jefferson in the Declaration of Independence, "that all men are created equal, that they are endowed by their Creator with certain unalienable rights, that among these are Life, Liberty, and the pursuit of happiness"—have continued to challenge and inspire each new generation of Americans.

The body of the Constitution was made up of seven numbered Articles. Articles I, II, and III highlighted the Founders commitment to fundamental ideas including **separation of powers**, **checks and balances**, and **bicameralism**. Articles IV and VI dealt with federal relations, while V and VII dealt with the processes for amendment and ratification.

separation of powers The idea that distinctive types of governmental power, most obviously the legislative and executive powers, and later the judicial power, should be placed in separate hands.

checks and balances The idea that government powers should be distributed to permit each branch of government to check and balance the other branches.

bicameralism A two-house, as opposed to a unicameral or one-house, legislature.

Article I: The Legislative Branch. It was widely assumed that the legislature would be the core of the new government and that its powers and responsibilities needed to be laid out with care. Article I, section 1, states: "All legislative Powers herein granted shall be vested in a Congress of the United States, which shall consist of a Senate and House of Representatives." This language seems a stark adoption of separation of powers theory, although the bicameral design shows that the idea of checks and balances was not ignored. Sections 2 through 6 are largely given over to legislative housekeeping.

Section 7 lays out the president's role in the legislative process. The president has the right to review all legislation before it becomes law. If he concurs, he signs the legislation; if he strongly opposes the judgment of the legislature, he can veto the legislation subject to an override by two-thirds of each house or he can ignore the legislation, in which case it becomes law after ten days. Both bicameralism and the presidential veto were intended as checks on the legislature's ability to act rashly.

Section 8 of Article I describes the powers of the Congress. What makes Article I, section 8, utterly fascinating is that it begins by listing seventeen specific congressional powers. Foremost among these **enumerated powers** are the powers to levy taxes and to control commerce. The right to tax has been central to the growth of national power, but, as we shall see more fully in Chapter 2, the obscure sounding commerce power has supported increasingly broad national authority as well. Most of the remaining enumerated powers involve financial and monetary policy and regulation and the right to raise and support an army and navy. Section 8 closes with language that has come to be known as the **"necessary and proper" clause:** "To make all Laws which shall be necessary and proper for carrying into Execution the foregoing Powers, and all other Powers vested by this Constitution in the Government of the United States, or in any Department or Officer thereof." To many, the broad sweep of the "necessary and proper" clause seemed to defeat the purpose of a finite list of enumerated powers.

enumerated powers The specifically listed or enumerated powers of Congress found in Article I, section 8, of the Constitution.

"necessary and proper" clause The last paragraph of Article I, section 8, of the Constitution, which states that Congress may make all laws deemed necessary and proper to carry into execution the powers specifically enumerated in Article I, section 8.

Article II: The Executive Branch.   Article II, section 1, declares that "The executive Power shall be vested in a President of the United States of America." It also describes the process by which the president will be selected, the qualifications of the office, the succession of the vice president in the case of presidential death or incapacity, and the presidential oath. Section 2 describes one set of powers that is explicitly granted to the president and another set that is granted to the president "with the Advice and Consent of the Senate." The first set of powers is modest indeed. The president serves as commander in chief of the army and navy, may require the opinions in writing of the principal officers of the executive branch, and may grant reprieves and pardons for offenses against the United States. With the **advice and consent** of two-thirds of the senators present, the president can conclude treaties, and with the approval of a simple majority of the Senate he can appoint ambassadors, members of the Supreme Court, and other public ministers and administrative officers of the United States.

advice and consent Article II, section 2, of the Constitution requires the president to seek the advice and consent of the Senate in appointing Supreme Court justices, senior officials of the executive branch, and ambassadors, and in ratifying treaties with foreign nations.

Section 3 provides several opportunities for presidential influence but gives no additional powers. The president is required to give the Congress, from time to time, information on the "State of the Union," and he is entitled to "recommend to their consideration such Measures as he shall judge necessary and expedient." Also in section 3 is a clause that charges the president to "take care that the Laws be faithfully executed." The **"take care" clause** has been read by presidents since Abraham Lincoln as a command that they see that the laws of the United States are both faithfully executed by the government and obeyed by the citizenry. Finally, section 4, the impeachment clause, warns against misuse of power by the president and his associates and officers.

"take care" clause Article II, section 3, of the Constitution requires that the president "take care that the laws be faithfully executed."

Article III: The Judicial Branch.   Section 1 declares simply that "The judicial Power of the United States shall be vested in one supreme Court, and in such inferior Courts as the Congress may from time to time ordain and establish."

Section 2 sketches a very limited jurisdiction for the federal courts. The federal courts are to handle cases arising under the Constitution or federal laws and treaties; involving ambassadors and other public ministers; or involving the United States, two or more states, citizens of different states, and states with citizens of other states. Only in those unusual cases where the jurisdiction of a single state does not cover the parties involved do the federal courts have jurisdiction. The Supreme Court has original jurisdiction in cases involving ambassadors, other public ministers, and cases in which one or more states are involved. In all other cases, their jurisdiction is appellate.

Articles IV and VI: Federal Relations. Article IV provides for reciprocity between the states, for the admission of new states into the union, and for guarantees of **republican government** and protections against domestic violence in the states. Article IV, section 1, guarantees that **full faith and credit** will be given by each state to the legal acts of the other states. More generally, the full faith and credit clause, together with the **privileges and immunities clause** of Article IV, section 2, guarantees that normal social and economic transactions would have effect across state lines within the new nation. Article IV, section 3, guarantees that new states can be admitted into the union but that they will not be carved out of existing states or parts of existing states except with the consent of the states involved. Section 4, in direct response to the concern created by Shays's Rebellion, promises that "The United States shall guarantee to every State in this Union a Republican Form of Government, and shall protect each of them against Invasion; and on Application of the Legislature, or of the Executive (when the Legislature cannot be convened) against domestic Violence."

Article VI declares: "This Constitution, and the Laws of the United States which shall be made in Pursuance thereof; . . . shall be the supreme Law of the Land." Moreover, all public officials, "both of the United States and of the several States, shall be bound by Oath or Affirmation, to support this Constitution." The "supremacy clause" declared federal authority supreme within its authorized areas of responsibility. Nonetheless, Joseph F. Zimmerman, a leading scholar of American federalism, has noted, "The U.S. Constitution was the first written document in the world to provide for the distribution of significant powers between the national government and territorial governments."[24]

Article V: The Amendment Process. Article V outlines two methods by which amendments can be proposed and two methods by which they can be approved or rejected. Congress can, by a two-thirds vote of both houses, propose amendments to the Constitution, or, in response to a call from two-thirds of the state legislatures, must summon a convention to consider proposing amendments. Regardless of whether Congress or a convention proposes amendments, they must be ratified by the legislatures of three-fourths of the states or by special conventions called in three-fourths of the states (see Figure 1.1).

Although the Founders quite clearly wanted the Constitution to be subject to amendment, they just as clearly did not want to see it changed easily or often. In fact, the Constitution has been amended only twenty-seven times in two

republican government Mixed or balanced government that is based on the people but may retain residual elements of monarchical or aristocratic privilege. Americans of the colonial period were particularly impressed with the example of republican Rome.

full faith and credit Article IV, section 1, of the Constitution requires that each state give "full faith and credit" to the legal acts of the other states.

privileges and immunities clause Article IV, section 2, of the Constitution guarantees to the citizens of each state the "privileges and immunities" of the several states.

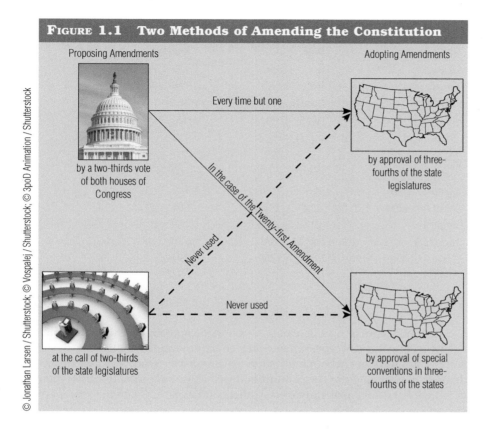

FIGURE 1.1 Two Methods of Amending the Constitution

Proposing Amendments

Adopting Amendments

Every time but one

In the case of the Twenty-first Amendment

Never used

Never used

by a two-thirds vote of both houses of Congress

by approval of three-fourths of the state legislatures

at the call of two-thirds of the state legislatures

by approval of special conventions in three-fourths of the states

hundred and thirty years. Congress has always exercised close control over the amendment process. All twenty-seven amendments to the Constitution were proposed by Congress. Congress has only once, in the case of the Twenty-first Amendment, chosen the state convention approach to considering amendments proposed by Congress. In every other case, Congress has specified that consideration of proposed amendments occur in the state legislatures.

THE STRUGGLE OVER RATIFICATION

The members of the Federal Convention made every effort to tilt the ratification process in favor of the proposed Constitution. They knew that if they followed the amendment process laid out in the Articles of Confederation—adoption by the Congress and "the legislatures of every State"—the prospects for ratification were literally zero. Therefore, the convention proposed a ratification process that included neither explicit congressional approval nor a role for the state legislatures.[25] The intent of the convention was that the Constitution "be submitted to a Convention of Delegates, chosen in each State by the People thereof, under the Recommendation of its Legislature, for their Assent and Ratification" (see Table 1.2).[26]

TABLE 1.2 State Ratification of the Proposed Constitution			
State	**Date**	**Approve**	**Reject**
Delaware	Dec. 7, 1787	30	0
Pennsylvania	Dec. 12, 1787	46	23
New Jersey	Dec. 18, 1787	38	0
Georgia	Jan. 2, 1788	26	0
Connecticut	Jan. 9, 1788	128	40
Massachusetts	Feb. 7, 1788	187	168
Maryland	Apr. 28, 1788	63	11
South Carolina	May 23, 1788	149	73
New Hampshire	June 21, 1788	57	47
Virginia	June 25, 1788	89	79
New York	July 26, 1788	30	27
North Carolina	Nov. 21, 1789	194	77
Rhode Island	May 29, 1790	34	32

Article VII of the proposed Constitution made approval by nine states sufficient to put the new government into effect among the approving states. Some states were overwhelmingly supportive and were ready to move immediately; others had grave reservations and wished to have time to gather their arguments and to watch early developments. Therefore, while the first wave of decisions took only a few weeks and several were unanimously positive, it took nearly seven months to secure the ninth ratification and two more years to secure the thirteenth.

Moreover, the vote in some major states was close; Massachusetts approved by 187 to 168, Virginia by 89 to 79, and New York had to vote twice. In the first vote, on June 17, 1788, the Constitution went down 19 to 46. After the Federalists rallied, agreeing to 31 proposed amendments, a second vote on July 26 narrowly succeeded 30 to 27.

Federalists Supporters of a stronger national government who favored ratification of the U.S. Constitution.

Anti-Federalists Opponents of a stronger national government who generally opposed ratification of the U.S. Constitution.

Federalists versus Anti-Federalists. Although **Federalists** supported the proposed Constitution and **Anti-Federalists** opposed it, they were not divided by deep and irreconcilable differences. Historian Ralph Ketcham noted that both Federalists and Anti-Federalists "were conditional democrats. They were for or against the ideas of majority rule, representation, broad suffrage, and so on insofar as those processes seemed more or less likely to result in order, freedom, justice, prosperity, and the other broad purposes of the Constitution."[27]

The problem was that the Federalists and Anti-Federalists disagreed about how the national government described in the proposed Constitution would actually work. Many Americans were concerned that the proposed Constitution was simply too powerful to leave their liberties secure. James Madison, Alexander Hamilton, and John Jay teamed up to write a series of newspaper columns intended to explain and support the new Constitution during the ratification struggle in New York. These columns, which came to be known as the *Federalist Papers*, turned the debate in New York in favor of the Constitution and were reprinted by supporters up and down the Atlantic coast.

The Federalists believed, as James Madison explained in Nos. 10, 48, and 51 of the *Federalist Papers*, that a large nation, an "extended republic" in the phrase of the day, made a powerful and stable national government possible if that government was wisely and carefully crafted. Extensive territory meant a broad diversity of groups and interests, no one of which, or no combination of which, would constitute a stable majority capable of oppressing a stable minority. Rather, the diversity of religious, social, economic, and regional interests would check and balance each other (*Federalist*, Nos. 10 and 51 are included in Appendix C in the back of this book).

If diversity means that no oppressive majority is likely to form in society and press its demands on government, then one has only to guard against oppressive tendencies arising within government itself. Madison and his colleagues believed that they had in fact guarded against governmental tyranny by constructing a careful system of limited and enumerated powers, by supplementing a pure separation of powers with appropriate checks and balances, and by leaving important governmental powers to the states and rights and liberties to the people.

The Anti-Federalists were not so sure. They thought that popular governments could exist only in "small republics" where the people could come together, as in county court days in the South or town meetings in New England, to conduct the public business. They did not believe that a nation as diverse as theirs could have a single public interest. Rather, they thought that sectional divisions would divide the national councils and that legislators serving so far from home would forget the interests of their constituents. The Anti-Federalists believed that the blessings of the Revolution—local people controlling local governments according to local needs, interests, and customs—would be endangered by a powerful national government.[28]

A Concession to the Opposition: The Bill of Rights. As the ratification debate progressed, Anti-Federalist opinion settled on the absence of a bill of rights as the fundamental deficiency of the proposed Constitution. The public was responsive to this criticism. The idea of rights and resistance to their violation had been a rallying cry for Americans since the mid-1760s.

What kind of bill of rights should be added to the new Constitution remained an open question for some time. Madison concluded that a bill of rights designed to secure the traditional rights of citizens could, assuming that its provisions did not weaken the legitimate powers of the government, win over those citizens still worried that the new government was too powerful. On September 28, 1789, largely due to Madison's efforts, Congress approved and sent to the states for ratification twelve amendments to the Constitution. Ten of these were approved and have come to be known as the **Bill of Rights**.

The Bill of Rights, broadly conceived, accomplished two things. First, it defined a preserve of personal autonomy, choice, and expression where government power should not intrude. The First Amendment offered the expansive

05 What role did the debate over a bill of rights play in the adoption of the U.S. Constitution?

Bill of Rights The first ten amendments to the U.S. Constitution, proposed by the first Federal Congress and ratified by the states in 1791, were intended to protect individual rights and liberties from action by the new national government.

Pro & Con

Do We Need a Bill of Rights?

The Federalists contended that adding a bill of rights to the Constitution was not only unnecessary, but positively dangerous. It was unnecessary, they asserted, for two reasons: first, because the structure of the Constitution was designed to protect the rights of the people through the principles of representation, separation of powers, bicameralism, checks and balances, and federalism; and second, because the Constitution was composed of enumerated powers and powers not given were retained by the people. It was positively dangerous because to list some rights might suggest that rights not listed were not retained or claimed by the people.

James Wilson, a leading member of the Philadelphia Convention and an important lawyer in that city, was the chief defender of the proposed Constitution in Pennsylvania. In his famous State House speech of October 6, 1787, Wilson presented an argument that became the standard Federalist case against adding a bill of rights to the Constitution. Wilson's "reserved powers theory" held that the Constitution provided for a government of limited and enumerated powers, so "every thing which is not given" to the national government "is reserved" by the people. Under these circumstances, Wilson contended, no bill of rights would be needed because the government had power to act only where power had been expressly granted.

Wilson further reasoned that "If we attempt an enumeration, everything that is not enumerated is presumed to be given. The consequence is that an imperfect enumeration would throw all implied power into the scale of the government; and the rights of the people would be rendered incomplete." Wilson was by no means the only prominent Federalist to oppose a bill of rights.

Anti-Federalists argued that the people demanded explicit protection for traditional rights including freedom of speech, press, religion, search and seizure, speedy trial, and more. If Federalists worried that a short list of rights might leave something off, make a long list. Besides, they argued, clear protection of some critical rights and liberties was better than none.

Eventually, Thomas Jefferson and others convinced James Madison of the importance of a national bill of rights. Madison then convinced his colleagues in the first House of Representatives that a bill of rights was necessary to "quiet that anxiety which prevails in the public mind" and to "stifle the voice of complaint, and make friends of many who doubted [the Constitution's] merits." The first ten amendments to the Constitution, known as the Bill of Rights, went into effect on December 15, 1791.

What do you think?
- If the Federalists had prevailed, and no bill of rights had been added to the Constitution, how might that have changed the course of our national development?
- Would those changes have been for good or ill?

PRO	CON
The people deserve a bill of rights	The Constitution's structure protects rights
Make a long list	Some rights might be left off any list
Protecting some rights is better than none	Powers not granted cannot be abused

assurance that "Congress shall make no law respecting an establishment of religion, or prohibiting the free exercise thereof; or abridging the freedom of speech, or of the press; or of the right of the people peaceably to assemble, and to petition the government for a redress of grievances."

Second, the Bill of Rights defined how persons would be subject to the power of government. Isolated individuals, especially common people, cannot stand up to the concentrated power of government unless that government is required to proceed slowly, carefully, and according to well-known rules and procedures. Hence, the Bill of Rights confirmed the rights to a speedy trial before an impartial jury, to confront witnesses, and to have the aid of counsel (Amendment 6). The Bill of Rights protected citizens against "unreasonable searches and seizures" (Amendment 4), double jeopardy and self-incrimination (Amendment 5), and excessive bail or cruel and unusual punishments (Amendment 8). The Ninth Amendment, like the Declaration of Independence, suggested that citizens may, likely do, have more rights than those specifically listed in the Constitution and its amendments. The Ninth Amendment said, "The enumeration in the Constitution, of certain rights, shall not be construed to deny or disparage others retained by the people." Finally, the Tenth Amendment declared that, "powers not delegated to the United States by the Constitution, nor prohibited to it by the states, are reserved to the states respectively, or to the people." These reassuring commitments encouraged citizens to give the new Constitution a chance. Just as Madison had hoped, support for the Constitution increased to near unanimity within a few years.

CONSIDERING CONSTITUTIONAL REFORM

The U.S. Constitution was written in an undemocratic age. The Founders did not intend to write a democratic constitution. They did not intend to treat poor white men, minorities, and women as equals. They intended to write a constitution that would check, balance, and limit political power while protecting the individual and property rights of white men.[29] While comfortable white Americans tend to slide over the narrow sense of equality in the Constitution, others do not. Thurgood Marshall, a top lawyer for the National Association for the Advancement of Colored People (NAACP) and the first black justice of the United States Supreme Court, appointed by President Lyndon Johnson in 1967, was invited on the 200th anniversary of the Constitution to give a speech celebrating the genius of the Founding Fathers and of the document they crafted. Justice Marshall both educated and discomfited his audience by moving quickly past praise for the Founders and the Constitution to take a clear-eyed view of the weaknesses and shortcomings of both.

Marshall said:

> I do not believe that the meaning of the Constitution was forever 'fixed' at the Philadelphia Convention. Nor do I find the wisdom, foresight, and sense of justice exhibited by the Framers particularly profound. To the contrary, the government they devised was defective from the start, requiring several amendments, a civil war, and momentous social transformation to attain the system of constitutional government, and its respect for the individual freedoms and human rights, we hold as fundamental today. When contemporary Americans cite 'The Constitution,' they invoke a concept that is vastly different from what the Framers barely began to construct two centuries ago.[30]

The Constitution, Marshall thought, had been, sometimes forcefully and still only partially, opened and democratized by successive generations of Americans.

In some eras of American politics, including the Revolutionary Era from the Boston Tea Party to Shays's Rebellion, but also including the anti-slavery movement, the rural populist insurgencies of the late nineteenth century, the women's suffrage movement, the urban troubles of the 1960s, and the populist energies that fueled the Bernie Sanders and Donald Trump campaigns in 2016, broad swathes of the people concluded that political elites had lost touch with common hopes and fears. Populist eras challenge the prevailing political assumptions, policy commitments, and their elite beneficiaries. Sometimes the challengers are beaten back, sometimes they drive change, but always they raise questions about whether the constitutional democracy constructed by our Founders is democratic enough to allow "the people" to be heard.

Advocates of the Founders' constitutional handiwork point to their wise intention to blunt popular passions with institutional limits and stout protections for minority rights. Critics of the U.S. Constitution find many of its key structural elements undemocratic and call for their removal or revision. Robert A. Dahl, perhaps the most prominent democratic theorist of the second half of the twentieth century, wrote a book in 2002 called *How Democratic Is the Constitution?* Dahl's answer was, "Not very." Dahl leveled particular criticism at the role of the Electoral College in presidential selection, the equal representation of the states in the Senate, and the power that judicial review gave judges to overturn the actions of elected executive and legislative officials.[31]

University of Texas law and government professor Sanford Levinson agreed with Dahl that the Electoral College, the Senate, and the federal courts were undemocratic in their origins and operations. In *Our Undemocratic Constitution* (2006), Levinson pointed out that most modern democratic nations are governed by untrammeled, unicameral, parliamentary majorities. Levinson contended that the slow and painful need to reach a consensus in our "tripartite" system of House, Senate, and presidency is an unnecessary and inefficient check on democratic governance. He called for, though he did not expect, a nationwide petition campaign demanding that Congress and the state legislatures authorize a new constitutional convention.[32]

Many agree with Dahl and Levinson that our politics are broken and the Constitution is the root cause. Others believe that the Electoral College, Senate, and Supreme Court are curiously configured and mildly undemocratic, but they do not believe that wholesale constitutional reform is necessary. What do you think?

Chapter Summary

During the eighteenth century, the population of the colonies doubled approximately every twenty years. As the economy grew and matured, domestic markets became increasingly important, and the desire for free access to international markets beyond Britain became more compelling. After British victory in the Seven Years War cleared the French threat from Canada, Americans could see less and less benefit from British intrusion into their economic and political lives.

Independence brought its own difficulties. The decade leading up to the Revolution was dominated by talk of British tyranny and American freedom. The argument was that American rights and liberties were threatened by the power of a distant government in London. Not surprisingly then, when Americans set about creating their own political institutions they sought to limit political power by keeping it local wherever possible. Where political power had to be exercised at a distance, as with the national government under the Articles of Confederation, it was made as modest as possible.

Yet, history suggested that popular political institutions were volatile and unstable. Shays's Rebellion convinced many that a more powerful national government was needed to stabilize politics in the states and to encourage national economic opportunity and development. The delegates that each state sent to the Constitutional Convention of 1787 understood quite clearly that they were to propose reforms that would secure the social, economic, and political stability of the new nation.

The delegates shared a number of broad principles that were rarely challenged in the convention. They agreed that written constitutions provide the surest guarantee of limited government. They agreed that federalism permits the assignment of power and responsibility to the level of government best suited to fulfill them efficiently and safely. They agreed that at both levels of the federal system—national and state—the principles of bicameralism, separation of powers, and checks and balances provide the best assurance that political power will be exercised in the public interest.

The delegates did, however, differ over the distribution of power within the federal system and how to ensure that their states and regions were well placed to exercise decisive influence in the new system. Men from small states believed that their interests would suffer if men from the large states dominated, and men from the South believed that their interests would suffer if men from the North dominated.

The Federal Constitution of 1787 reflected the particular configuration of ideas and interests present in the convention during the summer of 1787. As that configuration has changed and as ideas have asserted their steady influence, the Constitution has been brought to reflect more fully the values of liberty, equality, and opportunity that were so important to the rhetoric of the Revolution and so clearly stated by Thomas Jefferson and his colleagues in the Declaration of Independence. The Declaration of Independence remains an open invitation to those not enjoying the full fruits of liberty and equality to make their case for a fuller share.

Key Terms

advice and consent

Annapolis Convention

Anti-Federalists

Articles of Confederation

bicameralism

Bill of Rights

Boston Massacre

Boston Tea Party

checks and balances

Confederation Congress

Constitutional Convention

Continental Congress

Declaration of Independence

Declaratory Act

enumerated powers

Federalists

full faith and credit

individualism

Intolerable Acts

"necessary and proper" clause

New Jersey Plan

privileges and immunities clause

republican government

separation of powers

Shays's Rebellion

social contract theory

Stamp Act Congress

"take care" clause

Virginia Plan

Suggested Readings

Amar, Akhil Reed. *The Constitution Today: Timeless Lessons for the Issues of Our Era.* New York: Basic Books, 2016. Amar argues that the Constitution's promise of self-government put the U.S. on a path to expanded democracy, and that the lessons of the founding era can help to guide our thinking about modern problems.

Beeman, Richard. *Plain, Honest Men: The Making of the American Constitution.* New York: Random House, 2009. Beeman tells the story of the Constitution's drafting by highlighting the compromises that permitted success.

Gibson, Alan. *Understanding the Founding: The Crucial Questions.* Lawrence, KS: University Press of Kansas, 2007. Gibson explores the historical and intellectual influences on the Founders and the Constitution.

Hoock, Holger. *Scars of Independence: America's Violent Birth.* New York: Crown Publishing, 2017. Hoock highlights the physical, emotional, and intellectual violence of the Revolutionary War and the scars this violence left on the new nation.

Levinson, Sanford. *Our Undemocratic Constitution.* New York: Oxford University Press, 2006. Levinson contends that important provisions of the Constitution are insufficiently democratic.

Maier, Pauline. *Ratification: The People Debate the Constitution.* New York: Simon & Schuster, 2010. The first full account of the debate in the thirteen states over whether to approve the Constitution.

Wood, Gordon S. *Revolutionary Characters: What Made the Founders Different.* New York: Penguin, 2006. Wood offers eight brief but compelling biographies of leading Founders and two essays on the nature of their times.

Web Resources

1 www.archives.gov/
   The national archives provide a treasure trove of information on the Constitution. Click on "America's Historical Documents."

2 www.iep.utm.edu/locke/
   The Internet Encyclopedia of Philosophy provides a short biography, list of works, and links to the founder of British empiricism and social contract theory. The site includes links to other philosopher pages such as Thomas Hobbes.

3 www.lawmoose.com/internetlawlib/8.htm
   The complete text of *Federalist Papers* and other founding documents can be found at the Internet Law Library, formerly maintained by the U.S. House of Representatives.

4 www.constitutioncenter.org
   A non-partisan center focused on increasing knowledge and understanding of the U.S. Constitution.

5 www.constitution.org/afp/afp.htm
   The Constitution Society provides a good selection of anti-federalist writings opposing the Constitution and good directions to secondary literature.

6 www.youtube.com
   To get more information on the events and personalities of the Revolutionary and Constitutional Convention Eras, go to YouTube and type in your interest. Many fascinating clips are available.

Notes

1 Samuel H. Beer, *To Make a Nation: The Rediscovery of American Federalism* (Cambridge, MA: Harvard University Press, 1993), 64–65.
2 Thomas Hobbes, *Leviathan*, Michael Oakeshott, ed. (London: Collier Books, 1962), 100.
3 John Locke, *Two Treatises of Government*, Peter Laslett, ed. (New York: Cambridge University Press, 1960), 374–375.
4 Mark Hulliung, *The Social Contract in America: From the Revolution to the Current Age* (Lawrence, KS: University of Kansas Press, 2007).
5 Joyce Appleby, *Economic Thought and Ideology in Seventeenth-Century England* (Princeton, NJ: Princeton University Press, 1978), 80, 93.
6 Clinton Rossiter, *The First American Revolution* (New York: Harcourt Brace, 1956), 52, 56.
7 Desmond S. King and Rogers S. Smith, "Racial Orders in American Political Development," *American Political Science Review*, vol. 99, no. 1 (February 2005): 75–92.
8 J. Franklin Jameson, *The American Revolution Considered as a Social Movement* (Princeton, NJ: Princeton University Press, 1925), 9. See also Theda Skocpol, *States and Social Revolutions* (New York: Cambridge University Press, 1979).
9 Joseph F. Zimmerman, *Contemporary American Federalism: The Growth of National Power*, 2nd ed. (Albany, NY: State University of New York Press, 2008), 13.

10 See Jackson Turner Main, *The Sovereign States, 1775–1783* (New York: New Viewpoints, a division of Franklin Watts, 1973), 99–142, for a thorough treatment of the general structure and powers of American colonial political institutions.

11 Marc Egnal, "The Economic Development of the Thirteen Continental Colonies 1720 to 1775," *William and Mary Quarterly*, vol. 32, no. 2 (April 1975): 221; see also Gordon S. Wood, *The American Revolution* (New York: Modern Library, 2002), 12–16.

12 Thomas Jefferson quoted in Bernard Bailyn, *The Ideological Origins of the American Revolution* (Cambridge, MA: Harvard University Press, 1967), 118–143.

13 J. Franklin Jameson, *The American Revolution Considered as a Social Movement* (Princeton, NJ: Princeton University Press, 1925), 9.

14 *Journals of the Continental Congress, 1774–1789*, Worthington C. Ford, ed. (Washington, D.C.: U.S. Government Printing Office), 2: 22.

15 Donald S. Lutz, *Popular Consent and Popular Control: Whig Political Theory in the Early State Constitutions* (Baton Rouge, LA: Louisiana State University Press, 1980).

16 Leonard L. Richards, *Shays's Rebellion: The American Revolution's Last Battle* (Philadelphia, PA: University of Pennsylvania Press, 2003).

17 Richard Beeman, *Plain, Honest Men: The Making of the American Constitution* (New York: Random House, 2009).

18 David Robertson, *The Constitution and America's Destiny* (New York: Cambridge University Press, 2005).

19 Martin Diamond, *The Founding of the Democratic Republic* (Itasca, IL: Peacock, 1981), 16–18. See also Charles A. Beard, *An Economic Interpretation of the Constitution of the United States* (New York: Macmillan, 1913), 73–151.

20 Calvin C. Jillson, *Constitution-Making: Conflict and Consensus in the Federal Convention of 1787* (New York: Agathon, 1988), 1–17.

21 Gaillard Hunt, *The Writings of James Madison* (New York: Putnam, 1901), 2: 43, 134.

22 Max Farrand, *The Records of the Federal Convention of 1787* (New Haven, CT: Yale University Press, 1937), 1: 225–228.

23 Thornton Anderson, *Creating the Constitution: The Convention of 1787 and the First Congress* (University Park: PA, Pennsylvania State University Press, 1993).

24 Zimmerman, *Contemporary American Federalism*, 29.

25 Jack N. Rakove, *Original Meanings: Politics and Ideas in the Making of the Constitution* (New York: Random House, 1996), 106.

26 Farrand, *Records*, 2: 665.

27 Ralph Ketcham, *Framed for Posterity: The Enduring Philosophy of the Constitution* (Lawrence, KS: University of Kansas Press, 1993), 75.

28 David J. Siemers, *The Anti-Federalists: Men of Great Faith and Forbearance* (New York: Rowman and Littlefield, 2003).

29 Joseph J. Ellis, *Founding Brothers: The Revolutionary Generation* (New York: Alfred A. Knopf, 2001), 1–19.

30 John Nichols and Robert W. McChesney, *Dollarocracy: How the Money and Media Election Complex Is Destroying America* (New York: Nation Books, 2013), 260.

31 Robert A. Dahl, *How Democratic Is the American Constitution?* (New Haven, CT: Yale University Press, 2002), 15–20, 141–157.

32 Sanford Levinson, *Our Undemocratic Constitution* (New York: Oxford University Press, 2006), 12, 171–176.

Chapter 2

FEDERALISM AND THE AMERICAN CONSTITUTIONAL ORDER

Focus Questions: from reading to thinking

Q1 How did the meanings of the terms *federal* and *federalism* change over the course of the founding and early national periods?

Q2 What powers and responsibilities did the U.S. Constitution give the national government in relation to the states and to the states in relation to the national government?

Q3 How did the expansion and integration of the American economy shape the balance of governmental power and authority within the federal system?

Q4 What fiscal and political forces led to the change in American federalism called "devolution"?

Q5 Have the complexities of the twenty-first century rendered our government essentially national, or do state and local governments still have important roles to play?

The Constitution TODAY

IF MARIJUANA IS ILLEGAL, WHY ARE THEY SELLING IT IN CALIFORNIA?

Article VI (in part): "This Constitution, and the laws of the United States which shall be made in pursuance thereof . . . shall be the supreme law of the land."

Tenth Amendment: "The powers not delegated to the United States by the Constitution, nor prohibited by it to the states, are reserved to the states respectively, or to the people."

In 1970 the Congress passed and the president signed the Controlled Substances Act (CSA). The CSA declared marijuana, first made illegal in federal law in 1937, to be a Schedule I drug with a "high potential for abuse" and no legitimate medical use. The CSA is federal law to this day; yet new claims regarding the medical benefits of marijuana led California to enact a medical marijuana law in 1996. By 2017 medical marijuana was legal in twenty-nine states and D.C., but the Trump administration, led by Attorney General Jeff Sessions, has noted ominously that it is still illegal. Even under the Obama administration, when the number of pot shops in California proliferated beyond apparent medical needs, federal authorities cracked down. By 2017, eight states had upped the ante as citizen referenda approved marijuana use by any citizen over 21. Can federal and state laws conflict like this and, when they do, is not federal law supposed to prevail over state law? Yes, well usually, but occasionally federalism, the topic of this chapter, is messy.

The question of the relative priority of federal versus state law plagued the Founders during the Constitutional Convention, was one of the central issues over which ratification was fought, and has surfaced time and again throughout American history. In the 1860s we fought a bloody Civil War over just this issue—national versus state authority within the federal system.

For most of American history, the claims of state officials that federal officials construed their powers too broadly and infringed on state powers protected by the Tenth Amendment were taken seriously in the federal courts. All of that changed during the "Great Depression," in 1937 to be exact. President Franklin Roosevelt moved aggressively to deal with the depression, but the Supreme Court resisted, striking down major parts of his agenda. FDR responded by trying to "pack" the court with new and more compliant members. The court blinked, almost wholly abandoning its traditional role of limiting government regulation of the economy in favor of a focus on civil rights and liberties. The federal government initiated expansive social programs and an aggressive regulatory agenda. Only in the mid-1980s did the court begin to challenge federal powers, but only occasionally on the basis of the Tenth Amendment.

How then can states push back against unwelcome actions by the federal government? One option is through nullification, the idea that states can render federal laws null and void within their boundaries if they believe the laws are unconstitutional—meaning touching matters beyond the scope of the Congress's enumerated powers. To understand this claim we must distinguish between formal and informal nullification. Formal nullification would involve a state government declaring an act of Congress void and the federal courts upholding that claim under the "reserved rights" of the states in the Tenth Amendment. The Supreme Court has done so only twice in the last half century. In the most notable case, *Printz v. U.S.* (1997), the court struck down a provision of the Brady Handgun Violence Protection Act for requiring state officials to conduct background checks on persons seeking to buy a handgun.

Informal nullification, as with the case of medical marijuana or the broader marijuana use approved by Colorado, Washington, and a half a dozen other states, is more common and is well within the American traditions of political bargaining, popular democracy, and federalism. Informal nullification occurs in a variety of ways, most involving state and public reluctance to comply with a particular federal statute. State legislatures may pass contrary laws or decline to enforce federal mandates and the public may demonstrate an unwillingness to comply. If state authorities do not challenge federal authority directly, or do so carefully, federal authorities may react to the opposition by withdrawing the act or at least limiting enforcement.

FEDERALISM AND AMERICAN CONSTITUTIONAL THOUGHT

This chapter completes our discussion of the origins of American political ideals and institutions. In the previous chapter, we explored the Founders confidence in constitutional structure to limit, distribute, and check power awarded to government. In this chapter, we see that the Founders intended federalism to play a similar role. We explore the origins of the American federal system and ask how the tensions inherent in the federal structure have been managed historically and in our own time. In subsequent chapters, we regularly find federalism providing the context and terrain for the continuous struggle that is American politics (see Table 2.1).

TABLE 2.1 Strengths and Weaknesses of Federalism	
Strengths	**Weaknesses**
Limits concentrated national power	Leaves state power vulnerable
Encourages innovation by the states	Complex overlapping responsibilities
Encourages pluralism and citizen involvement	Lack of uniformity
National minorities may be subnational majorities	Encourages race to the bottom

A federal system divides political power and responsibility between national and subnational levels of government.[1] We describe how the nature of American federalism and the balance of power within it have evolved over time to address new issues and problems in a rapidly growing, increasingly complex, national and international environment.

Just as the Founders used separation of powers and checks and balances to allocate and limit executive, legislative, and judicial functions within the national government, they used federalism to allocate and limit political power and responsibility between levels of government. Some among the founding and later generations always wanted more power and initiative at the national level, others always wanted less. The struggle between and among national and state actors for the authority and resources to define and address the dominant issues of American political life has been and remains the drama of American federalism.

Modern American federalism involves a complicated array of authorities and actors. The nation now spans a continent and contains 330 million citizens. These citizens are served, at most recent count, by 90,107 governments within the federal system. There is, of course, only one national government. There are fifty state governments. Within the states are 3,031 county governments, 19,519 municipalities, 16,360 towns and townships, 12,880 school districts, and 38,266 special districts that deliver all manner of services.[2] As you read this chapter, think about the tremendous growth and change that our nation has undergone over the course of its history. Once just small colonies scattered along the Atlantic seaboard, the U.S. is now a global economic and military powerhouse. Is the federal system that the founding generation wrote into the Constitution still in force today? Has that federal system changed and, if so, when? How did the Constitution adapt to permit and even facilitate the evolution of our federal political structure? How healthy is contemporary American federalism and what are the system's prospects for effective governance in the twenty-first century?

Q1 How did the meanings of the terms *federal* and *federalism* change over the course of the founding and early national periods?

THE ORIGINAL MEANING OF FEDERALISM

Federalism is a very old idea. The word *federalism* and several closely related terms including *federal*, and *confederation* are drawn from the Latin root *foedus*, which means "treaty, compact, or covenant." The idea that people can establish lasting compacts or covenants among themselves by discussion and consent has been central to American political thought. Before the first Pilgrim stepped onto Plymouth Rock, the entire *Mayflower* company approved the famous Mayflower Compact to define the kind of society and government that they would have.

The great difficulty involved in thinking about government as resting on the ideas of compact or covenant is the obvious fragility of such an arrangement. Political scientist Samuel Beer remarked that, "Among the consequences of thinking of federal government as based on a contract was the idea of secession, 'the idea of simply breaking a disagreeable contract whenever any pretext of bad faith on the part of any other party arose.'"[3]

Nonetheless, the best thinking of their day told the Founders that governments over large territories had to take one of two forms. One was a consolidated or **unitary government** like the empires of the ancient world or the monarchies of Europe. These centralized states were subject to the will of one man or woman who could wield his or her power both offensively and defensively. The other was a **confederation** of smaller republics. The confederal solution left the individual republics fully sovereign, fully in control of their own domestic affairs, but pledged to coordinate their foreign affairs and to assist each other if attacked. Not surprisingly, confederations, including our own Articles of Confederation, proved to be weak and unstable in times of crisis.[4]

What made the choice between consolidation and confederation seem so stark was the idea of sovereignty—that in any political system, ultimate or final political authority must rest somewhere specific. In English history, disagreement about whether the king or Parliament was sovereign resulted in almost fifty years of civil war between 1640 and 1688. In the American case, it seemed that sovereignty had to be located either in a national government or in individual states that might then confederate together. The Articles of Confederation allocated specific modest powers to the Confederation Congress, but unambiguously left sovereignty with the individual states. Article II read: "Each state retains its sovereignty, Freedom and independence, and every Power, Jurisdiction and right, which is not by this confederation expressly delegated to the United States, in Congress

unitary government Centralized government subject to one authority as opposed to a federal system that divides power across national and subnational (state) governments.

confederation Loose governing arrangement in which separate republics or nations join together to coordinate foreign policy and defense but retain full control over their domestic affairs.

Library of Congress

Benjamin Franklin created this image of the separated serpent to convince his fellow colonists to unite, warning them to "Join or Die."

assembled." The powerful idea that several governments might operate in the same space and in relation to the same citizens if each was limited in its authority and jurisdiction was not yet widely understood or accepted.

The Constitutional Convention of 1787 set aside familiar names (confederation) and outdated assumptions (sovereignty) and let the problem that they were trying to solve guide their thinking in new directions.[5] Initially, James Madison and the supporters of the Virginia Plan called for a powerful national government capable of overriding the states where necessary. Madison's opponents rallied behind the New Jersey Plan's demand that the national government be grounded on the sovereignty of the states. Eventually, the convention came to understand, if only vaguely, that neither old model applied well to the new nation and that a new understanding of federalism was required.

FEDERALISM IN THE CONSTITUTION

Q2 What powers and responsibilities did the U.S. Constitution give the national government in relation to the states and to the states in relation to the national government?

The Founders' most fundamental insight was that the apparent choice between a consolidated national government and a loose confederation of sovereign states was false. The ideas of constitutionalism and limited government laid open the possibility that within a single territory there might be two sets of governments and two sets of public officials assigned clear and specific responsibilities and powers through written constitutions.[6]

Enumerated, Implied, and Inherent Powers

James Madison arrived at the Constitutional Convention determined to strengthen the national government. The Virginia Plan envisioned a national Congress with both a broad grant of legislative authority and the right to review, amend, or reject acts of the several state legislatures. This strong national federalism, in which the states would play a decidedly secondary role, was rejected in favor of a national Congress wielding specifically listed or enumerated powers. The nationalists' disappointment was assuaged somewhat by the Convention's adoption of the **supremacy clause** in Article VI. Article VI read in part: "This Constitution, and the laws of the United States which shall be made in pursuance thereof; and all treaties made, or which shall be made, under the authority of the United States, shall be the supreme law of the land; and the judges in every state shall be bound thereby; anything in the Constitution or laws of any State to the contrary notwithstanding." Moreover, all state officials were required to take an oath "to support this Constitution."

supremacy clause Article VI of the U.S. Constitution declares that the acts of the national government within its areas of legitimate authority will be supreme over the state constitutions and laws.

The enumerated powers of Congress are laid out in Article I, section 8, of the U.S. Constitution. Article I, section 8, lists seventeen enumerated powers, including the powers to tax, to regulate commerce and coinage, to declare war, and to raise armies and navies. In theory, Congress is limited to making law and policy within these areas of enumerated power. But other language in the Constitution seems to give Congress **implied powers** that go beyond its specifically enumerated powers. The closing paragraph of Article I, section 8, grants Congress the power to "make all laws which shall be necessary and proper for

implied powers Congressional powers not specifically mentioned among the enumerated powers, but which are reasonable and necessary to accomplish an enumerated end or activity.

carrying into execution" its enumerated powers. The "necessary and proper" clause, frequently referred to as the "elastic clause," suggests that Congress has a general authority beyond and in addition to its enumerated powers.

If the enumerated powers are fairly specific, and implied powers are somewhat broader but still must be a means to achieve enumerated purposes, the idea of inherent powers is only loosely related to specific constitutional provisions. Both Congress and the Supreme Court have accepted the idea, especially relating to the president and foreign affairs, that nationhood entails the right and necessity, without reference to specific language in the Constitution, to deal with other nations from a footing equal to theirs. In fact, these **inherent powers** of nationhood were what the Declaration of Independence referred to when it announced to the world: "That these United Colonies are, and of Right ought to be Free and Independent States; that . . . they have full Power to levy War, conclude Peace, contract Alliances, establish Commerce, and to do all other Acts and Things which Independent States may of right do."

inherent powers Powers argued to accrue to all sovereign nations, whether or not specified in the Constitution, allowing executives to take all actions required to defend the nation and protect its interests.

One example of presidential initiative, taken in threatening circumstances, but with no narrow constitutional authorization, will suffice to clarify the nature of inherent powers. Early in 1861 President Lincoln took several steps in the immediate wake of the secession of the southern states, including calling up additional troops and spending substantial sums of money, even though Congress was not in session and had not previously authorized these actions. When critics complained Lincoln simply asked, "Was it possible to lose the nation and yet preserve the Constitution?" Lincoln assumed that the answer was "no" and that his actions required no further justification.

Concurrent Powers

The idea of **concurrent powers** was central to the Founders' conception of a compound republic in which national and state governments exercise dual sovereignty. Dual sovereignty suggests that in some fields, such as the power to tax and borrow, to regulate commerce, to establish courts, and to build roads and highways, the national and state governments have concurrent powers. Both levels of the federal system are authorized to act in these and similar areas of law and policy. Your tax bill is a good example of a concurrent power. In all but seven states citizens must fill out income tax returns for both the national and state levels (and sometimes the local level, too).

concurrent powers Powers, such as the power to tax, that are available to both levels of the federal system and may be exercised by both in relation to the same body of citizens.

Powers Denied to the National Government

Article I, section 9, of the Constitution denied certain powers to the national government. Congress was forbidden to suspend normal legal processes except in cases of rebellion or grave public danger, to favor the commerce or ports of one state over another, to expend money unless lawfully appropriated, and to grant titles of nobility. Other limitations on national power have been added to the Constitution by amendment, but students should notice that this is a brief paragraph.

Powers Reserved to the States

The fundamental logic of American federalism is that the states possess complete power over matters not delegated to the national government and not denied them by the U.S. Constitution or by their own state constitutions. As Madison explained in Federalist Number 39, the jurisdiction of the Congress "extends to certain enumerated objects only, and leaves to the several States a residuary and inviolable sovereignty over all other objects."[7] Nonetheless, widespread concern that the new national government might encroach upon the powers of the states and the rights of their citizens led many to demand that protections be added to the Constitution itself. The first Congress initiated a process that led to adoption of ten amendments to the Constitution—the Bill of Rights—in 1791. The Tenth Amendment reads as follows: "The powers not delegated to the United States by the Constitution, nor prohibited by it to the states, are reserved to the states respectively, or to the people."

reserved powers The Tenth Amendment to the U.S. Constitution declares that powers not explicitly granted to the national government are reserved to the states or to the people.

Joseph Zimmerman has usefully divided the **reserved powers** of the states into three categories: "the police power, provision of services to citizens, ... and creation and control of local governments."[8] The "police power" covers regulation of individual and corporate activities in order to protect and enhance public health, welfare, safety, morals, and convenience. States also provide services such as police and fire protection, road construction, and education. Finally, local governments are created and regulated by the states.

Powers Denied to State Governments

The Founders wanted to be sure that the problems experienced under the Articles of Confederation, where individual states had antagonized dangerous foreign powers and tried to create economic advantages for their own citizens to the detriment of citizens of other states, were not repeated. Article I, section 10, of the U.S. Constitution forbids the states to enter into treaties or alliances either with each other or with foreign powers, to keep their own armies or navies, or to engage in war unless actually invaded. Foreign and military policy belongs to the national government. States are also forbidden to coin their own money, impair contracts, or tax imports or exports.

Federal Obligations to the States

The U.S. Constitution makes a series of explicit promises to the states. Most of these are found in Article IV, sections 3 and 4, and in Article V. The states are promised that their boundaries and their equal representation in the Senate will not be changed without their consent and that their republican governments will be protected from invasion and, at their request, from domestic violence.

When President Obama sought to loosen immigration restrictions by executive order, a broad coalition of conservative, mostly Republican-led, states sued in the federal courts to stop him. Here, Congressman Ruben Gallego (D-AZ), center, and Dolores Huerta, long-time union and Hispanic activist, rally before the Supreme Court in favor of Obama's policies.

Relations among the States

Article IV, sections 1 and 2, of the U.S. Constitution deal with interstate relations. Provisions require the states to respect each other's civil acts, deal fairly with each other's citizens, and return suspected criminals who flee from one state into another.

Full Faith and Credit.   Article IV, section 1, of the U.S. Constitution requires that "full faith and credit shall be given in each state to the public acts, records, and judicial proceedings of every other State." Stated most directly, "public acts are the civil statutes enacted by the state legislatures. Records are documents such as deeds, mortgages, and wills. Judicial proceedings are final civil court proceedings."[9] Through this simple provision, the Founders largely succeeded in creating a national legal system requiring the states to recognize and respect each other's legal acts and findings. Nonetheless, over the course of American history, social issues such as religious toleration, slavery, gay marriage, and, most recently, the decision by some states to permit marijuana use, have strained reciprocity and cooperation between the states.

Privileges and Immunities.   Article IV, section 2, of the U.S. Constitution declares that "The citizens of each state shall be entitled to all privileges and

Paul v. Virginia (1869) This decision declared that the privileges and immunities clause of the U.S. Constitution guaranteed citizens visiting, working, or conducting business in another state the same freedoms and legal protections that would be afforded to citizens of that state.

extradition Provision of Article IV, section 2, of the U.S. Constitution providing that persons accused of a crime in one state fleeing into another state shall be returned to the state in which the crime was committed.

immunities of citizens in the several states." The classic statement of the reasoning behind the privileges and immunities language was delivered by the Supreme Court in the 1869 case of *Paul v. Virginia*. The court explained that citizens visiting, working, or conducting business in states other than the one in which they normally reside have "the same freedom possessed by the citizens of those States in the acquisition and enjoyment of property and in the pursuit of happiness; and it secures them the equal protection of the laws."

Extradition.   Article IV, section 2, provides for a legal process called **extradition**: "A person charged in any state with treason, felony, or other crime, who shall flee from justice, and be found in another state, shall on demand of the executive authority of the state from which he fled, be delivered up, to be removed to the state having jurisdiction of the Crime."

Fundamentally, the Constitution left the states in charge of their own internal police and gave the national government responsibility for military and foreign policy. Yet, the Constitution also sought to lower trade and regulatory barriers among the several state economies to create a national economy, an American free trade zone that would stretch from Maine to Georgia and from the Atlantic coast to the farthest edge of western settlement. Not surprisingly, the boundary line between the national government's supremacy within its areas of constitutional responsibility and the states' reserve powers has been fuzzy, contested, and shifting. In fact, it is fair to say that the principal point of tension in thinking about American federalism is how to balance federal power, grounded in the elastic clause and the supremacy clause, and the powers reserved to the individual states by the Tenth Amendment. As we shall see, these tensions arose early and remain with us today.[10]

The Fluidity of American Federalism

If political power derived from the people, as the Founders believed that it did, the people need not cede sovereignty either to a consolidated national government or to loosely confederated sovereign states? James Madison made this point in *Federalist* No. 51 (see Appendix C). Madison explained: "In the compound republic of America, the power surrendered by the people is first divided between two distinct governments, and then the portion allotted to each is subdivided among distinct and separate departments. Hence, a double security arises to the rights of the people." After this double security is in place, Madison concluded, "Every thing beyond this, must be left to the prudence and firmness of the people; who, as they will hold the scales in their own hands, it is to be hoped, will always take care to preserve the constitutional equilibrium between the General and the State Governments."[11] Although Madison used the phrase, "the people," more narrowly than we would today, we easily recognize his description of constitutional democracy.

Madison made a second point about American federalism that we often ignore today because the work of the national government seems so big and important that the work of state and local governments by comparison seems less momentus. As we shall see, this was not true for most of American history and remains largely untrue today. Madison noted in *Federalist* No. 45 that; "The powers delegated by the proposed Constitution to the federal government, are few and defined. Those which are to remain in the State governments are numerous and indefinite."[12] Madison's point was that the states did most of the governing that touched people's lives. States had the lead on broad swaths of public policy, including, but not limited to: education, health care, welfare, law enforcement, economic development, regulation of the professions, elections, corporate and family law, and municipal regulation and zoning.

As a result, most political and legal disputes are initiated in the states and most, though not all, are resolved there. But oftentimes initial resolutions do not hold; circumstances change, old issues arise in new forms, and past winners lose on the next round. Woodrow Wilson, president of Princeton University in 1908 when he wrote *Constitutional Government in the United States* and later president of the United States, described federal relations this way: "The question of the relation of the States to the federal government is the cardinal question of our constitutional system.... It cannot, indeed, be settled by the opinion of any one generation, because it is the question of growth, and every successive stage of our political and economic development give it a new aspect, makes it a new question."[13]

Woodrow Wilson was correct to note that our federal system evolved as social change and economic development raised new questions and problems. Think, for example, about commercial regulation in the age of wagon haulage, compared to railroad, flight, and Internet movement of products. But there has been another aspect of federal politics and dispute resolution. While most policy fights do start at the state level, they often end up going back and forth between the state and national levels depending upon where the various parties to the fight think they have the best chance to win and that may change over time. If you are losing at the state level, try the federal level; losing at the federal level, back to the states.

Finally, federalism often extends policy fights through time as the parties, groups, and individuals who control the policy levers in Washington seek a national resolution while the losers seek shelter and sustenance in friendly states. State and regional political and policy variations rarely allow one party to rule everywhere. Opposition states, even when they are relatively few, provide a refuge where national minority parties and their policy goals are accepted and where they can plot a comeback in the next election.

While any number of major policy issues have been fought out within the American federal system, no issue has highlighted the political dynamics of federalism more starkly than race. Initially, race was described as a states' rights issue, but slavery was dramatically and violently nationalized by the Civil War and its outcome. Nonetheless, within little more than a decade, national attention faded and states across the South moved to enact "Jim Crow" segregation of the races. Not until the middle of the twentieth century did the federal government again move to make equal rights a national commitment. Again, resistance in the South and not only in the South was tenacious and the fight continues today. The fight for civil rights will be the topic of Chapter 4, so we will leave the details for later—but when we get there federalism will be a big part of the story.

DUAL FEDERALISM AND ITS CHALLENGERS

dual federalism Nineteenth-century federalism envisioned a federal system in which the two levels were sovereign in fairly distinct areas of responsibility with little overlap or shared authority.

American federalism has always been a story of conflict. **Dual federalism**, often referred to as layer-cake federalism, saw the nation and the several states as sovereign within their areas of constitutional responsibility, but with little policy overlap between them. During the nation's early history and, to a lesser extent, throughout the nation's history, dual federalism had two challengers, one a nation-centered federalism and the other a state-centered federalism.[14] The national vision of federalism was championed by a long series of American statesmen including Alexander Hamilton, Chief Justice John Marshall, Senator Henry Clay, and President Abraham Lincoln. The fundamental idea was that the nation preexisted the states and in fact called the states into existence in June of 1776 when the Continental Congress instructed the colonies to sever ties to England.

Q3 How did the expansion and integration of the American economy shape the balance of governmental power and authority within the federal system?

A second set of American statesmen took a different view. Thomas Jefferson, John C. Calhoun, the South's great antebellum political theorist, and President Jefferson Davis of the Confederate States of America all believed that the states preexisted the nation and created it by compact among themselves. On this state-centered vision of federalism, the original parties to the compact, that is, the individual states, could secede from the Union if the national government violated the compact by encroaching upon their sovereign prerogatives. Short of secession, states could nullify, or declare unenforceable within their boundaries, federal laws they believed fell outside Congress's Article II, section 8, enumerated powers.

The nation-centered and state-centered visions of federalism contested on even terms through the early decades of the country's history. However, as the industrial economy of New England outstripped the agrarian economy of the South during the 1840s and 1850s, state-centered federalism became increasingly isolated and strident. When Abraham Lincoln was elected president in 1860, the South seceded and two visions of American federalism faced off on the battlefields of the Civil War.[15]

Chief Justice John Marshall and National Federalism. As early as 1791, a federal court declared a Rhode Island state law unconstitutional, and in 1803 Chief Justice John Marshall, in the famous case of *Marbury v. Madison*, declared a section of an act of Congress, the Judiciary Act of 1789, to be unconstitutional. The broad result of the *Marbury* decision was to establish the Supreme Court as the final arbiter of what is and is not constitutional, and, hence, of the meaning, shape, and boundaries of American federalism.

Marbury v. Madison (1803) Chief Justice John Marshall derived the power of judicial review from the Constitution by reasoning that the document was supreme and therefore the court should invalidate legislative acts that run counter to it.

John Marshall, Chief Justice of the U.S. Supreme Court from 1801 to 1835, established the judiciary as a co-equal branch of the national government.

The importance of the Supreme Court's role as arbiter of the meaning of the Constitution was highlighted by the court's 1819 ruling in *McCulloch v. Maryland*. The issue in McCulloch, whether Congress could legitimately charter a bank, permitted the court to interpret the powers of Congress broadly and to limit state interference with them. No power to establish a bank appeared among the enumerated powers of Congress, so opponents of the bank, arguing from the state-centered or compact vision of federalism, denied that Congress

McCulloch v. Maryland (1819) The court announced an expansive reading of the "necessary and proper" clause, holding that Congress's Article I, section 8, enumerated powers imply unspecified but appropriate powers to carry them out.

had the power to create a bank at all. Chief Justice Marshall, writing from the nation-centered vision, rested the right of the Congress to establish and administer a bank on the "necessary and proper" clause. Marshall noted that Congress's enumerated powers included the power "to coin money" and "regulate the value thereof." He argued that the bank was an "appropriate," though perhaps not an "indispensable," means to this end. Marshall's classic interpretation of the "necessary and proper" clause made this point as follows: "Let the end be legitimate, let it be within the scope of the Constitution, and all means which are appropriate which are plainly adapted to the end, which are not prohibited, but consistent with the letter and spirit of the Constitution, are constitutional." This expansive interpretation of national power came at the expense of the Tenth Amendment "reserved powers" of the states.

A third decision completed Chief Justice Marshall's attempt to embed the nation-centered vision of federalism in the Constitution. The 1824 case of *Gibbons v. Ogden* dealt with the regulation of interstate commerce, that is, commerce conducted across state lines. While the court's interpretation of the commerce clause may seem arcane, even boring, it has been absolutely central to the expansion of national power from Chief Justice John Marshall's day to our own day.

Gibbons v. Ogden (1824) This decision employed an expansive reading of the commerce clause, the doctrine of the "continuous journey," to allow Congress to regulate commercial activity if any element of it crossed a state boundary.

The issue in *Gibbons* was whether a steamship company operating in a single state was in interstate commerce and subject to the regulatory powers of the Congress. Advocates of the state-centered vision said no. Marshall, writing for the majority, held that the Congress's power to regulate interstate commerce applied to navigation, even in a single state, if any of the passengers or goods being carried on the steamship were engaged in a "continuous journey" that found or would find them in interstate commerce. Clearly, this was a very expansive ruling because it is almost inconceivable that not a single person or piece of cargo on such a steamship had been or would later be in interstate commerce. These decisions laid the foundation for the triumph of national federalism, though it would be another century before the structure was fully built. In the meantime, Marshall's opponents would have their century-long day in the sun.

Chief Justice Roger Taney and the States. Upon John Marshall's death in 1835, President Andrew Jackson named Roger B. Taney to be the new chief justice, an office he held until 1863. Chief Justice Taney was a strong advocate of state-centered federalism and of a limited national government.

Chief Justice Taney's most infamous opinion was *Dred Scott v. Sandford* in 1857. Taney held that Congress had no right to prohibit a slave owner from taking his property, even his human property, into any state in the Union, even a free state, and holding that slave as property. The next year, in the Illinois Senate election of 1858, Senator Stephen A. Douglas argued that the deep American commitment to "popular sovereignty" meant that the citizens of individual states should be able to vote for or against slavery. Douglas's opponent, then

---

Struggling Toward Democracy

In a letter to William B. Giles on December 6, 1825, Thomas Jefferson wrote, "I see, as you do, and with the deepest affliction, the rapid strides with which the federal branch of our government is advancing toward the usurpation of all the rights reserved to the States."

What do you think?

- In what areas, if any, do you think the states' ability to govern is being threatened by the federal government?
- Does the increased size of the country now compared to the founding make the role of the federal government more or less important?

a little-known former congressman named Abraham Lincoln, argued for the right of the national government to limit slavery to those states where it currently existed. Lincoln lost.

The strong arguments by Taney and Douglas in favor of an expansive view of states' rights and the state-centered view of federalism helped set the stage for the Civil War. Northern opinion mobilized against the expansion of slavery and Lincoln rode that mobilization to the presidency in the election of 1860. The South seceded, the North resisted, and America went to war with itself over the nature of its federal Union.

FROM DUAL FEDERALISM TO COOPERATIVE FEDERALISM

Although the idea of the Constitution as a compact from which states might secede was a casualty of the Civil War, the idea of states' rights—a large and secure place for the states in the federal system—certainly was not. Congress did little to regulate state and local affairs until the Great Depression seemed to demand change in the broad character and basic structure of American federalism. After the 1930s American federalism was better described as cooperative federalism than as dual federalism.

The defining aspects of **cooperative federalism**, or marble-cake federalism as it is often called to highlight the sharing or mixing of national and state responsibility, have been nicely described by political scientist David Walker. Walker made two key points that distinguish cooperative federalism from dual federalism. In cooperative federalism, national, state, and local officials share "responsibilities for virtually all functions," and these "officials are not adversaries. They are colleagues."[16] Over time, however, concern about the national government's dominance of the federal system, usually by attaching mandates to federal funds provided to states and communities, has became a growing concern.

The Industrialization and Urbanization of America

Social change in America between the elections of Abraham Lincoln in 1860 and Franklin Roosevelt in 1932 was massive. During this period, the nation went from one mostly of small towns and isolated farms to one of burgeoning cities and large-scale industry. More important, the nation was bound ever more tightly into a web of commerce and communication, highlighted by railroads and the telegraph, that seemed to demand tending above the levels of states and communities. As the web of commerce expanded over the course of the nineteenth century and into the twentieth century, debate raged over the reach of congressional power channeled through the Constitution's commerce clause.

How could states, let alone localities, control and regulate a railroad that stretched across half a dozen states, or a steel, sugar, or tobacco trust that did

Dred Scott v. Sandford (1857) The court declared that African Americans, whether free or slave, were not citizens of the U.S. Moreover, slaves were property and could be carried into any state in the union, even a free state, and held as property.

cooperative federalism Mid-twentieth-century view of federalism in which national, state, and local governments share responsibilities for virtually all functions.

Pro & Con

The Continuing Relevance of States' Rights

The language of the U.S. Constitution is ambiguous about the relative power of the national and state governments. Although Article VI suggests national supremacy ("This Constitution, and the laws of the United States which shall be made in pursuance thereof . . . shall be the supreme law of the land"), the powers granted to Congress are enumerated rather than general. Moreover, the Tenth Amendment, adopted as part of the Bill of Rights in 1791, reads: "The powers not delegated to the United States by the Constitution, nor prohibited to it by the states, are reserved to the states respectively, or to the people."

Prior to the Civil War most discussions of the rights of the states in the new Union revolved around the ideas of nullification and secession. **Nullification** was the idea that a state could suspend within its borders the operation of an act of the national government with which it disagreed. **Secession** was the idea that a state might actually withdraw from the Union if it disagreed deeply with the general pattern of policy activity of the federal government.

Although the Civil War destroyed both nullification and secession as practical ideas within the American political system, the broader idea of states' rights retained its importance. Some now believe that the fights against the racism and poverty of the 1960s and 1970s, important though they may have been at the time, left behind programs that no longer work and a federal government too large and intrusive for the needs of the twenty-first century. Therefore, many, mostly conservatives, believe that federal money and authority should be transferred back to the states, closer to the problems that need to be solved and to the people in the best position to know how to solve them.

Some others, mostly liberals, worry that the old states' rights arguments for the virtues of local control will once again be used by powerful local majorities to ignore the needs of weaker local minorities and that, as in the past, the most vulnerable (women, blacks, gays) will be among the first to suffer. The modern opponents of states' rights claim that fairness and justice require that national standards be set and maintained, not just in the obvious area of equal rights for minorities and women, but also in such diverse areas as health, welfare, and education. Absent such standards, they believe, some states will do much less than others to assist their neediest citizens.

When President Obama and Democrat majorities in Congress passed Obamacare, Democrats across the nation cheered. When the Supreme Court upheld Obamacare but declared that the states could not be required to implement it, conservatives did not know whether to cheer or cry. Although there are principled reasons to stand for states' rights or national uniformity, there is also a long national tradition that the party that dominates Washington is comfortable with uniformity while the opposition party looks for partial victories in friendly states.[17]

What do you think?
- What are the pros and cons of allowing each state to decide what they want to do on critical issues like health care, legalization of marijuana, abortion, guns, prayer in schools, and other hotly debated issues?
- Why might liberals or conservatives have conflicting views of state–federal powers depending on the policy issue?

PRO	CON
State differences are real	Natural standards for justice are critical
Problems should be addressed close to home	Many problems require national coordination
States' rights no longer about secession	Local minorities are still vulnerable

business in every state in the Union? They simply could not. Yet, the Supreme Court declared in *U.S. v. E.C. Knight* (1895) that Congress's power to regulate interstate commerce did not reach manufacturing or production, only the transportation of goods across state lines. Hence, as the twentieth century dawned, the nation's largest businesses were beyond the reach of congressional and state regulation and control.

Theodore Roosevelt threatened "trust busting" to encourage large private sector actors to accept more federal oversight and President Woodrow Wilson secured passage of an income tax, just prior to World War I, but the Roaring 20s saw a renewed commitment to *laissez faire*. Not until Franklin Roosevelt rose to confront the Great Depression of the 1930s did the balance of American federalism begin a decisive shift of responsibility and authority to the national level.

nullification The claim prominent in the first half of the nineteenth century that states have the right to nullify or reject national acts that they believe to be beyond national constitutional authority.

secession The claim that states have the right to withdraw from the Union.

U.S. v. E.C. Knight (1895) The court held that Congress's power to regulate interstate commerce extended only to transportation of goods across state lines, not to manufacturing or production.

The Great Depression

Nothing made the fact that the American economy had become an integrated whole more clear than its collapse in late October 1929. "The Crash," in which the stock market lost almost a quarter of its value in two days of panic trading, began a decade of deep economic depression and persistent unemployment. Just as the depression eased, World War II erupted (see Figure 2.1).

FIGURE 2.1 Percent of Government Expenditures by Level of Government, 1902–2016

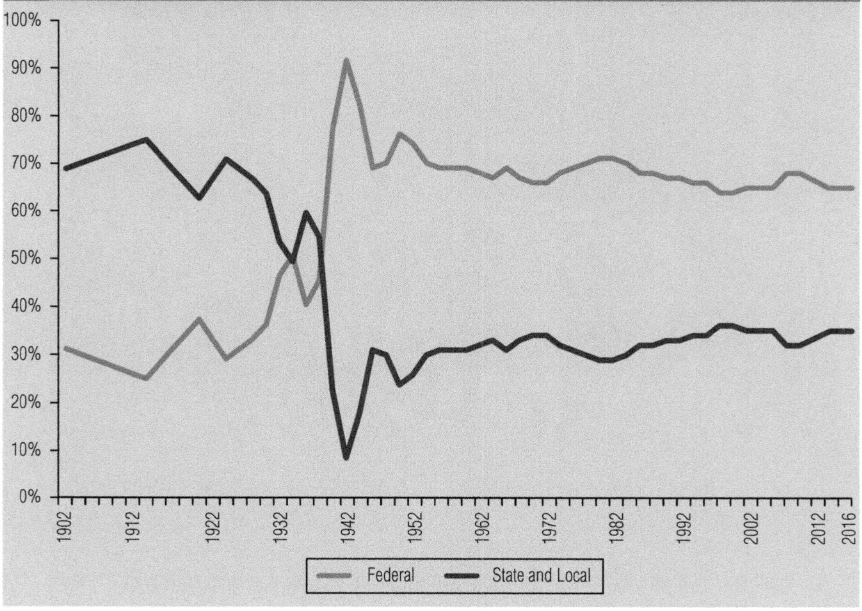

Source: Historical Statistics of the United States, Colonial Times to 1957 (Washington, D.C.: U.S. Department of Commerce, 1960), 711, Series Y254–257, and 726, Series Y536–546. Post-1960 figures come from Budget of the United States Government, Fiscal Year *2018*, Historical Tables (Washington, D.C.: Government Printing Office, 2018), Table 14.2.

The 1930s and 1940s were a period of national emergency. By the time Franklin Roosevelt assumed office early in 1933, the country had already been mired in depression for more than three years. The Depression was a national, even worldwide, economic collapse. The economy had declined by 40 percent from its 1929 high, and fully one-third of the workforce was unemployed. State and local governments were overwhelmed by the needs of their citizens. Roosevelt's dramatic response, known as the "New Deal" and initiated during his "first hundred days" in office, included "an extraordinary assumption of federal authority over the nation's economy and a major expansion of its commerce and taxing powers."[18] The Supreme Court, still committed to maintaining as much of the logic and operation of "dual federalism" as possible, declared much of it unconstitutional.

Roosevelt threatened to ask the Congress to expand the size of the Supreme Court so that he could "pack" it with new members more favorably disposed to his vision of an activist role for the federal government. The Supreme Court blinked. Some members changed their votes, a few retired, and Roosevelt soon had a Supreme Court that would bless a vastly expanded role for the federal government.

Getty Images/Universal Images Group

In the depths of the Great Depression, unemployed men line-up for free coffee and donuts. The Depression struck deep into the working and middle classes, even the upper classes – note that some of the men in line are well-dressed.

Wickard v. Filburn shows how far the Supreme Court had moved by 1942. Roosevelt's program for rejuvenating agricultural prices, the Agricultural Adjustment Act (AAA), regulated the acreage that farmers could plant. Roscoe Filburn was authorized to plant 11 acres of wheat on his Ohio farm. He planted 23 acres, arguing that the wheat from only 11 acres would be sold and the other 12 would feed livestock. The Supreme Court held that feeding the excess wheat to his own animals meant that he did not have to buy that wheat in the open market and that tiny effect on "interstate commerce" was enough to bring him under the purview of Congress's legitimate constitutional authority.[19] The balance between national and state authority within American federalism had shifted dramatically to the national level.

World War II drove the federal share of total government spending to 90 percent by 1944. When the war ended in 1945, the United States remained engaged in international politics, aided in the rebuilding of the European and Japanese economies and constructed a military alliance to confront Soviet expansionism. Although the federal share of total government spending fell below 60 percent in 1950, the Korean War of the early 1950s drove it back up toward 70 percent. It has ranged between 60 and 70 percent for the past half century. Moreover, consolidation of political authority at the national level involved domestic policy as much as it did foreign and national security policy.

Wickard v. Filburn (1942) The court rejected the narrow reading of the commerce power in *U.S. v. E.C. Knight* to return to the broader reading in Gibbons v. Ogden by which Congress could regulate virtually all commercial activity.

THE RISE OF FISCAL FEDERALISM

For most of American history, the limited congressional authority outlined in Article I, section 8, of the Constitution was understood to forbid national control of broad policy areas including education, health care, income and retirement security, and much more. Slowly, beginning with Theodore Roosevelt's "Square Deal" and picking up speed with Franklin Roosevelt's "New Deal," federal authorities highlighted the first clause of Article I, section 8, permitting Congress to "lay and collect taxes … to pay the debts and provide for the common defense and general welfare of the United States." Especially during the "Great Depression," need in the nation's states and communities seemed to call for an activist federal government.

The reach of the national government within the structure of American federalism continued to expand during the 1960s and early 1970s. The fuel that powered this new movement was national government money. The favored device for delivering national funds to states and localities was the **categorical grant**. Each categorical grant program offered state and local governments the opportunity to receive national funds if they would engage in a certain narrow activity and if they would do so in compliance with detailed mandates on eligibility, program design, service delivery, and reporting. Only five categorical grant programs were in place in 1900 and only fifteen by 1930. Fifteen more were added during FDR's first two terms as president, but major transfers of funds from the national government to state and local governments did not begin until after World War II.

categorical grant A program making national funds available to states and communities for a specific, often narrow, purpose and usually requiring a distinct application, implementation, and reporting procedure.

LBJ: Creative Federalism and Grants-in-Aid

By the time John Kennedy entered the White House in early 1961, 132 categorical grant programs were in operation. During the five years that Lyndon Johnson was president, he and his overwhelmingly Democratic Congresses passed more than two hundred new categorical grant programs covering the full range of U.S. domestic policy initiatives. **Creative federalism** was the term used to describe the range and breadth of Johnson administration activities.

The "Great Society" initiatives of the 1960s were driven, not just by Democratic activism in the White House and the Congress, but also by a federal judiciary determined to end racial discrimination and segregation, protect civil liberties, reform criminal justice procedures, and afford new protections to rights of the accused and convicted.[20] Every new federal grant program passed and every expansive judicial decision handed down increased the federal bureaucracy's range of regulatory control. By the time LBJ left office early in 1969, his opponents had begun to refer to creative federalism as **coercive federalism**.

Nixon: Revenue Sharing and the First New Federalism

Republican President Richard Nixon's "New Federalism" was intended to enhance the discretion of the states in deciding how best to use the financial resources they received from the national government. President Nixon undertook two major federalism initiatives. The first, called **special revenue sharing (SRS)** or **block grants**, bundled related sets of categorical grants into a single SRS or block grant program. States and localities were permitted to decide how to allocate the money across the eligible program activities. The second Nixon initiative, called **general revenue sharing (GRS)**, provided $30.2 billion to the fifty states and approximately thirty-eight thousand local governments over a five-year period. Unlike categorical grants or even block grants, general revenue sharing funds had few strings attached. States could set their own priorities.

The Process of "Devolution" in Contemporary Federalism

Not surprisingly, the rapid rise in federal transfers to the states over the past half century and more sharpened the long-running conflict between nation-centered and state-centered federalism. The modern version of this historical battle has been between "preemption" and "devolution." **Preemption** is the power of the national government, based on the "supremacy clause" in Article VI, to preempt or push aside state law. Joseph F. Zimmerman, one of the nation's leading federalism experts, has written that Congress passed 678 preemption statutes between 1790 and 2011 in policy areas ranging from banking and commerce to health care and the environment.[21] Fully 70 percent of them were passed after 1970.

creative federalism 1960s view of federalism that refers to LBJ's willingness to expand the range of federal programs to support state and local activities and to bring new, even nongovernmental, actors into the process.

coercive federalism A pejorative term to describe the federalism of the 1960s and 1970s, suggesting that the national government was using its financial muscle to coerce states into following national dictates as opposed to serving local needs.

special revenue sharing The Nixon administration developed block grants that bundled related categorical grants into a single grant to enhance state and local discretion over how the money was spent.

block grants Federal funds made available to states and communities in which they have discretion over how the money is spent within the broad substantive area covered by the block grant.

general revenue sharing Program enacted in 1974, discontinued in 1986, that provided basically unrestricted federal funds to states and localities to support activities that they judged to be of highest priority.

preemption The Article VI declaration that national statutes are "the supreme law of the land" allows Congress to preempt or displace state authority in areas where they choose to legislate.

Alternatively, **devolution** stems from the idea that the Tenth Amendment to the U.S. Constitution guarantees the states against undue intrusion by the national government. Supporters of devolution call for returning both authority and financial resources to the states so that they can deal with the issues that seem most critical to them.

Ronald Reagan, Bill Clinton, and George W. Bush all served as governors and all thought they knew how the national government should relate to the states. Ronald Reagan came to the presidency early in 1981 with a view of American federalism unlike that of any president since Herbert Hoover. Reagan's first inaugural address declared his "intention to curb the size and influence of the Federal establishment and to demand recognition of the distinction between the powers granted to the Federal Government and those reserved to the States or the people."

The Reagan administration concluded that the national and state governments were doing too much and would do less only if they had less money. The Reagan administration's signature tax cuts produced budget deficits and put very heavy pressure on domestic spending in general and on transfer payments to state and local governments in particular. States were dropped from general revenue sharing in 1980 and the program was allowed to lapse in 1986. "Federal outlays to state and local governments fell by 33 percent between 1980 and 1987."[22] State and local governments were left to decide whether to pick up the slack or take the heat for program cuts.

Bill Clinton thought that government had an important role to play in American life, but that many problems were better addressed by people in their states and communities. He sought to redirect both financial resources and programmatic responsibilities to the states. After 1994, President Clinton's desire to produce a balanced budget joined with the Republican Congress's desire to shift primary responsibility for social welfare policy from the national to the state level to produce a dramatic overhaul of federal relations.

President George W. Bush accelerated the process of moving financial resources and policy responsibility to the states, especially in the areas of education, health care, homeland security, and electoral reforms. However, like Reagan, Bush also cut taxes, and the resulting budget deficits put new pressure on federal support for the states.[23]

Just as momentously, in a series of narrow 5–4 judicial decisions, beginning with **U.S. v. Lopez** (1995) and extending through **U.S. v. Morrison** (2000), the Supreme Court moved to limit the ability of the president and Congress to use the commerce clause to push states in directions that they did not wish to go. In *Lopez*, the court decided that the national government's prohibition on guns near schools was too loosely connected to regulating commerce to be justified. Similarly, in *Morrison*, the court held that the 1994 Violence Against Women Act was unconstitutional because its impact on commerce was too remote to displace the rights of the states to legislate as they see fit in this area. *Lopez* and *Morrison* were the first cases in more than 70 years, since *Wickard v. Filburn* in 1942, in which the court struck down an attempt by Congress to regulate some realm of public activity under the commerce clause.

---

devolution The return of political authority from the national government to the states beginning in the 1970s and continuing today.

Q4 What fiscal and political forces led to the change in American federalism called "devolution"?

U.S. v. Lopez (1995) The court found that Congress's desire to forbid carrying handguns near schools was too loosely related to its power to regulate interstate commerce to stand. The police powers of the states cover such matters.

U.S. v. Morrison (2000) Citing *U.S. v. Lopez*, the court found that the Violence Against Women Act was too loosely related to Congress's power to regulate interstate commerce to stand.

A far larger battle broke out in 2010. Within five minutes of President Barack Obama signing the Affordable Care Act, universally known as Obamacare, Virginia's Republican attorney general, Ken Cuccinelli, filed suit contesting its constitutionality. Within weeks, 26 state attorneys general (mostly Republican), led by Florida's Bill McCollum, had joined Cuccinelli or filed similar suits. The attorneys general argued that the new law dramatically overreached on Congress's Article I, section 8 power to regulate interstate commerce by ordering that every person must have health insurance. They also argued that this vast new federal program would change the relationship between the federal and state governments in violation of the Tenth Amendment guarantees of the states' reserved powers.

Beginning in late 2010, several federal district and appellate courts declared the law constitutional while several others found part, usually the individual mandate, or all of the law unconstitutional. As the number of conflicting rulings among the lower courts grew, the U.S. Justice Department in September 2011 asked the U.S. Supreme Court to resolve the dispute. The Supreme Court heard an unprecedented five hours of oral arguments across three days in March 2012 and ruled in June, just as the 2012 general election campaign for president shifted into high gear.

Stunningly, Chief Justice John Roberts, writing for a narrow 5-4 majority, upheld most of Obamacare. To the great relief of Democrats and progressives, the court held that even though the commerce clause could not sustain the health care law, it was constitutional based on the Congress' power to tax. As if to balance the ledger with Republicans and conservatives, the court declared that the federal government could not require or unduly pressure the states into expanding their Medicaid programs to cover more of the poor. About twenty states, including large states with lots of uninsured poor, like Texas, refused to expand Medicaid, claiming that the burden on state budgets was too great. As a result, Obamacare was left hobbled but still standing.

By 2016, nearly 20 million citizens had been signed up for health insurance or had been added to Medicaid rolls in states that had approved expansion. Once the Supreme Court held Obamacare constitutional, Republican opposition began to shift and even to moderate. Some Republican governors, like Rick Scott of Florida or John Kasich of Ohio, approved Medicaid expansion and congressional leaders began to worry that taking coverage from those that had it was more politically dangerous than had been opposing the program before implementation. Nonetheless, when Donald Trump won the presidency in late 2016 and Republicans held majorities in both houses of Congress, they made Obamacare "repeal and replace" their top priority. They failed and Republican governors protecting their expanded Medicaid programs contributed to that failure.

Federalism was central to the fight over Obamacare. Soon after "repeal and replace" collapsed in Senate, Senator Marco Rubio (R-FL) explained that: "there are members here who understood the president's preference and were willing to vote against it anyway. . . . This is the Senate. Leadership sets the agenda, but senators vote in the interests of their states. . . . Republics are certainly interesting systems of government, but certainly (they're) better than dictatorship"[24] Yes, Senator, they are, a smiling James Madison might have replied.

The new Trump administration pursued devolution with a vengeance. One of Donald Trump's first actions as president, just five days after inauguration, was to sign an executive order banning "sanctuary cities" and threatening loss of federal grant money to those defying the order. While there was no formal definition of sanctuary cities, they are generally understood to be local governments that declare that they will not cooperate in the enforcement of federal immigration laws. Almost before the ink was dry on the president's executive order, several cities and immigrant advocacy groups, led by San Francisco, sued in federal court to have the order declared unconstitutional.

Paradoxically, Democratic and progressive opponents of the president's order went into court with legal arguments and precedents earlier touted by conservatives. For decades, conservatives had championed states' rights and the U.S. Constitution's Tenth Amendment as limits on federal authority over states and localities. As opponents noted, conservative icon Supreme Court Justice Antonin Scalia wrote in *Printz v. United States* (1997), a case challenging a federal mandate that states perform background checks as part of enforcing federal gun laws, "preservation of the States as independent and autonomous political entities" precludes "commandeering" state and local officials to enforce federal laws. Progressives were joyful when a U.S. district court judge held that Trump's attempt to command state resources to combat sanctuary cities was unconstitutional.

Similarly, on April 26, 2017, President Trump, during an executive order signing ceremony on education, declared, "For too long, the federal government has imposed its will on state and local governments.... Previous administrations have wrongfully forced states and schools to comply with federal whims.... The time has come to empower parents and teachers to make the decisions that help their students achieve success."[25] Many applauded, but when President Trump's 2018 budget proposed 50 percent cuts in state Medicaid funds by 2027, Republican governors, especially those who had expanded Medicaid as part of Obamacare, quickly lost their taste for devolution.[26] Nonetheless, the stark fact is that over the course of the twentieth century, the weight and focus of government in the United States shifted from the state and local levels to the national level.

> **Struggling Toward Democracy**
>
> State governments receive more than one-third of their general revenue directly from the federal government. State officials claim that strings attached to the federal funds limit their ability to confront state and local problems as they think best.
>
> **What do you think?**
> - When the federal government sends money to the states, do they have the right to define how it can be used or not?
> - Should the federal government withdraw its funding if states fail to comply?

THE FUTURE OF AMERICAN FEDERALISM

Federalism has been a part of American constitutionalism since several Puritan communities founded the New England Confederation in 1643. After more than 350 years of experience with federalism, one might think our commitment to it would be secure. It is not. Some wonder whether American federalism has been compromised, perhaps irreparably, by American economic development and, more recently, by the globalization of world communication, finance, and

Q5 Have the complexities of the twenty-first century rendered our government essentially national, or do state and local governments still have important roles to play?

trade structures. Some support the devolution of recent decades while others believe that globalization of commerce, the serious threat of global warming, international terrorism, and the pandemic threats of Aids and Ebola require more national authority, not less (see Table 2.2).

Social networks of all kinds must be tended. Consider the nation's transportation infrastructure. Highway systems, to say nothing of air traffic control systems, require management and integration above the level of towns, cities, and even states. Fundamentally, as societies and their economies grow and mature, more and more of their activities occur nationally and internationally.

For example, the North American Free Trade Agreement (NAFTA) signed by Canada, the United States, and Mexico in 1993 both permits free trade throughout North America and limits each nation's ability to manage its own internal trade and national labor markets. These rules effect states differently. Some Midwestern politicians claim that NAFTA has cost their states too many good, high paying, jobs while Texas politicians claim their state has benefited from increased cross-border trade. When the Trump administration moved to renegotiate NAFTA, some state leaders were supportive, others urged caution. Similarly, when the Trump administration decided to withdraw from the Paris climate change accords, California's Democratic governor, Jerry Brown, pledged to resist. These policy developments and responses pose great challenges to American federalism. Once again, the resilience of the American federal system will be tested.[27]

TABLE 2.2	The Evolution of American Federalism
Stages	**Events**
National Federalism	John Marshall appointed Chief Justice (1800) *Marbury v. Madison* establishes judicial review (1803) *McCulloch v. Maryland* defines "necessary and proper" (1819) *Gibbons v. Ogden* defines "interstate commerce" broadly (1824)
State Federalism	Roger B. Taney appointed Chief Justice (1835) *Dred Scott v. Sandford* lets states define property (1857) U.S. Civil War (1861–65)
Dual Federalism	*U.S. v. E.C. Knight* limits federal commerce power (1895) *Plessy v. Ferguson* limits federal citizenship rights (1896) Nineteenth Amendment approves federal income tax (1913)
Cooperative Federalism	FDR's New Deal (1935) *Wickard v. Filburn* expands federal commerce power (1941) LBJ's Great Society (1965) Nixon's Special Revenue Sharing (1972) Nixon's General Revenue Sharing (1974)
Devolution	Reagan's tax reform (1981) Clinton's welfare reform (1997) *U.S. v. Morrison* limits federal commerce power (2000) Obamacare approved; Medicaid expansion made discretionary (2012)

Chapter Summary

Federalism is a system of government that divides political power and responsibility between national and subnational levels of government. Initially, the distribution of political power described in the Constitution seemed to indicate that the national government would be responsible for dealing with foreign and military affairs and for economic coordination between the states and with foreign powers. The states would retain the power to deal with domestic affairs. The rights and liberties of the people would remain unfettered in broad areas where power had not been granted to either the national or subnational level of government.

However, as the nation grew in size and complexity, many issues that had once seemed appropriate for state or local resolution, such as building and tending a transportation system, seemed to require support and coordination from the national level. As problems seemed to move within the federal system, power within the federal system had to be redistributed or realigned. After the founding there were two historical eras during which power was redistributed dramatically upward within the American federal system: the Civil War era of the 1860s and the Depression era of the 1930s.

Both the 1860s and the 1930s marked distinctive phases in the integration of the American economy and society. In the two decades before the Civil War and the two after, a national structure of communication and transportation was developed. Railroads and telegraph not only permitted goods and information to move nationally, but also permitted the businesses and corporations that produced these goods and information to become national entities. By the time FDR assumed the presidency in March of 1933, most Americans had become convinced by their experience with the Depression that federal regulation of the economy needed to be enhanced.

FDR's "New Deal" and LBJ's "Great Society" initiatives involved the federal government in almost every area of policymaking. Many of these areas, including education, job training, health care, and welfare, had traditionally been the exclusive responsibilities of state and local governments. Initially, states and localities were too eager to receive the federal funds to worry much about the rules and regulations that accompanied them. However, the rules and regulations that seemed reasonable when there were thirty categorical grant programs in the 1930s seemed unreasonable as the number of such programs passed four hundred in the 1960s. The complexity of applying for, administering, and reporting on all of these grants worked a hardship on state and local governments.

By the late 1980s and early 1990s the problems of fiscal federalism and of American federalism in general had been redefined. Ronald Reagan thought that government at all levels of the federal system was too big, demanding, and expensive. Reagan sought to scale back governments at all levels by denying them funds. Although Bill Clinton sought to restore federal assistance to states and localities, he and the Republican Congress that he faced through most of his administration agreed that federal responsibilities as well as funds should be devolved to the states where possible.

In the latter half of the 1990s, Congress moved to reconstitute the federal system by repackaging dozens of social programs into block grants, cutting the funds allocated to them by up to 30 percent, and returning primary responsibility for them to the states. This policy reversal, called "devolution," in which President Bush joined enthusiastically, was the largest reallocation of authority within the federal system since LBJ's "Great Society" and perhaps since FDR's "New Deal." Nonetheless, it was reversed, at least temporarily, when the "Great Recession" of 2008–2009 strained state budgets and the Obama administration offered help as part of its stimulus strategy. Today, the federal government supplies 30 percent of the dollars spent by state and local governments.[28] The struggle within the American federal system for authority and resources is unending.

Key Terms

block grants	*Marbury v. Madison*
categorical grant	*McCulloch v. Maryland*
coercive federalism	nullification
concurrent powers	*Paul v. Virginia*
confederation	preemption
cooperative federalism	reserved powers
creative federalism	secession
devolution	special revenue sharing
Dred Scott v. Sandford	supremacy clause
dual federalism	unitary government
extradition	*U.S. v. E.C. Knight*
general revenue sharing	*U.S. v. Lopez*
Gibbons v. Ogden	*U.S. v. Morrison*
implied powers	*Wickard v. Filburn*
inherent powers	

Suggested Readings

Beer, Samuel H. *To Make a Nation: The Rediscovery of American Federalism.* Cambridge, MA: Harvard University Press, 1993. Beer traces thinking about federalism from the ancient world through the American founding period.

Karch, Andrew. *Democratic Laboratories: Policy Diffusion Among the States.* Ann Arbor: University of Michigan Press, 2007. Karch describes the influences on policy innovation and adoption among the states.

LaCroix, Alison L. *The Ideological Origins of American Federalism*. Cambridge, MA: Harvard University Press, 2010. LaCroix traces the roots of American federalism in law, theory, and practice.

Robertson, David Brian. *Federalism and the Making of America*. 2nd ed. New York: Routledge, 2018. Robertson shows how America's federal structure has shaped the nation's politics, especially in critical areas like economic policy and race.

Zimmerman, Joseph F. *Contemporary American Federalism: The Growth of National Power*. 2nd ed. Albany, NY: State University of New York Press, 2008. An excellent survey of the broad stages of the development of American federalism and of its contemporary strengths and weaknesses.

Web Resources

1 www.theamericanpartnership.com/federalism-links/
   This site highlights dozens of top websites dealing with federalism.

2 www.publius.oxfordjournals.org
   Home page for *Publius*, a scholarly journal dedicated to the study of federalism. The journal provides the reader with a better understanding of the dynamics of federal/state relations.

3 www.whitehouse.gov/omb/budget/
   If an individual has an interest in fiscal federalism, this website is of great assistance. The page provides access to current budget statistics as well as analytical and historical data and information.

4 www.ncsl.org
   The National Conference of State Legislators' (NCSL) home page offers links to information about state legislators, tax and budget issues, and general news relevant to state policymaking.

5 www.statelocalgov.net/index.cfm
   State and Local Government on the Net (SLGN) has links featuring various local governments within each state.

Notes

1 G. Ross Stephens and Nelson Wikstrom, *American Intergovernmental Relations: A Fragmented Federal Polity* (New York: Oxford University Press, 2007), 2–6.

2 Department of Commerce and Bureau of the Budget, *Statistical Abstract of the United States, 2012* (Washington, D.C.: U.S. Government Printing Office, 2012), table 428, 267.

3 Samuel H. Beer, *To Make a Nation: The Rediscovery of American Federalism* (Cambridge, MA: Harvard University Press, 1993), 223–224. Beer quotes briefly from Patrick Riley, "The Origins of Federal Theory in International Relations Ideas," *Polity*, vol. 6, no. 1 (Fall 1973): 97–98.

4 Joseph F. Zimmerman, *Contemporary American Federalism: The Growth of National Power*, 2nd ed. (Albany, NY: State University of New York Press, 2008), 2–4. See also Raymond A. Smith, *The American Anomaly: U.S. Politics and Government in Comparative Perspective*, 3rd ed. (New York: Routledge, 2013), 34–37.

5 Vincent Ostrom, *The Meaning of American Federalism: Constituting a Self-Governing Society* (San Francisco, CA: ICS Press, 1991), 45.

6 David Brian Robertson, *Federalism and the Making of America* (New York: Routledge, 2012), 31–33.

7 Edward Meade Earle, ed., *The Federalist* (New York: Modern Library, 1937), no. 39, 249.

8 Zimmerman, *Contemporary American Federalism*, 35.

9 Zimmerman, *Contemporary American Federalism*, 147-148.

10 Robertson, *Federalism and the Making of America*, 34.

11 Earle, ed., *The Federalist*, no. 51, 339, no. 31, 193.

12 Ibid., no. 45, 303.

13 Woodrow Wilson, *Constitutional Government in the United States* (New York: Columbia University Press, 1908), 173.

14 Bruce Ackerman, *We the People: Foundations* (Cambridge, MA: Harvard University Press, 1991), 40.

15 Edward S. Corwin, "The Passing of Dual Federalism," *Virginia Law Review*, vol. 36, no. 1 (February 1950): 4.

16 David B. Walker, *Toward a Functioning Federalism* (Cambridge, MA: Winthrop, 1981), 66.

17 David Brian Robertson, *Federalism and the Making of America* (New York: Routledge. 2012), 40, 151, 155, 171.

18 Walker, *Functioning Federalism*, 68.

19 Theodore J. Lowi, *The Personal President: Power Invested, Promise Unfulfilled* (Ithaca, NY: Cornell University Press, 1985), 49–50. See also Adam Liptak, "At Heart of Health Law Clash, a 1942 Case of a Farmer's Wheat," *New York Times*, March 20, 2012, A1, A14.

20 Ross Sandler and David Schoenbrod, *Democracy by Decree: What Happens When Courts Run Government* (New Haven, CT: Yale University Press, 2003), 13–34.

21 Joseph F. Zimmerman, *Congressional Preemption: Regulatory Federalism* (Albany, NY: State University of New York Press, 2005), 1–9; see also Zimmerman, "Congressional Preemption Trends," *The Book of the States*, 2012, vol. 44, 51–55.

22 Timothy Conlan, *New Federalism: Intergovernmental Reform from Nixon to Reagan* (Washington, D.C.: Brookings Institution, 1988), 153–154.

23 Jackie Calmes, "States Confront Fiscal Crisis," *Wall Street Journal*, December 18, 2003.

24 James Hohmann, "Daily 202: A Flawed Strategy," *Washington Post*, July 19, 2017.

25 White House, Office of the Press Secretary, "Remarks by President Trump at Signing of Executive Order on Federalism Education," April 26, 2017.

26 Julie Hirschfeld Davis, "Trump Budget Cuts Deeply Into Medicaid," *New York Times*, May 22, 2017, A1.

27 William T. Pound, "Federalism at the Crossroads," *State Legislatures*, June 2006, 18–20.

28 Roberton Williams and Yuri Shadunsky, "State and Local Tax Policy: What Are the Sources of Revenue for State Government," Tax Policy Center, May 7, 2013.

Chapter 3

CIVIL LIBERTIES
Democracy and the Expansion of Liberty's Realm

Focus Questions: from reading to thinking

Q1 How do civil liberties differ from civil rights?

Q2 Do our commitments to free speech and a free press conflict with our sense that flag burning should be prohibited or that pornography should be regulated?

Q3 Does our commitment to separation of church and state mean that no trace of religious sentiment or symbolism should emanate from government?

Q4 Should someone accused of a serious crime go free if police commit a procedural error during the investigation or during the arrest and questioning?

Q5 If we value civil liberties so highly, why do we keep so many people in prison?

The Constitution TODAY

THE SECOND AMENDMENT AND GUN RIGHTS IN AMERICA

Second Amendment: "A well regulated militia, being necessary to the security of a free state, the right of the people to keep and bear arms, shall not be infringed."

Mass shootings always return our attention to the role of guns in our society. Particularly tragic cases, like the Sandy Hook school shooting in which 20 six- and seven-year-olds were killed, the Charleston shooting at the Emanuel AME church in which 9 were killed, the Sutherland Springs church shootings in which 26 died, the Orlando shooting in which 49 gay and lesbian Latin night-clubbers were killed, and the slaughter at the outdoor concert on the Las Vegas strip, produce anguished debate but no real policy change. What does the Constitution say about the place of guns in our society?

The Second Amendment is strangely phrased and, for most of American history, its meaning was thought to be somewhat murky. Legal analysts, political scientists, and historians long debated whether the first two clauses of the Second Amendment, "A well regulated militia, being necessary to the security of a free state," modified or limited the straightforward declaration of the last two phrases of the Amendment, "the right of the people to keep and bear arms, shall not be infringed." If the first two phrases do modify and limit the second two, then perhaps the people only have a constitutional right to keep and bear arms consequent to militia service. But if the first two clauses of the Second Amendment do not express limits, then the right to keep and bear arms is much more full and stark.

The debate appears to be over, at least for now. In 2008, Justice Scalia declared for a Supreme Court divided 5 to 4 in a case called *District of Columbia v. Heller*, that "the Second Amendment protects an individual right to possess a firearm unconnected with service in a militia, and to use that arm for traditional lawful purposes, such as self-defense within the home." Heller was the Supreme Court's first unequivocal ruling that the Second Amendment right to bear arms was an individual right not connected to the collective responsibility of militia service. Moreover, hot on Heller's heels came *McDonald v. Chicago*, asking that the finding in Heller be applied in full against state and local gun laws. In 2010, in another 5–4 decision, with Justice Alito writing for the majority, the Supreme Court extended the Heller finding to a general limit on local, state, and federal intrusion on the individual right of citizens to keep and bear arms.

Two questions remain for us to ponder in light of the Supreme Court's decisions in *Heller* (2008) and *McDonald* (2010). First, was the Supreme Court correct in *Heller* to find that the Second Amendment right to bear arms was an individual right rather than a collective right related to militia service? It seems so, at least from an historical perspective. The court and a number of scholars point out that several founding period state constitutions had a straightforward right to bear arms. Moreover, the first version of the Second Amendment submitted to Congress by James Madison on June 8, 1789, read: "The right of the people to keep and bear arms shall not be infringed; a well armed and well regulated militia being the best security of a free country. . . . " A second version, submitted on August 17, read: "A well regulated militia, composed of the body of the people, being the best security of a free state, the right of the people to keep and bear arms shall not be infringed." On either of these readings, an individual right to bear arms seems clear. In the first it is baldly stated before the semicolon and in the second it is clear that the militia is composed of the whole adult male population.

Second, was the court right to apply the Second Amendment against states and localities? Until these two cases were decided, most gun ownership had been regulated by state constitutions and laws. For well over a century, in a series of cases including *U.S. v. Cruikshank* (1875), *Presser v. Illinois* (1886), *Miller v. Texas* (1894), and *U.S. v. Miller* (1939), the court held, as they said in *Cruikshank*, that "the Second Amendment . . . has no other effect than to restrict the powers of the national government." The argument in *McDonald* was that the right to bear arms is among the "privileges and immunities of citizens of the United States" protected against state and local incursion by the Fourteenth Amendment. The Supreme Court has now agreed with that argument.

Cases raising gun control questions will be in the federal courts for years as cities and states defend their restrictions on gun ownership and use, and federal judges struggle to add detail and specificity to the broad but vague right declared by the nation's high court.

CIVIL LIBERTIES, CIVIL RIGHTS, AND MAJORITY RULE

Constitutional democracy is democracy constrained. In Chapter 1 we described the Founders careful construction of a written constitution with separations of power, bicameralism, checks and balances, and judicial independence to tame power. In Chapter 2 we described federalism, the allocation of some power to the national government while the rest remains with the states or their people, as a constitutional device further to separate, check, and limit power. In this third chapter we describe how the Founders quickly came to believe that, even in a written constitution awarding limited powers, certain areas of personal autonomy, choice, and security—certain liberties—must simply be placed beyond the purview of government.

Q1 How do civil liberties differ from civil rights?

Civil liberties mark off areas of social life where we believe that government power should rarely intrude on the free choice of individuals. For example, our society has long, though not always, assumed that within the realm of religion, government should leave the individual alone—unless that individual believes that religion requires behavior like having several wives at once or treating controlled substances as sacraments. Throughout American history

civil liberties Areas of social life, including free speech, press, and religion, where the Constitution restricts or prohibits government intrusion on the free choice of individuals.

we have used our political institutions to draw lines between those areas of social life where individuals generally will be free to do as they please and those areas of social life where certain sorts of individual choices will be required or prohibited.

civil rights Areas of social life, such as the right to vote and to be free from racial discrimination, where the Constitution requires government to act to ensure that citizens are treated equally.

Civil rights, on the other hand, mark off those areas of social life where we believe that government must act, must intrude upon what individuals might otherwise choose to do, to ensure that all citizens are treated fairly. For example, we promise each other that whatever our external characteristics of race, ethnicity, or gender, each of us will get a fair chance to compete, succeed, and enjoy the benefits of our society. What makes the broad question of individual rights fascinating and also troubling is that although civil liberties and civil rights reinforce and strengthen each other at one level, at another they clash directly. Civil liberties will be the focus of this chapter, civil rights of the next.

In this chapter, we ask how civil liberties were conceived early in U.S. history and how our understanding of them has changed and expanded over time. We first look at freedom of expression as it relates to both speech and press, then at freedom of religion and conscience, and then at the protections afforded to criminal suspects and defendants. In each case, we see that our sense of what these liberties entail is much broader and more comprehensive than it was formerly. We also see that the battle to expand civil liberties has been fought over the familiar terrain of federalism. Though the states won many individual battles, in the end, the national government—mainly the Supreme Court—won the war by nationalizing much of civil liberties law. We conclude the chapter by asking how our commitment to civil liberties squares with the fact that the U.S. holds more people in jails and prisons that any other country in the world.

CIVIL LIBERTIES AND THE BILL OF RIGHTS

The men and women who colonized British North America fled Europe because the governments there would not permit them to pursue their religious, social, and economic lives as they saw fit. Not surprisingly, when these colonists turned to writing charters of government in America, they produced documents that explicitly defined the liberties of those—white men—they acknowledged as citizens. Some of the most famous of these colonial charters were the Massachusetts Body of Liberties (1641), the New York Charter of Liberties (1683), and the Pennsylvania Charter of Privileges (1701).

As the conflict with England intensified after 1765, Americans came increasingly to believe that British tyranny threatened their cherished liberties. Freedoms of speech and the press were restricted; homes, businesses, and property were searched and sometimes seized without benefit of specific warrants; the right to trial by a jury of one's peers was denied; and other threats to the security and safety of persons and property seemed imminent.

In the immediate wake of the Declaration of Independence, state after state produced new constitutions, many of which began with a preamble dedicated to enumerating and justifying the liberties of the people.[1] These charters were framed with recent British actions clearly in mind. They were, therefore, largely anti-government documents aimed at limiting and defining government power.

The Origins of the Bill of Rights

Chapter 1 explained the movement in the late 1780s for a new constitution. Even in the Constitutional Convention's final days, after a powerful new national government had taken shape, the wish of some delegates to add a bill of rights was rejected by a unanimous vote of the states. The delegates badly miscalculated how their failure to include a bill of rights in the new Constitution would be received by the public at large.

The Anti-Federalists, led by Patrick Henry in Virginia, seized upon the absence of a bill of rights as the key reason for their opposition to ratification. The demand for a bill of rights gained momentum as the ratification process proceeded. By the time the Virginia convention met in June 1788, nine states had already approved the Constitution, though several had added lists of recommended amendments. Virginia's narrow 89–79 ratification was secured only by the Federalists' promise to support amendments in the first Congress. James Madison's Baptist constituents were particularly concerned that the Anglican majority in Virginia might deny them religious freedom.

When Madison reached New York, the site of the first Congress, he set about drafting amendments to the Constitution. He had before him several state bills of rights and more than two hundred proposed amendments that had come from the states during the ratification process. By late August of 1788, he had guided a set of seventeen proposed amendments through the House of Representatives. The House concurred in the Senate's proposal to narrow the list to twelve, and these were submitted to the states for ratification in late September. Two of the proposed twelve amendments failed to win approval from the required three-fourths of the state legislatures.

However, ten amendments to the Constitution, the Bill of Rights, were approved and went into effect on December 15, 1791. The first eight amendments contain broad guarantees of individual liberty: freedom of religion, speech, press, and assembly; the right to keep and bear arms; protection for the privacy of the home; assurance against double jeopardy and compulsory self-incrimination; the right to counsel and to trial by jury; and freedom from cruel and unusual punishment. The Ninth Amendment provided that rights not specifically enumerated in the first eight amendments or elsewhere in the Constitution were not thereby lost, and the tenth assured that all powers not delegated to the national government were retained by the people or by the state governments.

The explicit language of some of the amendments (e.g., "Congress shall make no law" in the First Amendment) made it clear that the Bill of Rights was to apply only against the national government. The Supreme Court reiterated this view in the famous case of ***Barron v. Baltimore*** (1833). Chief Justice Marshall held "that the Bill of Rights limited the actions only of the federal government and not the states, thus making those who claimed that

Barron v. Baltimore The court held that the Bill of Rights applied to the federal government, not the states. As a result, individuals whose rights had been violated by state and local governments had to appeal to state constitutions, state judges, and local juries.

their rights had been violated by the state and local governments dependent on appeals to state constitutions, state judges, and local juries."[2] In fact, the Supreme Court did not move to enforce the individual liberties of the Bill of Rights against state and local governments until well into the twentieth century. Then the high court began a revolution in American federalism by slowly nationalizing civil liberties law.

As we shall see below, the Supreme Court held in the 1920s that the First Amendment freedoms of speech and press were protected against state action because they had been "incorporated" through the Fourteenth Amendment's declaration that "no state shall" deny its citizens "due process of law." In the 1947 case of *Adamson v. California*, Justice Hugo Black wrote a dissenting opinion, in which he was joined by three other justices, arguing for the total **incorporation** of the Bill of Rights into the Fourteenth Amendment. Justice Black argued that "no state could deprive its citizens of the privileges and protections of the Bill of Rights." Though Black failed to win total incorporation, the process of "selective incorporation" continued, most recently in the cases discussed above on the right to bear arms, so that today most provisions of the Bill of Rights constrain both federal and state governments (see Table 3.1).

incorporation The idea that many of the protections of the Bill of Rights originally meant to apply only against the national government applied against the states as well because they were "incorporated" into the Fourteenth Amendment's guarantee of "due process" of law.

Freedom of Expression: Speech and the Press

Freedom of expression is absolutely fundamental to the idea of popular government. Political participation, the open debate of policies and programs, and majority rule all depend on freedom of speech, press, and assembly. Yet, society's leaders, including public officials, have been reluctant to see themselves and their activities criticized from the soapbox or in the press. Popular majorities have been similarly reluctant to see their mainstream values flouted.

TABLE 3.1	The Incorporation Doctrine: A Timeline	
Provision	**Case**	**Year**
Freedom of Speech	*Gitlow v. New York*	1925
Freedom of the Press	*Near v. Minnesota*	1931
Freedom of Assembly	*DeJonge v. Oregon*	1937
Free Exercise of Religion	*Cantwell v. Connecticut*	1940
No Establishment of Religion	*Everson v. Board*	1947
Unreasonable Search and Seizure	*Mapp v. Ohio*	1961
Cruel and Unusual Punishment	*Robinson v. California*	1962
Right to Counsel	*Gideon v. Wainwright*	1963
Right to Petition	*Edwards v. South Carolina*	1963
Self-Incrimination	*Miranda v. Arizona*	1966
Speedy Trial	*Klopfer v. North Carolina*	1967
Right to Bear Arms	*McDonald v. Chicago*	2010

Not surprisingly, political leaders confident of majority support often move to suppress unpopular minority opinions. Sometimes the courts have upheld their actions, sometimes not. Should political leaders or popular majorities be able to limit expression that they think ill- advised or inconvenient? What circumstances might justify the government's limiting the right of citizens to express themselves as they see fit? These are fundamental questions in a free society and they have been center stage during the wars in Iraq and Afghanistan and in the broader war on terror. President Trump, more sensitive to personal and political slights even than most other politicians, announced a desire, as we shall see in more detail below, to reform libel laws to make it easier for those criticized to seek redress.

Q2 Do our commitments to free speech and a free press conflict with our sense that flag burning should be prohibited or that pornography should be regulated?

Freedom of Speech. As late as March 1919, in *Schenck v. United States*, the Supreme Court upheld the conviction of a prominent socialist for producing and mailing leaflets opposing U.S. involvement in World War I. Justice Oliver Wendell Holmes, writing for the Court's majority, argued that the right to free speech is never absolute and that Schenck's actions were punishable. Holmes's famous argument was that "the most stringent protection of free speech would not protect a man in falsely shouting fire in a theater." The distinction between protected and punishable speech, he wrote, is "whether the words used are used in such circumstances and are of such a nature as to create *a clear and present danger*." Critics argued that acts of protest such as Schenck's, which had only the most remote prospect of causing real disruption to society and government, should not be suppressed. Soon, Holmes came around to this view too.

The next major development in free speech law came in 1925 in the case of *Gitlow v. New York.* Benjamin Gitlow was a communist convicted under New York law for advocating the overthrow of democracy and capitalism in America. His lawyer contended that the New York law was unconstitutional because Gitlow's federal First Amendment right to free speech had been "incorporated" into the "due process" clause of the Fourteenth Amendment that applied to state actions. The court accepted the defense's incorporation argument, declaring that "we may and do assume that freedom of speech and of the press—which are protected by the First Amendment from abridgement by Congress—are among the fundamental personal rights and 'liberties' protected by the due process clause of the Fourteenth Amendment from impairment by the States." Simultaneously, however, the court relaxed Holmes's "clear and present danger" test to the more general "bad tendency" test. Any speech that had a "bad tendency," that might produce social or political turmoil even at some remote future point, could be punished.

Gitlow v. New York The court accepted the argument that the First Amendment limited state as well as federal action, but then applied a relaxed version of the "clear and present danger" test that allowed speech to be punished if it created a "bad tendency" to produce turmoil, even at some point in the remote future.

Holmes and his colleague, Louis Brandeis, responded in the 1927 case of *Whitney v. California*. Charlotte Whitney was convicted under California law of engaging in Communist Party organizational activities. Whitney lost when the Supreme Court upheld the California statute. Nonetheless, Brandeis argued in dissent that the danger that Whitney's actions represented was so distant that state action to suppress it was illegitimate. Brandeis wrote that "no danger flowing

---

Struggling Toward Democracy

Alexis de Tocqueville wrote in *Democracy in America*, "I know of no country in which there is so little independence of mind and real freedom of discussion as in America."

What do you think?
- What did Tocqueville mean by this?
- If it was true then, is it still true today?

from speech can be deemed clear and present, unless . . . serious injury to the state . . . [is] so imminent that it may befall before there is opportunity for full discussion.... Only an emergency can justify repression."

Not until *Brandenburg v. Ohio* (1969) did the court overrule *Whitney*. Clarence Brandenburg, and Ohio Ku Klux Klan leader, threatened the president and Congress for, he claimed, suppressing the "white, Caucasian race." He was arrested and convicted, but on appeal to the U.S. Supreme Court his conviction was overturned on the grounds that his words had not created the danger of "imminent lawless action." Reprehensible, yes; actually dangerous, no, so the state should not have punished the speech. In *Brandenburg*, the court finally adopted the "clear, present, and imminent danger test" offered by Brandeis and Holmes forty years earlier. This is a good place to pause long enough to note that the Constitution does not speak for itself—it requires interpretation by the Supreme Court. In the line of free speech cases just discussed, from Schenck and Gitlow to Brandenburg, the court obviously was groping for an interpretive rule, or test, or standard—clear and present danger, bad tendency, no, no, clear, present and imminent danger—to define the scope and range of free speech.

More recently, the court has moved well beyond the standard conceptions of free speech to protect forms of **symbolic speech** or speech-related activities including demonstrations, picketing, and protests. In 1989, the court found burning the American flag to be a speech-related act. In ***Texas v. Johnson***, the court held that, "If there is a bedrock principle underlying the First Amendment, it is that Government may not prohibit the expression of an idea simply because society finds the idea itself offensive or disagreeable." [3]

symbolic speech Speech-related acts, such as picketing or flag burning, that like actual speech are protected under the First Amendment because they involve the communication of ideas or opinions.

Texas v. Johnson This case upheld flag burning as protected expression or symbolic speech by applying the stringent clear and imminent danger test of *Brandenburg*.

Getty Images/NY Daily News/Todd Maisel

Protesters burn an American flag. The U.S. Supreme Court has declared that symbolic speech, including flag burning, is protected by the Constitution.

Interestingly, one class of persons—students—have limited free speech rights. The controlling precedent on the free speech rights of students is *Tinker v. Des Moines School District* (1969). Tinker held that students have a presumptive right to engage in political speech so long as that speech does not unduly disrupt the basic educational mission of the school. In 2007, a case called *Morse v. Frederick* came before the Supreme Court. Joseph Frederick, a high school student in Juneau, Alaska, was released from school to see the Olympic torch pass through town. Frederick attended the event and stretched a 14-foot banner, reading "Bong Hits 4 Jesus," across the parade route. Was this a school-sponsored event, at which his speech rights could be limited, or a public event, at which he could say what he pleased? Chief Justice John Roberts, writing for the majority, took the former view in finding for the school and upholding its punishment of Mr. Frederick for what they deemed to be a pro-drug message.

Unprotected Speech: The Cross Burning and Obscenity Examples. Even expansive views of free speech do not hold that absolutely all speech is constitutionally protected. In 2003, the Supreme Court held, in ***Virginia v. Black***, that cross burning, a traditional form of racial intimidation, was not speech protected by the Fourteenth Amendment. Justice Sandra Day O'Connor, writing for the court, noted that free speech rights "are not absolute.... [W]hen a cross burning is used to intimidate, few if any messages are more powerful." Most Americans probably agree that aggressive racial bullying, as in cross burning, should be illegal, but some consider such prohibitions to be "political correctness" run amuck.

Virginia v. Black The court ruled that cross burning, due to its historical ties to racial fear and intimidation, is not protected speech.

But what are we to make of the events in Charlottesville, Virginia, in August 2017. White nationalists, neo-Nazis, the KKK, and others rallied to protest a plan to take down a statue of Confederate General Robert E. Lee. Following a Friday night torchlight parade through the University of Virginia campus, white nationalists and counter-protestors clashed violently on Saturday, leaving one young woman dead and many injured when a white nationalist drove his car into a crowd of counter-protestors.

As President Trump pointed out, the protest by the white nationalists, neo-Nazis, and Klansmen was legal—they had a parade permit. In fact, the American Civil Liberties Union (ACLU) had gone to court the previous week to see that the city of Charlottesville did not deny the white nationalists their parade permit. The ACLU's position—often described as free speech absolutism—was that all speakers, even those from the fringes of the right and left, have a constitutional right to be heard in the public square. Others argue that political authorities actively should direct assembly and speech into channels where disruption and violence can be contained. What do you think? Do we have to—given America's fundamental constitutional guarantees—listen to neo-Nazis? What does *Brandenburg* say?

Another example of the limits of free expression involves the right of a community to protect its members from obscene materials. Obscenity, as a constitutional or legal issue, has always involved suppressing some expression, whether in speech, print, or art, in light of some community standard.

obscenity Sexually explicit material, whether spoken, written, or visual, that "taken as a whole . . . lacks serious literary, artistic, political, or scientific value."

Miller v. California The court allowed states and local communities greater latitude in defining and regulating obscenity.

The traditional test in American law followed a standard laid down in the nineteenth-century English case of *Regina v. Hicklin* (1868), in which the court asked "whether the *tendency* of the matter charged as **obscenity** is to *deprave and corrupt* those whose *minds are open* to such immoral influences."[4] This rule of law, that material could be found obscene on the basis of its "tendency" to "deprave and corrupt" those minds in the community most open to suggestion left great latitude to local community standards.

The modern standard in American law was established by a line of cases extending from *Roth v. United States* (1957) through **Miller v. California** (1973). *Miller* set out a three-part obscenity test: would the average person applying contemporary community standards find that the work taken as a whole (a) appeals to prurient interests; (b) depicts or describes sexual conduct in a patently offensive way; (c) and lacks serious literary, artistic, political, or scientific value? With the advent of the Internet, obscene materials became so pervasive that most prosecutors stopped bringing cases except in the area of child sexual exploitation. In 2007, the Supreme Court found the Protect Act of 2003, which outlawed trafficking in real or purported (i.e., computer-generated) child pornography, to be constitutional and not an infringement of First Amendment rights. Clearly, it is easier to say that obscenity is not protected speech than it is to define obscenity in a way that is both acceptable to the courts and understandable to most Americans.

Freedom of the Press.   Unaided speech can reach and potentially sway only a few people, whereas the same views expressed in print or distributed across the airwaves and the Internet can reach and potentially sway millions. Does government have a greater responsibility to screen and limit expression that can reach millions in seconds than it does speech that can reach only dozens or perhaps hundreds and never more than thousands? As we shall see, the answer is generally no.

No Prior Restraint versus Freedom to Publish.   There are two views of freedom of the press, one much broader than the other. One view is that the press should not be required to secure permission from the government before publication, that is, that there should be no **prior restraint** of the press, no censorship. The second and broader view of freedom of the press both prohibits prior restraint and severely limits the conditions under which one can seek legal redress after the fact for statements appearing in the press. The right to publish without "prior restraint" is of modest benefit if one has to worry about being punished after the fact.[5]

prior restraint Any limitation on publication requiring that permission be secured or approval be granted prior to publication. No prior restraint means no censorship or permission process that could hinder publication.

Near v. Minnesota This decision established an almost complete prohibition against prior restraint on publication by any agent or level of government.

Two cases established the modern Supreme Court's position on these two key aspects of press freedom. The first case, **Near v. Minnesota** (1931), established an almost complete prohibition against prior restraint on publication by any agent or level of government. Jay M. Near was the editor of a newspaper called the *Saturday Press*, which regularly attacked Minnesota public officials. One such public official was Floyd B. Olson. Tired of being pilloried in Near's paper, Olson tried to use a Minnesota public nuisance law to force the closure of the *Saturday Press*. The Supreme Court held that closing the paper would be a form of prior restraint and therefore was unconstitutional. Since *Near*, American courts have rejected requests for prior restraint of the press virtually out of hand.

New York Times v. Sullivan dealt with freedom to publish without fear of being sued or otherwise punished. On March 29, 1960, supporters of Dr. Martin Luther King Jr. took out a full-page advertisement in the *New York Times* claiming that Montgomery, Alabama, city officials had illegally harassed black protesters. L.B. Sullivan, the Montgomery city commissioner in charge of the police, sued the *New York Times* and others, claiming that the advertisement had libeled him with charges of "grave misconduct" and "improper actions and omissions as an official of the City of Montgomery."

Alabama courts, citing the potential damage done to Commissioner Sullivan's reputation, found against the *Times*. The *Times* appealed first to the Alabama Supreme Court, where it lost again, and then to the U.S. Supreme Court. Attorney Herbert Wechsler representing the *Times* argued that if Sullivan prevailed no newspaper would allow criticism of government policy or officials in its pages for fear that it might be sued if any aspect of the story offended a public official.

The Supreme Court found against Sullivan and for the *Times*. Justice Brennan, writing for the majority, contended that, "free public discussion of the stewardship of public officials was . . . a fundamental principle of the American form of government." Brennan and his colleagues knew that public officials able to intimidate their critics with the threat of legal action would be free from oversight and evaluation.

Most U.S. courts now recognize a "neutral report privilege" protecting journalists who report, without approval or disapproval, negative comments about politicians. Nonetheless, as candidate and now president, Donald Trump spoke many times about his desire "to open up our libel laws so when they [journalists] write purposely negative and horrible and false articles, we can sue them and win lots of money."[6] The president's lawyers knew, even if he did not, that since *Sullivan* the Supreme Court has privileged free and robust political speech over the pain that politicians, even presidents, might feel when harshly, and they might think falsely, criticized in the press.

Restrictions on Press Freedom: National Security. No freedom is without limits. Just as Justice Holmes noted that the right to free speech does not extend to falsely shouting "fire" in a crowded theater, others have noted that freedom of the press may be limited by national security concerns. However, even this potential reason for restricting press freedom have been very narrowly construed. For example, in the 1973 **Pentagon Papers Case**, the federal government went to court to constrain several newspapers including the *New York Times* and the *Washington Post* from publishing illegally obtained materials relating to the conduct of the Vietnam War. The Supreme Court declined to award the injunction, noting the heavy presumption against "prior restraint" of publication.

New York Times Co. v. Sullivan By concluding that a public official had to prove either "actual malice" or "reckless disregard for the truth" in order to be awarded damages in a libel case, the court essentially constructed a right not to be punished after the fact for what has been published.

Pentagon Papers Case Formally titled *New York Times Co. v. United States*. The court found that prior restraint violated the First Amendment unless imminent danger could be proven.

On the other hand, government officials often appeal to the press to withhold sensitive information, particularly in wartime. Oftentimes, the press will comply, at least for a time, if the government makes a plausible case. The Bush administration clashed repeatedly with the nation's leading newspapers, including the *New York Times*, *Los Angeles Times*, and *Washington Post* over stories about questionable intelligence, prisoner abuse, secret CIA prisons, surveillance of domestic communications, and international and domestic banking records. In each case, the administration claimed that publication would endanger national security and journalists pointed to the people's right to know what their government was doing.[7]

As a candidate, Barack Obama promised to roll back many of the Bush administration's most aggressive claims to national security authority because they "undermined the Constitution." But as president, Barack Obama was reluctant to disclaim these powers, especially in the area of domestic surveillance. Prior to 9/11 the FBI was required to secure approval, under the Foreign Intelligence Surveillance Act (FISA), for wiretapping or securing the phone records of Americans. After 9/11 the records of thousands of citizens were secured without warrants. In early 2010 the Obama administration's Office of Legal Counsel supported the FBI's claim that the right to obtain phone records without court approval still obtained.[8]

Freedom of Religion

Q3 Does our commitment to separation of church and state mean that no trace of religious sentiment or symbolism should emanate from government?

Nine of the thirteen colonies had state-sanctioned churches as the Revolution approached. Nonetheless, Jefferson's vision of a "wall of separation between Church and State" soon came to be the most visible image of church–state relations in American politics. Although this phrase has been repeated endlessly over the course of American political history, it has no obvious and decisive meaning.

There are three basic views about how the separation of church and state should be conceived and these are still hotly contested.[9] The first view calls for a strict separation in which government takes no notice of religion and permits no hint of religious sentiment or symbolism to attach to its actions. The second view holds that government may not favor one religion over another, and certainly not one over all of the others, but that it may provide general support and benefit to all religions. The third view contends that government should actively promote religion as beneficial to the nation's moral strength and health although once again, no religion or religions should be favored over others.

establishment clause The First Amendment to the Constitution says that "Congress shall make no law respecting an establishment of religion." This clearly means that Congress may not establish a national religion. There is an ongoing debate over how much, if any, contact is allowed between religion and government.

The Establishment Clause. The **establishment clause** of the First Amendment says "Congress shall make no law respecting an establishment of religion." This stark language has been taken to mean that the national government in general, and Congress in particular, may neither establish an official national religion nor favor one religion over the others. What is less clear is whether government, using tax dollars, public facilities, or moral suasion, may support, facilitate, or cooperate with religious groups even if government is equally supportive of all religious groups. The answer seems to be yes, but carefully.

The Supreme Court's clearest attempt to draw the line between constitutional and unconstitutional government involvement with religion came in *Lemon v. Kurtzman* (1971). The court developed a three-pronged test, widely known as the *Lemon* test, to determine the constitutionality of state aid to religious activities and institutions. The state program: (1) must have a secular purpose; (2) its principal effect must neither advance nor impede religion; and (3) it must not permit or encourage an "excessive entanglement" of church and state.

Governments wishing to provide support to children attending religious schools have long argued that the support is going to the children rather than to the schools and that some children merely receive their state support in a religious school setting. Recent rulings have increased public aid to parochial schools by allowing federal funds to be used for transportation, lunch programs, textbooks, computers, and other instructional equipment in religious schools.[10]

Teaching intelligent design in the public schools is a hot-button issue that has been in the news and in the courts. Religious conservatives in Dover, Pennsylvania won a majority on the local school board and mandated that intelligent design (the idea that nature is too complex to have developed randomly and evinces signs of a creator) be taught as an alternative to evolution in biology classes. Judge John E. Jones III of the federal district court in Harrisburg presided over the six-week trial. He declared that intelligent design was religion, not science, and teaching it in public school science classes was a violation of the First Amendment establishment clause.

In 2005, the Supreme Court decided two cases involving display of the Ten Commandments in public spaces. The court held that framed copies of the Ten Commandments on the walls of two Kentucky courthouses served as unconstitutional endorsements of religion, while a six-foot monument to the Ten Commandments on the grounds of the Texas state capitol among more than two dozen other statues was not an endorsement. Justice David Souter wrote that "the touchstone of our analysis is the principle that the First Amendment mandates government neutrality between religion and religion, and between religion and non-religion; . . . that liberty and social stability demand a religious tolerance that respects the religious views of all citizens."[11]

The establishment clause again became the focus of public debate when Donald Trump, first as a candidate and then as president, proposed what many came to call a "Muslim ban." In late 2015, Trump called for "a total and complete shutdown of Muslims entering the United States until our country's representatives can figure out what the hell is going on." One week after his inauguration, President Trump signed an executive order temporarily banning travellers from seven majority Muslim countries—Iraq, Syria, Iran, Sudan, Libya, Somalia, and Yemen. One week later, a federal judge in Seattle blocked the ban as a violation of the First Amendment prohibition of establishment of religion and discrimination among religions. In March a revised travel ban was again struck down. The president's lawyers continued to fight for the ban, but his own words from the campaign were hard to overcome. Finally, in June, the Supreme Court allowed a much watered-down ban to go into effect temporarily.[12]

Lemon v. Kurtzman This case established the *Lemon* test for state support of religion. Such support must be secular in purpose, not unduly advance or impede religion, and not involve "excessive entanglement" of the state with religion.

free exercise clause The First Amendment to the Constitution says Congress may not prohibit the "free exercise" of religion. The intent of the free exercise clause is to protect a wide range of religious observance and practice from political interference.

The Free Exercise Clause.   If the establishment clause is essentially about how much support or opposition the state can offer to institutionalized religion, the **free exercise clause** is about how completely free individuals must be to conduct their religious lives. The free exercise clause protects most, but not all, religious observances and practices from state interference.

The free exercise clause protects Americans in believing and asserting any religious principles they please. The court has long held, however, that actions are not beliefs. In *Reynolds v. U.S.* (1879), the court held that religiously inspired action, in this case the Mormon practice of plural marriage, is not protected by the free exercise privilege because it violates "otherwise valid law prohibiting conduct that the State is free to regulate" (i.e., marriage law). More recently, in *Employment Division v. Smith* (1990), a case in which two individuals were denied unemployment benefits after having been fired for sacramental peyote use, the court affirmed that illegal action, even if religiously motivated, enjoys no exemption from "generally applicable criminal law."

In 1993 Congress sought to support free exercise of religion and limit government intrusion by passing the Religious Freedom Restoration Act. The act forbade any level of government to "substantially burden" religious observance without showing a "compelling" need to do so and without selecting the "least restrictive means available." The Supreme Court struck down the Religious

This Bremerton, Washington, high school football coach, obscured near the center in blue, defied school district officials' orders to stop holding post-game prayers. The coach was fired and federal courts refused to reinstate him on grounds that he used his school position to press his particular religious views.

Freedom Restoration Act in 1997, declaring that it gave religious activity more protection against normal law and regulation than the First Amendment required. Finally, Presidents Clinton and Bush issued guidelines guaranteeing federal workers the right to express and reflect religious views at work.

Prayer in the Schools.   No issue in the broad area of separation of church and state has been as consistently contested as prayer in the schools. In 1962, the Supreme Court declared in *Engel v. Vitale* that "it is no part of the business of government to compose official prayers for any group of the American people to recite as part of a religious program carried on by government." *Engel* made clear that mandatory prayer in the public schools was unconstitutional. In 1982, the Supreme Court held that a Louisiana statute authorizing daily voluntary prayer in its public schools was unconstitutional. In 1994, the Ninth Circuit Court of Appeals in San Francisco declared a high school graduation prayer unconstitutional even though it was approved by a majority vote of the students. And in 2000, the Supreme Court held that organized, student-led prayers at high school football games constituted an unconstitutional establishment of religion.

On the other hand, no one in public schools was ever prohibited from praying privately. Private prayer—mostly before tests, to be sure—was always an option and much public prayer occurred among those who agreed and arranged to participate. Religious conservatives are, not surprisingly, always working to assure and even expand these rights. For example, in 2012, Florida passed a law allowing "inspirational messages" to be read during school assemblies and sporting events. And in 2013, Governor Phil Bryant of Mississippi signed a law instructing schools to develop policies allowing prayers over school intercoms and during ceremonies, like graduation, and sporting events. The governor suggested, "You might put on the program that this is not a state-sanctioned prayer if a prayer does break out at a football game or graduation."[13] Do you think judges will find that to be persuasive?

Both Presidents Bill Clinton and George W. Bush sought to clarify the complex and sensitive issue of prayer in public schools. Both issued statements through the Departments of Justice and Education, to ensure that school administrators were not unnecessarily and illegally discouraging religious activities in their schools. Basically, President Clinton made the point that student-initiated religious activity is subject to the same opportunities and limitations as are other nonacademic social and political activities. What students are permitted to do in support of their political or economic views, they may do in furtherance of their religious views, as long as other students are not coerced and school officials do not participate in the activity.

President Bush included provisions in the "No Child Left Behind Act" of 2001 requiring the Department of Education to ensure that schools were open to voluntary religious activity. Each state must declare that every school in the state is in compliance with national law and policy; failure to comply can trigger loss of federal funds.

Moreover, the Supreme Court and the Obama administration moved to exempt religious institutions from some aspects of laws that others must obey. The court declared in 2012 a "ministerial privilege" allowing churches to hire only within their own religion while other employers may not discriminate in hiring. Also in 2012, the Obama administration backed off, at least partially, when the Catholic Church and others complained that the new health care law required that they violate their religious principles by including birth control and abortion services in the health care plans they provided to employees.[14]

THE RIGHTS OF CRIMINAL DEFENDANTS

Q4 Should someone accused of a serious crime go free if police commit a procedural error during the investigation or during the arrest and questioning?

The fundamental question that arises in many people's minds over the rights of criminal defendants is why we should care about them? Why do we restrict our police and courts to a narrow range of specific procedures and methods for protecting us against those who would break the laws of our society? Fundamentally, we defend what we call "due process of law" even for the most heinous criminals because the treatment that we sanction for them might become the norm for the rest of us. We are protecting ourselves when we demand that no one be treated with cavalier brutality.

Judicial interest in the rights of the accused is more recent than one might imagine. Not until the 1960s did the Supreme Court move to regulate police, prosecutorial, and judicial conduct in the states. This was accomplished by incorporating Bill of Rights protections—for the right to counsel and a fair and speedy trial and against unreasonable searches and seizures, self-incrimination and double jeopardy, and cruel and unusual punishment—into the "due process" clause of the Fourteenth Amendment. Something of a rollback has been underway since the mid-1980s and many new questions have been raised by government actions undertaken as part of the war on terror.

unreasonable searches and seizures The Fourth Amendment to the Constitution guarantees that citizens will not be subject to unreasonable searches and seizures. A search must be authorized by a warrant secured on probable cause that specific, relevant evidence is to be found if a particular place is searched.

Searches, Seizures, and the Exclusionary Rule. The Fourth Amendment to the Constitution declares that "The right of the people to be secure in their persons, houses, papers, and effects, against **unreasonable searches and seizures**, shall not be violated, and no Warrants shall issue, but upon probable cause, supported by Oath or affirmation, and particularly describing the place to be searched, and the persons or things to be seized." Police cannot engage in general searches in the hope of uncovering wrongdoing. Traditionally, obtaining a search warrant required police to convince a judge that they have "probable cause" to believe that the search of a particular place would result in the seizure of particular items relevant to a specific crime.

exclusionary rule The exclusionary rule holds that evidence illegally obtained by police cannot be used in court. The Supreme Court established the exclusionary rule in regard to the federal authorities in *Weeks v. U.S.* (1914) and in regard to state authorities in *Mapp v. Ohio* (1961).

To encourage police to abide by these stringent rules, American courts enforced the **exclusionary rule**. Developed first in *Weeks v. U.S.* (1914) at the federal level and then applied to state officials in *Mapp v. Ohio* (1961), the exclusionary rule says that evidence illegally obtained will be "excluded" from use against the defendant at trial.[15] The pros and cons of the exclusionary rule have been clear from the beginning. Two prominent jurists, both future

Supreme Court justices, laid them out during the discussion of *Weeks*. Louis Brandeis explained the necessity of the rule by saying, "If the government becomes a lawbreaker, it breeds contempt for law." New York Court of Appeals Judge Benjamin Cardozo responded incredulously, "the criminal is to go free because the constable blundered."

Since the mid-1980s there has been considerable movement away from complete exclusion of tainted evidence. The Supreme Court held in 1984 that the exclusionary rule should be subject to a "good faith" exception. The government had long contended that officers acting on the "objectively reasonable" assumption that a warrant that they had obtained was good but was later found to be flawed should not lose their evidence. Another 1984 case, *Nix v. Williams*, held that evidence should be admitted even if it first came to light in an illegal search "If the prosecution can establish by a preponderance of evidence that the information ultimately or inevitably would have been discovered by lawful means." The "good faith" and "inevitable discovery" exceptions significantly eroded the exclusionary rule and the deterrence that it provided to illegal police conduct.

In 2006, the Supreme Court declared in *Hudson v. Michigan* that although the police failed to observe the "knock and announce" rule (central to the common law since the thirteenth century), they could still use evidence obtained at trial. Police arriving at the home of Booker T. Hudson Jr., announced their presence but did not knock and waited only seconds before entering through an unlocked door. The police discovered drugs in the home. Justice Scalia, writing for a 5–4 majority, was dismissive of the exclusionary rule, weighing "the right not to be intruded upon in one's nightclothes" against the "grave adverse consequences that exclusion of relevant incriminating evidence always entails."[16] Justice Kennedy, the swing vote in *Hudson*, signed the majority opinion, but he also wrote separately to declare that, "the continued operation of the 'exclusionary rule,' as settled and defined by our precedents, is not in doubt." Others were not so sure.

In 2009, Chief Justice Roberts, writing for a 5–4 court in *Herring v. U.S.*, struck another blow to the exclusionary rule. Bennie D. Herring went to the Coffee County, Alabama, Sheriff's office to check on an impounded truck. While inquiring into the truck, deputies asked the records clerk to check for outstanding warrants on Herring. The clerk reported an open felony warrant on Herring and he was arrested. Subsequent to the arrest, police found methamphetamine and an unloaded handgun on Herring. Almost immediately, the clerk corrected himself, reporting that the warrant on Herring had been recalled, but Herring was held anyway on the drug and weapons charges.

At trial, Herring's lawyer moved to have the case dismissed based on the "exclusionary rule." The trial court declined to dismiss the case and the appeals court agreed, citing the "good faith" exception to the exclusionary rule. Herring's appeal to the Supreme Court was decided in 2009. Chief Justice Roberts took the occasion to broaden exceptions to the exclusionary rule. Roberts wrote that, "To trigger the exclusionary rule, police misconduct must be sufficiently deliberate that exclusion can meaningfully deter it, and sufficiently culpable that

AP Photo/Russell Contreras

Albuquerque, New Mexico, police officers stop and frisk a man in an area where drug sales were suspected of taking place.

such deterrence is worth the price paid by the justice system."[17] The Court's finding that police misconduct must be both "deliberate" and "culpable," meaning ill-intended, seems to envision a cost/benefit balancing test rather than an automatic exclusion of tainted evidence.

Finally, on a related legal track, the Supreme Court decided a 2012 Fourth Amendment search and seizure case that updated this historic personal privacy right for the twenty-first century. Police suspected that Antoine Jones, a Washington D.C. nightclub owner, was involved in cocaine sales. As part of their investigation, the police secretly placed a GPS tracking device on Jones's Jeep Grand Cherokee to follow his movements. After a month of evidence gathering, Jones was arrested, convicted, and sentenced to life in prison. The U.S. Court of Appeals for the District of Columbia overturned the conviction and the U.S. Supreme Court agreed, declaring that police must secure a warrant because intensive tracking by GPS is a "search" within the meaning of the Fourth Amendment.[18]

right to counsel *Gideon v. Wainwright* (1963) declared that a person accused of a crime has the right to the assistance of a lawyer in preparing his or her defense. The right to counsel is part of the meaning of the Fourteenth Amendment's guarantee of "due process of law."

Right to Counsel.   The Sixth Amendment provides for a federal **right to counsel**. The rights of criminal defendants in state courts to the assistance of legal counsel during trial were established in *Gideon v. Wainwright* (1963). Clarence Earl Gideon was a 51-year-old man charged with breaking into the Bar Harbor Poolroom in Panama City, Florida. Gideon denied having broken into the pool hall and requested the assistance of counsel at his trial. Assistance was denied, and Gideon was convicted. He appealed, claiming that it was a violation of the "due process" clause of the Fourteenth Amendment to confront an untrained citizen with the complexity of the legal and judicial systems. The Supreme Court agreed that persons charged with crimes should have the right to counsel at state expense if they cannot afford to provide it for themselves, saying "In our adversary system of criminal justice, any person haled into court, who is too poor to hire a lawyer, cannot be assured a fair trial unless counsel is provided for him."

States do comply with the requirement to provide counsel to indigent defendants, but their budgets are often meager and their performances spotty. Fully 80 percent of defendants are too poor to afford their own lawyer, so they must depend upon public defenders or legal aid lawyers. Some public defenders handle as many as 2,000 cases a year, so the amount of time they can spend preparing for each case, let alone doing independent investigation of the circumstances surrounding the case, is minimal. Hence, many public defenders are reduced to negotiating plea bargains and guilty verdicts.[19]

Self-Incrimination. "Taking the Fifth" is the shorthand term for exercising one's Fifth Amendment right against **self-incrimination**. The Fifth Amendment reads in part, "nor shall any person . . . be compelled in any criminal case to be a witness against himself." As with the right to counsel, the Supreme Court has acted to ensure that the right against self-incrimination applies in state as well as federal courts, from the investigation stage of the legal process through arrest and trial. Since *Miranda v. Arizona* (1966), persons taken into custody must be specifically informed that they have the right to remain silent and that they cannot be questioned unless they waive that right. If the *Miranda* warning is not given, statements made by the accused cannot be used at trial.

The right against self-incrimination was strengthened in a 1986 case known as *Michigan v. Jackson. Michigan v. Jackson* held that police could not initiate questioning of a suspect who had a lawyer or who had asked for a lawyer until the lawyer was present. The Michigan case also held that defendants could not change their mind and agree to talk with police between the lawyer's appointment and arrival. But as with the search and seizure cases, the Supreme Court's recent rulings on self-incrimination represent a dialing back of the exclusionary rule to a more case-by-case "totality of the evidence" test.

The 2009 case of *Montejo v. Louisiana* began as an attempt to clarify whether a defendant had to affirmatively accept counsel for the Michigan prohibition on questioning to apply. Jesse Jay Montejo was convicted of murder in 2002. He had been appointed counsel, knew it, and did not ask to consult with counsel, before leading the police to the murder weapon. On appeal, Montejo claimed that the police should not have questioned him until his lawyer arrived. The Supreme Court declined simply to find that Montejo should have consulted with his lawyer before cooperating with the police.

self-incrimination The Fifth Amendment to the Constitution guarantees that one cannot be compelled "to be a witness against himself." Taking advantage of the right against self-incrimination is often called "taking the Fifth."

Pro & Con

Defending the USA Patriot Act (2001–Present)

Major Provisions of the USA Patriot Act

Improved Information Sharing

Allows greater information sharing between domestic law enforcement and the intelligence agencies.

Enhanced Surveillance Authority

Authorizes "sneak and peek" warrants with delayed notification to the target.

Authorizes "roving wiretaps" of all phones used by a target as opposed to tapping a specific phone number.

Expands FBI access to personal health, financial, and other records if agents certify foreign intelligence or antiterrorism activities.

Expands law enforcement's access to Internet routing, e-mail, and voice mail records and broadens Internet provider's responsibility to cooperate with authorities.

Strengthened Antiterrorism Laws

Expands the definition of domestic terrorism to include life-threatening activities designed to intimidate the public or to change government policy by threats, assassination, or mass destruction.

Expands the definition of what constitutes material support of terrorists and penalties attached.

Allows a federal judge to issue eavesdropping orders that can be executed anywhere in the country.

Following the Money

Gives intelligence agents access to financial records in international terrorism cases.

Permits expanded forfeiture in bulk-cash smuggling cases and cases against those planning or committing acts of terrorism in the United States.

The Debate over the Patriot Act

Passed only weeks after the 9/11 attacks, the USA Patriot Act has been controversial since its inception. The controversy was on stark display when Congress struggled over renewal of sixteen key provisions of the Patriot Act during 2005 and 2006. Its advocates, led by President Bush and Attorney General Alberto Gonzales, argued that the new powers were needed to defend the homeland and combat the threat of global terrorism. In April 2005, Attorney General Gonzales warned Congress that, "Al Qaeda and other terrorist groups still pose a grave threat to the security of the American people, and now is not the time to relinquish some of our most effective tools in this fight."

Critics on both the left and the right have expressed concerns about the Patriot Act and related national security laws and how these powers have been used.

Justice Scalia, writing for a 5–4 court, declared that, "It would be completely unjustified to presume that a defendant's consent to police-initiated interrogation was involuntary or coerced simply because he had previously been appointed a lawyer." Moreover, Scalia asserted that the benefits to police effectiveness far outweighed the cost to defendants' rights. "The considerable adverse effect of this (the *Michigan v. Jackson*) rule upon society's ability to solve crimes and bring criminals to justice far outweighs its capacity to prevent a genuinely coerced agreement to speak without counsel present."[21] In 2010, the Supreme Court limited Miranda rights a bit more by holding that

These powers of investigation, surveillance, and arrest press hard on the traditional rights and liberties that Americans have enjoyed. The point is frequently made that the terrorists have won if we become a more closed and fearful society. On the other hand, no one denies that the terrorists took advantage of our open society in wreaking the terrible destruction of 9/11. After a year-long debate, key provisions of the Patriot Act were renewed in March 2006.

Now nearly twenty years after 9/11, how should we be thinking about the relationship between security and liberty? Bush Attorney General Alberto Gonzales was right to point to the continuing terrorist threat but shouldn't we be at least a little bit surprised that Obama Attorney General Eric Holder takes much the same view. Scholars recall that every major war in our history—the Revolutionary War, the Civil War, World Wars I and II—produced restrictions on civil liberties that were later regretted and dismantled. But no president, conservative Republican or progressive Democrat can risk seeming to let down their guard against terrorist threats.[20]

This delicate balance between the liberty of individuals and the security of the nation returned to the front-burner with the 2013 revelations of National Security Agency (NSA) contractor Edward Snowden. Snowden released to the media and the public a vast array of secret documents showing a variety and scope of domestic and international surveillance not previously imagined. NSA, generally tasked with foreign surveillance and court-approved domestic surveillance related to its international responsibilities, was doing much more. The Snowden revelations showed NSA and related agencies to be sweeping up vast amounts of data, domestically and internationally, on phone, text, and Internet traffic. While most of this data was described as "metadata," not the full messages and not linked to individuals, the scope of the collection disturbed regular citizens as well as privacy advocates. The Obama administration responded with modest reforms, but a host of unanswered questions remain.

What do you think?
- Have we gone too far in sacrificing liberty to security in the Patriot Act?
- Or are the threats all too real and the sacrifices of personal liberty appropriately modest in your view?

PRO	CON
War on Terror demanded greater powers	National security challenges often elicit over-reaction
Protecting Americans must be top priority	Individual rights must not be sacrificed
The War on Terror is on-going	Perpetual war gives government too much power

suspects must explicitly invoke their right to remain silent and then follow through by remaining silent. Ambiguous invocations, as when a suspect initially declines to answer but later responds to some police questions, will be decided in favor of the police.[22]

Finally, much discussion of police and national security interrogation policy resolves around the famous "ticking time bomb" scenario. The question is posed—if you captured a terrorist, whether in the U.S. or outside, who was thought to have information about a bomb about to go off, do rules like Miranda rights and the Geneva Convention prohibitions on torture make sense? Something close to this hypothetical actually occurred in the wake of the Boston Marathon bombing in 2013. Four days after the bombing, Dzhokhar Tsarnaev, one of the two brothers who were the main perpetrators, was captured, seriously wounded, and questioned in his hospital bed without being read his Miranda rights. Federal authorities claimed a "public safety exemption" to the normal Miranda requirements. As in the "ticking time bomb" scenario, the claim was that there might be other plots afoot that the perpetrator—in this case Tsarnaev—might know about. There were not, but there might have been. What do you think of the "public safety exemption?" Too broad, or just common sense?[23]

cruel and unusual punishment The Eighth Amendment to the U.S. Constitution prohibits "cruel and unusual punishment." Historically, this language prohibited torture and other abuses. Today the key question is whether the death penalty should be declared to be cruel and unusual punishment.

Cruel and Unusual Punishment. The Eighth Amendment to the Constitution forbids **cruel and unusual punishment**. This provision was not terribly controversial until the 1960s when the National Association for the Advancement of Colored People (NAACP) convincingly made the case that the death penalty in America was applied arbitrarily and more frequently against blacks than against whites. The Supreme Court suspended the death penalty in *Furman v. Georgia* (1972) until states could reconsider and refine their procedures. Georgia's rewritten death penalty procedures were approved by the Supreme Court in *Gregg v. Georgia* (1976).

Although the United States is one of the few advanced industrial countries to employ the death penalty, the Supreme Court has been adamant that the death penalty is constitutional if fairly and reasonably applied. Hence, until recently, the debate revolved around issues of age and mental development—how young is too young to be executed and how mentally challenged is too challenged to be held responsible for your actions? In 1989, the Supreme Court held that executing young people at 16 or 17 was not "cruel and unusual." In 2005, in a case called *Roper v. Simmons*, the court reversed itself, citing evolving national and international standards, declaring that execution for crimes committed before age 18 was constitutionally prohibited. In 2012, the court declared that sentences of life without the possibility of parole also are unconstitutional for those under 18.[24]

Courts struggle with what it means to punish the mentally ill. The issue of executing the mentally challenged and the mentally ill who are convicted of serious crimes has been particularly vexing. All recognize that at some level of mental incapacity, an individual lacks the ability to form criminal intent or to assist in his or own defense or both. In *Atkins v. Virginia* (2002) the Supreme Court agreed that it was unconstitutionally cruel to execute the severely mentally challenged (IQ below 70), but little guidance was given on how to deal with the more common cases of mild to moderate limitations. In 2014, the Supreme Court declared that states could not simply declare those with IQs above 70 to be competent. A wider range of evidence had to be considered.[25]

Atkins v. Virginia The Supreme Court held that the execution of severely retarded persons violated the prohibition against "cruel and unusual punishment" in the Eighth Amendment.

Quite unexpectedly, a legal dispute erupted over whether the particular three-drug cocktail used to execute death row inmates in most states caused sufficient pain to be prohibited as "cruel and unusual." In 2007, the Supreme Court agreed to consider this question in a Kentucky case, *Baze v. Rees* (553 U.S. 35).

By the end of the year an informal moratorium on executions was in place awaiting the court's determination. In 2008, the court declared that lethal injection using the three-drug cocktail was constitutionally permissible. While the result was no great surprise, a concurring opinion by Associate Justice William Brennan created a stir. Brennan, then the court's oldest and longest serving member, at 88 with 33 years of service on the court, declared that the time had come to reconsider "the justification for the death penalty itself."[26] While there is growing unease about the death penalty, change will come slowly.

Civil Liberties, Prisons, and the Death Penalty

Paradoxically, while the American commitment to civil liberties is strong, so is the commitment to prisons and punishment. The Bill of Rights was added to the Constitution by the first Congress because many were concerned that a powerful national government might threaten individual liberty. Yet, today the United States, with less than 5 percent of the world's population, holds one-quarter of the world's prisoners, the most of any nation in the world.[27]

Q5 If we value civil liberties so highly, why do we keep so many people in prison?

Let's start with the number of state and federal prisoners held in the U.S. We have solid data going back nearly a century. In 1925, fewer than 92,000 prisoners were held by the federal and state governments. The numbers rose during the difficult depression years of the 1930, peaking at almost 180,000 in 1939, before falling back during the 1940s and early 1950s. The prison

AP Photo/Eric Risberg

A row of general population inmates move through California's San Quentin State Prison. Under federal pressure, overcrowding in California prisons has been reduced in recent years.

population stayed near 200,000 from the late 1950s through the early 1970s—and then it took off. In 1972, there were 196,092 federal and state prisoners in the U.S., by 1980 there were 316,000, by 1990 there were 740,000, by 2000 there were 1.33 million, and by 2015 there were 1.5 million.

Another way to think about the size of the federal and state prison population is in terms of prisoners per 100,000 of total population, also referred to as the incarceration rate (Figure 3.1). Population increases over time and so one would expect prison population to increase over time as well. If the prison population increased at the same rate as the general population, the incarceration rate would hold steady. It has not. In 1925, the incarceration rate was 79 per 100,000 of population. Again, the incarceration rate rose during the depression and then fell back during the 1940s and 1950s. The incarceration rate was 93 per 100,000 in 1972, 139 in 1980, 297 in 1990, 478 in 2000, and 458 in 2015. This is more than a six-fold increase in prisoners per 100,000 of population since 1925. The U.S. is number one in the world in incarceration rates. Russia is number two and the average for the world is about one-sixth the U.S. rate.[28]

Even more stunningly, when one adds those in local jails and on probation and parole to those in federal and state prisons, there are 6.7 million

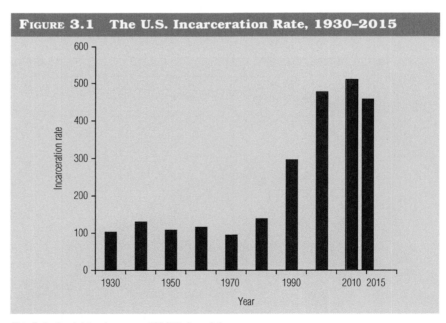

FIGURE 3.1   The U.S. Incarceration Rate, 1930–2015

Note: Federal and state prisoners per 100,000 of population.

Source: U.S. Census, *Statistical Abstract of the United States, 2003*, Mini-Historical Series, HS-24, Federal and State Prisoners by Jurisdiction, 1925–2001 and Bureau of Justice Statistics, Number of Sentenced Inmates Incarcerated, see http://www.ojp.usdoj.gov/bjs/glance/tables/incrttab.htm.

persons in the U.S. correctional system. This number has grown inexorably, increasing every year between 1982 and 2007. In 1982, the total corrections population was just under 2.2 million persons. By 1990 it was 4.35 million, by 2000 it was 6.45 million, and by 2007 it was 7.34 million. By 2015, the total number of persons in the U.S. corrections system had declined modestly to 6.7 million.[29] Just 1 in 89 women report to some element of the corrections system, while 1 in 18 men do. One in 11 blacks report to the corrections system, 1 in 27 Hispanics, and 1 in 45 whites report to some aspect of the corrections system.

Now, we come to the costs. In 2015, it cost the states $80 billion to control 6.7 million people in prisons and jails and on probation and parole. Prisons are obviously the most expensive element of the corrections system. It costs an average of $29,000 annually to hold an inmate, $2,750 per parolee, and $1,250 per probationer.[30] Not surprisingly, the loss of state revenues produced by the economic downturn of 2007–2009 led a number of states to reduce prison populations by moving offenders onto probation and parole programs.

Interestingly, crime rates, incarceration rates, and corrections expenses all increased during the 1970s and 1980s, but for the last two decades, even as crime rates fell, prison populations and cost continued to rise. Both violent crime and property crime rates doubled between 1960 and 1970. Violent crime rates increased from 161 per 100,000 persons in 1960 to 364 in 1970 and property crime rates increased from 1,726 per 100,000 persons to 3,621. Congress and the states responded with "get tough on crime" campaigns, criminalizing more behavior and lengthening sentences, especially in drug cases. Crime continued to rise for two more decades, cresting at 758 violent crimes per 100,000 persons in 1991 and 5,140 property crimes. But crime has been trending steadily downward since. In 2015 there were 373 violent crimes per 100,000 and 2,487 property crimes, essentially back to the early to mid-1970s levels.

So how should be think about the American commitments to civil liberties and to mass incarceration? Perhaps it is simply the case that someone uncivil enough to commit a serious crime deserves to lose his or her liberty. But surely the commitment to civil liberties—and to liberty more generally—should guide us toward a review of our incarceration policies and goals.

Chapter Summary

Most of the delegates to the Constitutional Convention did not believe that the new constitution they drafted needed a Bill of Rights. They believed the limited powers granted to the national government and the institutional safeguards, including bicameralism, separation of powers, and checks and balances, would be sufficient protection for the liberties of the people. Yet, during ratification it became clear that many citizens disagreed and worried that their liberties were insecure. Fortunately, James Madison and other strong supporters of the Constitution listened to these concerns and responded to them in the first Congress by crafting and securing adoption by the states of the Bill of Rights.

The Bill of Rights codified a broad consensus, informed both by British history and colonial American experience, that certain individual rights and liberties were necessary for a people to be and remain free. Foremost among them are the rights of conscience: the right to speak, write, publish, think, and believe what one will. The justly famous First Amendment further claims the right of people to come together to debate their opinions, join with others who share their views, and to appeal to government on behalf of their opinions. The Second Amendment declares the right to bear arms. The Fourth through the Eighth Amendments secure basic procedural and legal rights, including rights against unreasonable search and seizure, double jeopardy, self-incrimination, excessive bail, and cruel and unusual punishment, and the rights to a speedy trial before a jury of one's peers. The Ninth Amendment, intriguingly, says this list of rights may not be complete and other rights may obtain, while the Tenth says powers not given to the national government remain with the states and the people.

Until the 1920s, the Bill of Rights acted as a limit only on the national government, though most state constitutions included bills of rights that applied within those states. Since the 1920s, a process of "partial incorporation" has applied the freedoms in the Bill of Rights, beginning first with the freedoms of speech and the press, against the states through the "due process clause" of the Fourteenth Amendment. During the 1950s and 1960s, the Supreme Court, guided by Chief Justice Earl Warren, expanded freedoms of speech, press, assembly, and, more controversially, the rights of criminal defendants. More recently, the Rehnquist and Roberts counts have been trimming back the rights of criminal defendants in regard, for example, to search and seizure and the right against self-incrimination.

Finally, we asked why a country so dedicated to civil liberties would simultaneously have so many people in prison. The U.S. has 6.7 million people under the control of the corrections system, either incarcerated or on probation or parole. The U.S. has the largest prison population in the world. Moreover, though two-thirds of the nations in the world have abandoned capital punishment, the U.S. continues to employ the death penalty. The U.S. executed 23 people in 2017.

Key Terms

Atkins v. Virginia	*Gitlow v. New York*
Barron v. Baltimore	incorporation
civil liberties	*Lemon v. Kurtzman*
civil rights	*Miller v. California*
cruel and unusual punishment	*Near v. Minnesota*
establishment clause	*New York Times Co. v. Sullivan*
exclusionary rule	obscenity
free exercise clause	Pentagon Papers Case

prior restraint

right to counsel

self-incrimination

symbolic speech

Texas v. Johnson

unreasonable searches and seizures

Virginia v. Black

Suggested Readings

Amar, Akhil Reed, and Les Adams, *The Bill of Rights Primer: A Citizen's Guidebook to the American Bill of Rights.* New York: Skyhorse Publishing, 2015. The book describes the Bill of Rights and the liberties guaranteed therein as they have developed and evolved over the course of our history.

Griffith, R. Marie, *Moral Combat: How Sex Divided American Christians and Fractured American Politics.* New York: Basic Books, 2017. A cultural history of the prominence of issues relating to gender, sexuality, and procreation and their impact on our politics.

Healy, Thomas. *The Great Dissent: How Oliver Wendell Holmes Changed His Mind—And Changed the History of Free Speech in America.* New York: Metropolitan Books, 2013. The story of how Holmes' famous dissent in *Abrams v. United States* signalled his shift from a defender of government power to control dissident speech to a defender of the "free trade in ideas."

Houppert, Karen. *Chasing Gideon: The Elusive Quest for Poor People's Justice.* New York: The New Press, 2013. Houppert argues that the promise of legal representation for the poor, made in *Gideon v. Wainwright* (1963), has gone largely unfulfilled.

Waldman, Michael. *The Second Amendment: A Biography.* New York: Simon & Schuster, 2014. Waldman traces the history of the right to bear arms from its militia origins in the founding period to its status as an individual right today.

Web Resources

1 www.aclu.org
   The official home page of the American Civil Liberties Union, an organization dedicated to issues surrounding civil liberties. This page provides up-to-date news as well as discussions of legal decisions and the rights of individuals.

2 www.nationalgunrights.org
   National Gun Rights organization whose webpage provides original and secondary material in favor of gun rights.

3 www.deathpenaltyinfo.org
   This is the key website maintained by opponents of the death penalty. It contains data on executions going back to colonial times, broken down by year, state, region, and race.

4 www.bancroft.berkeley.edu/collections/meiklejohn/project.html
The Meiklejohn Civil Liberties Institute Archives contain briefs, transcripts, and opinions on major civil liberties cases since 1955.

5 www.freedomforum.org
Freedom Forum maintains a Web page offering current coverage of censorship, speech, and the press, including links to archives, the Newseum, and a report on the First Amendment.

Notes

1 James MacGregor Burns and Stewart Burns, *The People's Charter: The Pursuit of Rights in America* (New York: Vintage Books, 1993), 44.

2 Burns and Burns, *The People's Charter*, 199. See also Henry J. Abraham and Barbara A. Perry, *Freedom and the Court: Civil Rights and Liberties in the United States*, 8th ed. (Lawrence, KS: University Press of Kansas, 2003), 34–36.

3 For a little historical background on *Texas v. Johnson*, see Robert Wilonsky, "Hot Topic Ignited in Dallas," *Dallas Morning News*, November 20, 2016, 1B, 8B.

4 Abraham and Perry, *Freedom and the Court*, 237.

5 Anthony Lewis, *Make No Law: The Sullivan Case and the First Amendment* (New York: Vintage Books, 1991), 68. See also David W. Dunlap, "The Burden of Providing Truth: The Libel Suit that Kept Speech Free," *New York Times*, July 1, 2017, A2.

6 Adam Liptak, "Can Trump Change Libel Laws," *New York Times*, March 30, 2017.

7 Dean Baquet and Bill Keller, editors of the *New York Times* and *Los Angeles Times* respectively, "When Do We Publish a Secret?" *New York Times*, Op-Ed, July 1, 2006. See also Richard Stengel, managing editor of *Time*, July 10, 2006, 6.

8 Marisa Taylor, McClatchy Newspapers, "Administration Backing FBI Phone Policy," *Dallas Morning News*, January 23, 2010, A16.

9 The key debate is to be found in Michael J. Malbin, *Religion and Politics: The Intentions of the Authors of the First Amendment* (Washington, D.C.: American Enterprise Institute, 1978), and in Leonard W. Levy, *The Establishment Clause: Religion and the First Amendment* (New York: Macmillan, 1986).

10 Linda Greenhouse, "Justices Approve U.S. Financing of Religious Schools' Equipment," *New York Times*, National Edition, June 29, 2000, A21.

11 Linda Greenhouse, "Justices Allow a Commandment Display, Bar Others," *New York Times*, June 28, 2005, A1, A17.

12 Adam Liptak, "Court Rejects Revised Travel Ban as Sessions Vows to Appeal to Top." *New York Times*, May 26, 2017, A1, A19.

13 Kim Severson, "Mississippi Tells Public Schools to Develop Policies Allowing Prayers," *New York Times*, March 15, 2013, A12.

14 Adam Liptak, "Religious Groups Given Freer Hand on Employment," *New York Times*, January 12, 2012, A1, A3.

15 William Yardley, "Dollree Mapp Is Dead, Defied Search in Landmark Case," *New York Times*, December 10, 2014, A29.

16 Linda Greenhouse, "Court Limits Protection against Improper Entry," *New York Times*, June 16, 2006, A24.

17 Adam Liptak, "Supreme Court Edging Closer to Repeal of Evidence Rule," *New York Times*, January 31, 2009, A13.

18 Adam Liptak, "Justices Reject GPS Tracking in a Drug Case," *New York Times*, January 24, 2012, A1, A3.

19 Karen Houppert, *Chasing Gideon: The Elusive Quest for Poor People's Justice* (New York: The New Press, 2013).

20 Donald F. Kettl, *System under Stress* (Washington, D.C.: CQ Press, 2013).

21 Jesse J. Holland, AP, "Suspect Questioning Ruling Is Overturned," *Dallas Morning News*, May 27, 2009, A8.

22 Jess Bravin, "Justices Narrow Miranda Rule," *Wall Street Journal*, June 2, 2010, A2.

23 Ethan Bronner and Michael S. Schmidt, "In Questions at First, No Miranda for Suspect," *New York Times*, April 23, 2013, A13.

24 Adam Liptak and Ethan Bronner, "Mandatory Life Terms Barred for Juveniles in Murder Cases," *New York Times*, June 26, 2012, A1, A14.

25 Lizette Alvarez and John Schwartz, "After Justices' Ruling on I.Q., Hope for Death Row Reprieves," *New York Times*, May 31, 2014, A1, A3.

26 Linda Greenhouse, "After a 32-Year Journey, Justice Stevens Renounces Capital Punishment," *New York Times*, June 26, 2012, A20.

27 Pew Center for the States, "One in 31: The Long Reach of America's Corrections," March 2009.

28 E. Ann Carson, "Prisoners in 2014," U.S. Department of Justice, Bureau of Justice Statistics, September 2015.

29 Danielle Kaeble, "Correctional Population in the United States, 2014," U.S. Department of Justice, January 21, 2016.

30 Solomon Moore, "Study Shows High Cost of Criminal Corrections," *New York Times*, March 3, 2009, A13.

Chapter 4

CIVIL RIGHTS
Where Liberty and Equality Collide

Focus Questions: from reading to thinking

Q1 Where does the energy that drives social movements come from?

Q2 What role did the Supreme Court play in first limiting and then expanding civil rights for blacks?

Q3 Has Congress usually led or followed the Supreme Court on civil rights?

Q4 Does affirmative action to assist minorities and women inevitably mean reverse discrimination against white men?

Q5 What were the similarities and differences between the movements for racial and gender equality?

SEXUAL PRIVACY, THE NINTH AMENDMENT, AND UNENUMERATED RIGHTS

The Constitution TODAY

Ninth Amendment: "The enumeration in the Constitution, of certain rights, shall not be construed to deny or disparage others retained by the people."

The Ninth Amendment declares that we citizens may well have rights not explicitly enumerated in the U.S. Constitution. This seems like good news. But as you can imagine, the Ninth Amendment makes some people, including some Supreme Court justices, nervous. Broadly speaking, the idea of unenumerated rights makes conservatives wary and liberals giddy. What rights do you want to claim under the Ninth Amendment?

Recall that the Constitution did not initially have a Bill of Rights. Federalist proponents of the Constitution, the conservatives of the day, argued that since the document gave only certain enumerated powers to the national government, no specific protections of rights and liberties were needed. For example, they argued that because Congress was not granted the power to legislate on religion, there could be no need for protection of religious liberty. Anti-Federalist opponents of the Constitution, the populists of the day, argued that broad phrases like "promote the general welfare," "necessary and proper," and "supreme law of the land," raised the specter of a dangerously powerful national government. They wanted specific protections for religious and other liberties.

Proponents of the Constitution, led by James Madison in the first Congress, tried to assuage the concerns of opponents by adding a Bill of Rights. But adding a Bill of Rights raised the possibility that the list of rights specifically protected would be incomplete, one or more rights might be left off, or static, set once and for all. To address these concerns, Madison and the Congress added the Ninth Amendment (quoted above). OK, but what does it mean?

Most judges and scholars argue that the Ninth Amendment neither enhances nor limits other provisions of the Constitution. It acts principally as a rule of interpretation, saying that the absence in the Constitution of a claimed right cannot be taken by the court as proof that it does not exist. Still, judges and scholars are not of one mind about the Ninth Amendment. Justice Scalia, a conservative leader on the Supreme Court until his death in 2016, said the Ninth Amendment's "refusal to 'deny or disparage' other rights is far removed from affirming any one of them, and even further removed from authorizing judges to identify what they might be."

Though the Ninth Amendment has been evoked relatively infrequently by the courts, it has done some heavy lifting in recent decades. It has arisen in cases regarding sexual privacy, abortion, and gay rights. In *Griswold v. Connecticut* (1965), a law prohibiting contraception was struck down as a violation of marital privacy. Justice William O. Douglas, writing for a 7–2 majority, argued that while no explicit "right to privacy" appeared in the Constitution, rights mentioned in the First, Third, Fourth, Fifth, and Ninth Amendments, "have penumbras, formed by emanations from those guarantees that help give them life and substance." The idea that provisions of the

Constitution give off penumbras and emanations which sum to a right to sexual privacy has created some mirth among conservatives—but privacy is not a bad constitutional right to have.

In *Roe v. Wade* (1973), the U.S. District Court for the Northern District of Texas cited the "due process clause" of the Fourteenth Amendment and the Ninth Amendment in striking down Texas' abortion statute. Upon review, the Supreme Court declared that the Fourteenth Amendment was sufficient to protect a right to privacy encompassing abortion decisions during the early months of pregnancy. Justice Blackmun, writing for the majority, did not cite the Ninth Amendment but he did refer to the District Court's treatment of the Ninth Amendment respectfully. Finally, in *Lawrence v. Texas* (2003), in which the Supreme Court struck down sodomy laws in Texas and other states, Justice Kennedy cited Fourteenth Amendment protections to privacy, but Ninth Amendment claims were made as well.

Civil liberties and civil rights are the two brightest constellations in our constitutional firmament, and both have grown brighter over the more than 235 years of our national history. They are not, however, equally bright, and their relative glow has waxed and waned over time. Initially, the idea of liberty was dominant. Liberty required only that white men should be free to think and behave as they wished in broad stretches of social and economic life. Equality seemed to demand no more than that all white, male property holders be free to compete. But when issues of race and gender equality were raised, tensions escalated.

—————————◆◆×◆◆—————————

C ivil liberties restrict and control government power over individuals. Civil rights promise that government power will be used to ensure that individuals are treated equally and fairly by government and other individuals. Before the Civil War, civil liberties and civil rights seemed to be roughly the same thing and for white men they were very similar. The distinction became clearer after minorities and women began to claim the same liberties and rights available to white men.

Americans seldom stop to think that what made the struggle for minority and female rights so long and arduous was that the founding generation and several generations thereafter opposed them.[1] Moreover, law and policy governing relations between the races and genders, on slavery and marriage for example, were state matters, not national matters. Hence, even once attitudes about race and gender began to change for some people and in some regions of the country, the American federal structure meant that battles for equal rights had to be fought state by state and often on the most unfavorable terrain.[2]

In this chapter, we consider how the Civil War and its aftermath raised new issues of diversity, equality, and civil rights in America. First, we look at the stout resistance that white men put up even after the Civil War to claims by minorities and women for equal rights. Second, we explore the modern struggle for minority and gender equality. Third, we follow the debate over whether attempts to redress historical disadvantages of minorities and women through "affirmative action" must inevitably involve "reverse discrimination" against white men. These are some of the most contentious issues in contemporary American politics. In both cases, broad social movements lasting centuries were required to break through existing privileges and bring fundamental change.

SOCIAL MOVEMENTS IN AMERICAN POLITICS

Most politics are fairly predictable; the dominant party prevails, incumbents win, lobbyists have their way, and skeptical citizens turn their attention to family, work, and community. But sometimes political activity jumps the normal channels to cut new and broader channels for future politics. A **social movement** is a collective enterprise to change the organizational design or characteristic operating procedures of a society in order to produce changes in the way the society distributes opportunities and rewards. Genuine social movements aim to arouse large numbers of people alienated from the existing social order to force deep and permanent social change. The beneficiaries of the established order rarely give up without a fight, so social movements are always tumultuous.

Now, before proceeding, let's pause long enough to recall that the Founders constructed our constitutional democracy—with its separation of powers, checks and balances, bicameralism, the staggered terms of elected officials, the appointed judges, and federalism—to break the momentum of social movements. Social movements were the people rising up, sweeping past and perhaps over their elected representatives, to demand change in the structure and policy results of government. Shays's Rebellion, an uprising of indebted Massachusetts farmers, was one of the reasons that the Founders came together to strengthen government with a new constitution. So we should not be surprised to see that social movements, even those most Americans approve of today, like the movements for racial and gender equality, were spurned and ridiculed for generations after they made their first demands for change.

Social movements arise from the effect that socioeconomic development has on prominent social divisions including ideology, race, ethnicity, gender, and lifestyle preference. Often, compatible movements cooperate and coalesce as a wave of collective action passes through society. The mid-nineteenth-century movements in favor of emancipation of the slaves, women's rights, and temperance often shared members, leaders, and resources. Similarly, the mid-twentieth century movements for civil rights, women's rights, nuclear disarmament, and environmentalism shared members, resources, and even protest strategies.

Students of social movements argue that both the surges in movement activity during particular periods and the similarities between movements that occur simultaneously are explained by the presence of a dominant **frame** or organizing theme. The frame of the mid-nineteenth century—free labor,

Q1 Where does the energy that drives social movements come from?

social movement A collective enterprise to change the way society is organized and operates in order to produce changes in the way opportunities and rewards are distributed.

frame Dominant organizing frame or image, such as the equal rights image that motivated most of the movements of the 1960s and 1970s.

Pro & Con

Recognizing Gay Marriage

Some social movements, such as those demanding equality for racial and ethnic minorities and women, seem effectively permanent—we can trace them throughout our history. Other social movements, such as the demand for gay rights, including the right to marry, seem to many Americans to burst forth unexpectedly. While the demand for marriage equality may be relatively new, the demand for gay rights is not. The fact that it feels new to most heterosexual Americans only shows how thoroughly suppressed gay rights were until the last few decades.

Gay marriage statutes existed only in a few states as late as 2010 and all had been enacted since 2003. Advocates of gay rights, calling for full equality, contended that loving gay couples should be able to enjoy all the rights and privileges of marriage, just as loving heterosexual couples do. Opponents of gay marriage contended that marriage was the bedrock of human society and had always been understood to be between a man and a woman.

U.S. policy had, until recently, been to discourage but not forbid gay marriage. In 1996, Congress passed and President Bill Clinton signed the "Defense of Marriage Act" (DOMA) that defined marriage for the purposes of federal law as being between a man and a woman. The act further provided that, despite the Constitution's "full faith and credit clause," no state would be required to honor another state's same-sex marriages. In 2011, President Obama ordered the Justice Department not to enforce DOMA, but the law remained on the books. In May 2012 Vice President Biden and President Obama both declared, for the first time, that they supported gay marriage, and in 2014 Attorney General Eric Holder announced that a basket of federal benefits would be available to all married couples, gay and straight, in all states, whatever their state marriage laws might say. By 2016 thirty-seven states had approved gay marriage, though thirteen, mainly in the South, remained opposed.

Even as change toward gay marriage picked up speed at the state level, the pace of change in the federal courts was slow. In the June 2013 case of *United States v. Windsor*, the United States Supreme Court struck down the parts of DOMA denying federal benefits but stopped short of approving same sex marriage nationally. Gay rights advocates argued

entrepreneurship, and the right to contract—bound together the women's movement, the labor movement, and the abolition movement. The civil rights revolution of the past half century, in which most racial and ethnic groups, women, gays, the disabled, the elderly, and many others joined, was built around the equal rights frame.[3]

Social movements pose a twin threat to traditional political institutions like parties and interest groups and to the policies and programs they have developed for their constituents and supporters. The first threat is to policies, programs, and the existing flow of benefits. Movement supporters are dissatisfied with current policies and would change them. From the perspective of the status quo, change means that yesterday's insiders might become tomorrow's outsiders or at least that they might have to share benefits with a larger and more diverse group.

The second threat is potentially more serious. Social movements usually challenge not just policies but also the people, procedures, and institutions that

that this left a nation divided in which gay couples in the three-quarters of the states recognizing gay marriage had many rights still denied to gay couples in the one-quarter of states that still refused recognition to gay marriage. In January 2015, the U.S. Supreme Court agreed to hear a set of four cases starkly posing two questions. Must all fifty states permit marriage between same-sex couples, and, if not, must states that do not allow gay marriages respect legal marriages from other states? Arguments were held in April 2015 in the case of *Obergefell v. Hodges* and a decision was announced in June 2015. Justice Anthony Kennedy, for a court divided 5–4, declared same-sex marriage constitutionally and fully equal to heterosexual marriage. Kennedy wrote that marriage was a "liberty" that could not be denied gay couples. While the gay community celebrated this long-sought recognition,

conservative reaction on the court and more broadly was scathing.[4]

A Supreme Court decision may not, likely will not for many, end this fight. This leads some to ask whether courts are even the right vehicle for resolving divisive social issues like gay marriage. But if we do not use courts, that leaves only balky partisan legislatures. Can we, should we, ask gay couples to wait on legislatures to award them—maybe, at some point—equal rights?

What do you think?

- Should civil rights, rights to "due process" and "equal protection," be subject to majority vote?
- Should gay marriage be a constitutional right?
- If so, as a tactical matter, is this the right time to put this issue before this Supreme Court?

PRO	CON
Marriage is a human right	Marriage has always been heterosexual
The Constitution requires equal rights	States have always defined marriage
Public opinion is moving in favor	Red states are still strongly opposed

produced them. Naturally, the people, groups, and institutions that have controlled and benefited from the existing system resist changes for as long as they are able, grant reforms when they must, and occasionally are swept away if they cannot move far enough or fast enough in the direction of popular demands.

In our own time, social movements on the right, like the Tea Party movement and the Trumpian promise to drain the swamp, and on the left, like Occupy Wall Street and the Bernie Sanders campaign, pointed accusingly at corporate hegemony. But, just as the Founders intended, most social movements break up on the well-prepared defences of established privilege, or, if successful in gaining power, disappoint in actual policy and performance. Only a few social movements, such as those to which we now turn, persevere through ups and downs over the course of decades and even centuries to bring real change.

Rather than offering brief sketches of several contemporary social movements, we treat just two, but we treat them in depth. We treat the civil rights

Getty Images/Mark Wilson

Debate over the role of immigrants, legal and illegal, in the American society stirs deep emotions, especially in difficult economic times. Here pro-immigration activists demonstrate outside the White House.

movement and the movement for gender equality within American society. Neither movement was entirely successful. Social movements rarely achieve all of their aims. We will ask how and why the movement for black equality and women's rights movements arose, gained momentum, achieved their early success, and then declined before their final goals were reached.

SLAVERY AND ABOLITIONISM

Broad social change is almost always the hard and systematic work of decades, even centuries. To prevail, movement leaders and members must understand the constitutional terrain to be navigated. The constitution both holds out the prizes—citizenship, equality, the right to vote—that might be won and lays out the obstacles—separation of powers, checks and balances, federalism—that must be overcome to bring fundamental change.

abolitionist Advocates of slavery's abolition in the United States.

The **abolitionist** movement of the mid-nineteenth century, which sought to abolish slavery in the United States, was part of a wave of social reform that also promoted temperance, peace, and women's rights. Abolitionism had its origins in the patriot debates over freedom and independence during the revolution. But very few American patriots thought that blacks were entitled to freedom and independence in the same way that they were.

From independence to the coming of the Civil War the internal structure and rhythms of American life changed dramatically. During these years the population of the United States grew from less than three million to more than thirty million, while the percentage of the population that was black and enslaved held steady at about 15 percent.

The commitment of the Founders to freedom and independence led at least a few of them to dabble in emancipation after the Revolution. John Jay, Alexander Hamilton, and Benjamin Franklin founded the Pennsylvania Society for the Abolition of Slavery in 1784 and the New York Manumission Society in 1785. Many others thought that slavery was dying out and that no great effort was needed to hasten its demise. However, by 1810 the invention of the cotton gin had rejuvenated slavery by increasing the value of slaves and of their labor.

In 1817 the American Colonization Society was founded to promote the transportation of emancipated slaves to Liberia, the society's colony on the west coast of Africa. Making emancipation more attractive to whites by linking it to the idea of sending freed slaves back to Africa had the support of prominent white Americans from Jefferson to Lincoln, including James Madison, James Monroe, John Marshall, and Henry Clay.[5] Each of these great leaders thought that slavery was morally wrong, but none thought that white Americans would accept a biracial society in which blacks were treated as equal to whites. Few men, even few great men, think far beyond the parameters of the society they know. Do you?

The abolition movement took a more aggressive turn in the 1830s. In January 1831 William Lloyd Garrison published the first edition of *The Liberator* in Boston. In 1832 Garrison and eleven other white men founded the New England Anti-Slavery Society on a platform of immediate emancipation. In 1833 Garrison led his group into a coalition called the American Anti-Slavery Society (AASS).[6] By the middle of the 1830s the AASS claimed more than 200 local anti-slavery affiliates. In July 1835 more than 175,000 pamphlets were mailed from the New York post office into the southern states.

Reaction throughout the South, in Congress, and even in the North, was powerfully against the abolition movement. Congress passed and President Jackson signed legislation to limit the movement of incendiary pamphlets through the mails and in 1836 Congress passed a "gag rule" against the debate of anti-slavery petitions on the floor of Congress. Tensions rose and fell over the next two decades until the *Dred Scott* decision and the election of Abraham Lincoln as president unleashed the furies.

CIVIL RIGHTS AND THE CIVIL WAR AMENDMENTS

The stark question of civil rights for blacks came powerfully to the fore in the famous case of *Dred Scott v. Sandford* (1857), in the Civil War amendments to the Constitution, and in the Civil Rights Act of 1875. Chief Justice Roger B. Taney, writing for the court in the *Dred Scott* case, declared that white slave owners were at liberty to do as they wished with black slaves because blacks had "no rights which the white man was bound to respect." Dred Scott, a black slave from Virginia, was taken to Missouri and then by a new owner to the

Q2 What role did the Supreme Court play in first limiting and then expanding civil rights for blacks?

This statue on the grounds of the Texas state capital depicts slaves, male and female, learning of their freedom on June 19, 1865. Juneteenth celebrations occur in Texas annually.

free state of Illinois and later into the free territory of Wisconsin. Taney declared not only that Scott was not free as a result of being carried into free territory, but also that no black, slave or free, was a citizen either of a state or of the United States. The Civil War amendments to the Constitution were designed to assure former slaves that they did, in fact, have "rights that the white man was bound to respect." And finally, the Civil Rights Act of 1875 was part of the national government's attempt to define and enforce civil rights in post–Civil War America. But white opinion in the nation and its courts proved too powerful.

The Civil War Amendments

President Abraham Lincoln described the Civil War as "essentially a people's contest. [A] struggle for maintaining in the world that form and substance of government whose leading object is to elevate the condition of man—to lift artificial weights from all shoulders; to clear paths of laudable pursuit for all; to afford all an unfettered start, and a fair chance in the race of life."[7] As the war raged on, Lincoln set the end of slavery in motion with the Emancipation Proclamation.

Not until after the war did the Republican Party in Congress begin to define the rights that the former slaves would enjoy and how those rights would be guaranteed and protected. The Civil War amendments and the Civil Rights Act of 1875 laid out a promise of full equality. However, within little more than a decade all of these promises had been broken. By the end of the century "separate but equal" was constitutional doctrine, and by 1910 an American apartheid, Jim Crow segregation, was in place across the land. How did the promise of freedom erode so quickly?

The Thirteenth Amendment: Freedom.   The Thirteenth Amendment completed the work of emancipation. It reads: "Neither slavery nor involuntary servitude, except as a punishment for crime whereof the party shall have been duly convicted, shall exist within the United States, or any place subject to their jurisdiction." The Thirteenth Amendment went into effect on December 18, 1865.

The Fourteenth Amendment: Equality.   The Fourteenth Amendment sought to define, without ever mentioning them directly, the position of former slaves within American society. The key section of the Fourteenth Amendment reads: "All persons born or naturalized in the United States, and subject to the jurisdiction thereof, are citizens of the United States and the State wherein they reside. No State shall make or enforce any law which shall abridge the privileges or immunities of citizens of the United States; nor shall any State deprive any person of life, liberty, or property, without due process of law; nor deny to any person within its jurisdiction the equal protection of the laws." This broad and generous language went into effect on July 28, 1868.

The Fifteenth Amendment: Voting.   The Fifteenth Amendment sought to ensure that black men would be able to defend their rights and liberties at the ballot box. The Fifteenth Amendment, which went into effect on March 30, 1870, read: "The right of citizens of the United States to vote shall not be denied or abridged by the United States or any State on account of race, color, or previous condition of servitude." The vote, it was hoped, would be a powerful weapon that could be wielded in defense of rights and privileges awarded in the previous two amendments. For a time it seemed that this would be so, but that time proved short.

Early Supreme Court Interpretations.   Almost before the ink was dry on the Civil War amendments, the Supreme Court interpreted them in the narrowest possible terms. Soon thereafter, the Civil Rights Act of 1875 met the same fate. Precisely how the words of the Civil War amendments and the Civil Rights Act of 1875 were made tools of continued oppression and exclusion of blacks rather than powerful tools for black equality can be shown by looking at several key Supreme Court decisions.

The first decision did not even involve blacks. Nonetheless, its implications for the place of the newly freed blacks in the American society were immense. The **Slaughterhouse Cases** (1873) were brought by a group of white New Orleans butchers who claimed that the creation of a slaughterhouse monopoly by the Louisiana state legislature denied them the equal protection of the laws that the Fourteenth Amendment promised them as citizens of the United States.

Slaughterhouse Cases With this decision, the Supreme Court limited the impacts of the post–Civil War Amendments by defining U.S. citizenship narrowly and leaving the states to regulate domestic race relations.

Justice Samuel F. Miller, writing for the majority of a court divided 5–4, announced a view of federalism that understood national and state citizenships as essentially separate. Under Justice Miller's strict dual-federalist reading, national citizenship protected a citizen while traveling abroad, engaging in interstate or foreign commerce, or engaging in activities not within the jurisdiction of a single state. All other rights belonged to Americans as citizens of particular states. The *Slaughterhouse* decision meant that state governments would be allowed to define the domestic rights of their citizens, including their black citizens, as narrowly as they wished and the federal government would not interfere.

The first major test of the Civil Rights Act of 1875, which made most racial discrimination illegal, whether practiced by public institutions like governments or by private individuals, came in the **Civil Rights Cases** (1883). In an 8–1 decision, Justice John Marshall Harlan I dissenting, the Supreme Court declared the Civil Rights Act of 1875 to be unconstitutional. Justice Joseph P. Bradley explained that in the view of the court the Fourteenth Amendment prohibited discriminatory "state action" against blacks; it did not prohibit and could not reach the private discrimination of one individual against another. With this judgment, the federal government withdrew from the fight against private discrimination toward blacks.

Legal Segregation: *Plessy v. Ferguson*.   In 1890, the state of Louisiana passed a law requiring railroads to "provide equal but separate accommodations for the white and colored races" and requiring that "no person be permitted to occupy seats in coaches other than the ones assigned to his race." Homer Plessy, a citizen of Louisiana and one-eighth black, set out to test the law by boarding a train and occupying a seat in a car designated for white passengers. Following Plessy's arrest, his lawyer argued that the Louisiana statute violated the Thirteenth and Fourteenth Amendments, and most particularly the "equal protection" clause of the Fourteenth Amendment. The court upheld the Louisiana statute and, by implication, most other segregation statutes, noting that "the action was not discriminatory since the whites were separated just as much from blacks as the blacks were separated from the whites."

Justice Harlan again rose in dissent, pointing first to the obvious hypocrisy of the claim that segregation by race was no "badge of inferiority" for blacks subjected to it. Justice Harlan then went on to state the case for black equality that he believed was inherent in the Thirteenth and Fourteenth Amendments. He explained that "there is in this country no superior, dominant, ruling class of citizens . . . . Our Constitution is color blind, and neither knows nor tolerates classes among citizens. In respect of civil rights all citizens are equal before the law. The humblest is the peer of the most powerful. The law regards man as man, and takes no account of his . . . color when his civil rights . . . are involved." It would be more than half a century before these powerful words would be accepted by a majority of the nation's highest court.

The Modern Civil Rights Movement

The early twentieth century was a bleak time for civil rights in America. Not until the 1930s did forces begin to build both domestically and internationally that put the country on the road to desegregation by mid-century. However, looking back on the successes and failures of the modern civil rights movement, many Americans, both blacks and whites, are struck both by how much has changed on the surface and by how little has changed beneath the surface.[8] Many are sobered by the backsliding toward segregation that has occurred over the past four decades.

Desegregation: The Coming of *Brown v. Board of Education*. During the first decades of the twentieth century, Missouri, like several other border states and all of the states of the Deep South, ran a dual or segregated school system from kindergarten through college. However, as with most other segregated education systems, Missouri's did not provide a full range of advanced and professional degree programs at its black institutions. Therefore, upon graduation from Missouri's all-black Lincoln University in 1935, Lloyd Gaines sought admission to the University of Missouri's Law School. When Gaines was denied admission, he sued, claiming that his right to "equal protection of the laws" under the Fourteenth Amendment had been violated. The Supreme Court agreed in 1938 and informed the state of Missouri that it had to provide a separate law school or admit blacks to the University of Missouri Law School. The state responded by setting up a law school at Lincoln University.

Two landmark cases from 1950 raised the question of how equal separate facilities had to be. In *Sweatt v. Painter*, the court held that a law school set up to avoid admitting blacks to the University of Texas Law School was unacceptable because it was inferior in facilities, books, faculty, and in general quality of legal education and opportunities. *McLaurin v. Oklahoma* struck down an attempt to admit blacks to a white program on a "segregated basis." McLaurin was admitted to the University of Oklahoma's School of Education to pursue graduate study because no black universities in the state offered similar programs. However, he was restricted to a seat in an anteroom adjacent to the classroom and to an assigned space in the library and the cafeteria. The court supported McLaurin's contention that this treatment denied him "equal protection of the laws"[9]

The precedents established in *Gaines*, *Sweatt*, and *McLaurin* made the point that if facilities are to be separate, they must truly be equal. But could separate in fact be equal? In the landmark case of ***Brown v. Board of Education*** (1954), the U.S. Supreme Court was asked to take up precisely this question: Can separate be equal, or is separate inherently unequal and therefore discriminatory within the meaning of the "equal protection" clause of the Fourteenth Amendment? Arguing for the black complainants was Thurgood Marshall, chief counsel of the NAACP.

Brown v. Board of Education was before the court when conservative Chief Justice Fred M. Vinson died and was replaced by the liberal Republican former governor of California, Earl Warren. Chief Justice Warren thought that segregation had to be dismantled and that *Brown* was the right case to begin that process. Writing on behalf of a unanimous court, Warren reached back to resurrect Justice Harlan's dissent in *Plessy*. Warren wrote: "Segregation of white and colored children in public schools has a detrimental effect upon the colored children." Therefore, Warren concluded, "in the field of public education the doctrine of separate but equal has no place. Separate educational facilities are inherently unequal. . . . The plaintiffs . . . have been deprived of the equal protection of the laws guaranteed by the Fourteenth Amendment."

Before the decision in *Brown* was released to the public on May 17, 1954, seventeen states and the District of Columbia mandated segregation in their

Brown v. Board of Education This landmark case overturned *Plessy* and declared that separate was inherently unequal. Consequently, the segregation of public schools was unconstitutional.

Thurgood Marshall, chief counsel of the NAACP, became the first black associate justice of the U.S. Supreme Court.

03 Has Congress usually led or followed the Supreme Court on civil rights?

elementary and secondary schools. Although the District of Columbia and most of the border states complied with the instruction to desegregate their schools, the states of the Deep South dug in for a decade-long contest called "massive resistance."[10] As late as 1960, not a single black student attended a public school or university with whites in Alabama, Georgia, Louisiana, Mississippi, or South Carolina. Moreover, when John Kennedy took the oath of office as president of the United States early in 1961, fewer than 4 percent of voting-age blacks in Mississippi were registered to vote. The numbers were only slightly higher in the other southern states.

The Civil Rights Acts: 1964, 1965, and 1968. The Kennedy administration came under increasing pressure on the civil rights front during the "long, hot summer" of 1963 that culminated in the famous March on Washington in which 250,000 people participated. The highlight of the march was Martin Luther King Jr.'s "I Have a Dream" speech delivered from the steps of the Lincoln Memorial. The Kennedy administration responded to the demands of Dr. King and his followers by preparing legislation to supplement the Eisenhower administration's Civil Rights Act of 1957. That bill, the first major piece of civil rights legislation since Reconstruction, established the U.S. Civil Rights Commission and enhanced the Civil Rights Division of the Department of Justice.

In the wake of President Kennedy's assassination in November 1963, President Lyndon Johnson dramatically strengthened Kennedy's bill. The new bill came to be known as the Civil Rights Act of 1964. Its critical Title VI held that "No person in the United States shall, on the ground of race, color, or national origin, be excluded from participation in, be denied the benefit of, or be subjected to discrimination under any program or activity receiving Federal financial assistance."

Title VII of the act prohibited discrimination on the basis of race, color, sex, religion, or national origin by employers or labor unions in businesses with one hundred or more employees; prohibited segregation or denial of service in any public accommodation, including motels, restaurants, movie theaters, and sports facilities; and permitted the U.S. attorney general to represent citizens attempting to desegregate state-owned, -operated, or -managed facilities including public schools. An even more far-reaching civil rights act was passed in 1965. Finally, in April 1968, only days after the assassination of Martin Luther King Jr., Congress passed a law that forbade discrimination based on race, color, religion, or national origin in the sale or rental of housing.

AP Photo

Crowds gathered at the Lincoln Memorial on August 28, 1963, to hear civil rights speakers, including the Reverend Martin Luther King Jr. King delivered his famous "I Have a Dream" speech before a quarter of a million people.

The Elementary and Secondary Education Act (ESEA) of 1965. The ESEA provided federal education funds to school districts with large numbers of low-income students, provided that they were operating on a nondiscriminatory basis. The provision of federal money to support state and local programs, especially in education, seemed to break the back of segregation. Gerald Rosenberg noted that "financially strapped school districts found the lure of federal dollars irresistible . . . . And after federal money was received, the thought of losing it the next year, reducing budgets, slashing programs, firing staffs, was excruciating."[11] The most striking result of the movement of the Congress and the executive branch into the fray over desegregation was that the percentage of black school children attending school with whites in the South rose from 1.2 percent in 1964 to 91.3 percent in 1972.

The Voting Rights Act of 1965. The foundation of **Jim Crow** had been the near-total exclusion of blacks from southern state and local electorates and their limited participation in northern elections. A complicated array of rules and practices including literacy tests, poll taxes, white primaries, and grandfather clauses kept blacks, other minorities, and the poor more generally, from registering and voting in elections. The Voting Rights Act of 1965 prohibited these practices and sent federal marshals into southern states to assure that local election officials permitted all citizens to register to vote and to participate in elections. Ten million new black voters were on the rolls by 1970,

Jim Crow Jim Crow is the generic name for all of the laws and practices that enforced segregation of the races in the American South and elsewhere from the end of the nineteenth century to the middle of the twentieth century.

Q4 Does affirmative action to assist minorities and women inevitably mean reverse discrimination against white men?

affirmative action Policies and actions designed to make up for the effects of past discrimination by giving preferences today to specified racial, ethnic, and sexual groups.

direct discrimination Discrimination practiced directly by one individual against another.

reverse discrimination The idea that the provision of affirmative action advantages to members of protected classes must necessarily result in an unfair denial of benefits or advantages to white males.

and by 1984 black registration had passed white registration at 73 percent to 72 percent of those eligible. Large numbers of registered black voters simply could not be ignored by politicians expecting to remain in office.

Affirmative Action

The civil rights agenda of the 1950s and 1960s demanded equality of opportunity and nondiscrimination. These ideas were embedded as promises and guarantees in the civil rights and voting rights acts of the mid-1960s. **Affirmative action** envisions making up for the effects of past discrimination suffered by specified racial and sexual groups by giving their members preference today in admission to training and educational programs and in decisions concerning hiring, promotion, and firing on the job. Not surprisingly, nondiscrimination is an easier sell than is affirmative action.

Confronting Direct Discrimination. The Civil War amendments called for equality of rights and opportunities. Moreover, the Civil Rights Act of 1964 was carefully crafted to forbid both **direct discrimination** of one individual against another and racial preferences. Proponents of the Civil Rights Act of 1964 were very clear in assuring skeptical colleagues that the act offered redress only to specific individuals who could show that they had suffered direct discrimination as a result of racial bias. Numerous provisions of the Civil Rights Act of 1964 specifically prohibited racial quotas or hiring goals that might result in reverse discrimination against whites.

The Demand for Affirmative Action. Proponents of affirmative action argued that nondiscrimination and equality of opportunity, although certainly important, were not enough to ensure the full and meaningful participation of blacks and other minorities in the American society and economy. They argued that the current unequal status of blacks in America, to take the prime example, was a stark reflection of two centuries of slavery in which the products of black labor went to white slave owners and another century in which segregation was used to deny blacks access to opportunity and wealth. As we shall see below, during the late 1970s and 1980s the Supreme Court seemed to agree that some measure of affirmative action was required to promote justice in America. Still, many disagreed.

Claims of Reverse Discrimination. The first precedent-setting **reverse discrimination** case involved a man named Allan Bakke. Bakke was twice rejected for admission to the University of California at Davis Medical School even though on both occasions his academic credentials were superior to those of all of the minority students admitted under the school's affirmative action program. The medical school, like many other graduate and professional schools, set aside a number of seats, in this case sixteen out of about one hundred, for minorities and took the best minority candidates available. The remaining seats were awarded to the top candidates based on their academic credentials. Bakke sued the University of California at Davis Medical School and, in a case known as *Regents of the University of California v. Bakke* (1978), won—sort of.

Justice Lewis Powell, writing for a badly divided Supreme Court, held that the university had violated Bakke's Fourteenth Amendment right to equal protection of the laws and that he should be admitted to the medical school. Specifically, the court held in a narrow 5–4 decision that institutions could not set aside a specific number of seats for which only minorities were eligible. This stark denial of opportunity for whites to compete for these seats was unconstitutional. However, the court further held that race could be used as a "plus factor" in admission decisions if it were not the sole factor.

Regents of the University of California v. Bakke This landmark affirmative action case stated that race could be taken into account in admissions decisions as long as the institution did not set aside a specific number of seats for which only minorities were eligible.

Affirmative Action in the Workplace

One year after *Bakke* came *United Steelworkers of America v. Weber*. Kaiser Aluminum and the United Steelworkers had agreed that at least half of the thirteen slots in an on-the-job training program at Kaiser's Gramercy, Louisiana, plant would go to blacks. Brian Weber was denied a place in this training program on the basis of his race—he was white—so he sued the company and the union under Title VII of the Civil Rights Act of 1964. Title VII expressly prohibited discrimination in employment, forbidding any employer from granting "preferential treatment to any individual or to any group because of the race . . . of such individual or group."

Justice William Brennan, writing for the majority, upheld the affirmative action agreement reached by Kaiser and the United Steelworkers as a "voluntary" and "temporary" attempt by parties in the private economy to benefit black workers. Brennan argued that although the "letter" of the Civil Rights Act of 1964 required nondiscrimination, its "spirit" permitted voluntary agreements designed to improve the lot of blacks in the American economy. Associate Justice William Rehnquist, writing in dissent, accused the court of rejecting race-blind in favor of race-conscious standards for government policymaking and private behavior.

Throughout the 1980s, although quotas continued to be illegal, racial preferences and set-asides were accepted tools of affirmative action. Nonetheless, with Ronald Reagan's election to the presidency in 1980, the tide of opinion in favor of affirmative action began to ebb. By the time Reagan left the presidency in 1989, he had appointed more than half of the federal judiciary and affirmative action was under increasing pressure. Within a few years, a new majority seemed to be taking shape that was hostile to affirmative action.

Issues similar to the *Weber* case arose in a case called *Ricci v. DeStefano* (2009). Frank Ricci, a white New Haven fire fighter, finished sixth among 77 candidates taking a promotion exam. None of the 19 African-American candidates taking the exam qualified for promotion, so the city, fearing a discrimination lawsuit, threw out the results. Ricci and 17 other white fire fighters, including one Hispanic, sued claiming that they had been discriminated against on the basis of their race.

The Supreme Court, seeking to balance two provisions of Title VII of the 1964 Civil Rights Act, ultimately ruled for the white fire fighters. Title VII required both that employees not be treated differently on the basis of race and that promotion criteria and exams not have a "disparate impact" on members of one group. The white fire fighters, claiming differential treatment by race, prevailed. Justice Kennedy, writing for the Court's 5–4 conservative majority, observed that "the process was open and fair. The problem, of course, is that after the tests were completed, the raw racial results became the predominant rationale for the city's refusal to certify the results." As in other areas where race is involved, race can be a factor in the decision, but it cannot be the sole or driving factor.

Affirmative Action in Schools

A 2003 case dealing with undergraduate and law school admission criteria at the University of Michigan seemed to give affirmative action new life. At the undergraduate level, Michigan awarded 20 points to "underrepresented minorities" on a 150-point admissions index, while the law school used race as "one factor among many." As with the *Bakke* case 25 years earlier, white students with credentials superior to minority students who had been admitted sued, claiming that their Fourteenth Amendment right to equal protection of the laws and their 1964 Civil Rights Act promise of nondiscrimination had been violated.

The Michigan cases drew broad public attention. A long list of universities, major corporations, civic associations, military leaders, and others argued that programs like Michigan's to ensure a diverse student body were critical to their need for a diverse workforce, cadre of social leaders, and officer corps. More than three hundred organizations joined in 64 briefs filed in support of the university's affirmative action efforts. Fifteen briefs were filed on behalf of the plaintiffs, including one from the Bush administration, most claiming that affirmative action unconstitutionally harms whites and that diversity can be ensured by other, less objectionable means.

In the Michigan cases, the court narrowly upheld the law school's admissions process while striking down the specific point system used in the undergraduate admissions process. Justice Sandra Day O'Connor, writing for a narrow 5–4 majority in **Grutter v. Bollinger**, upheld the *Bakke* ruling that race can be a "plus factor" in admissions, but that firm quotas were unconstitutional. She particularly approved the law school admissions process as a "highly individualized, holistic review of each applicant's file," allowing race to play a role, but not in a "mechanical way." Justice O'Connor observed that "in a society like our own . . . race unfortunately still matters." Justice Thomas dissented, saying, "every time the government places citizens on racial registers and makes race relevant to the provision of burdens or benefits, it demeans us all."

Grutter v. Bollinger The court upheld *Bakke*, allowing affirmative action that takes race into account as one factor among many, but not in a rigid or mechanical way.

Yet, contentious issues like affirmative action remain perpetually open in American politics. *Grutter v. Bollinger* was a 5–4 case and Justice Sandra Day O'Connor, the deciding vote and author of the majority opinion, retired from the court. Two new members, Chief Justice Roberts and Justice Alito, expressed discomfort with affirmative action and moved quickly to limit it. By 2007, they were part of a narrow 5–4 majority declaring that public elementary and secondary school districts could not use race in assigning students to schools even if the purpose is to maintain racial integration.

This dramatic reversal of more than 50 years of desegregation policy in regard to public schools occurred in two cases. School boards in Louisville, Kentucky, and Seattle, Washington, sought to maintain racial balance within schools by managing transfer requests. Writing for the majority, Chief Justice Roberts declared the use of race in assigning students to school to be unconstitutional. He famously declared that "The way to stop discrimination on the basis of race is to stop discriminating on the basis of race." The court's proponents of affirmative action were stunned. In the principal dissenting opinion, Justice Breyer observed, speaking of the court's new members, Roberts and Alito, "It is not often in the law that so few have so quickly changed so much."

Nonetheless, the full impact of these opinions continue to play out. Though Justice Anthony Kennedy, the court's most frequent swing vote, joined the majority in the Louisville and Seattle public school cases, he wrote a separate opinion, declaring that while he thought the plans unconstitutional, he questioned the majority opinion's "all-too-unyielding insistence that race cannot be a factor in instances when, in my view, it may be taken into account."[12]

The concern of advocates of affirmative action was again heightened when Abigail Fisher, a white student denied admission to the University of Texas Law School, sued in 2008 claiming reverse discrimination. Fisher lost in the federal district court in Austin and in the generally conservative Fifth Circuit Court of Appeals, but observers immediately noted that turnover on the Supreme Court, most importantly Justice O'Connor's retirement and replacement by Justice Samuel Alito, had turned the 5–4 majority in *Grutter* in favor of affirmative action into a likely 5–4 majority against.[13] Though the Fisher case reached the Supreme Court twice and was not resolved until 2016, it finally was resolved in favour of affirmative action—narrowly tailored. Writing for a 4–3 majority, Justice Kennedy, to the surprise of many, upheld the University of Texas's use of race as a "factor of a factor of a factor" in its undergraduate admissions process.[14] Nonetheless, affirmative action remains a highly contested issue in American politics. We know that Supreme Court decisions are important, but they can often seem arcane. How much progress have we actually made toward racial equality?

While most white Americans focus on the progress made in civil rights law and policy in the modern era, many black Americans point to the narrowing of affirmative action programs and the often dire circumstances faced by many blacks in their communities and daily lives. Figure 4.1 presents data on family income by race going back seven decades, to just after World War II. The relative stability of the distribution of income by race and ethnicity in the United States over this period is striking. Although the categories used to describe non-whites changed over time, we can still get a pretty clear picture of the distribution of income by race and ethnicity since the late 1940s. Black

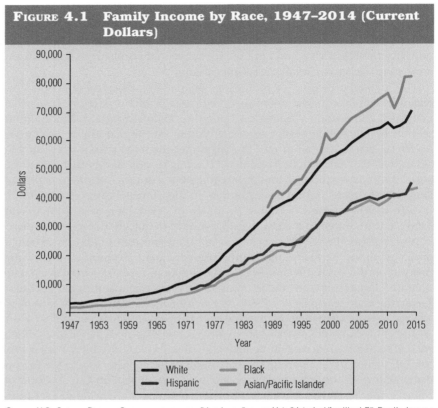

FIGURE **4.1** **Family Income by Race, 1947–2014 (Current Dollars)**

Source: U.S. Census Bureau. See www.census.gov/hhes/www/income/data/historical/families/ F5-Family Income by Race.

and Hispanic family income ran at about 55 percent of white family income through the early 1960s, jumped to about 60 percent in the mid-1960s, and has remained in a very tight range around 60 percent ever since. What, if anything, do these data mean for race in America and for the ongoing debate about affirmative action as public policy?

Black Lives Matter A social movement to stop violence against blacks and to demand investment in black people and communities.

The **Black Lives Matter** movement arose online in the wake of the 2012 shooting of Trayvon Martin, a black 17-year-old, in Sanford, Florida. The movement grew as other young black men were killed, often by police and frequently in ambiguous circumstances—depending upon the observer—and burst into full public view during the prolonged confrontation in Ferguson, Missouri. The Ferguson unrest began in the late summer of 2014 when a white police officer shot a young black man named Michael Brown. During subsequent months of upheaval, the police clamped down on Ferguson, with a militarized police presence and curfew, while the local black community countered that this precisely represented the official force and violence that threatened black lives.

More broadly, the Black Lives Matter movement demanded radical change well beyond affirmative action. The demand for reparations, for example, envisioned financial compensation to black people today for income and wealth stolen from ancestors during slavery and Jim Crow. The Black Lives Matter agenda also included systematic investment in black people and neighborhoods and an end to the disproportionate incarceration of young black men. Clearly, the civil rights debate is ongoing.

The Women's Rights Movement

If the question of black civil rights continue in turmoil, perhaps we can find more stable progress in the field of women's rights. As with black civil rights, there has been real progress. Social change, the evolution of the American society from rural to urban, from the dependence on strong backs to the need for strong minds, opened the door to enhanced rights for women.

From colonization throughout the nineteenth century, the place of women within the American society was defined by the legal concept of "coverture." **Coverture** was the rule of law whereby at marriage the husband and the wife became, in the phrase of the famous English jurist William Blackstone, "one person, and that person the husband." Coverture entailed the legal guardianship of women by men, their fathers before marriage and their husbands after marriage. During the first half of the nineteenth century, married women could not own or inherit property, control their own wages, sue or be sued in court, divorce drunk or abusive husbands, or have custody of their children if their husbands divorced them. Single women over 21, widows, and divorced women had more autonomy, but being alone generally meant poverty and exclusion.

Throughout the nineteenth century and into the 1970s, progress was slow because women were split on how best to frame their demands for change. Society has always socialized men and women to somewhat different roles. In the nineteenth century, men and women were seen as fitted for "separate spheres," men for the workplace and women for the home. More conservative women accepted broad gender differences and simply called for incremental changes—better education, fairer property and inheritance rights, and more protection against abusive husbands. These "difference feminists" were often scandalized by "equality feminists" who demanded full equality with men in society, the economy, and politics.

Sometimes difference feminists and equality feminists could work together and sometimes they could not. While Congress and the president eventually joined a united women's movement to support suffrage in 1920, the Supreme Court did not abandon its separate spheres perspective until the 1970s.[15] This ground is still contested.

Organization and Protest. If any great social movement can be said to have begun at a specific place and time, the women's movement in America began at Seneca Falls, New York, in 1848. The Seneca Falls Convention on women's rights produced two great products: one a statement of principles and demands, entitled a "Declaration of Sentiments," and the other a political alliance between

coverture A legal concept, transferred to America as part of English common law, holding that upon marriage the husband and the wife become "one person, and that person the husband."

Q5 What were the similarities and differences between the movements for racial and gender equality?

Seneca Falls Convention Momentous 1848 meeting of women's rights advocates, often credited with initiating the movement, in Seneca Falls, New York.

Elizabeth Cady Stanton and Susan B. Anthony and their allies and associates, including Lucretia Mott, Lucy Stone, and Sojourner Truth.

In the decade prior to the Civil War Stanton and Anthony worked to improve the legal status of women. They succeeded in winning greater economic rights for women in New York State, assuring that married women could own property and control their wages if they worked outside the home. After the war progress came slowly. The federal courts were consistent in upholding state and federal laws that barred women from the practice of law (*Bradwell v. Illinois*, 1872), voting (*U.S. v. Anthony*, 1873), and jury service (*Strauder v. West Virginia*, 1880).

During the second half of the nineteenth century, competing women's groups pursuing different strategies fought for a wide range of social, economic, and political rights. Women slowly gained the right to own and inherit property, control their wages, make contracts, sue in their own names, and have joint custody of children following divorce. Yet even as the end of the nineteenth century approached, women rarely had the right to vote, serve on juries, or attend professional schools. Moreover, some issues including sex outside marriage, birth control, and divorce, all seen as threats to the traditional family, were too controversial for most women's groups to touch.[16]

The final push for suffrage began in 1890. The women's movement narrowed its focus and expanded its alliances. First, Stanton's broad equal rights agenda was set aside in favor of a more singular focus on female suffrage. Second, two rival organizations, the National Woman Suffrage Association (NWSA), led by Stanton and Anthony, and the more conservative American Woman Suffrage Association (AWSA), led by Lucy Stone, merged in 1890 to become the National American Woman Suffrage Association (NAWSA). NAWSA convinced other important groups, like Frances Willard's Women's Christian Temperance Union, Jane Addams's settlement house movement, Consumers' Leagues, and the General Federation of Women's Clubs, that they could more readily accomplish their goals if women had the vote.

The suffrage bandwagon began to roll as Washington state approved female suffrage in 1910, California in 1911, and Arizona, Kansas, and Oregon in 1912. By the end of the decade half of the states allowed women to vote, but Congress and the Wilson administration remained ambivalent. Alice Paul laid siege to the powers that be in Washington, D.C., leading direct action confrontations including demonstrations, picketing of the White House, arrests, and starvation strikes. Finally, in June of 1919, at President Wilson's explicit urging, the Senate approved the Nineteenth Amendment. Thirty-six states ratified the amendment, and it went into effect on August 26, 1920. It reads: "The right of citizens of the United States to vote shall not be denied or abridged by the United States or by any State on account of sex."

Once suffrage was achieved in 1920, the women's movement lost much of its focus and direction until the 1960s. Nonetheless, broad-scale social and economic change including urbanization, expanded educational opportunities, and the steady growth of the service sector of the economy opened new opportunities for women. Still, in 1950, only about one-third of adult women worked for wages and they made less than half, about 48 percent, of what men made.[17]

By the early 1960s, women working in and watching the civil rights and antiwar movements arrived at two conclusions: that they knew how to organize a protest and that they had a great deal to protest about. Women drew on the themes of individual rights and equal opportunity that were so central to the civil rights movement to understand their own oppression. President John F. Kennedy's Commission on the Status of Women provided detailed evidence of social and economic discrimination against women in its 1963 annual report. Almost simultaneously, Betty Friedan's *The Feminine Mystique* identified the psychological impact that having few social or economic opportunities had on talented and well-educated women as "the problem with no name." Women's church groups, civic and service groups, and book clubs became forums for political discussion, networking, and consciousness raising.

When the Commission on the Status of Women proved unable or unwilling to press equal rights for women, several of the commission's leaders formed the National Organization for Women (NOW). NOW's charter promised "To take action to bring women into full participation in the mainstream of American society now, assuming all of the privileges and responsibilities thereof in truly equal partnership with men." NOW won important victories in the 1970s, fought to protect them throughout the 1980s and 1990s, and remains the focal point of the women's movement today.

Equal Rights and Personal Control.   NOW held its first annual convention in 1967. The convention produced a Women's Bill of Rights, which among many other things, called for an **Equal Rights Amendment (ERA)** to the Constitution and for women's control over family planning and procreation issues. The ERA was first introduced into the Congress in 1923 and was consistently reintroduced and largely ignored for most of the next fifty years. Slowly, the equal rights arguments of the civil rights and women's rights movements began to change the political consciousness of America. In 1970, the House of Representatives held hearings on the ERA, with many women members of the House speaking passionately on its behalf, and in August 1970 the House voted in favor of the ERA by a margin of 350 to 15. Although the Senate moved more slowly, on March 22, 1972, it approved the ERA by a vote of 84 to 8. The ERA read: "Equality of rights under the law shall not be denied or abridged by the United States or by any State on account of sex." Within days of Senate approval, half a dozen states unanimously ratified the ERA, and within a year twenty-four states had ratified. Most observers believed that eventually thirty-eight states would ratify and the ERA would be added to the Constitution.

Equal Rights Amendment (ERA) The ERA, first considered by Congress in 1923 and proposed in 1972 as a constitutional amendment guaranteeing gender equality, fell three votes short of ratification.

NOW's 1967 Women's Bill of Rights also called for removal of restrictive abortion laws. The National Abortion Rights Action League (NARAL) was formed in 1969 to focus exclusively on securing women's access to abortion services. Abortion law was the preserve of the states, so initially both NOW and NARAL focused their efforts at the state level. But state-by-state reform efforts had always been slow and uncertain. NOW and NARAL activists sought a Supreme Court judgment in favor of a woman's right to choose that would apply throughout the United States.

Roe v. Wade A 1973 Texas
case that struck down state abortion
restrictions by declaring that a woman's
right to privacy included access to
abortion services.

In 1973 the justices of the U.S. Supreme Court declared in *Roe v. Wade* that the Constitution guaranteed a "right to privacy" that included a woman's right to choose abortion. Justice Harry Blackmun, writing for a court divided 7–2, described a broad right to privacy residing in the "Fourteenth Amendment's concept of personal liberty and restrictions upon state action" that included a woman's right to choose abortion. Although Blackmun did not deny that states had a legitimate interest in regulating some aspects of the provision of abortion services, the decision in *Roe v. Wade* invalidated, in whole or in part, the abortion laws in forty-six states and the District of Columbia.

Passage of the ERA by Congress and announcement of *Roe v. Wade* by the Supreme Court, both in 1973, marked the high point of the twentieth century tide in favor of women's rights. However, as with most social movements, successful mobilization bred counter-mobilization.

Counter-mobilization, Conflict, and Stalemate. Liberal women's successful activism sparked a counter-mobilization among conservative women. Building on the organizational base of conservative religious and political groups, Phyllis Schlafly founded STOP ERA in 1972 and then the more broad-based Eagle Forum in 1975. Aided by Beverly LeHaye's Concerned Women of America (CWA), Schlafly's Eagle Forum warned that the traditional roles of wife and mother as well as the health of the traditional family were endangered by the ERA. Ronald Reagan's presidential campaign in 1980 affirmed and broadened conservative opposition to the ERA. Jane Mansbridge, a leading student of the effort to pass the ERA, concluded that "The campaign against the ERA succeeded because it shifted debate away from equal rights and focused it on the possibility that the ERA might bring . . . changes in women's roles and behavior."[18] The ERA died in 1982, three states short of the thirty-eight needed to ratify.

The attempts by conservative women and their allies to roll back abortion rights have been firm and steady. Within months of the *Roe v. Wade* decision, state legislatures were swamped with demands that limitations including counseling mandates, waiting periods, spousal and parental notification requirements, and doctor reporting requirements be placed on a woman's right to choose. Throughout the 1980s and 1990s state legislatures passed restrictions and limitations on women's access to abortion services. Conservative Reagan appointees on the federal bench threatened not just to let stand state restrictions, but to overturn *Roe v. Wade* in its entirety. Moreover, both pro-choice and pro-life advocates took to the streets to press their respective cases.

Tension peaked in 1992 when the administration of the first President Bush joined the state of Pennsylvania and dozens of pro-life groups including the Eagle Forum, the U.S. Catholic Conference, and the National Right to Life Committee to support regulations designed to make abortions in Pennsylvania more difficult. Pro-choice groups, led by NOW, NARAL, and the National Women's Political Caucus, called women into the streets and nearly 700,000 women joined the March for Women's Lives in Washington on April 5, 1992. The case at issue was called *Planned Parenthood of Southeastern Pennsylvania v. Casey*. The court allowed Pennsylvania restrictive regulations to stand but refused to overturn *Roe*.

AP Photo

On June 21, 1982, as time ran out for states to approve the Equal Rights Amendment (ERA), the Florida Senate voted 22 to 16 against. These ERA supporters, streaming out of the capitol to a planned protest rally, shouted "vote them out."

For more than a decade, the abortion battle focused on a specific technique, called "partial birth abortion," that opponents considered particularly objectionable. It is a late-term procedure used to abort a nearly fully formed fetus. During the 1990s, Congress twice voted to ban the procedure, but President Clinton blocked them both times. Meanwhile, thirty-one states adopted partial birth abortion bans between 1995 and 2000, before the Supreme Court struck them down as "an undue burden" on a woman's right to abortion services. In response, Congress passed a slightly revised ban and President Bush signed it into law. The Supreme Court reversed field and upheld the Partial Birth Abortion Act by a narrow 5–4 margin.

Justice Anthony Kennedy wrote the majority opinion in *Gonzales v. Carhart* (2007), declaring that the "act expresses respect for the dignity of human life." Justice Kennedy's opinion emphasized the "ethical and moral concerns" surrounding abortion in general and partial birth abortion in particular. Some women were particularly dismayed by the majority opinion's declaration that banning partial birth abortion saved women from making a choice that they might later come to regret. Justice Ruth Bader Ginsberg, writing in opposition, said, "This way of thinking reflects ancient notions of women's place in the family and under the Constitution—ideas that have long since been discredited."[19]

But pendulums swing both ways. In 2016, the Supreme Court, with Justice Kennedy again the decisive vote in a 5–3 decision, struck down Texas

On January 21, 2017, the day after Donald Trump was inaugurated as president, the Women's March on Washington and similar marches around the country brought million of women into the streets in protest. Here women protest in Seattle. The sign is a response to Donald Trump's campaign description of Hillary Clinton as "a nasty woman."

abortion restrictions as an "undue burden" on women's right to choose abortion. Texas law required that doctors providing abortions have admitting privileges in nearby hospitals and required hospital-like standards for abortion clinics. Texas officials claimed that their goals were to protect women's health and the life of the unborn. Justice Stephen Breyer, writing for the majority and citing _Planned Parenthood v. Casey_, declared that the Texas restrictions "provide few if any health benefits for women,. . . and constitute an 'undue burden' on their constitutional right" to seek abortion services.[20] The battle over abortion is not over.

Women in Schools and Colleges. The Education Act of 1972, in its now-famous Title IX, forbade discrimination based on gender in any education program receiving federal funds. Title IX had its greatest direct impact by advancing equality in the funding of college sports programs, but women have experienced rapid progress toward educational equality. In the early 1980s, women reached parity with men in college attendance. In 2014 women received fully 57 percent of college bachelor's degrees and 60 percent of master's degrees. Similar progress is apparent at the level of professional and doctoral education. Women now receive 49 percent of professional (law, medicine, accounting, etc.) and 52 percent of Ph.D. degrees.[21] These important trends in women's educational achievement have begun to translate into enhanced career options and increased earnings.

Struggling Toward Democracy

In 2015, U.S. men, employed full-time, year round, made an average of $51,212 while women made 80 percent of that, or $40,742.

What do you think?

- Is this evidence of discrimination or of different choices freely made by men and women?

Women in the Workplace. Today women still lag behind men once they leave school and enter the workplace but the gap is narrowing (see Figure 4.2). Many occupations remain gender-specific. As late as 2015, women still comprised 97 percent of all kindergarten teachers and 94 percent of dental assistants, 95 percent of all secretaries, child care workers, and dieticians, 89 percent of all maids and cleaners. At the other end of the economic status and income spectrum, women comprised 9 percent of airline pilots, 15 percent of engineers, 38 percent of physicians, and 35 percent of lawyers.[22] Moreover, the jobs that men hold tend much more commonly to include retirement benefits and those retirement benefits tend to pay out at higher rates.

Progress is evident for women in the workforce and seems to be picking up speed. In 1970 43 percent of women worked for wages, they made an average of 52 percent of what men made, and just 4 percent of married women earned

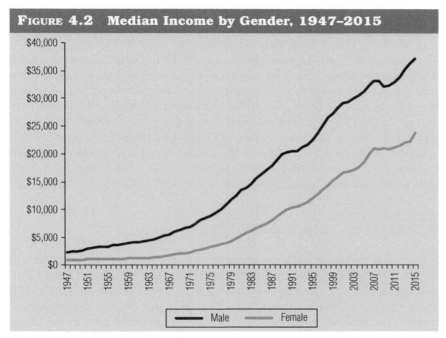

FIGURE 4.2   Median Income by Gender, 1947–2015

Source: U.S. Census. See www.census.gov/data/tables/time-series/demo/income-poverty/historical-income-people. html. Table P-5 Regions—People by Median Income and Sex.

more than their husbands. By 2015, 57 percent of adult women and 58 percent of married women worked for wages and made 81 percent of what men made. Moreover, almost one-third, 29 percent, of working women make more than do their husbands.[23]

Still, gains are not equality. There is still a "glass ceiling" that blocks most women from rising to the level of the executive suite. In 2017, just 27 Fortune 500 companies were headed by women and only 19 percent of board seats were held by women. Many in the women's rights movement doubt that opportunity in the absence of affirmative action will produce true equality within an acceptable time frame.

Moreover, the sexual harassment scandals that erupted in 2017 have exposed the deeper social injustices beneath the female wage gap and the struggle over reproductive rights. In early October 2017 rumors about movie producer Harvey Weinstein that had circulated in Hollywood for decades became dramatically public. A *New York Times* article reported that Weinstein had pressured dozens of women for sex. No one was particularly surprised to hear that sex, voluntary and not, pervaded Hollywood, but the Weinstein revelations seemed more than usually sordid. Soon he was fired by the company that bore his name, but the fires that consumed him soon became a national conflagration.

By year's end, other male Hollywood luminaries, media stars, corporate leaders, and politicians at all levels had been accused of sexual misbehavior and had been forced from their high places. In quick succession, NBC *Today* show host Matt Lauer, Amazon Studios CEO Roy Price, and Minnesota senator and former *Saturday Night Live* comedian Al Franken, as well as half a dozen U.S. House members resigned from office or declared that they would not stand for reelection. Many declared this a watershed moment in the nation's cultural life and it was indeed stunning, but the discussions of racial and gender equality throughout this chapter suggest that progress comes over time and that resistance must be anticipated and that backsliding is not uncommon. Such moments are valuable and progress can and has been made, but the struggle over social fundamentals like race, gender, and sexuality are permanent.

Chapter Summary

Social movements are collective enterprises to change the structure of society in order to produce changes in the way the society distributes opportunities and rewards. Social movements arise in response to dissatisfaction with some broad dimension of social life, like the place, role, and prospects of women or minorities or the treatment of fundamental substantive issues like peace or the environment. Social movements rarely achieve their goals quickly or completely. They wax and wane, rise and fall, rush forward and then are pushed back, over the course of decades, even centuries.

Two of the great civil rights struggles in American history have been conducted by and on behalf of minorities, especially blacks, and women. Organized opposition to slavery in America hardly existed prior to the Revolutionary War, but talk of freedom and independence highlighted the anomaly of slavery. Abolition societies arose and grew, but not until after the Civil War had done its gory work were white Americans required to think in detail about what freedom for blacks would mean. Most whites drew back from black equality, but over the next century Congress and the courts wrestled over what the principles embedded in our Constitution and laws really meant. Finally, in the second half of the twentieth century, the courts and Congress joined, in fits and starts and often half-heartedly, to acknowledge black equality.

The civil rights movement showed others—women, Hispanics, Asians, Native-Americans, the disabled, gays, and transsexuals—the processes and means by which rights can be pursued. The women's rights movement fought for equality not from the depths of slavery but from a still broad denial of freedom and opportunity. The demand for equal rights first voiced at the Seneca Falls Convention of 1848 had to wait for the right to vote secured by the Nineteenth Amendment, only to see the ERA denied in the early 1980s. Nonetheless, Congress has passed many laws requiring equal treatment of women in education and in the workplace; yet women still make less than men even as they have come to have more education.

Finally, the broad phrases of the Constitution are not enough to assure that all Americans are treated equally. Social movements struggle over decades, sometimes centuries, to reshape the public mind and elite opinion on what the Constitution requires America to be. The process by which the public mind and elite opinion are shaped, across the generations and in our own time, is called political socialization—to which we turn in Chapter 5.

Key Terms

abolitionist

affirmative action

Black Lives Matter

Brown v. Board of Education

Civil Rights Cases

coverture

direct discrimination

Equal Rights Amendment

frame

Grutter v. Bollinger

Jim Crow

Plessy v. Ferguson

Regents of the University of California v. Bakke

reverse discrimination

Roe v. Wade

Seneca Falls Convention

Slaughterhouse Cases

social movement

Suggested Readings

Branch, Taylor. *The King Years: Moments in the Civil Rights Movement*. New York: Simon & Schuster, 2013. A Pulitzer prize-winning author sets Martin Luther King's goals and accomplishments in historical context.

Chemerinsky, Erwin. *The Conservative Assault on the Constitution*. New York: Simon & Schuster, 2011. Chemerinsky argues that the Supreme Court has shifted dramatically to the right, limiting the scope of constitutional protections to all Americans.

Davis, Theodore J., Jr. *Black Politics Today: The Era of Socioeconomic Transition*. New York: Routledge, 2012. Davis traces black politics from the civil rights movement of the 1950s and 1960s to the more complicated contemporary period in which economic success and failure threaten to divide the black community.

Sandberg, Sheryl. *Lean In: Women, Work, and the Will to Lead*. New York: Knopf, 2013. Senior Facebook executive offered controversial advice to women in the workplace and in leadership roles.

Piven, Francis Fox, and Richard A. Cloward. *Poor People's Movements: Why They Succeed, How They Fail*. New York: Vintage Books, 1979. This classic study argues that movement leaders would do better to ride the early surge of movement energy as far as it will go rather than leave the streets prematurely to build institutions.

Web Resources

1 www.womhist.alexanderstreet.com
This interesting page provides text to primary documents relating to women's and other social movements between 1600 and the present.

2 www.usdoj.gov/crt/
The federal government has passed a number of statutes barring discrimination by employers and established the Civil Rights Division of the Justice Department to enforce these antidiscrimination statutes. This page provides a mission statement, a listing of cases, and a discussion of discrimination.

3 www.naacp.org
This is the website of the nation's premier civil rights organization.

4 www.now.org
This is the website of the nation's premier women's rights organization. The website includes discussion of key issues, including reproductive rights, economic justice, violence against women, and events.

5 www.eagleforum.org
Eagle Forum is a conservative interest group supporting family values, small government, low taxes, and a strong national defense. It was founded by Phyllis Schlafly in 1967 as a counterweight to the National Organization for Women.

Notes

1 Dorothy E. McBride and Janine A. Parry, *Women's Rights in the U.S.A.*, 4th ed. (New York: Routledge, 2011), 19.
2 David Brian Robertson, *Federalism and the Making of America* (New York: Routledge, 2012), 57–58.
3 Sidney G. Tarrow, *Power in Movement: Social Movements and Contentious Politics*, 3rd ed. (New York: Cambridge University Press, 2011), 153–157. See also F. Chris Garcia and Gabriel R. Sanchez, *Hispanics and the U.S. Political System: Moving into the Mainstream* (Upper Saddle River, NJ: Pearson, 2008), 49.
4 Adam Liptak, "4 Dissents Attest to Deep Divide on Court," *New York Times*, June 27, 2015, A1, A11.
5 Robert William Fogel, *Without Consent or Contract* (New York: W.W. Norton, 1989), 303–304.
6 Eric Foner, *Politics and Ideology in the Age of the Civil War* (New York: Oxford University Press, 1980), 62.
7 Speech by Abraham Lincoln delivered to the Congress on July 4, 1861.
8 Derrick Bell, *Faces at the Bottom of the Well* (New York: Basic Books, 1992), 12.
9 Alfred H. Kelly, Winfred A. Harbison, and Herman Belz, *The American Constitution: Its Origins and Development*, 7th ed. (New York: Norton, 1991), 2: 586.

10 Michael Janofsky, "A New Hope for Dreams Suspended by Segregation," *New York Times*, July 31, 2005, A1, A14.

11 Gerald N. Rosenberg, *The Hollow Hope: Can Courts Bring about Social Change?* (Chicago: University of Chicago Press, 1991), 99, and related tables, 98–100.

12 Linda Greenhouse, "Justices, 5–4, Limit Use of Race for School Integration Plans," *New York Times*, June 29, 2007, A1, A20.

13 Adam Liptak, "Justices Take Up Race as a Factor in College Entry," *New York Times*, February 22, 2012, A1, A13.

14 Robert Barnes, "Supreme Court Upholds University of Texas Affirmative Action Admissions," *Washington Post*, June 23, 2016.

15 Dorothy E. McBride and Janine A. Perry, *Women's Rights in the USA: Policy Debates and Gender Roles*, 4th ed. (New York: Routledge, 2011), 47–48.

16 Sara M. Evans, *Born for Liberty: A History of Women in America*, 2nd ed. (New York: Free Press, 1997), 93–143.

17 Nancy E. McGlen and Karen O'Connor, *Women, Politics, and American Society*, 2nd ed. (Upper Saddle River, NJ: Prentice-Hall, 1998), 11, 117, 177–181; Evans, *Born for Liberty*, 301–303.

18 Jane J. Mansbridge, *Why We Lost the ERA* (Chicago: University of Chicago Press, 1986), 20.

19 Linda Greenhouse, "In Reversal of Course, Justices 5–4, Back Ban on Abortion Method," *New York Times*, April 19, 2007, A1.

20 Robert Barnes and Mark Berman, "Supreme Court Strikes Down Texas Abortion Clinic Restrictions," *New York Times*, June, 27, 2016.

21 U.S. Census Bureau, *Statistical Abstract of the United States, 2017* (Washington, D.C.: U.S. Government Printing Office, 2017), table 314.

22 U.S. Census Bureau, *Statistical Abstract, 2017*, table 639, 408–412.

23 U.S. Census Bureau, *Statistical Abstract, 2017*, table 618. See also "Women in the Labor Force: A Databook," 2015. U.S. Department of Labor, Bureau of Labor Statistics, December 2015, Report 1034, Table 26, 87.

Chapter 5

SHAPING AMERICANS
Political Socialization, Public Opinion, and the Media

Focus Questions: from reading to thinking

Q1   What does it mean to say that America is the only country in the world based on a creed—on principles and ideals?

Q2   Where do individual Americans get their opinions about politics, and what are the forces that shape those opinions?

Q3   How do the media shape the ideas and information that citizens have about their world?

Q4   How well informed and well organized is public opinion in America today?

Q5   What does it mean to be liberal or conservative, libertarian or populist, in America today?

WHAT EXPLAINS THE U.S. COMMITMENT TO THE DEATH PENALTY?

The **Constitution** TODAY

Eighth Amendment: "Excessive bail shall not be required, nor excessive fines imposed, nor cruel and unusual punishments inflicted."

For more than a decade, Bianca Jagger, 1960s bad girl, fashion icon, first wife of ageless rocker Mick Jagger, and human rights activist, has been a Goodwill Ambassador in the Council of Europe's fight against the death penalty. Her main target has been the United States. The Council of Europe, established in the immediate wake of World War II, is now a 47-member regional organization opposed by charter to the death penalty. No member country has employed the death penalty since the late 1990s.

How is it that the U.S. views the death penalty so differently than its closest allies and now stands as one of the practice's last defenders and regular users in the world? Perhaps because Europe in the twentieth century saw government-sanctioned death wholesale, not just in war, but in the far more heinous example of the Holocaust. Death in war, while obviously state-sanctioned, can be seen as necessary, even noble. But the Holocaust, state-sanctioned killing of millions of innocents, done by and to Europeans, created a revulsion not as directly felt in the United States. Our state-sanctioned killing, the death penalty, was more democratic, something the public visited on its miscreant members. It remains legal today.

In a February 2010 speech in Geneva, Ambassador Jagger explained Europe's post–World War II commitment to abolition of the death penalty, saying,

> Since it was founded in 1949 the Council of Europe has played a leading role as a guardian of our fundamental rights and freedoms . . . . In 1989, abolition of the death penalty was made a prerequisite of accession for all new member states . . . . The idea now is to spread these values to the rest of the world, starting with the two countries that enjoy observer status to the Council of Europe: the United States and Japan. . . . I am shocked and appalled at the unabated . . . application of the death penalty in the U.S., China, Iran, North Korea, Saudi Arabia, Iraq, Vietnam, Afghanistan, Japan, Yemen, and Somalia among others.

Think about this list for a moment—except for the U.S. and Japan, this is a list of the world's rogue states—precisely Jagger's point, right!

But the U.S. is unblinking in its commitment to the justice and utility of the death penalty. Gallup has long shown a fairly steady, though slightly declining in recent years, support for the death penalty in the U.S, rejecting Jagger's declaration that "The death penalty is the ultimate denial of human rights, a pre-meditated and cold-blooded killing of a human being by the state." Nonetheless, the U.S. has been sensitive to the charge made by Jagger and others that "The death penalty is unfair, arbitrary and capricious often based on jurisprudence fraught with racial discrimination and judicial bias." In fact, the Supreme Court struck down the death penalty on just these grounds in *Furman v. Georgia* (1972). A popular backlash and hastily revised state and federal statutes led the court to reinstate the death penalty in *Gregg v. Georgia* (1976). Still, in recent years the court has prohibited execution of the mentally challenged (IQ under 70) and the young (under 18).

Finally, though the United States seems unlikely to abolish the death penalty anytime soon, some parts of the country have already done so. The Death Penalty Information Center reports that since 1976 when the death penalty was reinstituted, 1,185 inmates have been executed in the South, while only 4 have been executed in the Northeast. The Midwest and West fall in between, at 179 and 85, respectively, but it is the difference between the Northeast and the South that commands attention.

This chapter will raise important questions about American political culture and how the country's residents form political opinions. But as you read the chapter bear in mind that culture and opinions are not always monolithic across the entire nation; they often diverge along regional or other lines.

<table>
<tr><td>

Struggling Toward Democracy

Alexis de Tocqueville described the American political culture as: "*habits of the heart* . . . the various notions and opinions current among men and . . . those ideas which constitute their character of mind."

What do you think?

- What are the "habits of the heart" that define our culture today?
- Should cultures evolve, or are fundamental principles permanent?

</td></tr>
</table>

POLITICAL INFORMATION IN AMERICA

Earlier chapters introduced the basic ideas—liberty, equality, opportunity, limited government, the rule of law—and the basic constitutional design—separation of powers, checks and balances, federalism—of American politics. In this chapter, we ask how widely those broad ideas about government and politics are accepted today, how and how well they are transmitted from one generation to the next, and what contemporary Americans think about the major political issues of the day.

How do people, especially young people, come by their political views? Do different kinds of people, considered in terms of categories like age, sex, race, income, and region, hold similar views, or do they hold moderately, perhaps even completely, different views? What roles do family, schools, and the media play in shaping social and political views? How coherent are the opinions that Americans hold on public issues? These are important questions because democracy assumes political participation by an informed citizenry.

Brief definitions of three important concepts—political culture, political socialization, and public opinion—will help us understand how Americans come by their ideas about politics and public life. The term **political culture** refers to patterns of thought and behavior that are widely held in a society and that define the relationships of citizens to their government and to each other in matters affecting politics and public affairs.[1] Our political culture has long been referred to as the *American Creed*. Both terms refer to the ideas of the American founding: liberty, equality, opportunity, popular sovereignty, limited government, the rule of law, and the like.

political culture Patterns of thought and behavior that are widely held in a society and that refer to the relationships of citizens to their government and to each other in matters affecting politics and public affairs.

Political socialization refers to the process by which the central tenets of the political culture are communicated and absorbed. Political socialization is the process by which the next generation of children and the next wave of immigrants come to understand, accept, and approve the existing political system and the procedures and institutions through which it operates.[2] In the main, political socialization is a conservative process because, it reproduces in new citizens the dominant political ideas of the culture.

political socialization The process by which the central tenets of the political culture are transmitted from those immersed in it to those, such as children and immigrants, who are not.

Public opinion is the distribution of citizen opinion on particular matters of public concern or interest. Because the American political culture operates at a fairly general level, and political socialization impacts blacks somewhat differently than whites and women somewhat differently than men, public opinion varies on and across the major issues of the day. Now we turn to the origins of the American political culture, then to political socialization, and then to the nature and content of public opinion in America today. Throughout this chapter we ponder the role of the media in shaping political information and ideas.

public opinion The distribution of citizen opinion on matters of public concern or interest.

POLITICAL CULTURE: DEFINING THE "AMERICAN CREED"

Colonial Americans drew on their European cultural and intellectual heritage to create communities that then developed and evolved in interaction with the vast and wealthy continent itself. By the late eighteenth century, America's

Q1 What does it mean to say that America is the only country in the world based on a creed—on principles and ideals?

AP Photo/Richard Drew

The politically connected, whether in government or out, go on television news and opinion shows to make their case on the major issues of the day. Here Fox News host Sean Hannity talks with Donald Trump, Jr., about the inquiry into Russian interference in the 2016 presidential election.

basic self-image, its broad political culture was set. Thomas Jefferson and his colleagues in the Congress of 1776 drew heavily on John Locke in grounding the new nation's independence on the declaration that "all Men are created equal, that they are endowed by their Creator with certain unalienable Rights, that among these are Life, Liberty, and the pursuit of Happiness." The Declaration of Independence put liberty, equality, and opportunity at the core of the American Creed.[3] As we shall see below and throughout this book, these creedal values were aspirations, not realities, in the founding generation and remain so in our own.

Contemporary analysts still point to the same familiar ideas and concepts as fundamental to the American Creed. One prominent scholar, Samuel Huntington, concluded his study of the American Creed by declaring that "the same core values appear in virtually all analyses: liberty, equality, individualism, democracy, and the rule of law." Another, Seymour Martin Lipset, concluded that "the American Creed can be described in five terms: liberty, egalitarianism, individualism, populism, and *laissez faire.*"[4] These ideas form the basis of the American political culture and are almost universally approved within the American society.

POLITICAL SOCIALIZATION: WHERE OUR IDEAS ABOUT POLITICS COME FROM

How are the broad ideas of the American political culture taught by one generation of Americans to the next? Political scientist Fred Greenstein described political socialization as the study of "(1) who (2) learns what (3) from whom (4) under what circumstances (5) with what effects."[5] Greenstein's fundamental interest was in how young children acquire their first impressions of politics and political leaders. More recently scholars have asked the extent to which early political learning can or cannot be modified as people move through the life cycle. Do people change their political views as they experience school, work, marriage, family, retirement, and old age? Do poor children who get rich in adult life change political assumptions and beliefs?

Agents of Socialization

Q2 Where do individual Americans get their opinions about politics, and what are the forces that shape those opinions?

How does it happen that the vast majority of Americans come to believe that market competition is the best way to organize an economy, that elections are the best way to pick political leaders, and that the flag, the White House, the Lincoln memorial, and the Capitol dome represent a political heritage and culture worth passing on, worth defending, even worth dying for? As we shall see, while political socialization is a powerful process, much of it takes place informally, below the radar screen, almost automatically. Neither those who teach nor those who learn are much aware that they are doing it.

agents of socialization The persons, such as parents and teachers, and settings, such as families and schools, that carry out the political socialization process.

Agents of socialization are the persons by whom and the settings in which the process of political socialization is accomplished. Persons include parents, family, friends, teachers, coworkers, and associates of various kinds, as well as those whose views are transmitted through the media and online. Settings include homes, churches, schools, workplaces, clubs, union halls, and professional associations.

New technology, like the Internet and social media, and new uses of old technology, like talk radio, allow geographically disparate groups to form around and act on shared interests. Rush Limbaugh's "ditto heads" learn a coherent ideology and arguments supporting their positions by tuning in every day. www.Meetup.com, YouTube, Facebook, and President Trump's Twitter feed allow like-minded people to find each other and share enthusiasms, ideas, and plans. And where like-minded people do not find each other, pollsters, political strategists, and niche marketers work to identify people with shared values and interests so that they can target them with political information designed to mobilize them to political action.[6]

Family, School, and Work.   Everyone agrees that the first and most important agent of political socialization is the family. Virtually all American families teach respect for democracy and capitalism, but they differ on the lessons they teach regarding participation, partisanship, politics, and public policy. Studies show that about 70 percent of married couples share the same party affiliation or are both independents Most of the rest are partisans married to independents and fewer than 10 percent of married couples are Democrat and Republican.[7] Still, parents rarely sit young children down and tell them that they are Democrats and not Republicans, or vice versa, but children learn just as effectively by overhearing their parents, observing their actions and reactions, and sensing their party affiliation.

Over the past half century, scholars have consistently shown that high school and college-age young people generally adopt their parents' partisan identification. If both parents share the same party affiliation, Democrat or Republican, 60 to 65 percent of young people adopt the family partisanship, about 30 percent abandon it for an independent stance, while only about 10 percent join the opposition party. Young people from those uncommon households where Mom is a Democrat and Dad is a Republican or vice versa scatter with remarkable uniformity across Democrat, Republican, and independent categories. In households where both parents are independents, the children choose independent status at least two-thirds of the time, while the remaining one-third divide equally between the Democrats and the Republicans.[8]

Schools also play an important role in early political socialization. School curricula lay down layer after layer of American history, civics, and social studies. Students learn patriotic songs and rituals, they learn about political heroes such as Washington and Lincoln, and they cast their first presidential straw ballots. Moreover, schools, even elementary schools, offer a broader horizon than the family. Respect for diversity, equality, fair play, toleration, majority rule, and minority rights are required for the first time in a setting where people actually differ.

Teacher Robyn Harris instructs her second-grade students on a multiculturalism educational activity in her Yakima, Washington, classroom. Schools, like homes, are settings in which American values are taught to the next generation.

Fred Greenstein's seminal work with schoolchildren in New Haven in the late 1950s and early 1960s remains fascinating even today. Greenstein found that children begin to learn about politics in their elementary school years. Second graders can name the president. Over the remainder of the grade school years, children become aware of other branches of government and other levels of government. Initially, children see Congress as the president's "helpers." By eighth grade, they know that Congress can differ with the president and that this is how the system is supposed to work. Subsequent scholarly work over many decades, best summarized by Robert Erikson and Kent Tedin in their classic *American Public Opinion*, affirms "the primacy principle" that early learning has staying power. Still early views are not set in stone. Students begin their college careers somewhat more liberal than the adult population and become somewhat more liberal still by their senior year. Scholars attribute this to education challenging stereotypes and prejudices and to the diversity of the college environment.[9] Childhood political socialization can be deepened or partially reshaped during "the impressionable years" of 17 to 29.[10] Socialization continues after early adulthood, but early foundations are deeply set.

Work has both general and specific effects on political socialization. In fact, employment, quite apart from the nature of the job, has a profound effect on a person's political outlook. Having a job is one's ticket to participate in a whole range of social and political processes. Having a good job teaches confidence that carries over into political activity. Unemployment, particularly chronic unemployment, takes away the status, time, opportunity, and confidence that political participation requires. Not surprisingly, studies show that higher income people are more aware of politics, issues, and candidates than are lower income people. The wealthy are socialized to a more active political life than are the poor.[11]

After the family and maybe schools, the media are among the most powerful shapers of the American political culture and public opinion. But family and schools are personal and local, so one senior scholar of the media and politics has noted that, "for many Americans, the media are their only contact with the world of public affairs."[12] In a sense, this is obvious—we do not all live in Washington D.C., so we cannot have personal knowledge of what Congress and the president are doing. But it also means that everything— everything—we know about what is going on in Washington, let alone the rest of the world, we learn through the media. Are you comfortable with that thought? Can we depend upon the media to provide the news and information we need to be responsible democratic citizens? Let's explore the media landscape in a little more depth.

The Modern Media

The modern media form an increasingly complex, diffuse, but interactive information production and distribution system. The modern media include more than fourteen hundred daily newspapers, seven thousand weeklies, fifteen thousand journals and magazines, twenty-six hundred book publishers, ten thousand radio stations, and twenty-seven hundred cable and television stations. Many companies like Google, Twitter, and iTunes specialize in presenting and managing information on the World Wide Web.

The media landscape constantly evolves. Newspaper and magazine readership has been on the decline for decades. Fewer than 90 million Americans, about 40 percent of the 230 million Americans over the age of 16, receive a daily-newspaper. Slightly more, about 120 million people, receive a Sunday paper. Twenty percent of these spend less than 30 minutes scanning headlines and checking out the sports scores, market statistics, and weather forecasts before they move on. That leaves only about one quarter of adults who can be said to read a paper each day.

A 2012 study by the Pew Research Center for the People and the Press found that younger Americans spend only half the time older Americans spend following the news. A 2016 Pew study found that those under 30 were disconnected from newspapers and increasingly from television. Just 5 percent of those under 30 said that they often read a newspaper and just 27 percent said they often watch television news. By contrast, 72 percent of adults 50–64 years old and 85 percent of those over 65 often watched television news. Younger Americans, at least those who are consuming news, are twice as likely to do so online (50 percent) as they are on television (27 percent).[13]

Many Americans listen to radio at some point during the day. All news and politically-oriented talk radio have proliferated in recent years. Conservative domination of talk radio is led by Rush Limbaugh's "ditto-head" audience of

13.3 million a week. Liberals tend to gravitate toward National Public Radio (NPR), whose *Morning Edition* has an audience of 13 million a week, but Rush enjoys an advantage because NPR's programming is not explicitly ideological.

Fully 98.5 percent of American homes have one or more television sets on for an average of seven hours each day. Americans watch a lot of TV, but they do not watch a lot of news. While 24 million Americans tune in the nightly news on one of the three major networks on an average day, that is about one-tenth of adult Americans. All three networks focus their attention on the major events of the day in Washington, in the nation's major cities, foreign capitals, and the most visible foreign or domestic trouble spot of the moment. TV news-magazines such as *60 Minutes, 20/20,* and *Dateline* provide softer and more sensational fare. The Sunday morning interview shows led by *Meet the Press* are rigorously substantive, but their audiences are quite small.

Nonetheless, almost 85 percent of American homes have cable or satellite TV and many packages offer hundreds of channels. Despite the proliferation of new media channels, the transition from old to new media is not as rapid or complete as one might expect. First, no matter how many channels people have on their cable package, they tend to regularly use only about fifteen. Most viewers have a comfort zone that includes both old media and new. Second, with the partial exception of cable news, the new media do little original reporting. Rather, they offer analysis and commentary on news gathered elsewhere. The major networks' response to the rise of cable has been to embrace them. All of the broadcast networks have a growing list of cable holdings and cooperative relationships.

Finally, many now claim to get their news from the Internet and talk radio.[14] Is this possible? Can a person be well and thoroughly informed based on information gleaned from the Internet and talk radio? Yes and no, but certainly not without careful effort. Talk radio should be viewed as entertainment as much as information, as should cable news, though to a somewhat lesser degree, and the Internet should be scanned broadly and then mined deeply. No one, whether they read newspapers, watch broadcast television or cable news, or surf the net, should be dependent upon one or even a few sources of news and information. Only when you get roughly the same story from a number of credible sources on a major issue—health care reform, the safety of the banks, or global climate change—can you be confident that you "understand" the issue.

The strengths and weaknesses of social media have been highlighted by Donald Trump's use of Twitter, first as a candidate and then as our first "twitter president." The strength of social media, particularly as a political communication and messaging device, are its openness, immediacy, and spontaneity. It has the potential to display the personal, emotional, and even the joyful side of high public officials that the average citizen rarely if ever gets to see. Citizens might come away from such social media experiences, especially a series of encounters over time, with a sense that they know, trust, and understand the official—the president—better.

The weaknesses of social media as a political tool, especially if great care is not taken, are obvious because they are its strengths—openness, immediacy, and spontaneity—misunderstood and misused. All of us are well-advised to think before we speak, but that is all the more important for a political leader, especially one with 20 million Twitter followers (Katy Perry has 100 million followers; sorry Mr. President). A careless tweet can spread misinformation, stir emotions, and deepen divisions.

Most agree that President Trump would be better off if he tweeted less, but where are our real social and political needs and interests here? Is it more important for the public to see the president's initial thoughts and emotions on important matters or only to hear about the final policies once the discussions have been held and the choices made? Can a president roil public emotions by tweet one day and then bring the country together or console it in tragedy the next day? We are finding out in real time.

MEDIA INFLUENCE AND THE POLITICAL AGENDA

The traditional media—newspapers, magazines, and television—select from among all the things that happen in our country and the world and present a very thin slice to us as news. The new media—talk radio, personal electronics, and the Web—repackage, interpret, and critique the product of politics and the traditional media. In this section, we see how citizens receive and process the news that is presented to them. We find that the media not only present information, but they raise certain issues and not others, and they suggest how the issues that they raise should be understood. As a result, the media play a significant role in shaping public opinion in the United States.[15]

Q3 How do the media shape the ideas and information that citizens have about their world?

Where Does the Public Get Its News? For most people, politics and public affairs play an occasional and usually secondary role in their lives. Their attention is normally focused on their jobs and families, and during their free time they turn not to politics but to leisure, sports, and entertainment. They may catch snatches of news and pieces of information throughout the day if the news is on while they dress, as they glance over the morning paper, listen to the car radio on the way home from work, or hear parts of the evening news over conversation at dinner. Most Americans get their news from more than one source, but asked by Gallup in 2016 for their main source of news—43 percent said they look to TV, 26 percent said the Internet, 5 percent said newspapers, and 4 percent the radio.[17] An appreciable number of viewers, many of them young, prefer the pseudonews of Stephen Colbert to the "real" news of David Muir. What media do you pay particular attention to and what are you looking for from those particular media sources?

Moreover, the way that the media gather and report the news makes it difficult for citizens to see patterns and relationships. The media are focused on the events of the day: who said what about the

Struggling Toward Democracy

Some scholars and media analysts have argued that new media—the Internet, the Web—are powerfully democratic, allowing all of us to express our ideas and opinions.

What do you think?

- What does it mean for the democratic potential of "new media" that they originate little news, instead circulating or linking to news created by the "old media" stalwarts of print and broadcast?

- What other value, then, does new media have in a democracy?

Pro & Con

Is the Media Biased?

The American media are frequently condemned both as unduly liberal and as hopelessly conservative. How can this be? Some critics cite surveys of print and electronic journalists that consistently show that journalists identify themselves as liberals in higher proportions than do American citizens in general and that they tend to vote for Democratic candidates for president in much higher proportions than do Americans in general. Others argue that editors, publishers, and owners—those who manage, control, and own the media—tend to be more conservative than Americans in general. Moreover, newspapers have traditionally endorsed candidates for office and have usually, though not in 2016, favored Republicans.

This ongoing battle over bias in the media has new champions who have made their cases in new books. Tim Groseclose's *Left Turn: How Liberal Media Bias Distorts the American Mind* (2012) used advanced statistical techniques to demonstrate that most U.S. media outlets lean left and that this affects what voters think and how they act. John Nichols and Robert W. McChesney in *Dollarocracy: How the Money and Media Election Complex Is Destroying America* (2013) argue that aggressive wealth, mostly right leaning and conservative, works through the media to dominate

our electoral and democratic processes. As consumers of the media's product, we should all keep in mind that journalists' values are always present, even when they try to manage and control them, and during elections the power of money is evident.

The structure of the news media also plays a substantial role in how they work. Two major factors help to explain why traditional news organizations gather and disseminate the news in cautious and predictable ways. First, news organizations are or are part of large, bureaucratic, for-profit corporations that make money by selling space or time to advertisers. Network executives who thought they were losing viewers and the advertising dollars that pursue them because of the content of their news programs would make immediate changes.

Second, both the print and electronic media must efficiently organize and assign work to their reporters, editors, and production people. This requires both deadlines and beats. Deadlines are required because a morning paper must be on doorsteps by 6 a.m. and the evening news must go on precisely at its scheduled time. Moreover, reporters are assigned to news beats that usually revolve around institutions like the White House, the State Department, the county court house or police station where news is expected to occur on a regular basis. Having committed these resources, editors and producers have

latest act of random violence, the most recent unemployment figures, or the latest campaign poll or candidate promise. Citizens, with most of their attention directed elsewhere, may have heard about the latest isolated event or statement, but will not have the time, inclination, or related information to place it within an appropriate and meaningful context. Only citizens who already have high levels of information on a particular topic can readily make sense of the next piece of information that they receive on that topic. To the uninformed citizen, a new piece of information on a complex topic makes no sense and is likely to be ignored.[18]

How then do the media, and especially the electronic media, affect how citizens understand, think about, and evaluate their government and its officials? The broad answer to this question was famously delivered by Bernard Cohen

fake news Fake news is an all-purpose epithet that may refer to false stories that appear in the media or just to stories someone does not like.

little choice but to report what happened on the main beats each day.

The new media of talk radio, cable, and Internet with their smaller, but more intense, 24 × 7 audiences are edgier, more personality-driven, and more overtly ideological. But they are "mom and pop" operations when compared with the hundreds, even thousands, of people employed by traditional media giants. Breitbart News, with a couple dozen reporters and bureaus in London, Jerusalem, Texas, and California, is expanding and has been credited with a substantial impact on the 2016 presidential election. Headed by former Trump political strategist Steve Bannon, Breitbart advocated for Trump and against Hillary Clinton. According to the journalist Joshua Green, Bannon created, "an infrastructure of conservative organizations that together would work, sometimes in tandem with mainstream media outlets, to stop... the 2016 Democratic nominee: Hillary Clinton."[16] Certainly the Democrats had their own media advocates, but they were not as well organized and hard-hitting. So, yes, some media is biased.

In recent times, the charge of **"fake news"** has overtaken traditional arguments about media bias. Fake news can take several forms, including false stories circulated to discredit individuals or even for monetary gain. Fake news is not new—accounts of false news stories plaguing political figures go all the way back to the time of George Washington. But during the 2016 election cycle, so many stories of dubious origin surfaced to disrupt the campaign and electoral process that some, regardless of political persuasion, had a difficult time sorting out fake news from real news. Added to that, then-candidate and now President Trump co-opted the term to brand as "fake news" any news with which he disagreed. As a result, legitimate news sources have reaffirmed long-time standards of journalistic best practice including vigilant fact-checking, multi-level corroboration, separating news from opinion pieces, and enhancing news reporting transparency. Such time-tested norms are the surest bulwark against the universe of "alternative facts" on the Internet and even in the White House press room.

PRO	CON
Most reporters admit to voting Democrat	The media are businesses that focus on the bottom line
Credible studies have purported to find bias	No business wants to offend customers
Some media outlets clearly proclaim their biases	Journalists have a professional commitment to objectivity

in 1963 and has been affirmed many times since: "The press . . . may not be successful much of the time in telling people what to think, but it is stunningly successful in telling its readers what to think about."[19]

The media have at least four broad effects on what and how the public thinks about government, politics, and politicians. The first is an **educational effect** as the public learns from and is informed by what it hears and sees in the media. The second is an **agenda-setting effect** as the public's attention is directed toward issues to which the media give special or disproportionate attention. The third is a **framing effect** as the way that the media present the issue suggests who or what should be held responsible for the current state of affairs and for addressing it if need be. The fourth is a **persuasion effect** whereby the media can occasionally change the substance of what citizens believe or think they know.

educational effect The public learns from what it sees discussed in the media and cannot learn, obviously, about issues that are not taken up by the media.

agenda-setting effect The extent to which the amount of media coverage of an issue affects the public's attention to and interest in that issue.

framing effect The way an issue is framed or presented in the media, either episodically or thematically, suggests to the public where the praise or blame should be laid.

persuasion effect The way an issue is presented by the media can sometimes change the substance of what people think about the issue.

The leading contemporary analysts of the effect of television news on what Americans know about politics and of how that knowledge is structured are political scientists Shanto Iyengar and Donald Kinder. Iyengar and Kinder summarized their path-breaking book, *News That Matters: Television and Public Opinion*, first published in 1987 and updated in 2010, by writing, "the power of television news . . . appears to rest not on persuasion but on commanding the public's attention (agenda-setting) and defining criteria underlying the public's judgment (priming)."[20]

Iyengar and Kinder and others have shown that the more attention television news gives to a particular issue, whether that issue is crime, economic performance, or war, the higher that issue rises in the public's ranking of important issues facing the nation. Even more intriguingly, Iyengar and Kinder distinguish two general ways in which television news reports present or frame an issue. Framing can be predominantly episodic or thematic. A television news report on poverty that is framed episodically might involve pictures of or interviews with one or several poor people describing the difficulties of their situation. A report framed thematically might involve an analyst or official explaining the extent of poverty in the country and whether it is increasing or decreasing.

Episodic framing leads to placing responsibility for poverty on the individual poor person, whereas thematic framing leads to placing responsibility on society and government. Iyengar notes that "since television news is heavily episodic, its effect is generally to induce attributions of responsibility to individual victims or perpetrators rather than to broad social forces."[21] Episodic framing discourages the public from seeing the connections between issues and from attributing responsibility for the patterns to elected officials and political institutions.

Political operatives, of course, know all of this and so struggle mightily to shape the media narrative to the benefit of their clients. Politicians have long had media advisers on their campaign staffs, but over the past several decades media advisers have become central to the daily political struggle. Frank Luntz, a Republican media specialist, has been at this longer and more effectively than anyone else. In 1994, Luntz helped Republicans, led by Newt Gingrich, develop their Contract With America and learn to talk about issues in new ways. The inheritance tax became the death tax, tax cuts became tax relief, and drilling for oil became exploring for energy. Luntz's 2006 book, *Words That Work: It's Not What You Say, It's What People Hear*, is well worth a read. Democrats have their own message gurus, led by George Lakoff, author of *Moral Politics: How Liberals and Conservatives Think*, but the Republicans got there first and have generally been more effective in framing the national political debate—socialized medicine anyone? How about death panels?

The media, like the schools, provide pervasive and continuous support to effective political socialization simply by routinely reporting political and economic events. The president's latest statements, the work of the Congress, and the latest Supreme Court decisions are all reported on the evening news and in the morning papers. Trade figures, corporate profits, and the rise and fall of the stock market are reported in ways that assume the fundamental legitimacy of democratic capitalism. Even talk radio and the Internet offer few hints that politics or economics might be organized differently. In this sense, political socialization is a conservative process. But sometimes, big events and personalities break through normal processes and expectations to create broad change.

The Impacts of Transformative Events and Personalities.   Political socialization is the broadly effective process by which families, schools, and the media transmit the American political culture to young people and newcomers, but that broad process of cultural teaching and learning, of memory and renewal, can be disrupted. Some events including wars, economic upheavals, social turmoil, and political scandal can transform the way people see and understand their society. Depending upon how these challenges are handled by political leaders, the nation's faith in its political culture, its confidence in its basic ideals and institutions, is renewed and strengthened or called into doubt and weakened.

Abraham Lincoln held the nation together through a terrible Civil War, and Franklin Delano Roosevelt did the same through a dozen years of economic depression and world war. Both gave the Americans who witnessed their virtuoso political performances the confidence to confront their world forcefully and for the most part successfully. Alternatively, leaders that misperceive or mismanage the major threats of their time, as Herbert Hoover misperceived the threat posed by the Great Depression of the 1930s, may raise doubts about the viability of the nation's most basic political assumptions. Leaders facing crises must respond effectively to challenges and do so in ways that protect and strengthen the nation's basic principles. Moreover, successful presidents can strengthen their party brand and attract a new generation of supporters, as FDR and Ronald Reagan did, while failed presidents, like Herbert Hoover and Jimmy Carter, can haunt their party for years.

THE NATURE OF PUBLIC OPINION IN THE UNITED STATES

The agents of socialization discussed above, although they all work within a general American political culture revolving around capitalism and democracy, do not teach the same lessons to all members of society. The poor and the wealthy are

In his famous "fireside chats," President Franklin Roosevelt used radio to educate and reassure Americans through a dozen years of economic depression and world war. Though modern presidents still use radio, they depend more heavily on television when they need to address the nation.

socialized to different roles; minorities are socialized differently than whites, and women are socialized differently than men. Conservatives draw on different media sources than do liberals. Hence, public opinion varies across a wide range of social group characteristics.[22] Public opinion, in its most general formulation, is simply the current distribution of citizen opinion on matters of public concern or interest.

Before we can discuss public opinion in detail, we must address a prior question. How do we measure public opinion and how confident should we be in those measurements? Once we understand how public opinion is measured, we can ask how attitudes and opinions vary within the American public by class, race, ethnicity, and gender.

Public Opinion Polling

Citizens have always wondered how others see the leading candidates and major issues of the day. But modern polling, based on probability sampling, is a post–World War II invention. **Probability sampling** is based on a statistical model in which every person in the target population has an equal or known chance of being selected for the sample to be polled. In a simple probability sample, all members of the population have an equal chance of being selected. In a stratified probability sample, the population is first divided by some theoretically relevant characteristic—like gender, income, or likelihood of voting—and then the population is randomly sampled within each category. Pollsters have understood for more than half a century that a well-constructed national sample of just 1,000 persons produces results that have a sampling error of +/– 3 percent with a confidence interval of 95 percent. What do these ominous phrases, sampling error and confidence interval, actually mean?[23]

Assume we had a well-designed poll of 1,000 adults telling us that 60 percent of them approved a certain policy. Remember, we have not asked all adults whether they support the policy, just a carefully selected sample of them, so we know that our 60 percent result is unlikely to be precise. The 3 percent sampling error is the pollster's admission, or at least sampling theory's admission, that in a sample of 1,000 the results could be off as much as 3 percent either way—so maybe not precisely 60 percent, but somewhere between 57 and 63 percent support the policy. The 95 percent confidence interval is another admission. It says that if you polled 100 similarly drawn samples, at least 95 of them would produce results in that 57 to 63 percent range; meaning that the remaining 5 might be off by more than 3 percent either way.[24] None of this means that polls are always wrong, just that even well-constructed polls can be off within a certain known range and should be interpreted appropriately.

On the other hand, consumers of polling information should also keep in mind that not all polls are trying to be accurate.[25] Some polls strive for accuracy, some have other purposes, and some attempt to mislead. Sophisticated consumers of polls, as you are about to become, know how to tell the difference.

probability sampling A sampling model in which every person in the target population has an identical chance of being selected for the sample to be polled.

Should Citizens Believe Polls?   Many Americans are skeptical about polls and there are some good reasons to be skeptical. Doubts about polls were deepened when virtually every major national poll forecast a two- to five-point Hillary Clinton win anchored by a blue wall of traditionally Democratic states in the upper Midwest. On election night, though Clinton narrowly prevailed in the popular vote, Trump took Pennsylvania, Wisconsin, and Michigan—all states in which the polls had Clinton leading. How could the pollsters have gotten it so wrong?

Polls are not easy to conduct well, and the increasing use of answering machines, caller identification devices, cell phones, and the general unwillingness of citizens to respond to surveys make it more difficult. Moreover, campaigns must develop a "turnout model," an educated guess about how the actual electorate—those who will actually turn up to vote – will look. The Clinton campaign "turnout model," meaning the campaign's best estimate as to how many whites, blacks, Hispanics, etc. would turn out on election day, was off. They estimated fewer whites and more minorities than actually showed up on election day—and they lost, at least in the Electoral College. Political pros also know that poll results can be shaped and manipulated by the order in which questions are asked and by the way that they are phrased.[26]

Still, skepticism should be directed toward some polls more than others. As a general rule, citizens can trust polls from organizations that have reputational incentives to be accurate—major polling organizations like Gallup, major news outlets like ABC and the *New York Times*, and major research organizations like the Pew Charitable Trusts. Citizens might well mistrust polls from groups that pop up in the middle of a campaign or that have a dog in the fight—an advocacy group, candidate, SuperPAC, or political party.

push poll A push poll is not a real poll; instead it is designed to influence voters by providing negative, often, false information.

Variations in Political Socialization and Public Opinion by Class, Race, and Gender

What then do reputable polls tell us about how citizens differ in regard to politics and public opinion by class, race, ethnicity, and gender? Broadly, the more thoroughly and comfortably integrated a person is into the community and society, the more likely he or she is to be politically active. Wealthy, well educated, professionals tend to be engaged in lots of ways, and not just voting, while those for whom life is more difficult tend to be less active politically.

Class.   Poor children enter school with fewer skills than wealthy children and less is expected of them. Extensive research, summarized by Chris Garcia and Gabriel Sanchez, reported that schools serving children of the working class and poor "are less involved in preparing future leaders, and instead emphasize the importance of becoming good law-abiding citizens, paying taxes, serving one's country, and similar 'subject' rather than participant . . . styles."[27] Many studies have shown that these early differences in knowledge and confidence can translate into differences in political participation that last a lifetime.

The most recent National Election Study found that poor adults were only about half as likely as the wealthy, 22 percent to 38 percent, to say that they paid attention to public affairs "most of the time." But they were 14 points more likely, 52 percent to 38 percent, to agree with the statement that "people don't have a say in what government does." The poor believe, rightly in many cases, that society and government do not move to their commands.

Race. An important book, entitled *Black Politics Today*, by political scientist Theodore J. Davis, reported that 81 percent of blacks felt that society had not dealt fairly with their racial group (only 15 percent of whites agreed), 76 percent thought government should spend more to improve conditions among blacks (only 27 percent of whites agreed), and 55 percent felt that there still was a fair amount of discrimination against blacks (only 28 percent of whites agreed).[28]

In the 2012 presidential election, Obama won with a remarkable 93 percent of black votes, 71 percent of Hispanics, but just 39 percent of whites. In 2016, Clinton narrowly lost while polling 88 percent of black votes, 65 percent of Hispanic votes, and 37 percent of white votes—all down just a bit from Obama's totals four years earlier. Not surprisingly, blacks and whites have tended to differ on a broad range of policy issues, sometimes quite dramatically. Blacks are more supportive of government spending on health care, education, and job training than whites and less supportive of spending for defense and corporate subsidies. For example, over the last three decades, blacks have been 30 to 40

AP Photo/ SIPPL Sipa USA/Pacific Press/Erik McGregor

In 2016, Black Lives Matter activists, here confronting New York City police, also sought to hold presidential candidates, especially Democrats Hillary Clinton and Bernie Sanders, accountable for highlighting black opportunity and security.

points more favorable than whites to the idea that government should guarantee fair treatment in jobs. Scholars explain the cohesion of black opinion by positing a "linked-fate" hypothesis in which blacks stand uniformly against racial discrimination because each individual knows that if it occurs he or she will be impacted by it.

Ethnicity.   Until recently, Hispanic Americans were less likely than blacks to feel that discrimination was a major problem for their community. In a 2002 Pew Hispanic Center poll, 47 percent of Hispanics claimed that discrimination was a major problem. But by 2010, after several years of public debate about immigration and border control, 61 percent believed that it was and another 24 percent believed it was at least a minor problem.[29]

Hispanics favor special efforts to remedy past discrimination and help minorities get ahead by 76 percent to 14 percent and favor a bigger government offering a wider array of services by 75 percent to 16 percent. On the other hand, Hispanics are twice as likely as non-Hispanics, 44 percent compared to 22 percent, to think that abortion should be illegal.[30] Hispanic public opinion is often said to reflect an "in-between" community, with life experiences and attitudes in-between those of blacks and whites.

Asian-Americans, after Hispanics, are the fastest growing racial and ethnic minority in the nation. Asians currently make up about 5 percent of the population. In a recent major survey, 32 percent of Asians claimed a Democratic Party affiliation, 12 percent claimed a Republican affiliation, 19 percent were Independent, and 35 percent were non-partisan. Chinese, Filipino, Indians, Japanese, and Koreans tend to lean Democratic, while Vietnamese tend to lean Republican. Both Hispanics and Asians vote about 2 to 1 Democrat.

Gender.   Similar differences, although not so large and across a narrower set of issues, exist between men and women. Women have consistently been more supportive than men of gun control, stern punishments for drunk driving, and spending on education and health care, and less supportive of capital punishment at home and the use of force abroad. Women oppose force at home and abroad about 10 percent more than men and favor the "moralistic" position on domestic issues about 3 or 4 percent more consistently than men.[31]

The terrorist attacks of September 11, 2001, and the subsequent conflicts with Al-Queda, Afghanistan, and Iraq put these historical differences between men and women on stark display. In early September 2001, just prior to the attacks, 41 percent of men, but only 24 percent of women, favored additional defense spending. In the immediate wake of the 9/11 attacks, support for increased defense spending among men increased to 53 percent, but among women it nearly doubled to 47 percent, still 6 points below men. Nonetheless, only a year and a half later, as war with Iraq loomed in late February 2003, women were about 10 percent less willing than men to consider the potential costs in troops and treasure acceptable.[32] And in late 2011, as most troops were being withdrawn from Iraq and the Afghan War ground on, men remained 17 points more supportive of the war than women, 43 percent to 26 percent.[33]

In later chapters we will see how variations in political socialization by class, race, ethnicity, and gender affect partisan identification and voting throughout a lifetime.

Properties of Public Opinion

Although public opinion differs across class, race, and gender lines, it also displays a number of general properties or characteristics. Public opinion scholars distinguish between elites, often called "opinion leaders" or the "attentive public" and the mass public. Opinion leaders are those few, usually thought of as around 10 percent of the adult population, who follow public affairs closely and know a good deal about them. These people possess a lot of well-organized and readily accessible information about politics and public policy; they know the leading actors, the major issues, and the key policy choices.[34]

Members of the mass public, on the other hand, are busy with work and family and do not spend their free time puzzling over political issues. What they learn about politics comes in disconnected bits and pieces that do not add up to a coherent view of the political world. Not surprisingly, "opinion leaders" can easily slip into the view that it is good that the mass public listens to the well-informed. But sometimes the public loses confidence in the elites and this opens the door for an insurgent, like Donald Trump, to run an "us against them" campaign on behalf of the people against the interests. Such insurgencies have occurred irregularly in American history; traditional elites fight back and usually win, eventually, but tumult is the order of the day in the meantime. Feel familiar!

How Detailed Is Public Opinion?   The first aspect of public opinion that we must note is its lack of detail for most Americans. In one sense, most Americans "know" very little about politics, public policy, and political leaders. For example, in survey after survey over the past fifty years, most Americans knew who the president was (usually 95 percent plus) and almost as many could identify the vice president. Only about half of adult Americans knew that there were two U.S. senators from their state, could identify the majority party in the House and Senate, or could name their representative in Congress. Less than 10 percent could name the chief justice of the Supreme Court or the chairman of the Federal Reserve Board.[35]

Q4 How well informed and well organized is public opinion in America today?

Can you name the chief justice of the Supreme Court? Does it matter? How much specific information do citizens need to evaluate government and to decide whether they approve of its performance? Do citizens need to know who the chief justice is to be able to decide whether they like what the court has done on civil rights, on the rights of persons accused of crimes, or on school prayer? Some suggest that detailed knowledge is not required because citizens quite sensibly make broader judgments, based on partisanship and ideology, about how political and other national institutions are doing. Others worry that too many citizens aggressively reject scientific and other expert opinion when they conflict with their partisan and ideological preferences.[36]

Softening this picture just a bit is research that distinguishes between recall and recognition. Unassisted recall involves simply remembering your member of Congress's name, which only about one-third of citizens can do. But many more citizens are able to recognize the name of their member from a list of several names.[37] Unaided recall is hard, but many political activities, like voting, involve the easier task of recognition—so maybe citizens and voters are not in such bad shape after all.

General Principles versus Real Choices. A second worrisome aspect of public opinion is that there is often a wide gap between the general principles that citizens claim to hold and specific choices they make in their communities. The most famous evidence of this gap comes from a study done by political scientists James M. Prothro and Charles M. Grigg in the late 1950s. Many more recent studies confirm these findings with minor revisions. Prothro and Grigg found 95 to 98 percent support for majority rule, minority rights, and free speech. However, they found that only 44 percent of respondents were prepared to let a communist speak in their community and only 63 percent were prepared to let someone with antireligious views speak. Prothro and Grigg concluded that when one moves from general principles of the American political culture to specific applications of those principles, "consensus breaks down completely."[38]

The puzzling relationship between general principles and specific cases has spawned a great deal of research. Generally, findings confirm broad respect for the nation's general principles, but deep uncertainty about how they should apply in specific cases. Important research by James Gibson suggested that whether respondents initially gave a tolerant or intolerant response to a specific case, their minds could easily be changed by the presentation of counterarguments. Though the relationship between general principles and specific cases seems tentative, on some broad issues of fairness and inclusion, public opinion has clearly changed.[39]

For example, opinion on whether white and black children should attend the same schools has moved from only 30 percent responding yes in 1930 to more than 90 percent responding yes by the early 1980s.[40] Even more striking, the Gallup organization has been asking Americans whether they would be willing to vote for a woman for president since 1937. In 1937 only 33 percent said yes. The number rose to 48 percent in 1949, 57 percent by 1967, 82 percent by 1989, and 92 percent in 2015. A similar path was traced by willingness to vote for a black candidate for president. It began at 38 percent in 1958 and reached 92 percent by 2015.[41]

The Ambivalence of Public Opinion. On some issues, such as broad equity issues regarding minorities and women, the last eight decades have seen a slow, steady, and apparently permanent improvement that represents a fuller

---

Struggling Toward Democracy

There is debate over how well citizens need to be informed about details of the current political environment to act politically.

What do you think?

- What does it mean for our democracy that at any given time nearly half of adults do not know which party has majority control of the U.S. House of Representatives?

- How much do citizens need to know about government and politics to play a meaningful role in them?

realization of the basic principles of our political culture. On the other hand, as was suggested earlier, public opinion reflects a deep ambivalence on the part of the American people across a wide range of issues. Several examples will suffice to make a number of related points.

Perhaps the classic example of policy ambivalence in American politics has to do with abortion and the circumstances under which it should be available. About 55 percent of Americans believe that human life begins at conception (at the moment that the male sperm fertilizes the female egg), but only about 20 percent of Americans believe that abortion should be illegal in all cases. This suggests that 35 percent of Americans are in the uncomfortable position of believing that ending young human life is sometimes necessary. Extensive polling suggests that about 30 percent of Americans think abortion should always be legal, 50 percent think it should sometimes be legal, and about 20 percent say it should always be illegal.[42] In the end, most Americans want abortions to be available with restrictions. In fact, almost 85 percent of Americans want abortion to be available when a woman's life is in danger and more than 75 percent want it available when a woman's health is in danger or a pregnancy results from rape or incest. On the other hand, 88 percent of Americans want doctors to inform women of alternatives to abortion, 78 percent favor a 24-hour waiting period, and 73 percent want parental consent for women under eighteen.

Moreover, Americans are ambivalent about government in general. One long-running survey suggests that public satisfaction with American politics

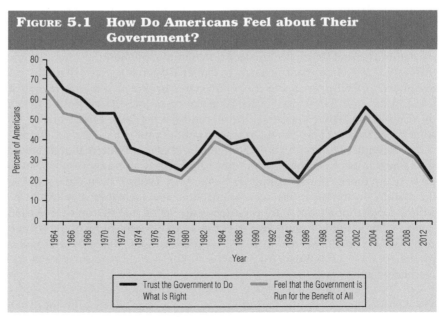

FIGURE 5.1 How Do Americans Feel about Their Government?

Source: The ANES Guide to Public Opinion and Electoral Behavior at www.electionstudies.org/nesguide/toptable/tab5a_1.htmand-electionstudies.org/nesguide/toptable/tab5a_2.htm.

and public life shows a clear decline though it moves up and down in broad waves. The Pew Research Center has pulled together data from many credible sources asking, "How much of the time do you think you can trust the government in Washington to do what is right?" In 1964, 77 percent of those polled answered, "just about always" or "most of the time," whereas only 22 percent answered, "some of the time" or "none of the time." An early low point was reached in 1994 when only 19 percent registered trust in the national government and an astounding 77 percent said it could be trusted only some of the time or not at all. From there, trust in government slowly rebounded through the 1990s before soaring 12 points in the wake of 9/11. In late 2001, 54 percent responded, "just about always" or "most of the time," while only 44 percent responded, "some of the time" or "none of the time." As Figure 5.1 so clearly shows, trust has subsided since.

Political Ideology and the Coherence of Public Opinion

We have seen that most Americans do not pay close attention to politics. Nonetheless, some Americans know more about politics, some a great deal more, than others do, and this small subset of citizens shapes the politics of the country.[43] The people who participate fully in American politics and who make and react to public policy are generally people whose interests, livelihoods, and futures depend upon it in some direct fashion. They are, of course, politicians and senior bureaucrats, but they are also business, media, and education elites for whom understanding the implications of particular political choices is a full-time job. These elites help set the assumptions, terms, and standards by which others understand and interpret the political spectacle. The average citizen, on the other hand, with only a modest education, an hourly wage, and limited savings and investments, is much less likely to be motivated to explore the complexities of interest rates, trade deficits, and whether the dollar is falling against the Euro.

How Many Americans Think in Ideological Terms?   A **political ideology** is an organized and coherent set of ideas that forms a perspective on the political world and how it works. In some nations, the ideological spectrum is quite broad, stretching from traditional monarchists on the right to communists on the left. In the United States, the ideological spectrum is bound by a political culture that highlights democracy and capitalism. Nonetheless, this still leaves room for Americans to differ on how large a role government should play in the nation's social and economic life.

Most public discussions of politics among partisans, politicians, and the media assume that liberalism and conservatism define the political fight in America. When asked, many Americans do place themselves within a liberal/conservative context. In 2012, 33 percent identified as conservative, 21 percent as liberal, but 24 percent of respondents placed themselves in the middle of

political ideology An organized and coherent set of ideas that forms a perspective on the political world and how it works.

Q5 What does it mean to be liberal or conservative, libertarian or populist, in America today?

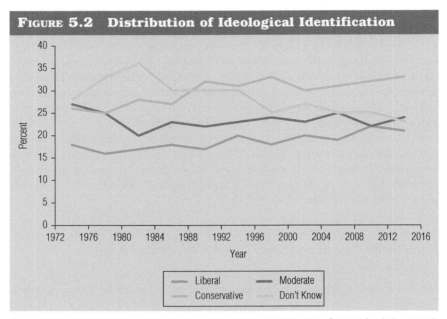

FIGURE 5.2 Distribution of Ideological Identification

Source: ANES website at http://www.electionstudies.org/nesguide/toptable/tab3_1.htm. For ease of analysis, extremely liberal, liberal, and slightly liberal were collapsed to liberal; extremely conservative, conservative, and slightly conservative were collapsed to conservative; don't know and haven't thought about it were collapsed to don't know.

that spectrum, calling themselves moderates, and 23 percent simply refused to locate themselves on the spectrum at all.

The apparent clarity of the traditional liberal/conservative ideological spectrum is muddied by the fact that the widely respected General Social Survey has reported since 1972 that most Americans say they want smaller government and lower taxes *and* they want to spend more, not less, on most government activities. In 2016, although 56 percent of respondents thought their federal income taxes were too high, most favored increased spending on education (73 percent), the poor (72 percent), protecting the environment (64 percent), health (64 percent), social security (60 percent), among other programs.[44] This is a classic paradox in American public opinion.

A book by Christopher Ellis and James Stimson, entitled *Ideology in America*, has sought to unwind this paradox by explaining that a majority of Americans are "symbolically" conservative (they self-identify as conservatives) and "operationally" liberal (they support government services and spending). Moreover, they show that while liberals are generally consistent in policy terms, conservatives tend to be less so. Many conservatives are attracted to the conservative label because they read it to mean careful, thoughtful, and responsible. Others read it to reflect a commitment to traditional social and religious values about family and sexuality. Nonetheless, many of these conservatives support an active government working to improve services and solve problems.[45]

FIGURE 5.3	A Two-Dimensional View of Political Ideology in America

		Government Intervention in Economic Affairs	
		For	Against
Expansion of Personal Freedoms	For	Liberal	Libertarian
	Against	Populist	Conservative

Source: William S. Maddox and Stuart A. Lilie, *Beyond Liberal and Conservative: Reassessing the Political Spectrum* (Washington, D.C.: Cato Institute, 1984), p. 5.

Ideological Types in the United States.   Other scholars contend that the traditional distinction between liberals and conservatives does not capture the range and variety of political ideology in America. William Maddox and Stuart Lilie were among the first to argue that the ideological spectrum in the United States is best understood along two dimensions rather than one. Americans differ both on the role of government in the economy and on the extent of government involvement in securing and expanding personal freedoms. Figure 5.2 clearly shows that conservatives have outnumbered liberals for decades."[46]

Broadly, a **liberal** favors taxes high enough for government to deliver a crucial range of services including education, health care, job training, and other supports to all who need them. Liberals also favor government action to expand and protect individual rights including the rights of minorities, women, and gays to enjoy the full range of opportunities and choices offered by American life.

A **conservative** favors smaller, less expensive, government that protects property, personal security, and social order. Conservatives believe that markets and competition distribute opportunities and rewards to individuals in society far better than government. On the other hand, conservatives believe that government should foster religion, morality, the family, and law as the bases for social order. Hence, conservatives often favor increased spending on the military and police as well as legal regulation of pornography, abortion, affirmative action, and sexual activity.

A **libertarian** favors the maximum of human freedom and personal choice consonant with social order. Hence, libertarians often agree with conservatives that government should be small and inexpensive, but with liberals that women should be able to choose abortions and gays should be able to choose their marriage partners. Libertarians favor a government limited to national defense, the protection of persons and property, and little more.

A **populist** favors an activist government, but expects it to defend the traditional social order. Hence, populists tend to agree with liberals on the size of government and the range of its activities and with conservatives on the importance of traditional social and religious mores. Populists usually want government to be active in supporting individual opportunity and

liberal A liberal generally favors government involvement in economic activity and social life to assure equal opportunity and assistance to those in need.

conservative A conservative generally favors small government, low taxes, deregulation, and the use of market incentives instead of government programs and mandates where possible.

libertarian A libertarian generally favors minimal government involvement in the social and economic lives of individuals and believes that government should be limited mostly to defense and public safety.

populist A populist generally favors government involvement in the economy to assure growth and opportunity but opposes government protection of individual liberties that seem to threaten traditional values.

advancement, to provide access to education, health care, job training, and unemployment compensation when it is needed. They usually oppose social changes, whether in regard to minorities or women, that run ahead of traditional values and local norms.

Have you thought much about where you fit on the ideological spectrum (see Figure 5.3)? Are you a liberal or a conservative, libertarian or populist?

PONDERING REFORM POSSIBILITIES

Given what we know about political socialization, polling, public opinion, and the media, what reforms, if any, would improve the workings of our democracy? Should we, for example, reform our elementary and secondary schools, our colleges and universities for that matter, to better educate students about our political institutions, how they operate, and who runs them and works within them? Or is that dangerously close to indoctrination? What do young people need to know to play a full and productive role in our society and in its politics?

How about immigrants? Immigration, legal and illegal, has been a divisive issue in our recent politics. How easy or difficult should it be to earn citizenship in our nation? What do immigrants need to know about American history, institutions, and politics to fulfill the role of citizen? Does one have to be able to speak English to play an informed and productive role in American life?

Should we be concerned that only about 10 percent of the American public plays an attentive and well-informed role? Should we be grateful, or perhaps at least relieved, that these "opinion leaders" guide their less well-informed citizen brethren, or are they usurping the role that self-governing citizens should play for themselves? These are interesting and important questions, but they remind us that changing what citizens know is a daunting, probably impossible, task.

Chapter Summary

This chapter asked how people come by the political information they have, how much of it they have, and how well it is organized. We found that the process of political socialization is quite effective at transmitting the broad principles of the American political culture—respect for democratic institutions, majority rule, minority rights, diversity, and competition—from one generation to the next. On the other hand, numerous studies show that most Americans pay so little attention to politics that their opinions are loosely held, often inconsistent, and subject to frequent change.

Political socialization is the process by which the fundamental norms and expectations of the society concerning politics are passed from one generation to the next. Early studies of political socialization were focused on the roles and relative impact of parents, families, work settings, social groups, and the media on the political information and attitudes acquired by children and adolescents.

More recently, studies have focused upon how early socialization responds to an individual's movement through the life cycle and to social, political, and economic change, turmoil, and crisis.

We have seen several troublesome developments in how the information that the media report is received and used by citizens and how it affects their views of society and politics. For example, we have seen that the media's penchant for conflict framing sours citizens' evaluations of politics and politicians. Moreover, episodic, as opposed to thematic, framing of issues like poverty leads to harsher evaluations of some groups of people than others. Specifically, depicting individual cases of black poverty leads to higher levels of assumed individual responsibility than does depicting identical cases of white poverty.[47]

Beyond what Americans think about particular issues, the academic study of public opinion is also interested in how much people know, how well organized that information is, and how it is employed in political life. Most Americans are not very interested in politics and do not follow it closely. As a result, public opinion displays a number of properties that some find worrisome. First, the opinions that many Americans hold on political issues are based on very little information. Second, there is often a gap between the principles that people claim to approve and the choices that they make in their own lives and communities. Third, Americans demonstrate a pervasive ambiguity in their thinking about public issues such as abortion, welfare, and government spending.

Most of the time, public opinion in the United States is shaped by the top 10 percent of the population who think consistently and systematically about politics and public affairs. These are the political elites, the media and educational elites who watch and study them, and the corporate and social elites whose jobs and incomes are directly affected by politics and public policy. When this elite is united, as it has been in recent decades on equal rights for minorities and women, all of the information and arguments reaching the general population are uniform, and broad public opinion will conform to it. When the elite divides, as it frequently does on issues like affirmative action and size of government, the public will receive mixed signals and will be divided as well.

Key Terms

agents of socialization	persuasion effect
agenda-setting effect	political culture
conservative	political ideology
educational effect	political socialization
fake news	populist
framing effect	probability sampling
liberal	public opinion
libertarian	push poll

Suggested Readings

Asher, Herbert. *Polling and the Public: What Every Citizen Should Know.* 8th ed. Washington, D.C.: CQ Press, 2010. Asher seeks to make citizens better consumers of polls by describing their design, methodological issues, and interpretation.

Bejarano, Christina E. *The Latina Gender Gap in U.S. Politics.* New York: Routledge, 2014. Latinos are rising in U.S. politics, but Bejarano notes that female Latinos, Latinas, are more involved politically than their male counterparts.

Bode, Leticia, et al., *Words That Matter: How the News and Social Media Shaped the 2016 Presidential Campaign.* Washington, D.C.: Brookings Institution Press, 2018. Bode and her colleagues assess how the news media covered the 2016 campaign and whether that coverage helped voters to understand and choose between the candidates.

Ellis, Christopher and James A. Stimson. *Ideology in America.* New York: Cambridge University Press, 2012. This book explains why so many Americans call themselves conservatives but still support active government and oppose spending cuts.

Erikson, Robert S. and Kent L. Tedin. *American Public Opinion.* 10th ed. New York: Routledge, 2019. The leading general text on American public opinion.

Patterson, Thomas E. *Informing the News: The Need for Knowledge-Based Journalism.* New York: Vintage Books, 2013. Calls for a journalism that does not hide behind false objectivity but gives the public the facts they need to make the democracy work.

Sunstein, Cass R. *#Republic: Divided Democracy in the Age of Social Media.* Princeton, NJ: Princeton University Press, 2017. This book explores the impact on our society of the melding of psychology, technology, and politics.

Web Resources

1 www.cnn.com/politics/
   This website is operated by CNN and is dedicated to providing news and features concerning politics. It provides up-to-date political information.

2 www.fair.org
   Official home page of Fairness and Accuracy in Reporting. This organization is a media watchdog group that reports on the performance of media outlets.

3 www.electionstudies.org/nesguide/nesguide.htm
   The major academic survey of voting behavior in U.S. national election is done by the National Election Studies (NES). The site gives online access to tables and graphs that reveal the trends in public opinion.

4 www.gallup.com
  The Gallup organization website affords use of an enormous number of polls and analyses, both current and archived.

5 www.typology.people-press.org/
  This is the website for the Pew Research Center for the People and the Press. Take the survey to see where you fit in the political typology.

6 www.csmonitor.com
  A prestigious newspaper with national stature. It is an excellent source for domestic and international news coverage.

Notes

1 See, for example, Donald J. Devine, *Political Culture of the United States* (Boston, MA: Little, Brown, 1972); and Herbert McClosky and John Zaller, *The American Ethos: Public Attitudes toward Capitalism and Democracy* (Cambridge, MA: Harvard University Press, 1984), 17.

2 Fred I. Greenstein, *Children and Politics*, rev. ed. (New Haven, CT: Yale University Press, 1969), 157–158. See also David Easton and Jack Dennis, *Children in the Political System* (New York: McGraw-Hill, 1969).

3 Gunnar Myrdal, *An American Dilemma: The Negro Problem and Modern Democracy* (New York: Harper and Brothers, 1944), I: 4, 8.

4 Samuel P. Huntington, *American Politics: The Politics of Disharmony* (Cambridge, MA: Harvard University Press, 1981), 14–15; Seymour Martin Lipset, *American Exceptionalism: A Double-Edged Sword* (New York: Norton, 1996), 19.

5 Greenstein, *Children and Politics*, 12.

6 Jeffrey M. Berry and Sarah Sobieraj, *The Outrage Industry: Political Opinion Media and the New Incivility* (New York: Oxford University Press, 2014).

7 Eitan Hersh, *FiveThirtyEight*, "How Many Republicans Marry Democrats?," June 28, 2016.

8 Frank J. Sorauf, *Party Politics in America*, 2nd ed. (Boston, MA: Little, Brown, 1972), 144. See also M. Kent Jennings and Richard G. Niemi, *Generations and Politics: A Panel Study of Young Adults and Their Parents* (Princeton, NJ: Princeton University Press, 1981), especially chapter 4. More recently, see M. Kent Jennings, Laura Stoker, and Jake Bowers, "Politics across Generations: Family Transmission Reexamined," *Journal of Politics*, vol. 71, No. 3, July 2009, 782–799.

9 Robert S. Erikson and Kent L. Tedin, *American Public Opinion*, 9th ed. (New York: Longman, 2015), 135.

10 Erikson and Tedin, *American Public Opinion*, 123–125.

11 Jan E. Leighley and Jonathan Nagler, *Who Votes Now? Demographics, Issues, Inequality and Turnout in the United States* (Princeton, NJ: Princeton University Press, 2014), 128, 135. Michele Lamont and Mario Small, *Culture and Inequality* (New York: W.W. Norton, 2008).

12 Shanto Ayengar, *Media Politics: A Citizens' Guide* (New York: W.W. Norton, 2011), 2.

13 Pew Research Center, "Pathways to News," July 7, 2016. See also Thomas E. Patterson, *Informing the News: The Need for Knowledge-Based Journalism* (New York: Vintage Books, 2013), 132–133.

14 Pew Research Center for the People and the Press, "Internet Gains on Television as Public's Main News Source," January 4, 2011, http://www.people-press. org/2011/01/04/internet-gains-on-television.

15 Amber E. Boydstun, *Making the News: Politics, the Media, and Agenda-Setting* (Chicago: University of Chicago Press, 2013), 12, 24.

16 Joshua Green, *Devil's Bargain: Steve Bannon, Donald Trump, and the Storming of the Presidency* (New York: Penguin Books, 2017), 47.

17 Gallup, "Americans Increasingly Turn to Specific Sources for News," July 8, 2016.

18 Patterson, *Informing the News*, 84.

19 Bernard C. Cohen, *The Press and Foreign Policy* (Princeton, NJ: Princeton University Press, 1963), 13.

20 Shanto Iyengar and Donald R. Kinder, *News That Matters: Television and American Opinion*, updated edition (Chicago, University of Chicago Press, 2010), 117.

21 Shanto Iyengar, *Is Anyone Responsible? How Television Frames Potitical Issues* (Chicago: University of Chicago Press, 1991), 124–125. See also Patterson, *Informing the News*, 91–92.

22 Deborah J. Schildkraut, "Defining American Identity in the Twenty-First Century: How Much 'There' Is There?" *Journal of Politics*, vol. 69, no. 3 (August 2007): 597–615.

23 Erikson and Tedin, *American Public Opinion*, 28–30.

24 Jack Rosenthal, "Precisely False vs. Approximately False: A Reader's Guide to Polls," *New York Times*, August 7, 2006, Wk 10.

25 Nate Silver, "Spin and Bias Are the Norm in Campaigns' Internal Polling," *New York Times*, December 3, 2012, A17.

26 Nate Cohn, "Election Review: Why Crucial State Polls Turned Out to Be Wrong," *New York Times*, June 1, 2017, A12.

27 F. Chris Garcia and Gabriel R. Sanchez, *Hispanics and the U.S. Political System: Moving into the Mainstream* (Upper Saddle River, NJ: Pearson, 2008), 107.

28 Theodore J. Davis, Jr., *Black Politics Today: The Era of Socioeconomic Transition* (New York: Routledge, 2012), 35, 40, 72. See also Andrew Romano and Allison Samuels, "Is Obama Making It Worse," *Newsweek*, April 16, 2012, 40–42.

29 Mark Hugo Lopez, Rich Morin, and Paul Taylor, "Illegal Immigration Backlash Worries, Divides Latinos," Pew Hispanic Center, October 28, 2010.

30 Simon Romero and Janet Elder, "Hispanics Optimistic About Life, Poll Finds," *Dallas Morning News*, March 6, 2003, 9A. Adam Nagourney and Janet Elder, "Hispanics Back Big Government and Bush, Too," *New York Times*, August 3, 2003, Yt 1, 14.

31 Adam J. Berinsky, *In Time of War: Understanding American Public Opinion from World War II to Iraq* (Chicago: University of Chicago Press, 2009).

32 Pew Research Center for the People and the Press and the Council on Foreign Relations, Calendar and Correspondence, December 2001, 14. New York Times/ CBS News poll, *New York Times*, February 23, 2003, Wk 5.

33 CNN/ORC Poll, October 28, 2011, Question 15 at http://iz.cdn.turner.com/ cnn/2011/images/10/28/rel17h.pdf.

34 James A. Stimson, *Tides of Consent: How Opinion Movements Shape American Politics* (New York: Cambridge University Press, 2004).

35 Erikson and Tedin, *American Public Opinion*, 58–59.

36 Tom Nichols, *The Death of Expertise: The Campaign Against Established Knowledge and Why It Matters* (New York: Oxford University Press, 2017).

37 Erikson and Tedin, *American Public Opinion*, 59.

38 James M. Prothro and Charles M. Grigg, "Fundamental Principles of Democracy: Bases of Agreement and Disagreement," *Journal of Politics*, vol. 22, no. 2 (May 1960): 276–294. See also John Sides, "The 40-Year Decline in the Tolerance of College Students Graphed," *Washington Post*, March 9, 2017.

39 Darren Davis and Brian Silver, "Civil Liberties versus Security," *American Journal of Political Science*, 48, no. 1, (Jan. 2004), 28-46.

40 Richard J. Niemi, John Mueller, and Tom W. Smith, *Trends in Public Opinion: A Compendium of Survey Data* (New York: Greenwood Press, 1989), 22–23, 180.

41 The Gallup Organization, "In U.S. Socialist Presidential Candidates Least Appealing," June 22, 2015.

42 http://www.pollingreport.com/abortion.htm. See also the poll archive at http:// www.youdebate.com/abortion.htm.

43 John R. Zaller, *The Nature and Origins of Mass Opinion* (New York: Cambridge University Press, 1992).

44 Tom Raum, "Study: We Talk of Austerity, Want New Spending," *Dallas Morning News*, March 9, 2013, A11.

45 Christopher Ellis and James A. Stimson, *Ideology in America* (New York: Cambridge University Press, 2012). See also Robert S. Erikson, Michael B. Mackuen, and James A. Stimson, *The Macro Polity* (New York: Cambridge University Press, 2002), 223–230.

46 William S. Maddox and Stuart A. Lilie, *Beyond Liberal and Conservative: Reassessing the Political Spectrum* (Washington, D.C.: Cato Institute, 1984), 59.

47 Shanto Iyengar, *Is Anyone Responsible? How Television Frames Political Issues* (Chicago: University of Chicago Press, 1991), 67–68.

Chapter 6

FACTIONS TODAY
Interest Groups and Political Parties

Focus Questions: from reading to thinking

Q1 What types of interest groups are most influential in American politics?

Q2 How do interest groups try to influence public policy?

Q3 What role do lobbyists play in the political process?

Q4 Are American political parties in decline and, if so, should we be worried about it?

Q5 Are interest groups or political parties the best vehicle for representing citizen opinion to government?

THE FIRST AMENDMENT RIGHTS TO ASSEMBLE AND PETITION, AND THEIR LIMITS

The Constitution TODAY

First Amendment (in part): "Congress shall make no law. . . abridging the right of the people peaceably to assemble, and to petition the government for a redress of grievances."

Citizen protest, usually peaceful, sometimes not, is a constant running through American history from the Boston Massacre, through the civil rights marches of the 1960s, to the Tea Party, Occupy Wall Street (OWS), and Black Lives Matter movements of recent years. Authorities almost always push back against protesters; usually it is the protesters that give in, but sometimes it is the authorities who are forced to retreat.

On September 17, 2011, several hundred protesters, calling themselves the Occupy Wall Street (OWS) movement, occupied Zuccotti Park in the financial district of lower Manhattan. OWS was a grassroots movement; it had no leadership structure, made decisions by direct democracy, and articulated a diffuse set of complaints including social injustice, economic inequality, and corporate dominance of government. Nonetheless, their signature slogan, "We are the 99 percent," protesting the greed of the 1 percent, captured the nation's attention.

Within a month, the OWS movement had spread to all of America's large cities and to hundreds of smaller cities and towns. Soon, police forces around the U.S. were moving in on OWS encampments, sometimes gently, sometimes forcefully, usually citing violations of city laws and codes, to break up the camps. OWS resisted government attempts to end their occupations by citing the First Amendment "right of the people peaceably to assemble, and to petition the government for a redress of grievances." Protesters always believe that the right to assemble and petition should be viewed broadly, but city governments and the police are the established order, so no one should be too surprised that their patience with protest is limited.

"The right of the people peaceably to assemble" means that citizens may gather in public to share their views, hear from each other, and organize for further action. The right "to petition the government for a redress of grievances" means that, individually or in groups, citizens have the right to address complaints, criticisms, and demands for change to public officials. These First Amendment rights are the foundation for modern interest group and political party organization, but they have much broader application as well.

Until well into the twentieth century, First Amendment limits applied only against the national government (recall that the First Amendment begins, "Congress shall make no law") unless individual state constitutions provided similar protections. In the late 1930s the Supreme Court began using the "due process clause" of the Fourteenth Amendment to limit the actions of state and local governments as well. The modern meaning of the right to peaceably assemble was established in *Dejonge v. Oregon* (1937). Oregon had made it a crime for radicals, in this case communists, to meet. The Supreme Court held that "peaceable assembly for lawful discussion cannot be made a crime." Justice Oliver Wendell Holmes made the even more challenging point that the constitution protected "free thought—not free thought for those who agree with us but freedom for the thought that we hate."

Freedom for the thought that we hate does not come naturally. *National Socialist party v. Skokie* (1977) was decided by the U.S. Court of Appeals for the Seventh Circuit. The U.S. Supreme Court agreed with the ruling of the Seventh Circuit and so declined to hear an appeal. The facts of this remarkable case are that public officials in Skokie, Illinois, had passed ordinances trying to prohibit a march by American Nazis, swastikas and all, through the small city of Skokie near Chicago. The Nazis wanted to parade in Skokie because it was home to many Jews, some of whom were Holocaust survivors. Drawing on Justice Holmes' "freedom for the thought that we hate" argument, Judge Bernard Decker held that "It is better to allow those who preach racial hate to expend their venom in rhetoric rather than to be panicked into. . . permitting the government to decide what its citizens must say and hear." Does that sound right to you? Some would argue that excluding Nazi hate speech, or speech directed against blacks, gays, or Muslims from the public square is no great loss.

Still, as with most rights, there are limits on the right to assemble and express one's views publicly. Courts have upheld the rights of cities to require permits and control the size, location or route, and timing of gatherings, parades, demonstrations, and similar events. In the case of the OWS movement, Zuccotti Park was a private park to which the public usually had access, which makes it a little murky, but many of the Occupy sites around the country clearly were public property.

INTEREST GROUPS AND POLITICAL PARTIES

In previous chapters we saw that most Americans share a broad commitment to ideas like individualism, liberty, equality, democracy, constitutionalism, and the rule of law. These commitments are said to be embodied in a political system built around openness, fairness, due process, freedom of speech and assembly, and the rights of citizens to petition their government for redress of grievances. But beneath this broad agreement on basic principles are politics and the struggle for political advantage. So how do individuals who see politics similarly come together to press their opinions on society and government. As we shall see, the answer is that citizens who share interests relevant to politics come together in interest groups and political parties. The founding generation knew this and it gave them great pause. They were deeply skeptical of what James Madison called "factions" because they believed that there was a public interest and a common good and that statesmen might discover and act upon them. Factions, groups, and parties reflected divisions and disagreements within the governing class and perhaps the public about the nature, even the existence, of the common good.

In this chapter we describe the interest group system in America, the types of groups that form, the resources they bring to the political fight, and the tactics they employ to get their way. We also discuss the role of political parties, both major parties, Republicans and Democrats, and minor or third parties, in our politics. We close the chapter by assessing the relative strengths and weaknesses of interest groups, minor parties, and major parties in representing citizen opinions and interests.

We begin from the simple observation that every society has insiders and outsiders. The insiders are the voters and the members of interest groups and political parties whose mostly mainstream views are represented in and reflected by the political system. The outsiders are the citizens who may or may not vote, may or may not belong to interest groups or political parties, but whose views are seen as unorthodox or radical and are regularly ignored and sometimes suppressed by the political system and the broader society.

Usually, the insiders dominate. Interest groups and their lobbyists engage elected and appointed officials every day. They offer advice, information, and support to assure that their views are heard and their interests addressed. Some interest groups, though not most, are closely identified with one party or the other—the Chamber of Commerce with the Republicans and the AFL-CIO with the Democrats—so they join in the electoral fray with all they have. Most hang back during elections in order to preserve the option of working

In testimony before the Senate Finance Committee, U.S. Chamber of Commerce President Tom Donohue and AFL-CIO President Richard Trumka (right) clashed over tax policy.

closely with whoever comes out on top. Once the ballots are counted and the winners take office, politics as usual continues largely as before. Democratic insiders may replace Republican insiders, as they did when the Obama administration arrived in Washington in 2009, or Republican insiders may return, as they did with the triumphant House Republicans in 2011, but many Americans see little real difference. Occasionally, as in 2016, the outsiders rise up and demand that the political system be changed to better represent them and reflect their views, interests, and needs. But as Donald Trump and we now see, the system resists.

INTEREST GROUPS IN AMERICAN POLITICS

The American Founders were keenly aware that, at least since the ancient Greeks and Romans, students of politics had warned that social divisions of class, party, and group threaten political stability. James Madison called all of these social divisions "factions" and declared a faction to be "a number of citizens . . . who are united by . . . some common impulse of passion, or of interest, adverse to . . . the permanent and aggregate interests of the community."[1] The most prominent contemporary definition of **interest groups** comes from David B. Truman's classic study of the governmental process. In terms similar to Madison's, Truman defined an interest group as "any group that, on the basis of one or more shared attitudes, makes certain claims upon other groups in the society."[2] Others highlight the interplay of interest groups and government. Graham Wilson noted that "interest groups are generally defined as organizations, separate from government though often in close partnership with government, which attempt to influence public policy."[3]

interest groups Organizations based on shared interests that attempt to influence society and government to act in ways consonant with the organization's interests.

The obvious presence and influence of interest groups in U.S. politics have led politicians and scholars to ask whether interest groups strengthen or weaken democracy. One perspective, **elitism**, contends that effective, well-funded interest groups are much more likely to form, win access, and exercise influence on behalf of the interests of the wealthy and the prominent than of the poor and the humble. The other, **pluralism**, suggests that interest groups represent the interests of citizens to government and that the struggle between groups produces a reasonable policy balance. But let us also keep in mind that in unsettled times populist candidates can, as Donald Trump showed, run effectively against the implications of both elitism and pluralism. The rallying cry of populism has always been "the people" against "the elites," with elites being both congressional leaders and the lobbyist representatives of the "interests." The call to "drain the swamp" is a challenge to insiders in general in the name of a people who have "had enough."

elitism The belief that the interest group structure of American politics is skewed toward the interest of the wealthy.

pluralism The belief that the interest group structure of American politics produces a reasonable policy balance.

Let us keep the insights of elitism, pluralism, and populism in mind as we explore three key aspects of the interest groups in America. First, we describe the variety of interest groups now active in American politics. Second, we ask what resources lead to influence for groups. And third, we ask what strategies interest groups use to affect the policymaking process.

The Rise of Interest Groups

Social change and economic development alter the environments in which people live, work, and govern. Initially, it was assumed by David Truman and many others that as change adversely affects people's interests they naturally and automatically formed groups to protect themselves. In recent decades, scholars like Mancur Olson, Jack Walker, Robert Salisbury, Frank Baumgartner, and Dan Tichenor showed that some kinds of groups form more easily than others and that the group system is more complicated and diverse than previously thought.[4] Business, corporate, and professional interests are well represented. On the other hand, it takes the support of wealthy patrons, foundations, and even government agencies to encourage groups to form around and fight for interests—the poor, the disabled, children, and the mentally challenged—that otherwise might not form so readily or fight so effectively.

A couple of quick examples will help make the point that some potential interest groups form more easily and fully than others. First, the pharmaceutical industry is fairly concentrated, with just a few dozen major drug companies leading the way, and a large sum of money at stake. They care a great deal about the length and expense of the government's drug testing and approval process. They are highly organized and very effective. Civil rights groups, consumer safety groups, and environmental groups, on the other hand, though they have huge potential membership—after all, we all want clean air—often attract only a small fraction of their potential members into the group as dues paying members.

Why wouldn't environmental groups form and be powerful if we all want clean air? Because, scholars have explained, the benefit—clean air—is non-excludable. If only some join the environmental group, pay their dues, and some policy success leads to cleaner air, the non-joiners cannot be excluded from breathing the cleaner air. They are called "free-riders" in the interest group literature and we are all free-riders in the sense that we benefit from the efforts of many groups—clean government groups, consumer safety groups, or education reform groups—that we do not join and actively support. Do you see why the drug companies might form a group, contribute funds to it, hire lobbyists, and win their policy battles more readily than environmental groups or consumer safety groups?

Types of Interest Groups

The most comprehensive study of interest groups in America comes from the work of Frank Baumgartner and Beth Leech. In 1959, the *Encyclopedia of Associations* listed fewer than 6,000 groups. Today the same source lists over 25,000. These groups now spend about $3.5 billion each year lobbying Congress and the executive branch. Baumgartner and Leech summarize an extensive literature showing that fully three-quarters of the group system reflects occupational interests. Almost 40 percent of interest groups are private sector occupational groups, including corporate, business, and labor interests, and

Q1 What types of interest groups are most influential in American politics?

about 35 percent are public sector, not-for-profit, groups, drawing members from educational, health, religious, science, and public affairs occupations. The remaining 25 percent of the interest group system are public interest and citizen membership groups. These draw members based on substantive interests, such as consumer, environmental, or international affairs, and member attributes such as ideology, partisanship, race, ethnicity, and gender.

Not surprisingly, given the wide array of interest groups in our society, organizations and individuals have an equally wide array of reasons for joining interest groups. Scholars have sorted these reasons into three broad categories: material benefits, purposive benefits, and solidary benefits. Material benefits are the real and tangible benefits, like lower taxes, lighter regulation, higher wages, and group insurance rates that often come with or are at least hoped to result from group membership. Purposive benefits refer to the substantive, partisan, and ideological goals, like fighting hunger, supporting Republicans, or battling socialists that might lead a person to join a group. And solidary benefits are the simple joys and social rewards of meeting, getting to know, and working with like-minded people. Organizations and persons often join interest groups for a mix of reasons, but anticipation of material, purposive, and solidary or social benefits are almost always among them.

Private and Public Sector Occupational Groups. Groups representing the economic interests of their members are the oldest as well as the most numerous members of the interest group system. Such groups form early and in large numbers because members share clearly defined interests that can be helped or hurt in significant ways by the actions of other groups, the government, or the market in general.

The business community has always been the most thoroughly organized part of the interest group system because it has natural advantages of money, organization, and expertise. In fact, the political-economist Charles E. Lindblom famously used the phrase "the privileged position of business" to describe the place of businesses and corporations in capitalist or market economies. Not only do businessmen serve in prominent roles in government, government policy is carefully designed to stimulate business and employment. Elected officials know that their tenure in office depends on a healthy economy and they listen closely when leading business figures talk about what policies will most likely produce the desired results.[5]

peak associations Peak associations, like the U.S. Chamber of Commerce, represent the general interests of business.

Peak Associations represent the interests of business in general. The National Association of Manufacturers (NAM) traces its roots to a meeting held in Cincinnati in January 1895. The NAM is the nation's largest industrial trade association, with 14,000 members. The national Chamber of Commerce, the principal voice of small business in the United States, was founded in 1912. The national organization now includes nearly 3,000 affiliated state and local chambers and an underlying membership of more than 3 million businesses. The newest major group representing American business is the Business Roundtable formed in 1972. The Roundtable is open only to America's largest companies—160 of the

Fortune 500 largest corporations were founding members—and is a forum for discussion of their shared concerns and interests.

Of the peak business associations, the Chamber of Commerce is the most politically dynamic and aggressive. The Chamber has been headed since 1997 by 80-year-old Thomas Donahue. Donahue manages an annual budget of $250 million and a staff of 500, including scores of lobbyists, economists, researchers and analysts, and communications experts. The Chamber spent $104 million on lobbying in 2016, far more than the $65 million spent by the number two National Association of Realtors. Donahue was paid just over $6 million in 2016. From the perspective of American business, government programs and regulations threaten many interests, so it makes a lot of sense to spend the money needed to influence those programs and regulations.[6]

Almost 6,000 **trade associations** bring together companies in a single business, commercial, and industrial sector. These trade associations go by such familiar names as the Aerospace Industries Association, the American Electronics Association, the American Petroleum Institute, and the Automobile Manufacturers Association. Moreover, many individual corporations are large, wealthy, and diverse enough to constitute formidable concentrations of interest by themselves. Names such as American Airlines, AT&T, Bank of America, General Motors, IBM, General Electric, Microsoft, and Google come immediately to mind.

trade associations Associations formed by businesses and related interests involved in the same commercial, trade, or industrial sector.

The modern labor movement began with the formation of the American Federation of Labor (AFL) in 1886. The AFL was a federation of skilled trade or craft unions including the Brick Layers, Carpenters, Cigar Makers, Glass Workers, Pipe Fitters, and Tool and Die Makers. Samuel Gompers of the Cigar Makers was the AFL's first president. The Congress of Industrial Organizations (CIO), first headed by John L. Lewis of the United Mine Workers, was formed in 1935. George Meany of the Carpenters, head of the AFL from the mid-1940s, helped engineer a merger of the AFL and CIO in 1955 and became the first president of the new **AFL-CIO.**

AFL-CIO Formed in 1955 when the American Federation of Labor joined with the Congress of Industrial Organizations, the 12.5 million member AFL-CIO is the largest labor organization in the United States.

The AFL-CIO declined from 20 million members in 1980 to 15 million in 1995. John Sweeney's election as AFL-CIO president in 1995 promised a new focus on recruitment; instead, membership continued to decline. In 2009, the AFL-CIO elected Richard Trumka as its president. Trumka, Secretary-Treasurer of the AFL-CIO and former president of the United Mineworkers, promised once again to focus intently on union organization and expansion. Despite their best efforts, the Great Recession of 2009 hit unions hard, driving AFL-CIO membership down to 12.5 million in 2017.

In recent decades, while private sector unions have slipped, public sector unions have expanded. While only 10.7 percent of all U.S. workers belong to unions, 35 percent of public sector workers belong to unions. About 35 percent of teachers are union members, with the 3 million member National Education Association (NEA) and the 1.5 million member American Federation of Teachers (AFT), an AFL-CIO affiliate, being the largest and most active. Nonetheless, the

---

Struggling Toward Democracy

Just 10.7 percent of American workers belong to labor unions, down from 24 percent in 1970 and 35 percent in 1955.
What do you think?
- What are the implications, positive and negative, for the American society and economy of the decline of labor unions?
- Why do you think labor unions have seen such precipitous declines?

Great Recession of 2009 provided an opening for several Republican governors, led by Scott Walker of Wisconsin and John Kasich of Ohio, successfully to push legislation limiting public sector unions.

Major professional associations, like those that serve lawyers, doctors, social workers, academics, and others formed in the late nineteenth and early twentieth centuries. These professional associations formed to set standards and design admission requirements, share information of general interest, and protect member interests against competitors and government regulators at the local, state, and national levels. The American Bar Association (ABA) was established in 1876; many of the nation's academic and scholarly associations were organized in the two decades that followed; and the American Medical Association (AMA) was founded in 1901. These professional associations derive influence from the respect that society awards to their members and from the expertise or specialized knowledge that they possess.

Public Interest and Citizen Groups.   Most private sector and some public sector occupation groups have economic or professional assets, money, expertise, and sometimes numbers to trade for government attention and assistance. The public interest movement, comprised of a diffuse set of membership groups, law firms, think tanks, lobbying groups, and community organizations, depends more on information and publicity to make both business executives and government bureaucrats look beyond narrow self-interests to the broader public interest. Political scientist Ronald Hrebenar defines public interest groups as groups pursuing goods that cannot be made available to some without generally being made available to all.[7] Such goods include honest government, safer toys, highways, and workplaces, and cleaner air and water.

Two of the most famous public interest groups are Common Cause and Ralph Nader's collection of Public Citizen groups. Common Cause was established as a "people's lobby" in 1970 by John Gardner, a former Johnson administration official. It focuses on "structure and process" issues such as ethics laws, open government laws, and campaign finance reform.[8] Nader's Public Citizen (1971) groups, of which Congress Watch is the most well known, lobby Congress and the executive branch on a wide range of consumer issues. Other public interest groups include the Wilderness Society, the League of Women Voters, the Young Americans for Freedom, and the Free Congress Foundation. Although it is hard to argue against the importance of pristine wilderness, clean air, and frugal and efficient government, the public interest movement is frequently criticized for limiting itself to an upper middle-class agenda.

Major elements of American society are not well represented either by economic groups or by consumer and public interest groups. Minorities and women, for example, have often felt that they must organize to demand access to America's economic mainstream before occupational and consumer groups can be of much assistance to them. Nonetheless, civil rights organizations, such as the NAACP, the Urban League, the Southern Christian Leadership Conference (SCLC), the League of United Latin American Citizens (LULAC), and the Native American Rights Fund (NARF) work to assure opportunity and fair treatment for the groups from which their members are drawn. Similarly, the National Organization for Women (NOW) has sought to assure women's rights in society, before the law, in the workplace, and in regard to procreation and reproduction.

Interest Group Resources

Different interest groups bring different resources to bear in pursuit of their goals. Some groups have millions of members. Others, like the American Bar Association (ABA), have fewer members, but the members they have are wealthy and have professional expertise upon which the government must draw. Still others like Common Cause and Congress Watch draw their strength from strong leadership, a membership intensely committed to the goals of the organization, and tight networks of strategic alliances with other groups pursuing related interests. In this section we explore the mix of resources available to American interest groups.

Q2 How do interest groups try to influence public policy?

Size of Membership.   Large groups such as the 38 million member American Association of Retired Persons (AARP) or the 12.5 million member AFL-CIO demand attention simply because of their size. Ultimately, however, both unity and coverage must accompany size if it is to have its full effect.

American unions provide good examples of how the influence that might flow from size can be compromised by a lack of unity within a group and a lack of coverage. If the membership of a group is divided over policy or over candidates in an election, that group will carry less weight than it otherwise might. Coverage is just as important as cohesion. The ABA claims fewer than half of lawyers and the AMA claims only about one-quarter of doctors as members. Public interest and consumer groups include only tiny fractions of potential members if one assumes that all citizens or all consumers are potential members.

Intensity of Membership.   Large majorities of Americans favor some form of gun control and some access to abortion services. However, well-organized and intensely interested minorities can often overcome unorganized majorities. The 5 million member National Rifle Association (NRA), whose clout represents both its size and its intensity, strongly opposes most limitations on the rights of gun owners. Similarly, much of the Right to Life movement favors outright prohibitions of abortion services. Both groups are sufficiently well organized, funded, and motivated that their influence over government decision making in areas of interest to their members is greater than their simple numbers would suggest.

Financial Resources of Members.   Money, like numbers and intensity, is critical to interest group success. Scholars point out that "quality leadership, access to political decision makers, a favorable public image, and a hardworking and knowledgeable staff are just some of the resources that can be purchased with

Getty Images/Justin Sullivan

Attendees at the 2013 National Rifle Association (NRA) convention in Houston visit one of 500 exhibits. Seventy thousand people attended the three-day meeting. A committed membership is a key source of interest group influence.

the careful expenditure of adequate amounts of money."[9] Money helps groups both organize internally and exercise influence externally.

Businesses, interest groups, and labor unions spend $260 million a month on lobbying the federal government. The Open Secrets website tracks lobbying in great detail. In 2015, interest groups spent a record $3.23 billion on lobbying. Three business sectors, pharmaceuticals and health products ($240 million), finance, insurance, and real estate ($159 million), and energy and natural resources ($132 million) led the pack. In 2016, when overall spending dropped slightly, to $3.15 billion, the same three sectors again led.[10]

Prestige and Expertise of Members. Some groups—business, labor, and professional groups, for example—are in better positions than other groups— consumer, wilderness, and civil rights groups, for example—to claim decisive or exclusive expertise. Most members of Congress and most citizens feel that they have enough personal insight and experience to have opinions on whether we need more national forests or stronger affirmative action laws. Most members of Congress and most citizens do not feel competent to set waste disposal policy without input from the chemical industry or drug approval guidelines without input from the pharmaceutical industry.

Organization and Leadership. Interest groups are organized either as unitary organizations or as federations. Common Cause, the NRA, NAACP, and NOW are unitary. Members belong directly to the organization, and there is a single level of administrative structure, usually a national office or headquarters. Although the organization may have local chapters, they are all directed from the national headquarters. Federations, on the other hand, are made up of member organizations that have a substantial degree of independence. In general, unitary organizations are more energetic and coherent than federations.

Different kinds of organizations also require different kinds of leaders. Charismatic leaders, of whom Martin Luther King Jr. is the most frequently cited example, lead by force of personality and will. Entrepreneurial leaders, of whom Ralph Nader and Tom Donahue are good examples, lead by energy, creativity, and strategic sense. Charismatic and entrepreneurial leaders are particularly common in unitary membership organizations, where their energy and ideas can fuel the entire organization. Managers are more common in federated organizations, where consensus must be negotiated among the leaders and members of the constituent organizations.

Some interest groups also have extensive staffs who provide analysis, policy, and legal support to their leaders. The pharmaceutical and health products lobby has more than 1,300 registered lobbyists in Washington and they spent $246 million on lobbying in 2016, more than any other industry. The National Rifle Association (NRA) has a Washington staff of over 460 persons and the American Petroleum Institute has a Washington staff of 400.

The Role of Lobbyists. **Lobbyists** attempt to influence government decision making in ways that benefit or at least avoid harm to those they represent. Traditionally, the chief instrument of influence for most lobbyists is information that is useful to policymakers in deciding how to proceed on the issues before them. Lobbyists provide information that supports their positions and withhold or suppress information that seems to argue against their positions. Decision makers such as members of Congress must hope that the contest for influence between and among lobbyists will produce enough diverse information to present a reasonably full and accurate picture.

lobbyists Hired agents who seek to influence government decision making in ways that benefit or limit harm to their clients.

The very top lobbyists often move back and forth, through what is referred to as the "revolving door," between important roles in government and lucrative lobbying jobs. Former congressman Billy Tauzin was a Democrat from Louisiana's third congressional district from 1980 to 1995 before switching to the Republican Party and serving until 2005. Tauzin declined to run for reelection in 2004 and instead became President and CEO of PhRMA, the trade and lobby association for the pharmaceutical industry, from 2005 to 2010. With his broad contacts in Congress and the clout of the pharmaceutical industry behind him, he played a central role in assuring that the Obamacare program that emerged from Congress in 2009 and early 2010 was acceptable to the drug companies. For his services, PhRMA paid Tauzin $11.6 million in 2010. Known as the "Tauzin line," this remains the top lobbyist salary on record.[11] Over the last two decades, nearly half of the senators and House members who left Congress stayed in Washington to lobby.[12] Many former high-ranking elected officials, military officers, and bureaucrats also act as lobbyists after they retire or leave office.

Q3 What role do lobbyists play in the political process?

Struggling Toward Democracy

Nearly half of U.S. congressmen and senators who leave office remain in Washington as lobbyists.
What do you think?
- Is this their right as citizens or is it a threat to our democracy?
- Should there be limits on the public role of former elected officials?

Family ties are also common between public officials and lobbyists. Literally dozens of legislators and their senior staffers are married to lobbyists. Increasingly, as legislators serve in Congress into their seventies, eighties, and beyond, their grown children join the lobby. Separating family life from business is difficult when you eat together, relax together, and even sleep together.[13]

The Trump administration has raised old issues and invented some new ones. Corey Lewandowski, Trump's first campaign manager, was fired during the campaign and immediately established his own political consulting business. Former Lt. Gen. Michael Flynn, the campaign's chief foreign policy adviser and President Trump's first national security adviser, was fired after a month for undisclosed foreign contacts and lobbying activities. And what to make of the president's family, Ivanka Trump and her husband Jared Kushner in the White House while their siblings run the family businesses. How would you distinguish potential conflicts of interest, meaning political decisions and choices that aid or advantage the family businesses, from innocuous family chit chat?

Interest Group Goals and Strategies

Most interest groups seek to gather, shape, and disseminate information in the hope of beneficially influencing the opinions and behavior of policymakers and, often, the public. Interest groups employ a fairly standard set of tools in their work. They gather information; consult with government officials; testify before committees, boards, and commissions; participate in campaigns and elections; organize and deploy their members; conduct public education; and build coalitions. Most interest groups do not engage in all of these activities with the same frequency and confidence. Depending on the type of group and the nature of its resources, some groups employ an "inside" strategy and some an "outside" strategy. Both aim to influence public officials, but in different ways.

inside strategy Lobbying strategies usually involving direct contact with elected and appointed officials or their staff to shape their view of issues.

Inside Lobbying. The goal of an **inside strategy** is to convince the elected and appointed officials, usually by means of close and quiet consultation, to develop or modify a policy or to take some action in the interpretation or implementation of a policy that would serve the interests of a group and its members. Since most of Congress's work is done in committee, lobbyists focus there as well. Committees debate pending legislation, adding, modifying, or dropping provisions as they go and lobbyists work hard to have a role in this process. Lobbyists also attend and may testify or present evidence at administrative hearings where laws or regulations affecting their clients may be under discussion and review. Lobbyists need to know what is happening in relation to their clients' concerns at all times and affect the process where they can.

Interest groups pursuing an inside strategy explicitly attempt to establish an exchange relationship, a relationship of mutual assistance and advantage, with government officials. Fundamentally, the exchange is information and financial contributions for access and influence. Interest groups and their lobbyist representatives provide government decision makers with useful information about how a proposed change might actually work and about how it would be received in relevant policy communities and publics. Public officials offer lobbyists access to and some influence, sometimes a great deal of influence, over the policymaking process. At a cruder level, campaign contributions are exchanged for targeted legislative benefits, about which we will hear more in our discussion of Congress.

Outside Lobbying. An **outside strategy** may involve media advertising designed to educate the public, or letter-writing, phone, and fax campaigns by interest group members and others designed to impress public officials with the breadth and depth of concern in the public over a particular issue. The range of outsider strategies may go beyond education campaigns and electioneering to protest and civil disobedience. Protests, demonstrations, and sometimes even violence are weapons of last resort, usually employed only by the poor and the weak. The classic example of the effectiveness of protests and demonstrations is the civil rights movement of the 1950s and early 1960s. The pictures of demonstrators under assault by water cannon, mounted police, and dogs confronted Americans with the tremendous gap between promises of liberty and opportunity and the reality of black lives.

Outside lobbying is a way to step up the pressure on public officials by showing that concern in the public is widespread. Elected officials are particularly sensitive to the opinions of persons who care enough to write a personal

outside strategy Lobbying strategies intended to inform and shape public opinion as an indirect way of influencing policymakers.

AP Photo/SIPPL Sipa USA/Erik McGregor

Supporters of "Rise and Resist" demonstrate against the Trump administration health care program outside the Trump International Hotel and Tower in New York City. People in the streets will often get lawmakers' attention when a quiet meeting in their office will not.

letter, make a phone call, or show up with signs outside a congressman's office. When demonstrations attract the media, demonstrators get to express their concerns to the broader public and elected officials have to answer uncomfortable questions, often on the record. Lobbying often works, but there are other tools in the interest group toolbox.[14]

Litigation. Interest groups that fail to influence public officials directly or indirectly by influencing public opinion may turn to the courts. Litigation, which is another name for bringing a case in court, is time-consuming and expensive. Few interest groups have experienced litigators on staff, though some, like the Chamber of Commerce, NAACP, and the Sierra Club, certainly do. Others must either hire a public affairs law firm or join a coalition of like-minded groups that includes such a firm.

The purpose of most interest group **litigation** is to demand a beneficial policy change or forestall an adverse change. Famously, from the 1930s through the 1960s, the NAACP, unable to move the political branches of the government toward equal rights, initiated a series of court cases that eventually brought down segregation and other forms of overt discrimination. The National Organization for Women (NOW), the Mexican-American Legal Defense and Education Fund (MALDEF), and, more recently, the gay rights Lambda Legal Defense and Education Fund, all followed similar strategies.

litigation Bringing a case in court for the purpose of demanding a beneficial policy change or avoiding an adverse change.

AP Photo/Rex Features

Former neuro-surgeon Ben Carson, a candidate for the Republican presidential nomination, addressed the 2016 Conservative Political Action Conference (CPAC). The conference, a project of the American Conservative Union, brings together conservative politicians, pundits, and activists for three days of speeches and workshops. CPAC exemplifies the "party as social network" idea.

POLITICAL PARTIES IN THE UNITED STATES

The distinguishing characteristic of a **political party** has always been that its candidates compete in elections in the hope of winning executive branch offices and majority control of legislatures. Parties recruit and screen candidates, offer platforms, contest elections, and, if they win, attempt to implement their campaign promises. The losing party acts as a watchdog, criticizes the governing party, exposes corruption and abuse of power, and prepares for the next election. Contemporary students of political parties have generally agreed with E.E. Schattschneider that modern democratic politics are unthinkable except in terms of parties. Table 6.1 highlights the several key roles played by parties in our politics.

political party An organization designed to elect government officeholders under a given label.

While the basic goals of American political parties—winning office, controlling public policy, keeping an eye on the opposition—seem clear, scholars disagree about the origins and driving dynamics of parties. Some scholars call for principled or responsible political parties. The "responsible party model" holds that parties should be clear about what they stand for so voters can know what they will get if they put that party in office. Responsible parties campaign on coherent and detailed platforms, seek to implement them if elected, and stand to be judged on them when they seek reelection.[15]

Other scholars see political parties as loose coalitions of like-minded social groups and interests. In this view, parties are "big tents," with the Democratic tent sheltering mostly liberal to moderate people and interests and the Republican tent sheltering mostly moderate to conservative people and interests. Both tents have their flaps up so that new members and new groups can enter.[16]

TABLE 6.1 Political Parties in Democratic Politics

1 Parties provide channels through which ordinary citizens can affect the course of government.
2 Parties give political leaders reliable bases on which to build support for their programs in the legislature and among the general electorate.
3 Parties offer a means for organizing dissent against the policies of an incumbent administration.
4 Parties, to protect their own rights of free expression, are natural guardians of civil liberties.
5 Parties "keep each other honest," since each party has a political interest in exposing corruption, deception, and abuses of authority by its opposition.
6 Parties perform many of the chores of democracy, such as getting voters registered and to the polls, disseminating information, and organizing public meetings for expression of opinion.
7 Parties recruit and screen candidates for public office, from local election officials to president of the United States.
8 Parties spur the development of new ideas.

Source: A. James Reichley, *The Life of the Parties: A History of American Political Parties* (New York: Rowman & Littlefield, 2000), 340.

Still other scholars reject both the responsible party and big tent models. They argue that parties are best seen as "social networks" of party officials, candidates, officeholders, and voters, but also supportive interest groups, social movements, campaign consultants, donors, and partisan elements of the media. The danger, of course, is that parties as social networks become so porous and easily penetrable that they stand for little. Donald Trump's nomination and election have often been described as a "hostile takeover" of the Republican Party that might change the party brand on issues from national security to trade to taxes. Parties always balance commitment to their traditional principles with adaptation to a new leader's policy views and campaign promises. But party brands can be muddied if the changes are too great or too abrupt.[17] As we shall see below, each of these perspectives on American parties provides insights as we look at parties and partisanship in campaigns, elections, and governance.

We now turn to the place of parties in the American political system. First, we assess the state of modern political parties in the electorate, as organizations, and in the government. Second, we assess the special role that minor parties play in American politics and how they, together with the interest groups discussed above, relate to and affect the performance of the major parties. Third, we ask what changes the future is likely to hold for American political parties and how we can expect parties to respond to those changes. Finally, we ask whether specific reforms might improve the performance of parties.

THE STATE OF POLITICAL PARTIES IN THE UNITED STATES

party in the electorate The voters who identify more or less directly and consistently with a political party.

party organization The permanent structure of party offices and officials who administer the party apparatus on a day-to-day basis.

party in government The officeholders, both elected and partisan-appointed officials, who ran under or have been associated with the party label.

What is the state of the major political parties in the United States today? We will look at them in each of three classic roles: **party in the electorate, party organization**, and **party in government**.[18] We shall see that parties have been strengthening among the voters, stronger in government, and still stronger as national and, increasingly, as state and local organizations. In fact, a "partisan conflict index" maintained by the Federal Reserve Bank of Philadelphia and Professor Marina Azzimonti of Stony Brook University show partisan conflict to be at all-time highs. The index, constructed from searches for partisan conflict stories in newspaper databases back to 1891, show high levels of conflict in the 1890s and 1900s, moderating from World War I (1914–17) through the mid-1960s, before beginning a steady climb. Early twentieth-century conflict levels were matched in the 1970s and 1980s, with all-time highs reached during the Obama years. How Donald Trump will affect these levels of partisan conflict remain to be seen.[19]

Party in the Electorate

There are two main descriptions of how citizens adopt partisan preferences and update them over time. One has its roots in the 1960 classic, *The American Voter*, which presented party identification as a deep-seated psychological commitment, established early and remaining quite stable over time. Partisans might defect in a given election or move from the partisan ranks into the independent ranks, but few jump from one party to the other and stay. An alternative view, offered by Morris Fiorina, sees partisanship as more a rational calculation than a stable psychological commitment. Fiorina explained partisanship as a "running tally" of positive and negative evaluations of party candidates and policies. A voter whose running tally points consistently toward one party may look like they have made a "standing decision" for that party, but if evidence shifts eventually so may the tally and ultimately the voter's partisan identification. Both views offer insights and should be kept in mind as we think about how voters interact with political parties.[20]

Party Identification: The Ties Loosen. The political science literature refers to the commitment of individual voters to their political party as **party identification**. For nearly seventy years, the Survey Research Center (SRC) at the University of Michigan has asked voters the following questions: Generally speaking, do you usually think of yourself as a Republican, a Democrat, an independent, or what? (If Republican or Democrat) Would you call yourself a strong (Republican or Democrat) or a not very strong (Republican or Democrat)? (If Independent) Do you think of yourself as closer to the Republican Party or to the Democratic Party? Answers to these questions distinguish voters who consider themselves stronger and weaker identifiers with one or the other of the major parties, independents who lean toward one of the major parties, and pure independents. Findings are reported in a seven-point scale and a simpler three-point scale.

First, we look at the seven-point scale (see Table 6.2). Only a few fairly straightforward points need to be made about variations in the distribution of party identification over the past seventy years. First, note the continuing breadth

party identification The emotional and intellectual commitment of a voter to his or her preferred party.

Q4 Are American political parties in decline and, if so, should we be worried about it?

TABLE 6.2 Party Identification in the Electorate, 1952–2016 (Seven-Point Scale)

	'52	'54	'56	'58	'60	'62	'64	'66	'68	'70	'72	'74	'76	'78	'80	'82	'84	'86	'88	'90	'92	'94	'96	'98	'00	'02	'04	'08	'12	'16
SD	23	23	22	28	21	24	27	18	20	20	15	18	15	15	18	20	17	18	18	20	18	15	18	19	19	17	17	19	20	18
WD	26	26	24	23	26	24	25	28	26	24	25	21	25	24	23	24	20	22	18	19	17	18	19	18	15	17	16	15	13	13
ID	10	9	7	7	6	8	9	9	10	10	11	13	12	14	11	11	11	10	12	12	14	13	14	14	15	16	17	17	16	15
I	5	8	9	8	10	8	8	12	11	13	15	18	16	16	15	13	13	14	12	12	13	11	10	12	13	7	10	11	10	10
IR	8	6	9	5	7	6	6	7	9	8	10	9	10	10	10	8	12	11	13	12	12	12	12	11	13	13	12	12	18	16
WR	14	15	15	17	14	17	14	15	15	15	13	14	14	13	14	14	15	15	14	15	14	15	15	16	12	16	12	13	11	12
SR	14	13	16	12	16	13	11	10	10	9	10	8	9	8	9	10	12	11	14	10	11	15	12	10	12	15	16	13	13	15

SD = Strong Democrat; WD = Weak Democrat; ID = Independent Democrat; I = Independent; IR = Independent Republican; WR = Weak Republican; SR = Strong Republican

Source: American National Election Studies. http://electionstudies.org/nesguide/toptable/tab2a_1.htm. I am grateful to Professor David Hopkins of the Boston College Political Science Department for providing the 2016 data.

and depth of the Democrats' "Roosevelt coalition" through the mid-1960s. Combining strong and weak partisans, we see that Democrats claimed 45 to 50 percent of the electorate, whereas the Republicans, even while Eisenhower was winning two easy elections in 1952 and 1956, claimed less than 30 percent, and independents remained around 23 percent.

Second, the late 1960s and 1970s saw both major parties give up chunks of their partisan base to the independent category. Lyndon Johnson's broad victory over Barry Goldwater in 1964 and the Watergate scandal and forced resignation of President Richard Nixon in 1973 pushed Republican Party identification under 25 percent, where it remained into the 1980s. Simultaneously, the cumulative effect of the turmoil of the late 1960s and early 1970s including the Vietnam War, social unrest, and economic stagnation shaved a full 10 percent off the Democratic base.

Third, the proportion of voters identifying themselves as independents rose from a steady 23 percent as late as 1964, to 30 percent in 1968, and to 37 percent in 1976, where it has remained relatively stable for decades. Recent figures show that 41 percent of voters identify themselves as independents, whereas only 31 percent identify themselves as Democrats and 28 percent as Republicans. These developments are often presented as evidence that the electorate has become less partisan, more willing to look at candidates from both major parties, and hence that American elections are decided by a large, floating, independent vote. Other evidence suggests a different interpretation.

Partisan Identification: The Scales Rebalance.   First, an extensive literature suggests that the broad category of "Independent" is more structured, more connected to party, than commonly understood.[21] Not surprisingly, strong partisans tend to turn out at high rates and to vote overwhelmingly for the nominees of their party. Weak partisans turn out at somewhat lower rates and are somewhat less loyal to the candidates of their party. Interestingly, however, independent leaners tend to behave very much like the weak identifiers of the party toward which they lean. They turn out at the same rates and are just as loyal. Only pure independents tend to split their votes between the major parties, and they turn out at lower rates than partisans and leaners.[22]

Table 6.3 presents a picture that better reflects partisan behavior. Independent leaners are allocated to the parties toward which they lean, leaving only the pure independents in the Independent category. Now we see that the number of pure independents tripled, rising from 5 percent to 15 percent between 1952 and 1976, before receding to 10–15 percent from 1980 onward. Democratic numbers, counting leaners, have fallen 10 or 15 points since the mid-1960s. Despite Democratic losses, the Republicans made little headway until the early 1980s. Ronald Reagan's reelection victory in 1984 expanded the Republican Party to about 40 percent of the electorate, where it stayed until ticking up to 44 percent in 2016.[23] The Democrats enjoyed a significant advantage in party registration during the 2008 election cycle, and a smaller but still significant advantage in 2012, but the Republicans had their own advantages.

TABLE 6.3   Party Identification in the Electorate, 1952–2016 (Three-Point Scale)

	'52	'54	'56	'58	'60	'62	'64	'66	'68	'70	'72	'74	'76	'78	'80	'82	'84	'86	'88	'90	'92	'94	'96	'98	'00	'02	'04	'08	'12	'16
D + L	59	58	52	58	53	56	62	55	56	54	51	52	51	54	52	55	48	50	47	52	50	47	52	51	50	49	50	51	49	46
I		5	8	9	8	10	8	8	12	11	13	15	18	16	16	15	13	13	14	12	12	13	11	10	12	13	7	10	11	10	10
R + L	36	34	39	34	37	36	31	32	33	33	34	31	33	30	33	32	40	36	41	36	37	41	38	37	37	43	41	37	41	44

D + L = Democrats + Leaners; I = Independents; R + L = Republicans + Leaners

Source: American National Election Studies. http://www.electionstudies.org/nesguide/toptable/tab2a_2.htm.

Historically, the Democrats needed a lead just to stay even. Partisan balance meant Republican advantage. At every level of partisan identification, strong, weak, and leaners, Republicans were 5 or 6 percentage points more likely to turn out and until 1996 they were 5 to 10 points more likely to stick with the candidates of their party. With the transition of conservative white southerners from the Democratic Party to the Republican Party now complete, Democrats are more uniformly liberal and Republicans uniformly conservative. In recent election cycles, both Democrats and Republicans have voted consistently for the nominee of their party.[24]

In fact, 2016 shaped up as a close election in which the Republican Party, opposing what they called a "third Obama term" for Democratic front-runner Hillary Clinton, might have had a slight advantage. The nomination of Donald Trump and his outsider campaign promised great change while Hillary Clinton's nomination signaled more of the same rather than change. A slow but steady economic recovery on the Obama watch, as well as turmoil domestically and internationally, left many voters uneasy and skeptical. Both major party candidates were unpopular.

But on election night, 92 percent of each party's identifiers voted for the candidate of their party. Nonetheless, Trump showed unexpected strength, especially in the traditionally Democratic upper Midwest. Though Clinton won the popular vote, Trump won comfortably in the decisive Electoral College. Republicans, though with slightly narrowed margins, held both the House and the Senate. Post-election, the Senate had 52 Republicans, 46 Democrats, and 2 Independents who leaned Democrat. The House remained in Republican hands 241 to 194.

The 2016 election highlighted deep divisions within both major parties, though the Republican divisions did seem deeper and more dangerous. Democrats were divided between the more entrenched institutional wing of the party, led by Hillary Clinton, and the insurgent wing, headed by Bernie Sanders. Sanders accused, with substantial evidence, the Democratic National Committee (DNC) of favoring Clinton and the Clintonites noted that Sanders only officially became a Democrat late in the campaign. The Democratic Party has moved further left, toward Sanders' universal health care and free college tuition positions, but many moderate Democrats wonder whether those progressive positions can carry a national election.

The Republican Party divisions, deepening since the Tea Party insurgency began in 2010, cleave traditional leaders like Senate majority leader Mitch McConnell from insurgents like Senator Ted Cruz. Those divisions threatened to split the party apart when Donald Trump defeated more than a dozen well-known Republican governors and senators with an unremitting populist message to win the party's nomination. Trump's unexpected win put Republican divisions under the additional pressure of governing in Washington. All parties experience internal divisions. Sometimes these internal battles create new energy in the party, but at other times they hobble the party and provide an open door to the opposition.

Party Organizations

What do parties look like in the twenty-first century? The traditional party organization was conceived as a pyramid rising from a broad base of local precincts through a series of intermediate layers—ward, city, county, congressional district, and state central committee—to the national committees and conventions of both parties. Well into the 1960s, the locus of activity and influence within the party organizations was much nearer the base than the tip of the pyramid. No longer. Modern parties focus on developing and managing partisan social networks that identify, train, and support candidates to win office and take policy control of government.

Local Party Organizations. The heyday of local party organization was in the two decades on either side of the beginning of the twentieth century. Some local party organizations, often called "machines" by their detractors, controlled hundreds and even thousands of patronage jobs and lucrative city and county contracts. Because the organizations controlled the voters, they could slate candidates, discipline officeholders who did not toe the line, and reward the party faithful with offices and opportunities.

Over the course of the twentieth century, and especially in its last three decades, several powerful trends served to hollow out most local party organizations. The first was bringing government jobs under civil service regulation. Civil service regulation of government jobs spread throughout the federal workforce by the 1930s and through most state and local governments by the 1970s and 1980s. The second was the movement toward nonpartisan local elections. The idea was that citizens suffer when local politics is a partisan scramble for patronage and that a more efficient and business-like approach to local problems is possible if candidates remove their party labels and run on issues and expertise. Nearly three-quarters of local elections in the United States today are nonpartisan.

The third trend was technology. By 1960, presidential candidates were using television to take political messages directly to voters in their homes. By 1980, all candidates for statewide offices and many at the local level were employing

Pro & Con

Black Commitment to the Democratic Party

For more than half a century, blacks have given about 90 percent of their votes to Democratic candidates for president and Congress. No other racial or ethnic group has been as deeply committed to one of the major parties over the other as blacks have been to the Democratic Party.

We must first note that this close connection between blacks and the Democratic Party is very curious historically. Consider, after all, that the Democratic Party was the party of the South and slavery during the Civil War and the party most identified with southern racial segregation into the 1960s. Consider also that the Republican Party came into existence in the 1850s as an antislavery party and that it was the Republican Party, the party of Abraham Lincoln and the Emancipation Proclamation, that fought a great civil war to end slavery.

Nonetheless, in the 1930s and then more decisively in the 1960s, black voters left the Republican Party for the Democratic Party. The connection made between the Kennedy brothers and Martin Luther King Jr. during the 1960 campaign and the social activism of the Johnson administration were especially heartening to black citizens. Then the Civil Rights Acts of 1964 and 1965, the Voting Rights Act of 1965, and the whole package of Great Society initiatives—in education, housing, welfare, health care, and job training—firmly attached blacks to what they took to be a new Democratic Party committed to equal rights.

What are the pluses and minuses of the nearly exclusive commitment of blacks to the Democratic Party? Among the pluses are at least the following. First, the Democratic Party's philosophy and programs have been responsive to the needs and interests of blacks. The Democratic Party created and defended the American welfare state and affirmative action. Second, the Democratic Party has been receptive to blacks with political aspirations. In 2008 and 2012, the Democrats elected and then reelected Barack Obama president of the United States. All but 3 of the 49 black members of Congress are Democrats.

Among the minuses are at least the following. First, Democrats—including Barack Obama—have been reluctant to have their campaigns too closely identified with the black community for fear of scaring away white voters. Second, the fact that both major parties know that most blacks will vote Democrat means that there is no bidding for their votes. Third, the wholesale commitment of blacks to the Democratic Party means that they are almost completely without access when Republicans win.

What do you think?
- How do you read the balance of the pluses and minuses?
- Does the near exclusive commitment of blacks to the Democratic Party enhance or detract from their political clout?

PRO	CON
Democrats have been more responsive	Democrats often take blacks for granted
Democrats support public services and affirmative action	Blacks are isolated when Democrats lose
Most black elected officials are Democrats	Republicans have no incentive to bid for black votes

television as the central component of their campaigns. While "local organizations are still essential for managing some aspects of campaigns, such as carrying on registration drives, arranging rallies, setting up phone banks, facilitating use of absentee ballots, and turning out the vote on election day," more and more campaigning is conducted over the head of the local party structure.[25]

Fifty State Organizations.   At the top of the party structure in each of the fifty states are a Democratic Central Committee and a Republican Central Committee. Although these state central committees still perform a number of traditional tasks, they have evolved remarkably in the last three decades. The traditional responsibilities of the state committees included organizing the state party caucuses and convention, drafting the state party platform, allocating campaign funds, and selecting the state party's national convention and national committee delegates.

On the other hand, few state parties still run large patronage operations or organize and support slates of candidates for statewide office. State party organizations have moved from a focus on electoral mobilization to a focus on campaign management. State party organizations all over the country now offer technical advice to candidates, campaign managers, and workers. The state parties train activists to manage voter lists, run phone banks, do mass mailings, organize election-day turnout, and raise, manage, and account for funds as required by state and federal law.

The National Party Organizations.   The Republican and Democratic National Committees, as well as the House and Senate Republican and Democratic campaign committees, are stronger and more active than at any previous point in their histories. The campaign committees raise funds and provide campaign services to their incumbent members of the House and Senate. Although the McCain–Feingold campaign finance reforms slowed "soft money" contributions to the national parties and campaign committees, they are still far more vibrant and capable than in past decades.

The modern national committees, although they certainly expand and contract their operations with the election cycle, engage in continuous party support and development activity. They recruit and train candidates and their staffs and pay for polling and issues research, media production, fundraising, consulting, and the ongoing administrative expenses of the operation. Candidates have become dependent on the services provided by the national committees.

Party in Government

Party in government is composed of the officeholders—both elected and appointed officials—who ran under or have been associated with the party label. Parties present alternative programs to the public during election campaigns and try to enact them once they gain office. Usually, this means the president's program, but it can mean the program of the majority party in Congress, especially if they do not hold the presidency.

Promoting the President's Program. The idea that the president should present a program to the Congress each year is relatively new. Prior to the New Deal, the majority party's program was as likely to come from the Congress as it was from the White House. Now, however, **presidential support** measures the president's ability to get his program through the Congress and consistently convince his partisans in Congress to support that program (see Figure 6.1).

Congressional voting records show that when presidents enjoy majorities in both houses of the Congress, as Democratic presidents Kennedy, Johnson, Carter, Clinton, and Obama and Republican President George W. Bush did during all or part of their terms, they are successful more than 80 percent of the time. Presidents whose partisans control at least one house of the Congress, as Republican presidents Eisenhower and Reagan did, do nearly as well, at almost 75 percent. Presidents who find both houses of the Congress controlled by the other party, as Republican presidents Nixon, Ford, George H.W. Bush, and as George W. Bush and Democrat Barack Obama did in their final two years, face tough sledding, achieving success only about 60 percent of the time. President Trump, though he enjoyed Republican majorities in both houses of Congress, struggled through his first year, achieving tax reform just before Christmas.

President George W. Bush's support scores during 2001 and 2002, his first two years in office, although Congress was evenly divided and control of the Senate shifted from Republican to Democrat and back again, averaged 88 percent, the highest since LBJ in 1964 and 1965. His support scores remained near 80 percent from 2003 to 2006. In November 2006, Republicans lost control

presidential support Each year *Congressional Quarterly* reports the proportion of votes in Congress on which the president took a clear position and Congress supported him.

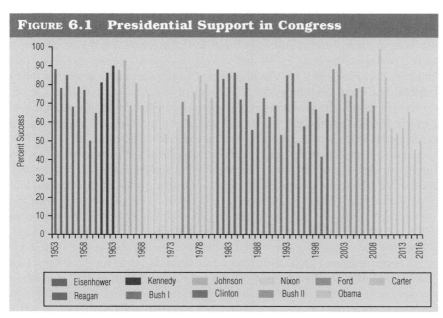

FIGURE **6.1** **Presidential Support in Congress**

Source: Congressional Quarterly Weekly Report, February 8, 2016.

of both houses of Congress and Bush's personal popularity touched all-time lows. His 2007 support score plunged to 38 percent, tied with Bill Clinton's post-Lewinsky 1999 low for the worst presidential support scores of the past half century. It recovered modestly, to 48 percent, in 2008.

Barack Obama's first year presidential support score was an astounding 97 percent. That is the highest on record; higher than LBJ's in 1964 and 1965, higher than Clinton's in 1993 and 1994, and higher even than George W. Bush's in 2001 and 2002. Presidents almost always do best in their first couple of years and then the political gravity of difficult problems, partial solutions, and familiarity, pull them down. Obama's success rate slipped to a still very respectable 86 percent in 2010, but after Republicans took control of the House in 2011 it languished in the mid-50s. In 2016, it slipped to just 50 percent.

The Loyal Opposition.   The role of loyal opposition falls to the leaders of the party in Congress that does not control the presidency. If this party is also a minority in Congress, as Republicans were during the first years of the Obama presidency and Democrats were early in the Trump administration, its leaders are mostly restricted to organizing dissent and raising questions about the president's program. Though if the opposition holds together and is adamant, they can, as Republicans did in 2009 and 2010 and Democrats did in 2017, reshape important parts of the president's program. If this party holds a majority in one house of the Congress, as Republicans did after 2011, it can more effectively bargain with the president on his program. If the party holds majorities in both houses of the Congress, it may well be in a position to offer a program of its own.

party unity Each year *Congressional Quarterly* reports the proportion of votes in the House and Senate on which a majority of one party lines up against a majority of the other party.

In general, **party unity** in Congress—defined as the proportion of votes on which the majority of one party lines up against a majority of the other party— was high during the 1950s and early 1960s, fell throughout the 1960s, and began to rise slowly in the early 1970s and then more rapidly during the 1980s (see Figure 6.2). During 1993, the first year of the first Clinton term, the proportion of partisan votes was an all-time high of 65 percent in the House and 67 percent in the Senate. Although this divisiveness moderated a bit in 1994, it shot to record highs in 1995 following the Republican capture of both houses of Congress: 73 percent of House votes and 69 percent of Senate votes were partisan.[26]

Partisanship declined markedly between 1996 and 1998, before the Clinton impeachment saga of late 1998 and early 1999 soaked the Congress in partisan rancor. President George W. Bush's determination to "change the tone in Washington" by "reaching across party lines" seemed to work initially. Partisan voting declined to 40 percent in the House and 55 percent in the Senate in 2001 and then to 43 percent in the House and 45 percent in the Senate in 2002. It did not last. Once the post-9/11 unity faded, partisanship surged in 2003 to 52 percent in the House and 67 percent in the Senate. From 2004 through 2008, party unity averaged about 53 percent in the House and 57 percent in the Senate.

Party unity in the House remained in its traditional range in 2009 and 2010, at 51 percent and 40 percent, while Senate party unity shot to all-time highs

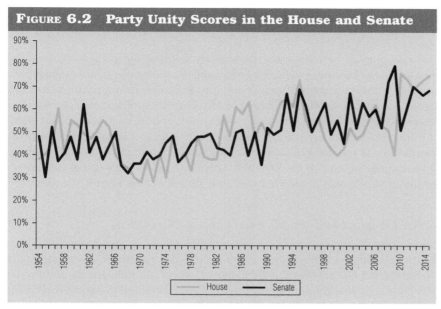

FIGURE **6.2** **Party Unity Scores in the House and Senate**

Source: Congressional Quarterly Weekly Report, February 8, 2016.

at 72 percent and 79 percent. Both Democrats and Republicans in the Senate were highly unified because the Democrats had just 60 votes, exactly the number needed to break a filibuster, and the Republicans needed all 40 of their votes and just one Democrat to sustain a filibuster and block the Democrats. In November 2010, Republicans swept to control of the House and narrowed the margin of Democratic control in the Senate. In 2011, House Republicans moved to block the Democratic agenda and to offer their own alternatives, driving House party unity scores to an all-time high of 76 percent. The more closely balanced Senate, 53 Democrats and 47 Republicans, was forced into occasional compromise, so party unity slipped back to 51 percent.

Though Obama won reelection in 2012, Republicans added majority control of the Senate to their control of the House and set about challenging the president for political and policy control of the government. During Obama's second term, party unity in the House averaged 73 percent while in the Senate it averaged 63 percent.

THE IMPACT OF MINOR PARTIES ON AMERICAN POLITICS

The United States is frequently described as a two-party system. In many ways it is: the Democratic and Republican parties have stood against each other since before the Civil War. They get most of the attention and win virtually all of the elections. But the United States as a two-party democracy is only part of the story. In this section, we define minor parties, describe their traditional role in

American politics, describe the barriers that the major parties throw up against them, and assess the recent history and future prospects of minor parties in American politics.

Major parties are the Democrats and Republicans, the parties that have the best chances of winning elections, organizing the government, and making public policy. **Minor parties** also seek support, stake out issue positions, and run candidates for election, but they generally have little chance of winning and everyone knows it. But sometimes, when the political stars line up just right, a third party can garner enough attention and votes to change the course of an election. In fact, many believe that the improved opportunities to communicate and organize offered by the Web and other new media suggest that the growth of minor parties may accelerate in the early decades of the twenty-first century.[27]

minor party A party that raises issues and offers candidates but has little chance of winning and organizing the government.

The Obstacles to Minor Party Success

Democrats and Republicans, in state legislatures and governors' offices, in Congress and the White House, wrote the rules governing elections in the United States. Not surprisingly then, these Democratic and Republican officials designed the American electoral system to favor them and to make life difficult for those who would challenge them.

The major parties have three main levels of defense against third party challenges. First, virtually all American elections are conducted in individual districts (often referred to as single-member districts) where the person getting the most votes (the plurality, though not necessarily a majority) wins. This is hard on minor parties.[28]

Second, most election rules are state rules. The states have made access to the ballot automatic for the major parties and difficult for minor parties. Frequently the number of valid voter signatures required to get a minor party candidate on the ballot is very high. At the end of the process of obtaining signatures, partisan election officials often disqualify many signatures for technical reasons. Even when third party candidates make it onto the ballot, the privileged top-of-the-ballot positions are usually reserved for the two major parties. Moreover, the petition process usually has to be redone for each new election cycle.

Even higher hurdles exist for a third party candidate for the presidency. To get on the ballots in all fifty states, a candidate must determine each state's rules and comply with them in detail. The ability of most third party candidates to raise money is miniscule compared to the two major party candidates. Third party candidates are barred from participating in presidential debates unless their support in the national polls is 15 percent (a rule made by the major party-sponsored Presidential Debate Commission). In a general election, the major party candidates raise hundreds of millions of dollars or receive tens of millions of dollars in public funds to run their campaigns, but third party candidates get nothing unless their parties achieved at least 5 percent of the vote in the last election (a rule made by the major party-dominated Federal Election Commission).

Struggling Toward Democracy

In 2016 "minor parties" got just 1.5 percent of the presidential vote.

What do you think?

- Is there a role for minor parties in U.S. politics and, if so, are they being allowed to play it?
- Is a protest vote for a third party candidate a "wasted" vote?

The major parties usually disdain even to notice the demands and machinations of the minor parties. Yet, if a minor party does begin to build momentum, the major parties react. Initially, they take half measures to try to drain off the emotion fueling the growing third party. If that fails, one or both of the major parties will adopt one or more of the key issue positions of the third party. These third party actions and major party reactions were on stark display during recent presidential election cycles as Gary Johnson, Jill Stein, and others took their shots at challenging the primacy of the two major parties in American politics.

Senator Ted Cruz (R-TX) speaks to supporters during a Tea Party rally in front of the U.S. Capitol in Washington, D.C. The Tea Party is not a major party like the Republicans. Is it a minor party, interest group, or something else?

Yet, at least once in American history a "minor" party broke through to displace one of the major parties. By 1860, the Whig Party had confronted the Democratic Party for more than two decades, winning the presidency twice. But in 1860, riding anti-slavery emotion in the North, the Republican Party displaced the Whigs to become the Democrat's new major party opponent. Some prominent analysts, including the historian Michael Beschloss, Bill Kristol, the editor of the conservative *Weekly Standard*, and former Trump political strategist Steve Bannon, suggest the potential for a divided Republican Party to spawn a new third party. Others suggest that the populist Bernie Sanders wing of the Democratic Party might break away from the more traditional Clinton wing of the party. How likely do such party splits seem to you?[29]

THE RELATIONSHIP OF INTEREST GROUPS TO POLITICAL PARTIES IN THE UNITED STATES

In this chapter we discussed interest groups and major and minor political parties. All three are institutional mechanisms for bringing together groups of citizens to promote interests, ideas, and shared goals. In a society like ours, based on freedoms of speech, press, and association, with the technical ability to communicate improving every day, interest groups and minor parties are likely to proliferate and the major parties are likely to remain strong. Americans will have more and more ways to join with like-minded fellow citizens to make their views known and to press them on government.

Q5 Are interest groups or political parties the best vehicle for representing citizen opinion to government?

As our political world grows more complicated, we must distinguish between interest groups and political parties and remember what each can and cannot do. Interest groups generally press their members' views on government, whichever political party happens to control government at the time.

Minor parties rarely win office and almost never win the top offices in government, but they do challenge the major parties and raise issues that might not otherwise get a hearing. Interest groups and minor parties may seem similar, but interest groups focus their attention on influencing government while minor parties often scorn traditional politics and policymaking and spend their energy on educating and organizing the public. Major parties offer candidates for all or most offices from the local to the national level in the hope of winning executive offices and legislative majorities so that they can run the government and make policy.

Finally, though interest groups and political parties compete for a limited supply of political talent, energy, and money, they also complement each other in critical ways. Political parties play the dominant role during elections and when government is being organized. Interest groups are at their most influential, perhaps even dominant, during the normal course of government business—during legislative hearings, program design, and bureaucratic rule-making and policy implementation. Political parties construct the broad public agenda; interest groups shape its details in ways acceptable and often beneficial to interest group goals.

Chapter Summary

The Founders were concerned that factions, because they reflect divisions within the community, would make the public interest and the common good more difficult to define and pursue. Madison hoped that the sheer size of the United States would limit the possibility that people with shared interests could come together to press their case on government. In the intervening two centuries, however, technological developments have rendered Madison's hope illusory.

All of the institutions that we have described in this chapter—business and labor groups, professional and volunteer associations, citizens' groups, major and minor political parties—serve to link groups of citizens to their government and to the political realm. Interest groups, which are often narrow and highly focused, try to influence the development and implementation of policies that affect their members. Interest groups draw upon resources including group size, money, intensity, and leadership to press their case on government. They usually prefer an insider strategy of quiet lobbying but are sometimes forced into an outside strategy of grassroots campaigning and protest.

Political parties compete in elections in the hope of winning majority control of government so that they can affect the full range of policymaking and implementation. The national parties have become exceptionally efficient at fundraising, campaign management, and advertising. As a result of closer connections between candidates and party organizations, parties have also become more cohesive and consistent forces in government. Two-thirds of voters claim partisan labels and in most major elections more than 90 percent of partisans vote for the candidate of their party. The emotional attachment of voters to political parties is stronger than it has been in decades.

The standard democratic politics of groups and parties serves the interests of most citizens most of the time. Minor parties and protest movements arise when increasing numbers of people conclude that the political system is simply unwilling or incapable of dealing with a set of critical issues about which they feel deeply. Minor parties raise new issues or demand new solutions to old issues. They organize, argue the issues, and run candidates, but have little chance of winning. However, sometimes, as with Ross Perot in 1992 or Ralph Nader in 2000, they gain enough attention to change the course of an election and to demand that the major parties respond.

Key Terms

AFL-CIO

elitism

inside strategy

interest groups

litigation

lobbyists

minor party

outside strategy

party identification

party in government

party in the electorate

party organization

party unity

peak associations

pluralism

political party

presidential support

trade associations

Suggested Readings

Cigler, Allan J. and Burdett A. Loomis. *Interest Group Politics*, 9th ed. Washington, D.C.: CQ Press, 2015. A leading general introduction to the study of interest groups.

Flanigan, William H., Nancy H. Zingale, Elizabeth A. Theiss-Moore, and Michael W. Wagner. *Political Behavior of the American Electorate*. 13th ed. Washington, D.C.: Sage, 2014. Classic overview of the partisanship and political behavior of the U.S. electorate.

Gibson, Joseph. *Persuading Congress: A Practical Guide to Parlaying an Understanding of Congressional Folkways and Dynamics into Successful Advocacy on Capitol Hill*. TheCapitol.net, 2010. Former top staffer on the House Judiciary Committee describes the nuts and bolts of effective lobbying.

Gray, Virginia, David Lowrey, and Jennifer Benz, *Interest Groups and Health Care Reform Across the United States*. Washington, D.C.: Georgetown University Press, 2013. Review of the Affordable Care Act and how it was dealt with in the states.

Hanjal, Zoltan L. and Taeku Lee. *Why Americans Don't Join the Party: Race, Immigration, and the Failure (of Political Parties) to Engage the Electorate*. Princeton, NJ: Princeton University Press, 2011. Explores the reasons immigrants and minorities do not readily connect to the major parties and how they might better be addressed.

Hershey, Marjorie R. *Party Politics in America*. 17th ed. New York: Routledge, 2017. This leading textbook on American political parties describes parties as they operate in the electorate, as organizations, and in government.

Lowery, David and Holly Brasher. *Organized Interests and American Government*. Prospect Heights, IL: Waveland Press, 2011. Explores how organized interests try to exercise influence and asks whether these activities are as negative as they as they are often portrayed.

Web Resources

1 www.naacp.org
   Official website of the National Association for the Advancement of Colored People (NAACP). This page provides a wealth of information about the organization that spearheaded much of the civil rights movement of the 1950s and 1960s.

2 www.opensecrets.com
   This is the leading website tracking campaign contributions by candidate, industry, party and much more.

3 www.citizen.org
   Public Citizen, founded by Ralph Nader in 1971, is a site that informs the activist and consumer about safety issues that are discussed in Congress such as drugs, medical devices, cleaner energy sources, automotive safety, and fair trade. The organization has the goal of maintaining a more open and democratic government by serving the public as a "Congress Watch."

4 www.democrats.org/index.html
   This serves as the official website of the Democratic National Committee. It includes party news and information on how to become involved in the party. It also provides discussion topics concerning legislative and issue positions.

5 www.gop.org
   Official website of the Republican National Committee. It includes information on how to become involved with the GOP. It also contains information on organizations and profiles of elected officials.

Notes

1 James Madison, *The Federalist* (New York: Modern College Library Edition, 1937), no. 10, 54.
2 David B. Truman, *The Governmental Process: Political Interests and Public Opinion* (New York: Knopf, 1958), 33.
3 Graham Wilson, *Interest Groups* (Cambridge, MA: Blackwell, 1990), 1.
4 Mancur Olson, *The Logic of Collective Action* (Cambridge, MA: Harvard University Press, 1965); Jack L. Walker, *Mobilizing Interest Groups in America* (Ann Arbor, MI: University of Michigan Press, 1991).
5 Charles E. Lindblom, *Politics and Markets* (New York: Basic Books, 1977), 170–188.

6 Sheryl Gay Stolberg, "The Pugnacious Builder of the Business Lobby," *New York Times*, June 21, 2013, BU1, BU6.

7 Ronald J. Hrebenar, *Interest Group Politics in America*, 3rd ed. (Armonk, NY: Sharpe, 1997), 315.

8 Lawrence S. Rothenberg, *Linking Citizens to Government: Interest Group Politics at Common Cause* (New York: Cambridge University Press, 1992), 32.

9 Hrebenar, *Interest Group Politics in America*, 72.

10 http://www.opensecrets.org/lobbyists/overview.asp.

11 Mark Leibovich, "Eric Cantor Is on the Market," *New York Times Magazine*, July 20, 2014, 12–13.

12 Public Citizen study cited in a *New York Times* editorial, "A Richer Life Beckons Congress," August 8, 2005, A18. See also Lawrence Lessig, *Republic Lost: How Money Corrupts Congress—and a Plan to Stop It* (New York: Twelve, 2011), 99, 123.

13 John Soloman, "Lawmakers' Lobbying Spouses Avoid Hill Reforms," *Washington Post*, January 17, 2007, A1.

14 Ken Kollman, *Outside Lobbying* (Princeton, NJ: Princeton University Press, 1998).

15 James MacGregor Burns, *The Deadlock of Democracy* (Englewood Cliffs, NJ: Prentice-Hall, 1963), Chapters 9 and 10.

16 Austin Ranney, *Curing the Mischiefs of Faction* (Berkeley, CA: University of California Press, 1975), 202.

17 Jan-Werner Muller, *What Is Populism?* (Philadelphia, PA: University of Pennsylvania Press, 2010), 78–79.

18 Marjorie R. Hershey, *Party Politics in America*, 16th ed. (New York: Routledge, 2016), 5–9.

19 Jeff Sommer, "Political Strife Is High, but the Market Doesn't Care," *New York Times*, July 23, 2017, Bu3.

20 Robert S. Erikson and Kent L. Tedin, *American Public Opinion*, 9th ed. (New York: Pearson, 2015), 81–82.

21 Erikson and Tedin, *America Public Opinion*, 81. See also Michael S. Lewis-Beck, William G. Jacoby, Helmut Norpoth, and Herbert F. Weisberg, *The American Voter Revisited* (Ann Arbor, MI: University of Michigan Press, 2008), 126–130.

22 William H. Flanigan and Nancy H. Zingale, *Political Behavior of the American Electorate*, 13th ed. (Washington, D.C.: CQ Press, 2015), 113–118. See also Lynn Vavreck, "The Power of Political Ignorance," *New York Times*, May 25, 2014, 45R.

23 Pew Research Center Publications, "Obama's 2010 Challenge: Wake Up Liberals, Calm Down Independents," December 17, 2009.

24 Erikson and Tedin, *American Public Opinion*, 146.

25 A. James Reichley, *The Life of the Parties: A History of American Political Parties* (New York: Rowman & Littlefield, 2000), 321.

26 Scot Schraufnagel, *Third Party Blues: The Truth and Consequences of Two-Party Dominance* (New York: Routledge, 2011), 7.

27 Danielle Allen and Jennifer S. Light, ed., *From Voice to Influence: Understanding Citizenship in a Digital Age* (Chicago: University of Chicago Press, 2015), 19.

28 John F. Bibby and L. Sandy Maisel, *Two Parties—or More* (Boulder, CO: Westview Press, 2002), 55–78.

29 Jeremy W. Peters, "Many See Potential in Trump For Future Third Party," *New York Times*, September 12, 2017, A18.

Chapter 7

DEMOCRACY'S MOMENT
Voting, Campaigns, and Elections

Focus Questions: from reading to thinking

Q1 Why do so many Americans fail to vote even in important elections like those for Congress, governor, or president?

Q2 How do those who do vote decide which of the parties and candidates to vote for?

Q3 Who chooses to run for political office, and how do they organize their campaigns?

Q4 How does the campaign for the presidency differ from campaigns for other offices that are less visible, powerful, and prestigious?

Q5 Does money dominate presidential elections?

IS THE ELECTORAL COLLEGE OUTDATED?

Article II, section 1 (in part): "Each state shall appoint, in such manner as the Legislature thereof may direct, a number of electors, equal to the whole number of Senators and Representatives to which the state may be entitled in the Congress:. . . The electors shall meet in their respective states, and vote by ballot . . . The person having the greatest number of votes shall be the President . . ."

The Constitution TODAY

No issue so puzzled the Founders as how to select the president. Most of the delegates to the Constitutional Convention knew that they did not want a king; what they did not know was how to design a national executive strong enough to guide the nation but not so strong that he might dominate it. They debated presidential selection longer than any other issue and, late in convention and eager to go home, left us with a process that vexes us to this day.

For months, the Founders debated two broad approaches. A few delegates, including the venerable Benjamin Franklin, did argue that the people should select the president. But most delegates so doubted the ability of common people to make the momentus choice of president that they searched for some—any—alternative. In the end, they settled on a form of elite selection—the Electoral College. Each state legislature would select a number of the state's leading citizens, equal to the number of the state's senators and U.S. House members, to vote for president. The top two vote-getters would be president and vice president.

Ominously, the Electoral College misfired almost immediately. In the election of 1800, the incumbent Federalist President John Adams was challenged by Thomas Jefferson and Jefferson's vice presidential choice, Aaron Burr. The Jefferson–Burr campaign did their work too well. All 73 electors voting for Jefferson also voted for Burr, while Adams got 65 votes and his vice presidential running mate got 64. Though everyone knew that Jefferson was running for president and Burr for vice president, they both got 73 votes and Burr, a scoundrel, did not immediately step back. Jefferson ultimately prevailed and Congress quickly passed and the states ratified a constitutional amendment instructing electors to cast separate votes for president and vice president. That solved the particular problem but others arose.

In 1824, Andrew Jackson won the most popular and electoral votes for president, but not a majority, and Congress famously appointed John Quincy Adams instead. Jackson railed against the Electoral College until and even after he won the presidency cleanly in 1828. Though mid-nineteenth-century elections were hotly contested, especially Lincoln's in 1860, the popular vote aligned with the electoral vote in each. Moreover, during the Civil War and Reconstruction, the Republican Party was dominant and the Democratic Party, the party of the South, was hobbled. As the nation emerged from the shadow of the Civil War, two-party competition returned. In two elections, 1876 and 1888, Democratic presidential candidates narrowly won the popular vote but Republican political advantages allowed them to carry the Electoral College and the presidency.

Then, for more than one hundred years, the Electoral College faded from the public imagination. Even in close elections, like Kennedy and Nixon in 1960, popular and electoral votes lined up. But in 2000 and 2016—two of our last five presidential elections—the candidate who lost the popular vote narrowly prevailed in the Electoral College and became president. George W. Bush in 2000 and Donald J. Trump in 2016 became president without incident because Americans respect, even if they don't quite understand, the constitutional provisions that produced those results. Nonetheless, and not surprisingly, there has been unease.

Two paths leading to popular selection of presidents have been proposed: one really hard and the other not quite so hard. The hard way would be to amend the Constitution, replacing the Electoral College with direct popular election of the president. Most close observers believe that a constitutional amendment, which would have to be ratified by three-quarters of the states, 38 of 50, would be blocked by small, rural, and lightly-populated states that are advantaged under the current system. That leaves a second path that proponents call the National Popular Vote Plan (NPV).

NPV proposes an interstate compact among states with a majority of electoral votes, at least 270 of 538, to award their electoral votes to the winner of the national popular vote. So far, eleven states with 165 electoral votes have adopted NPV and others are actively considering it. While our initial instinct, and maybe our firm conviction, might be that voters today should select the president, we should probably pause long enough to ask what could go wrong. So, what could go wrong? Does NPV sound like a good idea to you?

VOTING, CAMPAIGNS, AND ELECTIONS

Voting, campaigns, and elections are among the central structures and acts of democratic political life.[1] Election campaigns put alternative policies, programs, and politicians before voters for consideration and choice. However, fewer Americans take advantage of their rights to vote than do citizens in other advanced, industrial democracies.

During the colonial period, the electorate was restricted to white male property holders over the age of twenty-one. The slow addition of poor white males, then black males, then women, and finally young people between the ages of 18 and 21 now make virtually all adult American citizens eligible to vote.

But more than a third of eligible voters stay home even in presidential elections. We begin by asking who votes, who does not, and why. We then ask what motivates some Americans to stand for political office. We ask how congressional campaigns are organized and what accounts for the tremendous advantages that incumbents enjoy over their challengers. Finally, we ask how campaigns for the presidency—the top prize in American politics—are planned and executed from early organization and fundraising, through the long season of competition in state primaries and caucuses, to the national nominating conventions, to the general election where the voters make their final choice.

VOTING AND NONVOTING IN AMERICAN ELECTIONS

One of the great puzzles of American political life is that so many of us choose to ignore political rights for which citizens in other countries—China, Kenya, and Iran, just to name a few—still struggle and die. After all, no question is more fundamental to a free society than who gets to vote. Recall that the Founders were wary of direct democracy and, frankly, of the participation of the poor and the poorly educated in politics and governance. They knew and were comforted by the fact that republics since ancient Greece and Rome had employed limitations on **suffrage,** which is another term for the right to vote, as a way of balancing the interests of the few wealthy and the many poor.

Q1 Why do so many Americans fail to vote even in important elections like those for Congress, governor, or president?

suffrage Another term for the legal right to vote.

Discussions of voter turnout require several pieces of information. First, we have to know the size of the voting-age population (VAP). Then we ask what percentage of these people were eligible to vote (VEP) under the laws in force at the time and what percentage of those eligible to vote actually turned out on election day. **Voter turnout** is the percentage of the voting eligible population that actually turns out to vote on election day.

voter turnout That portion of the voting-eligible population that actually turns up to vote on election day.

Today, virtually all citizens over the age of eighteen, except the formally institutionalized and about 3.25 million former felons, are eligible to vote.[2] Turnout in 1996 and 2000 averaged slightly over 50 percent of eligible voters, but in 2004 rose to 61 percent and in 2008 to nearly 62 percent. In 2012, turnout dropped to just below 60 percent, and in 2016 it dropped again to 57 percent. Obviously, many Americans fail to put their legal eligibility to vote into effect.

What Might We Do to Increase Turnout?

Most analysts argue that the way the United States organizes and administers its voter registration system and conducts its elections does a lot to explain its low voter turnout rate. They contend that simplifying **voter registration** and voting is the key to increasing turnout. President Clinton and the Democratic Congress passed the National Voter Registration Act in 1993. The act, also called **Motor Voter,** allows Americans to register to vote at the same time they are doing other things, like getting their driver's license (hence the name *Motor Voter*), signing up for social services, or checking on their property taxes. Most states allow on-line registration. Voter registration is up since 1993, but just a bit.[3]

voter registration The process by which members of the voting-age population sign up, or register, to establish their right to cast a ballot on election day.

Motor Voter Popular name for the National Voter Registration Act of 1993. The act permits people to register to vote while they are doing other common tasks like getting or renewing their driver's licenses.

Other proposals for increasing turnout include reducing the number of elections in which voters are asked to participate by clustering national, state, and local elections on the same day. Elections might also be moved from the traditional Tuesday, a workday for most people, to a Saturday or a few days including a Saturday. Early voting, either in person or by mail ballot, is used in many jurisdictions, and same-day voter registration in a few; both serve to increase turnout moderately. Some advocate voter registration for high school seniors and a few call for mandatory voting.[4]

Not everyone agrees that ease of voter registration and voting is desirable. Republican state legislators in Indiana and three dozen others states passed laws requiring a government-issued photo ID, such as a passport or drivers' license, to vote. Republicans argue that illegal voting is a serious problem. Democrats argue that existing laws, which allow a wider range of documentation to prove residence, like an electric bill with a name and address on it, are sufficient and that requiring photo IDs will work a particular hardship on the poor, the elderly, and minorities. Beginning in 2013, federal courts in North Carolina and Texas began striking down strict voter ID laws as unconstitutional and the Supreme Court has upheld their findings. This fight is not over.

Finally, the vote counting debacle in Florida in the 2000 presidential election highlighted the question of whether votes were being accurately recorded and counted. To resolve these questions, Congress passed the Help America Vote Act (HAVA) in 2002. HAVA provided more than $4 billion dollars to replace outdated voting equipment, create statewide voter registration databases, and train election workers. No sooner was the new equipment installed than questions were raised about handicapped accessibility and the dependability of electronic voting equipment, especially when there was no paper trail to assure that votes were cast and counted as voters intended. In the wake of the 2016 presidential election, President Trump claimed that he lost the popular vote only because three to five million illegal votes were cast for Hillary Clinton. Though election officials and experts rejected Trump's claim, he appointed a commission to look into integrity of voter registration and voting in the U.S.

Two Decisions: Whether to Vote and for Whom to Vote

Q2 How do those who do vote decide which of the parties and candidates to vote for?

Registered voters still have two important decisions to make: whether to vote in a given election and, if they decide to vote, for whom to vote.[5] The first decision depends heavily on the kind of election it is. Voters are more likely to turn out if the offices at stake are important and visible; if the candidates are well known, popular, and attractive; if the main election is competitive; and if other key issues, such as hotly contested initiatives or referenda, are on the ballot. Not surprisingly, local elections among less-known candidates for minor offices draw fewer voters.

Who Votes, Who Stays Home?   Citizens of higher socioeconomic status (SES—a composite measure of education, income, and occupational status) vote, contribute time and money to campaigns, contact public officials, talk about politics with their friends and acquaintances, and engage in other political activities in greater numbers and more frequently than do citizens of lower socioeconomic status.[6]

TABLE 7.1 Voting Turnout by Population Characteristics, 1972–2016 (%)												
	1972	**1976**	**1980**	**1984**	**1988**	**1992**	**1996**	**2000**	**2004**	**2008**	**2012**	**2016**
Education												
8 Years or Less	47.4	44.1	42.6	42.9	36.7	35.1	28.1	26.8	23.6	23.4	21.6	18.3
Some High School	52.0	47.2	45.6	44.4	41.3	41.2	38.8	33.6	34.6	33.7	32.2	29.3
High School Grad	—	59.4	58.9	58.7	54.7	57.5	49.1	49.4	52.4	50.9	48.7	47.4
Some College	65.4	68.1	67.2	67.5	64.5	68.7	60.5	60.3	66.1	65.0	61.5	60.5
College Grad or More	78.8	79.8	79.9	79.1	77.6	81.0	73.0	72.0	74.2	73.3	71.7	71.0
Age												
18–20	48.3	38.0	35.7	36.7	33.2	38.5	31.2	28.4	41.0	41.0	35.1	37.0
21–24	50.7	45.6	43.1	43.5	38.3	45.7	33.4	35.4	42.5	46.6	40.0	42.0
25–34	59.7	55.4	54.6	54.5	48.0	53.2	43.1	43.7	46.9	48.5	46.1	46.0
35–44	66.3	63.3	64.4	63.5	61.3	63.6	54.9	55.0	56.9	55.2	52.9	53.0
45–64	70.8	68.7	69.3	69.8	67.9	70.0	64.4	64.1	66.6	65.0	63.4	61.7
65 and Over	63.5	62.2	65.1	67.7	68.8	70.1	67.0	67.6	68.9	68.1	69.7	68.5
Sex												
Male	64.1	59.6	59.1	59.0	56.4	60.2	52.8	53.1	56.3	55.7	54.4	53.8
Female	62.0	58.8	59.4	60.8	58.3	62.3	55.5	56.2	60.1	60.4	58.5	58.1
Race												
White	64.5	60.9	60.9	61.4	59.1	63.6	56.0	56.4	60.3	59.6	57.6	64.1
Black	52.1	48.7	50.5	55.8	51.5	54.0	50.6	53.5	56.3	60.8	62.0	55.9
Hispanic	37.4	31.8	29.9	32.6	28.8	28.9	26.7	27.5	28.0	31.6	31.8	32.5

Source: Department of Commerce, Bureau of the Census, *Statistical Abstract of the United States, 2014* (Washington, D.C.: U.S. Government Printing Office, 2013), Table 4.8. 2016 data is from U.S. Census, "Voting and Registration in the Election of November 2016". Author estimates for age.

Education is the most important component of socioeconomic status for influencing turnout. In fact, the data in Table 7.1 show that education is becoming an increasingly powerful determinant of turnout. Note that in the 1972 presidential election, 47.4 percent of people with less than eight years of schooling voted, whereas 78.8 percent of those with four or more years of college voted. This difference of more than 31 points is impressive. But then note that although turnout among the best educated dropped eight points between 1972 and 2016, it plummeted twenty-nine points, from 47.4 to 18.3, for the least educated. The well educated now vote at a rate more than three times that of the least educated.

Analysts point to three effects of education that facilitate political activity. First, education reduces the sense of complexity and mystery that surrounds politics and policymaking for many. Second, education makes citizens more able to anticipate the probable results for them of government actions on

AP Photo/Mary Altaffer

In the 2016 Democratic presidential nomination contest, young people were among Bernie Sanders's most fervent supporters. But as Table 7.1 shows, young people usually turn out in smaller numbers than older voters. Every campaign has both to identify their supporters and get them to the polls on election day.

matters such as taxes, trade policy, and interest rates. Third, highly educated citizens are confident that they have the knowledge and skills to influence government and that government listens to people like them.

Age, like education, is an important factor in discriminating between voters and nonvoters. Note in Table 7.1 that turnout among voters under 35 dropped 8 to 12 points between 1972 and 2016, whereas people 45 to 64 dropped 5 to 9 points, and older people voted 5 points more than they had in 1972. Although 2004 and 2008 recorded big increases in the youth vote over 2000, up 12 percent for voters 18–24 and up 5 percent for voters 25–34, they remained almost 20 points behind voters over 45. In 2012, the youth vote dropped back about 5 points, giving up about half the gains since 2000 and 2016 showed only slight improvement.

The relationship between gender and turnout has developed in interesting ways. Through the 1970s men voted in higher proportions than women, but women began to outvote men in 1980 and have incrementally increased the margin in most elections since. Women cast 53.6 percent of all votes in 2016. Race and ethnicity provide a final set of interesting comparisons.[7] Although white turnout dipped 7 percent between 1972 and 2012, turnout among blacks rose about 10 percent, putting black turnout 4.4 percent ahead of whites for just the second time (in 2008 it was 1 point ahead) in American history—the Obama effect. In 2016, white turnout jumped and black turnout slumped, restoring a traditional white advantage. Turnout among Hispanic voters in

2016 was just over 32 percent, whereas for blacks it was about 56 percent, and for whites it was 58 percent.[8]

How Do Voters Make Up Their Minds?   How do those who vote decide for whom to vote? Among the key factors that voters take into account are party identification, if they have one, party images and issue positions, and candidate attributes. Under most circumstances, voters respond positively to candidates they think are like themselves—in terms of social class, race, ethnicity, gender, even region— and, they hope, likely to see and understand the world as they do.[9] In the end, however, research suggests that voters make their decisions as much and perhaps more from gut reactions as from strictly rational calculations.

Party Identification.   Partisanship is the strongest and steadiest influence on the political behavior of individuals. Partisanship is a predisposition, often established in youth and maintained throughout adulthood, to favor one party over the other. Although this commitment can be shaken by the events and personalities of a particular election, all other things being equal, it will be the dominant influence on the voters' decision.

Strong partisans support the candidates of their party more consistently than do weak partisans, and they tend to make their decisions earlier in the electoral cycle. Party regulars listen almost exclusively to their own side in election campaigns, and hence they rarely change their minds during campaigns.[10] Strong partisans are also likely to be more interested in politics, to follow it more closely between elections, and to be better informed than weak partisans and independents. Thirty-four percent of votes were cast early in 2016 and most of those early voters were committed partisans.

Although independents now make up almost 40 percent of the electorate, two-thirds of independents admit that they "lean" toward the Democrats or the Republicans. These leaners behave more like partisans than like "pure" independents. Pure independents tend to have very little information about politics and to vote infrequently.[11] Hence, both major parties have learned to focus on holding their base rather than reaching out to the fairly small number of independent or swing voters.

Party and Candidate Positions.   Extensive polling data show that some issue information is fixed in the historical images of the two major parties. The Democrats are widely perceived to be more sensitive to the poor and minorities, social welfare issues, and income and employment issues. The Republicans are widely perceived to be better on issues of national security, crime, inflation, and business and regulatory policy. These party images stick in voters' minds and are hard to change.[12] As a result, elections that highlight race, crime, and national security (such as the Nixon elections of 1968 and 1972, the Reagan elections of 1980 and 1984, the Bush election of 2004, and Trump in 2016) tend to give Republicans the advantage, whereas elections that highlight the economic interests of the common person (such as the Clinton elections of

1992 and 1996 and the Obama elections of 2008 and 2012) tend to give Democrats the advantage.[13] However, if the party in power proves ineffectual, especially on their natural issues, voters may well decide to make a change.

The particular dynamics of individual elections encourage candidates to raise some issues and to try to keep others from coming to voters' attention. Candidates seek to raise issues that work to their advantage and to the disadvantage of their opponents and to bury issues that work to the advantage of their opponents and are a disadvantage to them. In general, however, candidates are constrained by positions that they have taken in the past and by the core positions of their party.

In 2016, Hillary Clinton ran on a platform of protecting and building upon what Democrats took to be Obama administration successes. Economic recovery, slower than anyone would like, but recovery nonetheless, Wall Street reform, and Obamacare were in place and Clinton promised to expand and improve them. She campaigned on experience in both domestic and international politics and policy. Donald Trump, a first-time candidate who rode a populist wave of white working-class anger to the Republican Party's presidential nomination, worried party elites because he did not seem tethered to past party doctrine and issue positions. Trump promised to build a wall to keep out illegal immigrants, ban Muslims, bring back jobs, and "Make America Great Again."

Candidate Attributes. Although partisanship and issue information remain important, attention to candidates and their personal traits and qualities has waned. Historically, voters wanted to know what kind of person a candidate was—was he or she a strong leader, of good moral character, experienced, and personable? —in order to gain some insight into how he or she would think, act, and react in office.[14]

For some candidates, such as Dwight Eisenhower and Ronald Reagan, qualities such as strength, honesty, and consistency were the foundation of their success. For others, such as Barry Goldwater, George McGovern, and Howard Dean, concerns about personal stability, judgment, and character were hurdles that they could not clear. Yet character is multifaceted, and questions about some aspects of a candidate's character can be overcome if other facets of that character seem to be attractive.

In 1992 and 1996, questions about Bill Clinton's character—in regard to business dealings such as Whitewater, sexual conduct with Gennifer Flowers, Paula Jones, and others, and his early history regarding marijuana and the draft—were widely discussed. Many voters looked past these questions about character to place greater weight on his seemingly deeper empathy for people and on policy proposals for addressing their problems.

In 2016, many voters saw a "lesser of two evils" choice. Hillary Clinton had been a national political figure for nearly three decades. She had been First Lady of the United States before being elected twice to the United States Senate from New York. She lost a closely contested race for the Democratic presidential nomination to Barack Obama in 2008 and then served four years as U.S. Secretary of State in Obama's first term. Voters saw her as experienced but as neither empathetic nor trustworthy. Thirty-eight percent of voters rated her favorably, while 55 percent rated her unfavorably.

Donald Trump, a real estate billionaire, reality television star, and a New York society and tabloid fixture for decades, executed a hostile take-over of the Republican Party. He entered the post-nomination phase of the election with poll ratings even worse than Clinton's. Just 30 percent of the public rated Trump favorably, while 64 percent rated him unfavorably. After Trump became president, observers waited for him to become "more presidential." When that did not happen, Trump's favorability ratings, eventually even with his base, declined. Even in a change election like 2016, voters and citizens want some sense that the president's character and capabilities will promote his or her success in the job.

POLITICAL CAMPAIGNS: AMBITION AND ORGANIZATION

Where do our political leaders, the people who sit on our city councils, in our state legislatures, in Congress, and even in the Oval Office, come from? What leads them to run for office? Most are driven to run for office and then to run for higher office by their own ambitions. Today politicians at the national level and increasingly those in the larger, more complex states and cities are careerists supported by teams of professional campaign managers and consultants. In this section, we focus on those who run for Congress. We ask what advantages incumbents enjoy, what difficulties challengers face, and how both organize and conduct their campaigns. Then we turn our attention to the big race—the race for the White House.

Q3 Who chooses to run for political office, and how do they organize their campaigns?

The Incumbency Advantage

We should not be terribly surprised to find that incumbent members of Congress usually win reelection. This incumbency advantage derives from the fact that incumbents are likely to be better known, more experienced, and have more established fundraising prospects than do their challengers.

On the other hand, we might reasonably be concerned to find that over the past six decades, House incumbents standing for reelection won more than 94 percent of the time and incumbent senators won over 82 percent of the time. Our concern might deepen to learn that more than 98 percent of House incumbents seeking reelection won in 1986, 1988, 1998, 2000, 2004, 2006, 2008, and 2012. More than 90 percent of senators seeking reelection won in 1990, 1994, 1996, 1998, 2004, and 2012. In 2014, Republicans retook the Senate, picking up nine new seats, and extended their House majority by winning thirteen new seats. Again, despite a big partisan win, this time for the Republicans, 96 percent of House incumbents and 82 percent of Senate incumbents were able to hold their seat.

In 2016, despite the populist candidacy of Donald Trump sweeping to a presidential win on election night, Hillary Clinton narrowly won the popular vote and Democrats picked up two Senate seats and seven House seats. Fully 90 percent of senators who chose to stand for reelection won, as did 97 percent of their House colleagues. Even in a tumultuous year, and few would deny that 2016 was that, incumbents have important advantages.

Name Recognition and Advertising. Voters like to vote for candidates they know, or at least know of, but they do not like to spend time getting to know candidates. As a result, more than half of eligible voters even at the height of a congressional campaign were unable to name either candidate running in their district, and only 22 percent of voters could name both candidates.[15] Voters who could name only one candidate almost always named the incumbent, and almost no one could name only the challenger.

Incumbent members of Congress control a variety of resources that come with the office, including a paid staff distributed between Washington and a number of home district offices, free postage from Washington (called the franking privilege), a travel allowance permitting approximately one trip a week home to the district, and a communication allowance. Members routinely mail newsletters and other information and advertisements throughout their district, and they maintain their district offices principally to handle constituent complaints and problems. These activities keep the names of Congress members before their constituents in a favorable light.

Fundraising Opportunities. Incumbent members of Congress raise campaign money both within their districts and from national interest group and party sources. Potential contributors know that incumbents almost always win, and no one likes to throw money away on an unknown challenger. As a result, campaign contributions flow much more readily to incumbents than to challengers. One recent study of congressional elections estimated that incumbency was worth about half a million dollars in additional contributions, mostly from business political action committees.[16]

National party sources want to protect their incumbents as a first priority, and interest groups want to make contributions to those most likely to be in a position to help them later. A study conducted by the Center for Responsive Politics reported just prior to the 2016 House elections that House incumbents seeking reelection had, on average, a seven-to-one advantage over their challengers in total campaign resources.[17]

Challengers and Their Challenges

Most challengers lack the visibility, organization, and resources to make a credible stand against an entrenched incumbent. Current officeholders seeking to move up to a higher office and former public officials make the best challengers because they are most likely to have the experience, fundraising ability, and contacts to assemble the organization and resources needed to make a strong showing, perhaps even to win. An experienced challenger—one who has held elective public office before and is trying to move up—is four times more likely than an inexperienced candidate to beat an incumbent member of Congress.[18]

National Influences. National influences on the prospects of congressional challengers come in two main forms. One is the national political and economic climate. The other is the national system of party committees, interest groups, campaign consultants, and SuperPACs. Experienced challengers run when the general prospects of their party look bright and step aside for the sacrificial lambs when the party's prospects look dim.[19] In 2006, President Bush was down in the polls, the Iraq War was going badly, and a majority of voters told pollsters that they were ready for a change. Democrats picked up 30 seats in the House and 6 in the Senate to take majority control of both for the first time since 1994.

In 2008, voters sent Obama to the White House and added 21 seats to the Democratic House majority and 8 more to the Senate majority. By 2010, it was President Obama who was down in the polls, the economy was limping and unemployment was stuck at 9.5 percent. Several former Republican congressmen, smelling blood, stepped forward to reclaim their seats and they were joined by high quality challengers to Democratic incumbents. Republicans picked up 63 seats in the House, more than they had lost in 2006 and 2008 combined, and 6 in the Senate. Smart politicians set sail for higher office when the political winds are at their back.

But 2016 was a hard year to read. Though unemployment had dropped to 5 percent and wages had begun to pick up, many voters were convinced that the economic gains had passed them by. Democrats were confident going into election night, but when the votes were tallied they had picked up just two Senate seats and seven House seats and Donald Trump was president.

Resources from the national level are critical to most congressional campaigns. National parties and interest groups rarely spend money just to make a statement of support. They give to candidates who have demonstrated that they can raise money in their own districts and who have connections to Washington through previous experience in Congress, the executive branch, the interest group structure, or congressional staff. Sponsorship by political figures already well known in Washington also helps to establish legitimacy.

Local Considerations. Candidates for whom the political climate is supportive and the necessary resources are available still need campaign skills, appropriate political experience, and local organization and support. Campaign skills are developed in prior electoral contests; appropriate political experience might mean service in the state legislature or city council; and local organization and support means familiarity with and influence within the local party, community, and interest group structure.[20]

Challengers must know the district within which they will run. They must know the voters, divisions or groups that exist among them, and how a majority might be created from them. They must also know the distribution of influence, prestige, and wealth in their district. These are the human and financial resources upon which a campaign must draw.

Running the Race

The American political process is more open than any other in the world. Nonetheless, the higher up the electoral system one goes, the more indirect the contact with voters becomes. At the local level, candidates and their supporters walk the neighborhoods; but in the cities and at the congressional, state, and national levels television and the Internet dominate and campaigns are run by teams of highly paid professional operatives and consultants.

Campaign Organization.　Members of the U.S. Congress are at the juncture of local and national politics. At the local level, congressional campaigns still depend heavily on candidates and volunteers who take the message directly to the voters by going door-to-door and by walking the neighborhoods and shopping malls. Volunteers also organize the district, distributing leaflets and bumper stickers, placing yard signs, sitting at telephone banks, working social media, and carpooling voters to the polls on election day. Most congressional campaigns rise or fall on the ability of local experts to identify, contact, and mobilize a candidate's likely supporters.[21]

In addition, most congressional campaigns, especially those for urban districts and Senate seats, seek the assistance of professional political consultants. A high-profile political consultant usually heads a seasoned organization that provides the candidate with information from polling and focus groups, provides debate preparation and opposition research, and handles scheduling, fundraising, and media. Respected campaign consultants also provide immediate credibility in Washington with the system of interest groups, party committees, and SuperPACs.

Crafting the Themes.　A campaign needs to know what likely voters think both of its candidate and of the major issues of the day so that the two can be related to maximum advantage. Baseline polling and focus groups are the sources of this kind of information. The key is to build on candidate strengths, protect against exploitation of weaknesses by the opposition, and try to highlight themes upon which the candidate and his or her party have a natural advantage.

Later in the campaign, sophisticated tracking polls, media technology, and political consultants allow candidates to stay in touch with and respond to the public mood day-to-day. **Micro targeting** is a process borrowed from corporate marketing in which political consultants sort voters into smaller and more precise target groups, using "public items like party affiliation, ZIP-code . . . and fairly detailed consumer preferences such as the car you drive, where you vacation and which entertainment you prefer. That information is augmented by surveys that link those traits and behaviors to attitudes on political and social issues." These huge databases, if properly constructed and analyzed, can generate probability

micro targeting Campaign consultants analyze dozens of pieces of demographic, political, and consumer data to determine what issues, themes, and arguments are likely to move a voter or group of similar voters toward a candidate.

estimates of who is most likely to volunteer, contribute, or turn out to vote for the campaign and its candidate.[22]

Campaigns seek to identify the mix of characteristics, preferences, and attitudes held by their supporters and then reach out in a highly targeted way to others that share that political DNA.[23]

Raising Money.   Successful candidates must combine local fundraising with the involvement of the national party and well-disposed independent groups. Local fundraising involves familiar techniques: breakfasts and lunches, picnics and cocktail parties, and visits by party leaders or other prominent figures on the candidate's or party's behalf. National fundraising moves beyond local or even statewide sources to tap the big money concentrations in Los Angeles, Dallas, Washington, and New York. As the cost of elections has continued to escalate, national sources have increasingly displaced local sources of funds. Successful Senate races in 2016 cost an average of $12 million, and successful House races averaged $1.5 million. Outside money, of course, added to these totals; sometimes it added a great deal. Remarkably, an open house seat in Georgia's 6th congressional district, just six months after Donald Trump's win, attracted national interest and cost an all-time record $55 million. The Republican, Karen Handel, narrowly won.

Fully 60 percent of campaign costs go for fundraising, that is, money spent to raise more money, and media and candidate marketing. The need to raise increasing amounts of money has produced "the 'permanent campaign,' with full-time staff, fundraising activities, and polling that helps candidates calculate their actions in office against the reactions of potential voters in future elections."[24]

RUNNING FOR THE PRESIDENCY

The presidency is the focal point of the American political system and, therefore, the ultimate goal of every American politician. The goal is implausible for most state and local politicians, but for sitting and former governors, senators, and leading members of the House, the question is almost never whether they want it, but how it might be accomplished.[25] What Donald Trump proved in 2016, whether permanently or not remains to be seen, is that the presidency may also be open to prominent cultural figures, non-politicians, with the self-confidence, visibility, and money to take the plunge. Mark Zuckerberg (Facebook), Howard Schultz (Starbucks), and Mark Cuban (Dallas Mavericks) are intrigued.

In this section, we ask how serious candidates for the presidency organize and run their campaigns. Presidential campaigns usually begin years before the actual election with a series of critical organizational steps that are largely invisible to the public. This organizational phase of the campaign is meant to prepare and position candidates for the usually brief and intense nomination phase, which begins in Iowa and New Hampshire in February, often is over by

Q4 How does the campaign for the presidency differ from campaigns for other offices that are less visible, powerful, and prestigious?

March, and formally culminates in the midsummer party nominating conventions. In 2008, the Republican nomination campaign followed this script, but the Democrats had an epic battle between Hillary Clinton and Barack Obama that stretched into June. In 2012, Democrats rested while the Republicans had an extended nomination battle between Mitt Romney, Rick Santorum, Newt Gingrich, and Ron Paul. In 2016, both parties fought into the spring to determine their nominees. The fall general election campaign is a national contest between the Democratic and Republican nominees, and occasionally, as with Ross Perot in 1992 and Ralph Nader in 2000, a third party candidate who attracts enough attention to change the character, and perhaps the result, of the race.

Early Organization and Fundraising

Even major political figures treat the decision to run for president as momentous. They know that years of preparation, often extending over several election cycles, are required to build the organizational, financial, and partisan support to mount an effective campaign. John McCain, the Republican nominee in 2008, was the normal case. First elected to the U.S. House of Representatives in 1982, to the Senate in 1986, he ran a strong race for the Republican presidential nomination in 2000 before being defeated by George W. Bush. He campaigned extensively for Bush in 2004 and declared early for the 2008 race. He had been around this track a time or two before.

Most politicians, even those of unquestioned national stature, who look at the possibility of running for president ultimately back away. But, an open race for the presidency, in which no incumbent president or vice president is in the field, is catnip to politicians of both parties.[26] In 2016, though Vice President Joe Biden flirted with running for months, he chose not to confront former First Lady, senator, and secretary of state Hillary Clinton. So formidable was Clinton thought to be that no major figure entered the race. Her opponents were all marginal figures in the Democratic Party. Bernie Sanders, the independent democratic socialist senator from Vermont, Martin O'Malley, the former governor of Maryland, former Virginia senator Jim Webb, and former Rhode Island senator and governor Lincoln Chafee entered the race.

On the Republican side, no fewer than seventeen candidates, most with at least budding national reputations, stepped forward. It was widely seen to be an impressive field. The presumed front-runner and early fundraising leader was former Florida governor Jeb Bush. The Bush family name gave him access to national networks of conservative policy experts, donors, and volunteers. Several more sitting and former governors, including Scott Walker of Wisconsin, Chris Christie of New Jersey, Bobby Jindal of Louisiana, Mike Huckabee of Arkansas, Rick Perry of Texas, John Kasich of Ohio, George Pataki of New York, and Jim Gilmore of Virginia, all entered the race. Four sitting senators, Lindsay Graham of South Carolina, Marco Rubio of Florida, Rand Paul of Kentucky, and Ted Cruz of Texas, as well as former senator Rick Santorum of Pennsylvania, jumped into the race. Three first-time candidates, billionaire Donald Trump, retired pediatric neurosurgeon Ben Carson, and retired business executive Carly Fiorina, completed the field.

Early money and an experienced campaign organization enhance a candidate's chances of being taken seriously by the media and allow time for systematic planning.[27] Clinton and Bush, the presumed front-runners, had full-blown campaigns and hundred million dollar war-chests in place months before they formally declared their decision to run. By early 2015 all of the major candidates had websites that offered candidate bios, campaign schedules, policy statements and speeches, chat rooms and message boards, and the always urgent appeal for campaign contributions. Candidates competed to sign up friends on Facebook and to keep their supporters entertained and informed with campaign videos on YouTube. Only Trump, who most political professionals thought a vanity candidate, not to be taken seriously, seemed to ignore all of the rules. Trump realized that while the old rules might apply to career politicians, like Jeb Bush, Marco Rubio, and Hillary Clinton, they did not apply to him.[28]

The Nomination Campaign

The modern presidential nomination campaign is a state-by-state series of primaries and caucuses, beginning with Iowa and New Hampshire in early February, concluding in the spring. A **primary** is a statewide election in which the voters select among the available candidates for their party's nomination. A closed primary is one in which only registered members of the party are allowed to participate, while an open primary is open to other voters as well. A **caucus** is organized as a set of small gatherings, face-to-face meetings, in which voters debate the merits of the candidates before selecting among them. The separate caucus votes are totaled to county, congressional district, or state totals, and the state's national convention delegate seats are divided accordingly.

Following the 2008 nomination process, many Republican leaders concluded that the long primary battle between Barack Obama and Hillary Clinton had energized the Democratic Party while Senator McCain's relatively early and easy victory had not hardened him for the campaign to come. So the Republican National Committee adopted new nomination rules to make the Republican process more like the Democratic process. Most importantly, for 2016 they switched the early events, those before March 15, from a winner-take-all process, where the candidate winning a state primary or caucus got all that state's delegates to the Republican nominating convention, to a proportional process where each candidate gets a share of the delegates equivalent to his/her share of the vote. States holding events after March 15 were allowed to run winner-take-all contests.

Republican rule changes also sought to avoid the **front-loading**—more and more states crowding to the front of the electoral calendar—that had plagued the 2008 nomination contest when 36 states voted before the end of February. The goals were to extend the nomination process, let more states have a say before the nominee was decided, energize the Republican base, and toughen

primary A preliminary election in which voters select candidates to stand under their party label in a later and definitive general election.

caucus Face-to-face meeting in which rank-and-file party members discuss and vote on candidates to stand for election to offices under the party label at a later general election.

front-loading The crowding of presidential primaries and caucuses into the early weeks of the nomination period.

up the eventual nominee. In 2012 and 2016, the rules allowed Iowa, New Hampshire, South Carolina, and Nevada to vote in February, while all others were to wait until March and incentives were offered to encourage some states to wait until April, May, and even June. In 2012, a half dozen eager states, led by Florida, Michigan, and Arizona, refused to comply, forcing Iowa, New Hampshire, and South Carolina back in January and disrupting the formal schedule. But in 2016 states complied and the process worked as intended.

Caucuses and Primaries.   In 2016, thirty-six states used primary elections to choose their convention delegates while a dozen used caucuses. Several states saw Democrats use one system and Republicans the other. By tradition, the first event is the Iowa caucuses (February 1, 2016), followed closely by the New Hampshire primary (February 9, 2016). These two states, even though they are small, rural, and homogeneous, play influential roles in the presidential selection process. To enhance the regional, racial, and ethnic diversity of the states earliest in the nomination process, a Nevada caucus and a South Carolina primary occur later in February.

While the Democratic Party field quickly shrank to two, Hillary Clinton and Bernie Sanders, the much larger Republican Party field took longer to distill. A few Republican candidates, like former governors George Pataki and Jim Gilmore, simply could not command the attention or the money to get a campaign started. Even major candidates like Wisconsin governor Scott Walker, former Texas governor Rick Perry, former Louisiana governor Bobby Jindal, and South Carolina senator Lindsay Graham left the field weeks or even months

AP Photo/Dave Weaver

Caucuses are small group, face-to-face, events. Here a voter speaks on behalf of their candidate at one of many sites during the 2016 Iowa caucuses.

before the first votes were cast. Once the voting started, casualties piled up quickly. In Iowa, Clinton and Sanders finished in a virtual tie, while on the Republican side Cruz beat Trump, 28 percent to 25 percent, with Rubio close behind at 24 percent. Huckabee, Paul, and Santorum dropped out.

A week later, in the New Hampshire primary, Sanders thumped Clinton, 60 percent to 38 percent, to signal that there was a long, tough, race ahead on the Democratic side. Among Republicans, Trump finished first with 35 percent of the vote, Ohio governor John Kasich beat expectations to finish second with 16 percent, while Cruz, Bush, and Rubio clustered at 11 or 12 percent. Fiorina and Christie withdrew. Clinton and Trump won both in Nevada and South Carolina and seemed poised to build on their leads as the first big multi-state test, the March 1 Super Tuesday voting, loomed. Of the eleven states voting on Super Tuesday, about two-thirds of them in the South, Clinton won seven states to Sanders's four, including most of the bigger, delegate-rich, states. On the Republican side, Trump won seven states to Cruz's three and Rubio's one. Texas senator Ted Cruz solidified his position as the principal alternative to Donald Trump and Dr. Ben Carson left the field.

During the first two weeks of March, Clinton and Trump continued to win and to build their delegate leads, but neither could put away their principal challengers. Five big states, Florida, Illinois, Missouri, North Carolina, and Ohio, voted on March 15. Again, the front-runners won, sometimes narrowly, and the field continued to thin as Rubio dropped out, but Cruz and Kasich, who won his home state of Ohio, vowed to continue the fight. During late March and early April, a series of lightly populated, mostly western, states went for the challengers, buoying their hopes, but not significantly changing the delegate math. In mid-April, the focus of the nomination fight shifted back East where the front-runners proved to be much stronger. New York went big for Clinton and Trump on April 19 and then on April 26 they both won Pennsylvania, effectively ending the nomination fights. Sanders laid off a third of his campaign staff but did not end his campaign, Kasich went quiet, and Cruz made his last stand in Indiana on May 3. When Trump won Indiana, Cruz and Kasich suspended their campaigns. Bernie Sanders continued his campaign through the D.C. primary on June 14 before grudgingly acknowledging Hillary Clinton as the Democratic Party nominee for president.

The Declining Importance of the Conventions. National party conventions were once scenes of high drama. National party leaders, regional leaders, and state "favorite sons" led their followers into the national convention and there struggled publicly, sometimes through dozens of ballots over several days, for the presidential nomination of their party. More recently, the national party conventions have ratified decisions made by the voters in their primaries and caucuses. The Democratic convention of 1952 was the last to take more than a single ballot to select its nominee, though the 2016 Republican convention had more drama than most.

In recent decades, **national party conventions** have become increasingly controlled and stylized events where the parties seek to present their best face

national party convention The Democratic and Republican Parties meet in national convention every four years, in the summer just prior to the presidential election, to choose a presidential candidate and adopt a party platform.

AP Photo/STAR MAX/IPx/Dennis Van Tine

Donald and Melania Trump, with members of their family, acknowledge the support of their party on the final night of the 2016 Republican National Convention.

to the voters. With the whole nation watching, the parties try to portray themselves as unified behind a leader and a program. They seek to highlight their key issues and themes, rouse their partisans to action, attract the attention of independent voters, and set the tone for the coming general election campaign. Convention coverage, which used to be almost gavel-to-gavel, was cut back to only three hours in prime time on the major networks. Since 2000, gavel-to-gavel prime time coverage has moved from the networks to cable channels like CNN, FOX, C-SPAN, and MSNBC.

The General Election Campaign

general election A final or definitive election in which candidates representing their respective parties contend for election to office.

The **general election** campaign is a national battle in which all of the states are equally in play at the same time and throughout the process. On the other hand, the logic and rules of the contest force the battle back to the states in certain fundamental ways. Most strikingly, as we saw so clearly in 2000 and 2016, the winner is not simply the candidate for whom the most people vote; rather, the winner is the candidate who gets the most votes in the Electoral College. Which raises several questions: what is the Electoral College, where did it come from, how does it work, and is it still useful today?

The Electoral College, a creation of the Founding Fathers, confuses and worries many Americans. The Founders were concerned that voters would not have enough information or judgment to select the nation's chief executive. They sought to leaven the voters' judgments with those of the political elite—the electors—in each state. Each state was assigned the number of electors equal to the number of seats in their congressional delegation. Since each state has two senators, no matter their population, this served to increase the influence of the smaller, less populous, states.

In modern times, electors no longer exercise independent judgment. They are simply party leaders who cast their votes to reflect the popular vote outcome in their state, but all of the state's electoral votes (except in the cases of Nebraska and Maine, which employ a slightly different process) still go to the winner of the popular vote, no matter how narrow that win is. This imperfect relationship between the popular vote and the Electoral College vote opens up the possibility, the reality in 2000 and 2016, that the winner of the popular vote and the Electoral College vote will differ—in which case the winner of the Electoral College vote is president. It happens only intermittently (the last time prior to 2016 was 2000 and the time before that was 1888), but every time it does, Americans scratch their collective heads and wonder what we are still doing with such a system. Still, because the less populous states benefit from the Electoral College system, it is unlikely to be changed any time soon.

Hence, the logic of the general election is not to pile up as many popular votes as possible. Rather, it is to win more votes than your opponent(s) in as many states as possible. Therefore, sound strategy dictates that candidates

AP Photo/Evan Vucci

After the Republican National Convention, while the Democrats were still meeting in their national convention in Philadelphia, Donald Trump and his vice presidential choice, Indiana governor Mike Pence, stumped through the key swing state of Virginia on July 25, 2016.

shift resources out of states where they are comfortably ahead (because they are going to get all of those states' electoral votes whether they win with 51 percent or 91 percent) to states that are still competitive and whose electoral votes they still might pick up with a little extra time, effort, or advertising money. In recent elections the "battleground" states have tended to be those with large blocs of electoral votes where both parties have been successful in recent elections. In the East, this would be states like Pennsylvania and Virginia, in the Midwest, states like Illinois, Michigan, and Ohio; and the big prize in the South is Florida. In the West, Colorado, Nevada, and New Mexico draw the attention of both parties (see Figure 7.1).

Therefore, general election campaigns are organized both to fight broad battles at the national level and to move resources between and among the states as the flow of the campaign and the changing strategic situation in each of the states seem to suggest. Each campaign has an inner circle of advisers close to the candidate who set strategy and a broader organization that executes the campaign plan.

The Campaign Organization.   Presidential campaigns vary somewhat in their organization, but in general the campaign chairperson organizes the

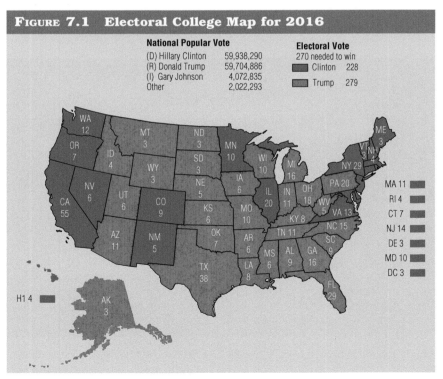

FIGURE 7.1   Electoral College Map for 2016

National Popular Vote
(D) Hillary Clinton	59,938,290
(R) Donald Trump	59,704,886
(I) Gary Johnson	4,072,835
Other	2,022,293

Electoral Vote
270 needed to win
Clinton   228
Trump   279

Source: Federal Election Commission.

broad operation and acts as liaison between and among the candidate, the party, the presidential campaign, and the congressional campaign committees. The campaign manager assists in setting general strategy, coordinates the state operations, and tries to keep the campaign on message. The finance chairperson runs the crucial fundraising operation. Recent campaigns, including those in 2016, have taken to using fancier titles, like senior political advisor or chief strategist, for their top officials, but they still play the traditional strategic planning and organizational roles.

A political director oversees the day-to-day operations, manages the ready response team (discussed below), and sees that resources are allocated and reallocated to achieve the best overall results. Every campaign also has a lead pollster, media consultants, data analysts, communications strategists and technicians, speechwriters, fundraisers, and schedulers.

The candidate's itinerary is set by the campaign scheduling team. The scheduling team's job is to get the candidate to those places and those events that will do him or her the most good. For example, the candidate's time would be better spent appearing before a group of swing voters in a state where he or she is two points ahead, or maybe even better, two points behind. After the site of a presidential candidate's visit has been determined, an advance team begins work to see that the candidate, an enthusiastic crowd, the media, and anything else required for a substantively and visually satisfying event are in place. The advance team's job is to ensure that the event generates the right message and feeling for both those attending and for the people who will read about it in the paper or see it on the television news.[29]

Finally, each national campaign has a ready response team. A **ready response team** is a group assigned to respond immediately and forcefully to any charge or comment from the opposition that, if left unattended, might harm the candidate. The 1992 Bill Clinton campaign organized a "war room" led by strategist James Carville to respond quickly and forcefully to any charges, inaccuracies, or slips by the George H.W. Bush reelection campaign. During the 1990s, candidates' war room operations were focused on managing the traditional print and electronic press.

Candidates now have a vastly more complex media landscape to manage. The year 2004 was the first presidential campaign in which all of the candidates had a presence on the Internet. Since 2008, candidates have sought to craft a hybrid media strategy by balancing "the decentralizing advantages of the Internet with traditional top-down campaign approaches, utilizing new media and online campaign techniques to secure their base while reaching less committed voters through television, direct mail, canvassing, and other traditional means."[30] All of the candidates in recent campaign cycles have had profile and friends pages on YouTube and Facebook, and they communicated constantly via Twitter and Tumblr.

The national campaign staff struggles to oversee a structure of campaign operatives that reaches to the state and local levels. The critical responsibility of these state and local operations is to identify and organize volunteers and voters, put up yard signs, and canvass door-to-door. After decades of

ready response team A group within a campaign staff that is assigned to respond immediately to any charge or negative comment made by the opposition or the media.

Q5 Does money dominate presidential elections?

concentrating on the "air wars" of the media campaign, the Republican Party in 2004 and both parties since have put new assets into their "ground game" or GOTV—get out the vote—efforts. Each party worked to create an army of volunteers, armed with electronic devices loaded with block-by-block voter identification information, to have front-porch contacts with as many potential voters as possible before the election. All of this, of course, takes a great deal of money.

Money and the Road to the White House

The modern legal basis for regulating the money that flows through presidential campaigns was laid in the early 1970s. The **Federal Election Campaign Act (FECA)** of 1971 and a series of strengthening amendments passed in 1974 set limits on the amount a presidential or vice presidential candidate could spend on his or her own campaign, limited individual contributions to federal campaigns including presidential campaigns to $1,000, and created a presidential election fund to support public financing of presidential elections. Presidential candidates accepting public financing had to abide by state-by-state spending limits during the nomination process. Each major party nominee then received a significant but limited amount for the general election contest. These strict rules have been slowly dismantled over recent decades.

Federal Election Campaign Act (FECA) Campaign reform legislation passed in 1971, with major amendments in 1974 and later, that required disclosure and set limits on campaign contributions and provided public funding of presidential elections.

In the latter half of the 1970s, two fairly large holes were poked in the FECA campaign finance system, one by the courts and the other by Congress. In 1976, the Supreme Court, in a case known as *Buckley v. Valeo*, declared provisions of the 1974 FECA amendments limiting the amounts that candidates could contribute to their own campaigns to be unconstitutional limitations on free speech. The court also held that political action committees (PACs) and other groups, as long as they did not coordinate their activities with a candidate's campaign, could spend as much as they wanted on campaign activities. In 1979, Congress passed amendments to FECA permitting political parties to raise unlimited amounts of money for party building, voter registration, and voter turnout activities. These unrestricted funds, unlike the limited amounts of money candidates were allowed to raise, were referred to as **soft money**.

Buckley v. Valeo (1976) This decision declared provisions of the 1974 Federal Election Campaign Act (FECA) limiting the amount that a candidate could contribute to his or her campaign to be an unconstitutional limitation on free speech.

During the 1990s, these and other holes in the campaign finance system allowed a flood of barely regulated money into presidential elections and spawned a movement for additional reform. In 1992 and 1996, Ross Perot drew on his extensive personal fortune to finance presidential campaigns, and in 1996 Steve Forbes did the same. Meanwhile, the presence of unregulated soft money in presidential campaigns burgeoned from $86 million in 1992, to $262 million in 1996, to $495 million in 2000. To many, the FECA system seemed broken (see Figure 7.2).

soft money Amendments to the FECA passed in 1979 allowed unlimited contribution to political parties for party building, voter registration, and voter turnout.

Senator John McCain's (R-AZ) focus on campaign finance during his 2000 presidential campaign and the subsequent corporate scandals of 2001 and 2002 broke open an ongoing debate over campaign finance reform. In March 2002, after a seven-year stalemate, Congress passed and President

Presidential candidates frequently campaign surrounded by their family because it is thought to soften and humanize them. What costs and benefits did Hillary Clinton face campaigning with her family as the first female party nominee and with a former president for a husband?

Bush reluctantly signed the **Bipartisan Campaign Reform Act (BCRA)**. BCRA, popularly known as McCain–Feingold after its chief Senate sponsors, John McCain (R-AZ) and Russ Feingold (D-WI), increased the allowable individual contribution from $1,000 to $2,000 and provided for future increases based on inflation. The maximum allowable contribution for 2016 was $2,700. The BCRA also banned soft money contributed to the national political parties and prohibited issue ads, less flatteringly referred to as "attack ads," within thirty days of a primary election and sixty days of a general election. Many expected the Supreme Court to strike down some or all of these limitations, just as it had in *Buckley* nearly thirty years earlier. Initially, the court upheld the BCRA, but in 2007 and even more decisively in 2010, after two changes in the composition of the court, it struck down key elements of the law.

Where Does the Money Come From?   Until 2008 the bulk of the money financing presidential campaigns flowed through the FECA system (now the BCRA system) either as private contributions subject to federal limits and matching or as general election grants to each of the major party candidates. BCRA provisions limited candidates operating within the federal campaign funding system to contributions of no more than $2,000, of which only $250 was subject to federal matching. To establish eligibility for federal

Bipartisan Campaign Reform Act (BCRA) Commonly known as McCain–Feingold, the 2002 BCRA was the first major revision of campaign finance laws since the early 1970s.

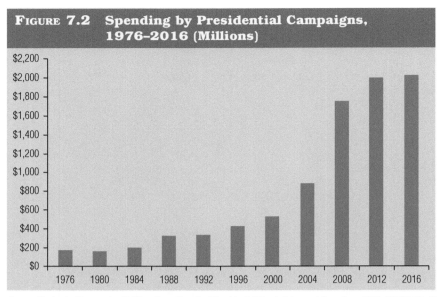

FIGURE **7.2** **Spending by Presidential Campaigns, 1976–2016 (Millions)**

Source: Center for Responsive Politics, Open Secrets, "Presidential Fundraising and Spending, 1976–2012," http://www.opensecrets.org/pres12/totals.php?cycle= Updated by the author.

matching funds, a candidate for the nomination of his or her party had to raise $100,000: $5,000 in twenty different states in amounts of no more than $250. Most of the candidates for president in 2008 stayed within the BCRA system, but Hillary Clinton, Barack Obama, and John McCain all opted out for the nomination phase.

Though Barack Obama and John McCain tentatively agreed in 2008 that if they were the nominees of their parties, they would give back contributions raised for the general election and take the public financing, Obama's extraordinary fundraising success during the nomination fight convinced him to forgo public funding for the general election campaign as well. McCain's fundraising lagged badly, so he did take federal funds. In 2012, neither the Obama reelection campaign nor the Romney campaign even thought about accepting, and being limited by, public funding.

President Obama and the Democratic National Committee and Mitt Romney and the Republican National Committee each raised and spent more than $1 billion for the 2012 campaign. The Democrats outraised the Republicans, but the $1 billion raised and spent by outside groups, the so-called SuperPACS and the even murkier non-profit "social welfare groups," leaned heavily to the Republicans. An additional $1.8 billion was spent by congressional campaigns, $430 million was spent by outside groups to effect congressional campaigns, and hundreds of millions in shadow money was spent off the books and never likely to be accounted for fully. The Center for Responsive Politics estimated that a total of $6 billion, a record, was spent on the 2012 elections.[31]

Though Donald Trump claimed to be worth as much as $10 billion and declared his willingness to spend up to $1 billion of his own money on the 2016 presidential race, he was out-raised by Hillary Clinton throughout the contest. Interestingly, Clinton's early fundraising was fueled by women. Close to half of her "bundlers," fundraisers who not only make their own contributions but solicit them from others and bundle all of the contributions together, were women and more than half of her early contributions came from women. Donald Trump's early fundraising lagged, both because he enjoyed so much free media and because many donors were reluctant to give to a billionaire.

Clinton began her fundraising in early 2015 when it looked like she would face the formidable Bush-family fundraising machine. Unlike Obama, Clinton allowed lobbyists to bundle for her and she embraced SuperPACs from the beginning. Clinton SuperPACs, joint fundraising with the Democratic Party, and her campaign raised $1.3 billion. Donald Trump began fundraising much later, not in earnest until he had nearly secured the nomination, and faced more skepticism from Republican mega-donors. The Trump campaign and related party and SuperPAC entities raised about $850 million. Entering the last month of the campaign, Clinton had about $150 million on-hand while Trump had about $75 million.[32] When the dust cleared, Clinton had won the popular vote, but Trump had won the Electoral College vote—and the White House.

McConnell v. F.E.C. The Supreme Court upheld all major elements of the Bipartisan Campaign Reform Act (BCRA) of 2002, including those permitting regulation of soft money and issue ads.

Citizens United v. F.E.C. Citizens United struck down the limits on corporate and union spending on elections that had been in *McCain v. Feingold* and other statutes going back to 1907.

CAMPAIGN AND ELECTION REFORM

Even a casual observer of recent American elections, from the Florida debacle in 2000 through the endless presidential campaign of 2016, will have wondered about reform. Is our election system secure and fair? Can we encourage more and better informed voting? How should we organize and fund our political campaigns, especially our presidential campaigns? And is the Electoral College still an integral part of our presidential election process, or a distracting vestige of the past?

First, how big a problem is electoral fraud in the U.S.? Thirty-six states have passed laws, some upheld by the Supreme Court, requiring voters to present government issued photo IDs to election officials before voting. Clearly, we do not want people voting illegally. But just as clearly, we do not want to throw obstacles in the way of legal voters, especially if we are truly worried about low turnout. And how should we respond to reports that Russian hackers broke into computers of the Democratic National Committee, the Rubio campaign, and twenty-one state voting systems.

Second, the U.S. is a democratic society with a free market economy, so we expect differentials in wealth and we know that people will spend their money to advance their preferences and interests. But Congress tried to limit the impact of big money by adopting public financing of presidential elections in the early 1970s. That system is now near collapse. While most major candidates abandoned public financing during the nomination phase of the 2008

Is the Supreme Court Right to See Money as Speech?

In a landmark decision known as *Buckley v. Valeo* (1976), the Supreme Court upheld Congress's right to set limits on the amount an individual can contribute to federal campaigns, but struck down limits on overall spending in campaigns, spending by candidates from their own personal wealth, and independent spending by individuals and groups on behalf of a candidate. The only spending limits left in place by the court were limits attached to voluntary acceptance of public funding. The limits generally held through the 1990s.

The Supreme Court reasoned in *Buckley* that campaign spending is speech intended to communicate ideas and as such is protected from government regulation by the First Amendment. The court held that "A restriction on the amount of money a person or group can spend on political communication during a campaign necessarily reduces the quantity of expression." The court further held that the only ground upon which campaign spending can explicitly be limited is to combat corruption defined as a "financial quid pro quo: dollars for political favors."

The 2002 McCain–Feingold legislation seemed to raise many of the same issues that the court had dealt with in *Buckley*—restrictions on political spending by groups and individuals through soft money contributions and issue ads in the period immediately before elections. Hence, McCain–Feingold was immediately challenged by a legal team assembled by Senator Mitch McConnell (R-KY), the bill's principal opponent in the Senate.

McConnell v. F.E.C. came before the Supreme Court on September 8, 2003. McConnell's legal team contended that the prohibition of soft money contributions by wealthy donors and interests, as well as the limitations on issue ads thirty days before primaries and sixty days before general elections, were unconstitutional limitations on free speech. The high court, divided 5–4, announced its decision on December 10, 2003. The majority opinion, written by Justices John Paul Stevens and Sandra Day O'Connor, rejected the First Amendment free speech claims of the opponents and upheld all of the major provisions of McCain–Feingold. Campaign spending as free speech seemed to have taken a blow.

In 2007, following two new Bush appointments to the Supreme Court, Chief Justice John Roberts in place of Chief Justice William Rehnquist, and, more importantly, Justice Samuel Alito in place of Justice Sandra Day O'Connor, the court reconsidered elements of McCain–Feingold in a case called *Federal Election Commission v. Wisconsin Right to Life, Inc. (551 U.S. 449)*. For a court once again divided 5–4, Chief Justice Roberts wrote, "Discussion of issues cannot be suppressed simply because the issues may also be pertinent in an election. Where the First Amendment is implicated, the tie goes to the speaker, not the censor." Writing for the dissenters, Justice David Souter

campaign, Barack Obama was the first major party candidate since 1972 to depend on private fundraising for the general election. In 2012 and 2016, both major candidates did so.

Third, some reform of the state-by-state primary and caucus presidential nomination system did take place before 2016, but other reforms remain under discussion. One proposal calls for regional contests—East, Midwest, South, and West, perhaps—with the regions rotating the order in which they vote from one election to the next. Another, known as the Delaware Plan, calls for the twelve least populous states to vote in March, the next thirteen in April, the next thirteen said, "After today, . . . the possibilities for regulating corporate and union campaign money are unclear." Senator McCain declared the decision "regrettable."[33]

The Supreme Court went out of its way to turn the case of *Citizens United v. Federal Election Commission* (2010) into a direct challenge to limits on corporations and unions spending on elections directly from their treasuries. Citizens United, a conservative advocacy group, produced an unrelentingly negative film, *Hillary: The Movie*, for release during Clinton's 2008 presidential nomination campaign. A trial judge found that the movie was a campaign commercial that could be prohibited within 30 days of a primary election under McCain–Feingold.

During oral arguments before the Supreme Court, Chief Justice Roberts asked, if the movie fell under the campaign finance law, how about a campaign book that urged readers to vote for or against a candidate? The government's lawyer, Deputy Solicitor General Malcolm Stewart, responded that such a book could be prohibited. Several justices worried that the government's reading of the McCain–Feingold statute was too broad and instructed the parties to brief the fundamental question of whether banning corporate spending on elections was an unconstitutional denial of corporate and union free speech rights. After reargument, the Supreme Court struck down most of the McCain–Feingold limits on corporate and unions campaign contributions.

Justice Kennedy, writing for the majority, declared: "If the First Amendment has any force, it prohibits Congress from fining or jailing citizens, or associations of citizens, for simply engaging in political speech." Many observers were stunned. One particularly interested observer, President Barack Obama, called the decision "a green light to a new stampede of special interest money . . . . It is a major victory for big oil, Wall Street banks, health insurance companies and other powerful interests . . . to drown out the voices of everyday Americans."[34]

What do you think?

- Is money speech?
- Should wealthy individuals, corporations, and unions be able to spend all that they want in election campaigns?
- If so, should they be able to say bluntly, vote for candidate X, or vote against candidate Y?
- If not, how do you justify telling a wealthy person, or a wealthy corporation or union for that matter, that they surpassed their limit of free speech?

PRO	CON
People have a right to express themselves	Our politics are awash in interested money
Spending to communicate is free speech	Big money can erode one-man-one-vote
Limiting speech is unconstitutional	Limits protect everyone's right to be heard

in May, and the twelve most populous states in June. That way, most voters would get to watch the candidates in earlier, smaller, contests before voting. More than half of citizens live in the twelve largest states and so would not vote until June. What do you think would be the pluses and minuses of these plans?

Finally, should we discard the Electoral College in favor of direct, popular, election of the president? Since the Electoral College is mandated in the Constitution and a constitutional amendment would be very difficult to pass, a shortcut has been proposed. States could simply pass a law requiring that their electoral votes to go, not to the winner of the statewide popular vote, as is now done, but to the winner of the national popular vote. If enough states, even just the dozen largest, made this change we would effectively select the president by popular vote without amending the Constitution. Interesting idea? Maybe, but it is still a long shot, though another disputed election like 2000 and 2016 might make it less so.

Chapter Summary

Campaigns and elections are the collective processes by which democracies choose the path that they will take into the future. Ideally, voting is the one opportunity made equally available to all members of the democracy to affect that critical decision. Yet, almost half of the voting-age population fails to participate even in presidential elections.

In this chapter we have seen that there are some fairly straightforward explanations for the generally low turnout in American elections. We leave citizens alone to figure out how to register to vote, whereas virtually every other wealthy democracy makes that a government responsibility, and a few even mandate voting. Motor Voter made it easier to register to vote, but about 90 million Americans of voting age did not cast ballots in 2016.

Those who do vote make their decisions between parties and candidates in light of a number of influences. Party identification is the most important influence for active partisans and leaners, particularly in low-information elections. In more visible campaigns, where more information is readily available, issue positions and candidate attributes can lead voters to abandon their standing party commitments at least for the current election.

Low turnout raises questions of democratic legitimacy. Stunningly high reelection rates raise questions of responsiveness and accountability. Incumbents benefit from advantages in personal visibility, political organization, and money. Challengers tend to do poorly unless they are experienced politicians able to raise money locally and attract the attention of the national party and PACs or unless they have great personal wealth. Still, some electoral climates, like 2006 for the Democrats and 2010 for the Republicans, are friendlier to challengers as the national currents run strongly against one party or the other.

The race for the presidency is the classic American election. It begins, mostly out of sight, with potential candidates building their own and assessing each other's organizational and financial prospects. Early money and an experienced organization are required to survive the grueling presidential nomination process. Each major party nominee is then presented to the American people in a highly stylized and thoroughly choreographed nominating convention in midsummer. The general election campaign then occurs between late summer and the first Tuesday in November. It is a national contest designed to produce both popular and Electoral College majorities.

Key Terms

Bipartisan Campaign Reform Act (BCRA)

Buckley v. Valeo

caucus

Citizens United v. F.E.C.

Federal Election Campaign Act (FECA)

front-loading

general election

McConnell v. F.E.C.

micro targeting

Motor Voter

national party convention

primary

ready response team

soft money

suffrage

voter registration

voter turnout

Suggested Readings

Dionne, E.J., Norman J. Ornstein, and Thomas E. Mann, *One Nation After Trump: A Guide For the Perplexed, the Disillusioned, the Desperate, and the Not Yet Deported.* New York: St. Martin's Press, 2017. The authors argue that the Constitution was never intended to or expected to produce a president like Donald Trump.

Dowling, Conor M. and Michael G. Miller. *SuperPAC: Money, Elections, and Voters after Citizens United.* New York: Routledge, 2014. Follows the origins and implications of the Citizens United case as they relate to the U.S. campaign finance system.

Fiorina, Morris P., *Unstable Majorities: Polarization, Party Sorting, and Political Stalemate.* Washington, D.C.: The Brookings Institution, 2017. Contends that a polarized political class no longer well represents the American public who are more moderate.

Richard Hasen, *Plutocrats United: Campaign Money, the Supreme Court, and the Distortion of American Elections.* New Haven, CT: Yale University Press, 2016. Hasen reviews the kinds of campaign finance reforms most likely to survive Supreme Court scrutiny and limit the impact of money on campaigns.

Polsby, Nelson W., Aaron Wildavsky, Steven Scheir, and David Hopkins. *Presidential Elections,* 14th ed. New York: Rowman & Littlefield, 2015. The standard work on the structure, process, and results of presidential elections historically and in the contemporary period.

Sunstein, Cass R. *Impeachment: A Citizen's Guide.* Cambridge, MA: Harvard University Press, 2017. Sunstein recounts the purposes, history, and precedents regarding impeachment.

Wattenberg, Martin P. *Is Voting for Young People?* 4th ed. New York: Routledge, 2016. Wattenberg argues that motivating young people to follow politics and to vote is a heavy lift, though he proposes ways to change that.

Wayne, Stephen J. *The Road to the White House 2016*. New York: Wadsworth, 2015. Like Polsby and Wildavsky, this book describes the process of running for election to the presidency.

Web Resources

1 www.fec.gov
The official website of the Federal Election Commission provides information on campaign contribution laws, how to register to vote, and election results for federal elections. It also gives national and state figures on registration and voter turnouts.

2 www.fairvote.org
Official website of the Center for Voting and Democracy. This organization is dedicated to educating the public about various international voting systems and how they affect voter turnout. It examines the idea of proportional representation in addition to the U.S. federal system of single-member districts.

3 www.realclearpolitics.com
A frequently updated gathering of the most important news stories, commentaries, blogs, videos, and polls.

4 www.opensecrets.org
This is the premier website for campaign contributions and candidate, party, and lobbyist spending.

5 www.sunlightfoundation.com
The Sunlight Foundation is a reform-minded watchdog on political spending.

Notes

1 M. Margaret Conway, *Political Participation in the United States*, 3rd ed. (Washington, D.C.: Congressional Quarterly Press, 2000), 3.
2 Sheryl Gay Stolberg and Erik Eckholm, "Virginia Felons Get Back Votes," *New York Times*, April 23, 2016, A1, A14.
3 U.S. Census Bureau, "Voting and Registration in the Election of November 2016," Table 2. Similar tables go back into the 1960s.
4 Matthew J. Streb, *Rethinking American Electoral Democracy* (New York: Routledge, 2008), 17–25. See also Kate Samuelson, "7 Ideas from Other Countries That Could Improve U.S. Elections," *Time*, November 14, 2016, p. 11.
5 Michael S. Lewis-Beck, William G. Jacoby, Helmut Norpoth, and Herbert F. Weisberg, *The American Voter Revisited* (Ann Arbor, MI: University of Michigan Press, 2008), 293–414.

6 Andrew Gelman, *Red State, Blue State, Rich State, Poor State* (Princeton, NJ: Princeton University Press, 2008), 144.

7 William H. Flanigan and Nancy H. Zingale, *Political Behavior of the American Electorate*, 13th ed. (Washington, D.C.: Congressional Quarterly Press, 2015), 73–84; Conway, *Political Participation in the United States*, 32–35.

8 Jan E. Leighley and Jonathan Nagler, *Who Votes Now? Demographics, Issues, Inequality and Turnout in the United States* (Princeton, NJ: Princeton University Press, 2014). See also Christine E. Bejarano, *The Latino Gender Gap in U.S. Politics* (New York: Routledge, 2014).

9 Richard R. Lau and David P. Redlawsk, *How Voters Decide: Information Processing in Electoral Campaigns* (New York: Cambridge University Press, 2006). See also Daniel Kahneman, *Thinking, Fast and Slow* (New York: Farrar, Straus, and Giroux, 2011), 90–91.

10 Stephen Ansolabehere and Shanto Iyengar, *Going Negative: How Political Advertisements Shrink and Polarize the Electorate* (New York: Free Press, 1995), 65–66. See also Arthur Lupia, *Uninformed: Why People Know So Little about Politics and What We Can Do about It* (New York: Oxford University Press, 2016), 11, 45.

11 Nelson W. Polsby, Aaron Wildavsky, Steven Schier, and David Hopkins, *Presidential Elections*, 15th ed. (Lanham, MD: Rowman & Littlefield, 2015), 16–17.

12 Samuel L. Popkin, *The Reasoning Voter: Communication and Persuasion in Presidential Campaigns* (Chicago: University of Chicago Press, 1991), 41, 57.

13 Gary C. Jacobson, *The Electoral Origins of Divided Government* (Boulder, CO: Westview Press, 1990), 112.

14 Ryan Lizza, "Battle Plans: How Obama Won," *The New Yorker*, November 17, 2008, 46–56.

15 Alan Ehrenhalt, *United States of Ambition: Politicians, Power, and the Pursuit of Office* (New York: Times Books, 1992), 9.

16 Alexander Fouirnaies and Andrew B. Hall, "The Financial Incumbency Advantage: Causes and Consequences," *Journal of Politics*, vol. 76, no. 3, May 2014, pp. 711–724.

17 http://www.opensecrets.org/news/201210/2012-election-spending-will-reach-6.html.

18 Jacobson, *The Electoral Origins of Divided Government*, 51.

19 Walter J. Stone, et al., "Candidate Entry, Voter Response and Partisan Tides in the 2002 and 2006 Elections," in Jeffrey J. Mondak and Donna-Gene Mitchell (eds.), *Fault Lines: Why the Republicans Lost Congress* (New York: Routledge, 2008).

20 David R. Mayhew, *Parties and Policies: How the American Government Works* (New Haven, CT: Yale University Press, 2008), 26.

21 Dennis W. Johnson, *Political Consultants in American Elections* (New York: Routledge, 2016), 1–43.

22 Eitan D. Hersh, *Hacking the Electorate: How Campaigns Perceive Voters* (New York: Cambridge University Press, 2015). See also Sasha Issenberg, *The Victory Lab: The Secret Science of Winning Campaigns* (New York: Broadway Books, 2012..

23 Dan Gilgoff, "Everyone Is a Special Interest: Microtargeters Study Who You Are and What You Like," *U.S. News and World Report*, September 25, 2006, 30–32. See also Johnson, *Political Consultants*, 186.

24 W. Lance Bennett, *The Governing Crisis: Media, Money, and Marketing in American Elections* (New York: St. Martin's Press, 1992), 145.

25 Barbara Norrander, *The Imperfect Primary* (New York: Routledge, 2010), 9–14.

26 Samuel L. Popkin, *The Candidate: What It Takes to Win—and Hold—the White House* (New York: Oxford University Press, 2012).

27 Polsby, et al., *Presidential Elections*, 90–101.

28 Joshua Green, *Devil's Bargain: Steve Bannon, Donald Trump, and the Storming of the Presidency* (New York: Penguin Books, 2017), 40.

29 Polsby, et al., *Presidential Elections*, 136–140.

30 Matthew R. Kerbel, *Netroots: Online Progressives and the Transformation of American Politics* (New York: Routledge, 2009), 9. See also Matthew R. Kerbel and Christopher J. Bowers, *Next Generation Netroots: Realignment and the Rise of the Internet Left* (New York: Routledge, 2016.

31 http://www.opensecrets.org/news/2012/10/2012-election-spending-will-reach-6.html.

32 Nicholas Confessore, "Clinton Doubles Trump: $150 Million on Hand," *New York Times*, October 16, 2016, Y19.

33 Linda Greenhouse, "Justices, In a 5 to 4 Decision, Back Campaign Finance Law That Curbs Contribution," *New York Times*, September 11, 2003.

34 Conor M. Dowling and Michael L. Miller, *SUPER PAC! Money, Elections, and Voters after Citizens United* (New York: Routledge, 2014), 31.

Chapter 8

CONGRESS
Partisanship, Polarization, and Gridlock

Focus Questions: from reading to thinking

Q1 What purposes were the Founders trying to serve by constructing and empowering the Congress as they did?

Q2 How does the committee system in Congress work to promote specialized knowledge and expertise among members?

Q3 What are the stages of consideration through which most legislation must pass to become a law?

Q4 What pressures operate on a member of Congress as he or she prepares to make an important legislative decision?

Q5 How serious has Congress been in its recent reform efforts?

The Constitution TODAY

THE CENSUS, REAPPORTIONMENT, AND GERRYMANDERING

Article I, section 2 (in part): "Representatives . . . shall be apportioned among the several states . . . according to their respective numbers. . . . The actual enumeration shall be made. . . every. . . ten years, in such manner as [Congress] shall by law direct."

Census results tell us how many people live in the United States and where they live. The population of each state determines how many seats in the U.S. House of Representatives that state gets. State legislatures then must redraw congressional, state legislative, and other district boundaries so that each contains an equal number of residents. Controlling the redistricting process allows lines to be drawn that advantage the dominant party and its candidates and disadvantage their opponents. The struggle over power is and has always been central to politics.

Elbridge Gerry was one of the first to see how redistricting could be used to partisan advantage. Gerry was a great man in his day. A graduate of Harvard College, he signed both the Declaration of Independence and the Articles of Confederation. He attended and took an active part in the Constitutional Convention but refused to sign the final document because it lacked a bill of rights. He died in 1814 while serving as vice president in the administration of President James Madison. Despite these achievements, Gerry is best remembered as the father of the Gerrymander. As Governor of Massachusetts, Gerry oversaw redrawing congressional district boundaries following the 1810 census. One of the oddly shaped districts, designed to maximize the electoral prospects of his Jeffersonian Democratic Party over the Federalists, reminded a local newspaper editor of a salamander—no, a **Gerrymander**! And the name stuck.

gerrymander Refers to the strange shape of some congressional districts that result when parties draw districts intended to maximize their political advantage.

Article I, section 2, of the Constitution says that the number of seats each state gets in the U.S. House of Representatives will be based on population as determined by an enumeration—what we call the census—conducted every ten years. Each state is guaranteed at least one seat in the House and then additional seats are awarded based on population. Through the 1910 census, as population grew, the size of the House was simply increased so that some states gained but few states ever lost seats. Following the 1910 census, which took place in the middle of a huge immigration surge, the size of the House was increased to 435 seats and fixed there by law. But fixing the size of the House at 435 made reapportionment a more contentious process. Now, if some states got additional seats because of population growth, other states had to lose seats. This reallocation of seats among the states is called reapportionment.

redistricting The redrawing of congressional district boundaries after each census.

Reapportionment, of course, is not the end of the process. **Redistricting,** that is redrawing congressional and other electoral district boundaries, must still be done and it is a complex and conflictual political process. Incumbents follow the process like hawks because if their district are to be changed, they want them made safer, not more competitive. The majority party obviously wants to protect its incumbents, but they may wish to take excess votes away from some of them to try to gain advantage in another district. Finally, the majority party tries to limit the clout of the minority party, either spreading their voters thinly across a number of districts or packing them into just a few districts.

The U.S. Supreme Court has laid out several legal requirements over the years for redistricting. First, each district must have equal numbers of residents. Second, districts should be as compact and contiguous as they reasonably can be. And third, districts may not reduce minority representation. But within these limits, modern computer technology allows levels of partisan manipulation and creativity that Elbridge Gerry could not have imagined.[1] Mapping census data onto precinct voting results from past elections allows redistricting experts to create districts whose partisan tendencies are known down to the city block and even the individual household. How these lines are drawn goes a long way toward determining partisan political advantage for the subsequent decade.

◆▸▸◀◀◆

THE UNITED STATES CONGRESS

Mark Twain, perhaps America's greatest humourist, was merciless in making fun of politicians in general and members of Congress in particular. Twain described members of Congress as the "only native American criminal class" and regaled his audiences with jokes like this: "Suppose you were an idiot. Suppose you were a member of Congress. But I repeat myself." Similar attitudes toward Congress can be heard any night in the monologues of Jimmy Kimmel, Stephen Colbert, Seth Meyers, and others.

What do we expect from Congress, and why does Congress have such a tough time meeting our expectations? Unfortunately, we expect several at least potentially incompatible things from Congress. First, we expect members of Congress to articulate the views and protect the interests of their constituents. Second, we expect Congress to stop talking at some point and enact a policy or program that works for the nation as a whole. As we shall see, Congress has a difficult time moving gracefully from discussion to decision and individual members of Congress have a difficult time lifting their gaze from local constituent interests to national interests.[2]

In this chapter, we ask and answer several important questions. First, what role did the Founders see for the Congress within the broader American political system? Second, how has Congress organized to do its work? Third, what are the key forces or influences that affect congressional deliberation and decision? Fourth, we describe the budgetary process as an example of how Congress works with the president and others to craft the nation's annual spending plan. And finally, we ask what reforms Congress has undergone in recent decades, and what reforms are now under discussion that might prove helpful?

ORIGINS AND POWERS OF THE CONGRESS

Q1 What purposes were the Founders trying to serve by constructing and empowering the Congress as they did?

The Founders drew their understanding of legislatures from English theory and practice and from watching and serving in their own colonial legislatures. During the late seventeenth century, the English political theorist John Locke deployed the ideas of "popular sovereignty" and "legislative supremacy" to justify the dominance of the Parliament and particularly of its lower house, the House of Commons.

popular sovereignty The idea that all legitimate governmental authority comes from the people and can be reclaimed by them if government becomes neglectful or abusive.

legislative supremacy The idea that the lawmaking authority in government should be supreme over the executive and judicial powers.

Popular sovereignty is the idea that all legitimate governmental authority comes from the consent of the people and that the people can reclaim that authority if government becomes neglectful or abusive of it. **Legislative supremacy** is the idea that the lawmaking power is supreme, or in Locke's words, that "what can give Law to another, must needs be superiour [sic] to him."[3] If the legislature makes law, and the executive and judiciary merely enforce and adjudicate its meaning, then the lawmaking or legislative power clearly is supreme. Americans began their own thinking about politics from these Lockean ideas of popular sovereignty and legislative supremacy.

Moreover, experience in colonial legislatures was consistently that of the people's representatives standing up to seemingly tyrannous royal governors. As tensions grew in the years immediately preceding the Revolution, Americans came to see all political power as dangerous and power held by any but the people's most direct representatives as especially dangerous.

Congress and the Constitution

The federal Constitution that went into effect in 1789 described a national government in which Congress was to play the central role. Article I comprises fully half of the Constitution and begins with the decisive statement that "All legislative Powers herein granted shall be vested in a Congress of the United States, which shall consist of a Senate and House of Representatives." Article I, section 8, enumerates the powers of Congress in seventeen specific clauses.

The first eight clauses gave Congress power to lay and collect taxes, borrow money on the credit of the United States, establish a national currency, regulate commerce, and establish post offices and post roads. A clause then permitted Congress to establish federal courts below the level of the Supreme Court. Seven clauses set Congress's power to punish violations of international law and illegal activity at sea, to declare war, and to raise, train, and equip armies, navies, and the state militias when in the national service. Congress was also given the power to exercise exclusive jurisdiction over a district, not to exceed ten miles square, in which to locate a national capital. Finally, the last clause of Article I, section 8, gives Congress the power "To make all Laws which shall be necessary and proper for carrying into Execution" the previously enumerated powers.[4]

Although the House and Senate have equal roles in the legislative process, each has a few specific powers and responsibilities. Article I, section 7, following both parliamentary and colonial precedents, declares that "All Bills for raising Revenue shall originate in the House of Representatives." The Senate is given the power and responsibility to try impeachments and to advise and consent on treaties, senior executive appointments, and nominations to the Supreme Court.

MEMBERSHIP AND SERVICE IN THE CONGRESS

The constitutional qualifications for service in the U.S. Congress are few and simple. They are age, citizenship, and residency. A member of the House of Representatives must be twenty-five years of age, have been a citizen of the United States for at least seven years, and be a resident of the state from which he or she is elected. A member of the Senate must be thirty years old, have been a citizen of the United States for nine years, and be a resident of the state from which he or she is elected. Moreover, neither the states nor Congress can add qualifications or limitations without amending the Constitution.

Though the constitutional qualifications of members have not changed at all since the first Congress, the kinds of people who serve in Congress and the nature of the congressional experience have changed a great deal. In the nineteenth century, members of Congress were almost all white men. They spent most of the year at home, often worked at regular jobs, and lived in Washington only when Congress was in session. Over the course of the twentieth century,

AP Photo/Zach Gibson

Surrounded by colleagues from the Congressional Black Caucus, Assistant Minority Leader James Clyburn (D-SC), discusses the group's reservations about President Trump's nomination of Alabama senator Jeff Sessions to be attorney general of the United States.

minorities and women became a growing presence in Congress. Congress meets year around, but with frequent recesses. Modern air travel allows members of Congress to spend almost every weekend and every recess back home.[5] Congress has averaged about 140 days in session each year since 2000, though it dropped to 132 days in 2015 and just 111 days in the election year of 2016.

Member Characteristics

The membership of Congress has always been drawn from the nation's economic, social, and educational elite. Members come disproportionately from the worlds of law and business, although lifetime public service has become increasingly common. Nearly all members have college degrees, and 75 percent have graduate degrees, with most of the graduate degrees being in law (J.D.) and business (M.B.A.). The presence of large numbers of lawyers in Congress is not surprising. Lawyers work in the law, and Congress makes laws. Moreover, lawyers can leave their practices with some ease, and the visibility of having served in Congress usually helps if they return to private practice.

Business careers work differently. Generally, members of Congress come from smaller, often private or family-owned, businesses. When a small business owner is elected to Congress, a spouse, brother, cousin, or partner can maintain the store, insurance agency, or pest control franchise. It is more difficult to get on and off the corporate ladder without losing ground to your colleagues and competitors. Therefore, one rarely finds members who have left senior positions in the corporate or financial world (unless they have retired or have no plans to return) to run for and serve in Congress.

AP Photo/House Television

Members of the U.S. House rise in bipartisan applause as Speaker Paul Ryan (R-WI) calls for unity in the wake of the June 2017 shooting at the Republican practice for the annual congressional baseball game.

Women now make up about 19 percent of the Congress, blacks make up about 9 percent and Hispanics about 7 percent. All are substantially underrepresented in relation to their presence in the population, especially women (see Figure 8.1). In the 115th Congress (2017–2019), eighty-three women served in the House and twenty-one in the Senate, no increase from the last session. The 115th Congress also saw forty-seven African American, thirty-four Latino, twelve Asian/Pacific Island, and two Native American members of the House. The Senate had two black members, four Hispanic members, and three Asian American members. About 29 percent of the members of Congress are Catholic, 8 percent are Jewish, 3 percent Mormon, and most of the remainder adhere to one or another of the Protestant denominations.

Finally, members commonly bring considerable political experience with them to Congress. Most members of the House of Representatives prepared for their runs for national office by serving first in local and state offices. Moreover, it is quite common for members of the House to "move up" to the Senate. As a result, half of U.S. House members had prior service in their state legislature and half of current senators served previously in the U.S. House. Another common path to the Senate is from statewide elective offices like governor. As a result, the average age of members of Congress is late-fifties, with senators averaging about five years older than members of the House.

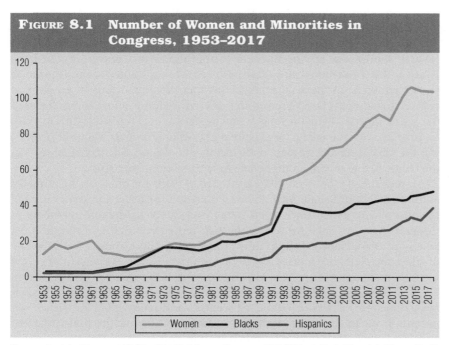

FIGURE 8.1 Number of Women and Minorities in Congress, 1953–2017

Sources: Ornstein, Mann, and Malbin, *Vital Statistics on Congress, 2008*, Tables 1.16, 1–17, and 1–18, pp. 43–45, and Harold W. Stanley and Richard G. Niemi, *Vital Statistics on American Politics, 2015–2016*, Table 5.2, pp. 197–200. Updated by the author.

While some members might make more money in the private sector, their congressional salaries and benefits make them among the most comfortable Americans. Members of the 115th Congress receive salaries of $174,000 and generous benefits. Members who serve in Congress for only five years receive modest pensions adjusted each year for inflation and lifetime health benefits. Longer service brings bigger pensions. In 2015, 620 former members drew pensions averaging around $74,000.[6] Texas Congressman Ralph Hall lost his last race and retired at 92, with 34 years in Congress, and an annual pension of $139,000. More than half of members of Congress—268 in all—have a net personal wealth of $1 million or more.[7]

Tenure, Incumbency, and Reelection

Through most of the nation's history, commitment to politics as a career was uncommon. Those who did take time from their real careers to serve in political office mostly chose state and even local office over service at the national level. Washington was a long way off and hard to get to. Hence, average congressional turnover was high, and average length of tenure was low.

During the nineteenth century, member turnover—that is, the proportion of new members from one Congress to the next—consistently ran at 40 to 50 percent. Turnover began to decline near the beginning of the twentieth century, and in the period after World War II the average tenure in office increased. Some members served for extraordinarily long times. Carl Hayden (D-AZ) served for fifteen years in the House and then for forty-two more in the Senate. John Dingell (D-MI), the longest serving member in the history of Congress, entered the House in 1955 and retired after 60 years in 2015. In early 2003, Strom Thurmond (R-SC) retired from the Senate at age 100 after more than forty-seven years of service. Robert Byrd (D-WV) served six years in the House before being elected to the Senate in 1959. Byrd, the longest serving senator in U.S. history, died in office on June 28, 2010 at age 92 (see Figure 8.2).[8] Senator Barbara Mikulski (D-MD) was the longest serving woman in the history of Congress. She served 10 years in the House before serving in the Senate from 1986 through 2016.

More generally, between 1946 and 2016, 94 percent of House incumbents and 82 percent of Senate incumbents who stood for reelection were returned to office.[9] Only twice since 1980, 1994 and 2010, have more members of Congress been defeated for reelection than retired voluntarily. Even in 2006, when the Democrats picked up thirty seats in the House and six in the Senate to take control of both houses for the first time since 1994, 94 percent of House incumbents standing for reelection and 79 percent of Senate incumbents won. 2010 was bloodier. Only 85 percent of senators and representatives who sought reelection were successful. While 37 senators and representatives retired voluntarily prior to the 2010 elections, 54 were defeated at the polls. In 2012 and 2014, reelection rates rebounded to traditional levels. Similarly, despite the upheaval at the top of the ticket created by Donald Trump's unexpected win, there was remarkably little tumult down ballot. Fully 97 percent of House incumbents and 90 percent of Senate incumbents retained their seats.

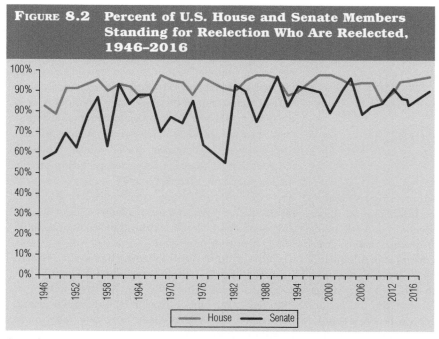

FIGURE 8.2 Percent of U.S. House and Senate Members Standing for Reelection Who Are Reelected, 1946–2016

Legend: House — Senate

Source: Ornstein, Mann, and Malbin, *Vital Statistics on Congress, 2008*, Tables 2.7 and 2–8, pp. 57–58 and Stanley and Niemi, *Vital Statistics on American Politics, 2015–2016*, Table 1.18, pp. 43–44. Updated by the author.

What explains these extraordinary reelection rates? Two classic works, David Mayhew's *Congress: The Electoral Connection* (1974) and Richard Fenno's *Congressmen in Committees* (1973), have long provided the foundation for our understanding of congressional motivation. Mayhew made a strong case that the dominant motivation of congressmen is reelection—without reelection nothing else in a congressional career is possible. Fenno made the equally compelling case that once reelection is secure, congressmen turn their attention either to policy influence or to broader power within the institution or to some combination of the two. Whatever choice they make, long-term success hinges on a series of successful reelection contests. Members stay focused on their reelection prospects.

HOW CONGRESS HAS ORGANIZED TO DO ITS WORK

Because of its larger size, the House came earlier and more completely to depend on strong leadership, internal organization, and adherence to explicit rules of procedure. The Senate remained more informal and individualistic. Fundamentally, the House operates by close enforcement of its rules, whereas the Senate operates by consensus (see Table 8.1).[10]

Should Representatives Represent Their Consciences or Their Constituents?

Modern thinking about the nature of representation is often traced to a famous speech by Edmund Burke (1729–1797), candidate for election to Parliament from Bristol, in November 1774. Democratic ideals were at large, but not yet widely accepted in Britain and her increasingly rebellious colonies in North America. The issue of "instructions," that is, whether voters could bind or instruct elected officials in the performance of their duties was much on people's minds. Burke's opponent had endorsed the idea of instructions and had promised to be bound by the wishes and views of his constituents if elected.

Hence, Burke felt constrained to speak to the issue of instructions and to the responsibility of a representative to his constituents. He did so in these memorable terms: "Certainly, gentlemen, it ought to be the happiness and glory of a representative to live in the strictest union, the closest correspondence, and the most unreserved communication with his constituents. Their wishes ought to have great weight with him; their opinion, high respect; their business, unremitted attention . . . . But his unbiassed [sic] opinion, his mature judgment, his enlightened conscience, he ought not to sacrifice to . . . any set of men living . . . your representative owes you, not his industry only, but his judgment; and he betrays, instead of serving you, if he sacrifices it to your opinion."

Still, stirring as Burke's rhetoric was and is, it essentially says that a representative should listen to his constituents but ultimately use his own judgment. Although many Americans of the founding generation, particularly the Federalist elite that gathered around Hamilton, accepted Burke's view, those who gathered around Jefferson held that legislatures should mirror the broader community and representatives should reflect the views and interests of their constituents.

Today we discuss these issues somewhat, but only somewhat, differently. Scholars use three terms—trustees,

TABLE 8.1 Differences between the House and the Senate		
	House	**Senate**
Term	Two years	Six years
Size	435	100
Special Role	Taxing and Spending Impeachment Charges	Treaties and Appointments Impeachment Trials
Rules	Rigid	Loose

The leading organizational features of the Congress are parties, committees, and legislative rules and procedures. Parties select the leaders and organize the members of Congress. Committees create a substantive division of labor within the Congress that permits it to discuss issues and make policy, oversee the executive bureaucracy, and serve the needs and interests of constituents. Finally, legislative rules and procedures define the order of events, who is entitled to participate at each stage, and which outcomes are permissible.

delegates, and politicos—to describe who or what modern representatives represent. Trustees, following Burke, believe that although they are responsible for listening to their constituents, they are sent to Congress to use their own knowledge and judgment in the broad public or national interest. Frequently, constituency and national interests will overlap, but where they do not, especially on critical issues, the **trustee** should—must—represent the national or public interest.

A **delegate** takes the mirror view of representation, seeing his or her role as reflecting the views and protecting the interests of constituents. A **politico** tends to move between trustee and delegate stances as issues, circumstances, and pressures vary. On issues about which their constituents are engaged and informed, politicos will often act like delegates. On issues that do not draw constituent attention, or on which constituent opinion is soft or split, politicos will have the latitude to act more like trustees and use their own judgment. In fact, every representative takes the national view on some issues and in regard to some aspects of his or her job, and the local or constituency view on others; but each representative also adopts a general approach and style that marks him or her as a trustee, a delegate, or a politico.

What do you think?
- Who or what should a representative represent?
- Are you comfortable with politicians using their own judgment even if they know that their constituents disagree?

PRO	CON
Representatives are accomplished people	Voters know what they think and want
Representatives study and debate the issues	Few issues come up unexpectedly
At least sometimes, representatives must take the broad view	Local views deserve a strong voice

The Role of Political Parties

Political parties span the separation of powers and integrate the disparate institutions and actors of the American political system. The Democratic and Republican parties field candidates and compete in elections at every level of the American political system. They offer programs and platforms designed to attract the attention and support of voters, and they are expected to implement these programs once elected.

It falls to the leaders of the majority party in Congress to organize their members, form committees, and control the floor so that as much of their program as possible will pass. Leaders of the minority party organize their members to influence and revise the programs being prepared by the majority and to obstruct their passage where influence is not possible. As we shall see below, the increasing partisanship of the past decade has rendered these traditional majority–minority relationships more deeply and consistently conflictual. The impact on the Senate has been particularly profound.

trustee A view of representation that says representatives should listen to their constituents but use their own expertise and judgment to make decisions about public issues.

delegate A view of representation that sees the representative's principal role as reflecting the views and protecting the interests of his or her own constituents.

politico A view of representation that sees representatives following constituent opinion when that is clear and his or her own judgment or political interest when constituency opinion is amorphous or divided.

Party Leaders: Responsibilities and Powers. Party leaders in Congress have responsibilities both inside the institution and in coordinating its activities with other actors and institutions like the president and the executive branch, interest groups, the media, and the public. Moreover, congressional leaders have both institutional and partisan roles and responsibilities.[11] Leaders must organize the chamber, collect and distribute information to members, schedule floor business, and consult and coordinate with the other chamber and the president. At the same time, leaders must organize their parties, promote party unity, ensure that party members are present on the floor for important votes, and provide campaign assistance to the party and its members.

The powers that leaders draw upon in fulfilling their responsibilities are both formal and informal.[12] The formal powers of leaders derive from the rules of each house. Leaders influence the appointment of committee chairs and of committee members, they control recognition of members on the floor and access of their bills to the floor, and they control the staff, space, and financial resources of the institution. The informal powers of leaders derive from their centrality to all that is happening. Leaders know what compromises are likely to be offered and accepted, what the leaders of the other house and the president think, and much more. Leaders also exercise considerable control over the stature and visibility of other members. Members with whom leaders consult and to whom they give important information gain in prestige and influence with their colleagues.

House of Representatives. The presiding officer of the House of Representatives is the Speaker of the House (see Figure 8.3). The Speaker is elected at the opening of each Congress by a vote of all the members, although in reality the majority party selects the Speaker on a straight party-line vote. Each party also selects a leader and an assistant leader, or whip.

The modern Speaker presides over the House and sets its agenda. He chairs the party committee that assigns members to committees; decides whether to refer legislation to one committee or to several; controls the Rules Committee, which determines whether and how a bill will reach the floor for debate; presides over debate on the floor of the House; and represents his party's positions to the president, the media, and the public. Paul Ryan (R-WI) assumed the Speaker's gavel in 2015.[13]

The Speaker's principal deputy is the majority leader. Although formally elected every two years by a secret ballot of the party caucus, the majority leader is usually a close ally of the Speaker. In the 114th Congress, California's Kevin McCarthy was elected majority leader. The majority leader is responsible, working with the Speaker, for setting the legislative agenda, maintaining communication with the committees and their leaders, informing members about the flow of major business onto the floor, and encouraging support for party positions and bills. The minority leader has little role in agenda setting or scheduling and is principally concerned with organizing her colleagues in committee and on the floor to win moderating adjustments in majority party bills. The closer the partisan balance in Congress, the more leverage the minority enjoys.

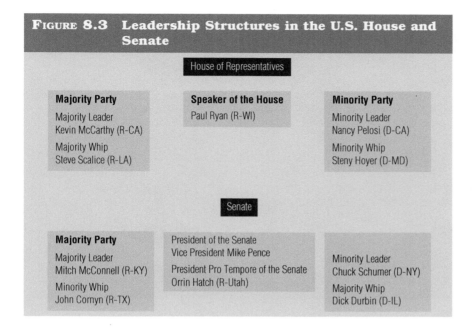

FIGURE 8.3 Leadership Structures in the U.S. House and Senate

House of Representatives

Majority Party

Majority Leader
Kevin McCarthy (R-CA)

Majority Whip
Steve Scalice (R-LA)

Speaker of the House
Paul Ryan (R-WI)

Minority Party

Minority Leader
Nancy Pelosi (D-CA)

Minority Whip
Steny Hoyer (D-MD)

Senate

Majority Party

Majority Leader
Mitch McConnell (R-KY)

Minority Whip
John Cornyn (R-TX)

President of the Senate
Vice President Mike Pence

President Pro Tempore of the Senate
Orrin Hatch (R-Utah)

Minority Leader
Chuck Schumer (D-NY)

Majority Whip
Dick Durbin (D-IL)

The majority whip's job is to encourage support among members of the majority party for the positions and legislation of the party, count votes, advise the senior leadership of the prospects for success or failure on the floor, and try, in general, to mobilize and turn out the majority party coalition on the issues critical to the party. The minority whip's job, of course, is to mobilize and hold together opposition to the majority's agenda.[14]

Senate. The Senate is as loosely organized and open as the House is highly organized and rulebound. The Senate normally operates by a running consensus called **unanimous consent**. Unanimous consent that the Senate proceed to a particular piece of business or proceed by a particular means, as the term so clearly suggests, can be denied by a single senator.

The Constitution declares that the vice president shall preside over the Senate, although without vote except in cases of a tie. Hence, vice presidents have rarely appeared in the Senate except when it seems that a tie vote on an important issue might provide an opportunity to resolve it in the administration's favor. The Constitution further provides that the Senate appoint a *president pro tempore* to preside in the absence of the vice president. This position has become entirely honorary and usually goes to the most senior member of the majority party. The Senate is actually presided over on any given day by a series of junior members of the majority party who exercise no personal influence over events on the floor.

The majority leader of the Senate is elected by the membership of the majority party, and the minority leader is elected by the membership of the minority

unanimous consent Legislative device by which the Senate sets aside its standard rules for a negotiated agreement on the order and conduct of business on the floor.

Here, in the informal setting of a sporting event, are the Republican and Democratic leaders of the House and Senate. They are (left to right) House Speaker Paul Ryan (R-WI), Senate Minority Leader Chuck Schumer (D-NY), House Minority Leader Nancy Pelosi (D-CA), and Senate Majority Leader Mitch McConnell (R-KY).

party. The majority leader, always in close consultation with the minority leader because of the collaborative nature of the Senate, sets the agenda for the Senate, oversees and manages debate on the floor, and brokers the many agreements, compromises, and deals by which the Senate disposes of its business.

Leading the Senate is an arduous and frustrating process even under the best of circumstances. The Senate's most famous and in many ways most accomplished majority leader was Lyndon Johnson (D-TX). In 1960, Johnson noted that "the only real power available to the leader is the power of persuasion. There is no patronage, no power to discipline, no authority to fire senators like the president can fire his members of Cabinet."[15]

The Development of the Committee System

Members of the early House and Senate were wary of committees. They preferred to set policy in open debate on the floor before selecting a committee to work out the details and frame a resolution or bill.[16] However, as the workload of the Congress grew, members came to realize that discussion of every issue on the floor was inefficient and time-consuming. By about 1820, both the Senate and the House had developed systems of permanent or standing committees. Most of Congress's work is done in its committees, so leaders, committee chairs, and members have struggled to influence if not control that work.

The Division of Labor. The committee system in Congress during most of the twentieth century represented a division of labor in which legislative work was distributed among stable groups of subject matter experts. Legislative work involves both enacting legislation and oversight and investigation of executive branch activities. An integrated set of norms and expectations promised members that if they concentrated on their committee work and developed deep expertise in these subject matter areas, they would be rewarded with influence. These understandings have broken down somewhat during the past several decades. Nonetheless, the division of legislative labor represented by the committee system is still a defining characteristic of the Congress.

Fixed Jurisdictions. The basis of the division of labor in Congress is the system of permanent standing committees with fixed committee jurisdictions. House rules require that legislation introduced into the House be considered in the committee or committees of appropriate jurisdiction before it is considered on the floor of the House. Senate procedures are similar but based more on precedent than formal rules. While committee jurisdictions are still generally respected, since the mid-1980s leaders have created special task forces to manage critical bills. Committee chairs and members are often involved, but they have less control than they would in the normal committee process.

Specialization. Traditionally, members of the House and, to a lesser extent, the Senate were expected to specialize (the **specialization norm**) in the work

Q2 How does the committee system in Congress work to promote specialized knowledge and expertise among members?

specialization norm The norm that encourages Congress members to specialize and develop expertise in the subject matter covered by their committee assignments.

Getty Images/CQ Roll Call/Bill Clark

Senator Chuck Schumer (D-NY) wades through a throng of reporters following his news conference on a critical Senate vote to raise the debt limit ceiling.

of their committees and to develop a subject matter expertise upon which the remainder of the body could depend. Members who complied with the specialization norm could expect to have their expertise honored if they were willing to reciprocate (the **reciprocity norm**) by deferring to the expertise of others. Hence, most subject matter areas in Congress are dominated by a few members who understand the process, know the issues inside and out, and know what can and cannot be done.

reciprocity norm Congressional norm promising that if members respect the views and expertise of members of other committees, their committee expertise will be respected as well.

seniority norm The norm that holds that the member of a congressional committee with the longest continuous service on the committee shall be its chair.

Seniority and Influence. The **seniority norm** traditionally provided that the majority party member with the longest continuous service on the committee be given the opportunity to chair the committee. It also provided that members, once assigned to a committee, could stay on the committee as long as they wished. The strength of the seniority system was that it reduced conflict; all members knew that their committee seats were secure and that they would move into positions of increasing influence as their seniority accumulated. The weakness of the system was that members advanced to key positions of committee leadership regardless of their talents or the compatibility of their views with the views of the leadership, their colleagues, or the country.

After the majority party leaders, committee chairs—and below them the chairs of important subcommittees—are the most influential members of Congress. Their influence flows from their long experience and deep knowledge of the subjects with which their committees deal, but also from their control over the resources of their committees and the subjects to which committee attention and resources are directed.

In the modern Congress, party leaders depend somewhat less on seniority and somewhat more on ideology, effectiveness, and fundraising prowess in selecting committee chairs. Though respect for seniority is less automatic than it once was, senior members are still the most active and effective legislators.[17]

Types of Committees. Committees are the principal vehicles through which the House and Senate do their legislative work. There are several different kinds of committees. The most important are the **standing committees** with fixed jurisdictions that automatically continue from one Congress to the next. The broadest distinction that can be made among standing committees is between authorizing committees and appropriating committees.

standing committees Permanent committees of the Congress enjoying fixed jurisdiction and continuing automatically from one Congress to the next.

authorizing committees House and Senate committees that develop or authorize particular policies or programs through legislation.

Authorizing committees produce legislation, policies, and programs. Some of these committees, such as Agriculture, Energy and Commerce, and Transportation, provide members with opportunities to bring specialized benefits back to their districts. Other committees, such as Foreign Affairs and Education and Labor, allow members to be centrally involved in making visible and important public policy.

The power committees of the Congress are those that set taxing and spending levels and determine when and if substantive measures come to the floor. The House Ways and Means Committee and the Senate Finance Committee set the tax rates and policies that determine the revenue available to government. **Appropriations committees** determine how much money will actually be spent on each government activity and program. The House Rules Committee determines which committee bills will come to the floor for final passage and under what circumstances. House rules define Appropriations, Ways and Means, and Rules as "exclusive" committees whose members cannot sit on other committees. The House and Senate Budget Committees are also important and powerful.

Select committees are temporary committees that go out of business unless specifically renewed at the beginning of each Congress. Select committees are usually charged to study and report on a particular topic but lack the legislative authority to receive or offer bills.

Joint committees are made up of members from the House and Senate assigned to do continuing analysis and oversight in a particular substantive area like aging. Joint committees do have authority to initiate legislation and are frequently continued from one Congress to the next. **Conference committees** are composed of members from both houses charged to resolve the differences between bills on the same topic passed in the separate chambers (see Table 8.2).

Because the Senate has about the same number of committees as the House with less than a quarter of the members, each senator must, of necessity, serve on more committees and subcommittees than a member of the House. In the 115th Congress, 2017–2018, senators served on an average of twelve committees and subcommittees, House members served or an average of six. Senators actually seek a wide range of committee assignments because this legitimates their access to the full range of issues likely to affect their states. Hence, senators tend to be more generalists than specialists.[18]

The Staff Structure. Each member of Congress stands at the center of a small business dedicated to assisting him or her in getting work done. Each member receives a member's representational allowance (MRA) each year to pay for the staffing and operation of his or her office. House members all receive essentially the same allowance, whereas senators receive allowances based on the populations of their states. House members receive about $1.27 million from which he or she hires a staff (which averages about twenty persons) and pays for such things as travel, computers, telecommunications, office equipment, supplies, and mail charges.

Senators receive varying amounts, depending on whether they represent sparsely settled states like Utah or populous states like California. Senate staff average about thirty-five and range from fifteen to seventy. Personnel accounts provide senators with $3 million to $4.8 million for personnel, depending on the sizes of the states they serve. Office expenses, again depending on the size of the senator's state, range from $121,000 to $454,000, while the mail allotment ranges from $32,000 to $300,000.[19]

appropriations committees House and Senate committees that appropriate or allocate specific funding levels to each government program or activity.

select committees Temporary committees of the Congress that go out of business once they complete their work or at the end of each Congress unless specifically renewed.

joint committees Congressional committees made up of members of both the House and the Senate and assigned to study a particular topic.

conference committees Committees composed of members of the House and Senate charged to resolve differences between the House and Senate versions of a bill.

TABLE 8.2 Major Committees in the Contemporary Congress	
House	**Senate**
Power Committees	**Power Committees**
Appropriations	Appropriations
Budget	Budget
Ways and Means	Finance
Rules	
Authorizing Committees	**Authorizing Committees**
Agriculture	Agriculture, Nutrition, and Forestry
Armed Services	Armed Services
Financial Services	Banking, Housing, and Urban Affairs
Energy and Commerce	Commerce, Science, and Transportation
Education and Labor	Health, Education, Labor, and Pensions
Homeland Security	Homeland Security and Governmental Affairs
Oversight and Government Reform	
House Administration	
Foreign Affairs	Foreign Relations
Judiciary	Judiciary
Natural Resources	Energy and Natural Resources
Science and Technology	Environment and Public Works
Small Business	Rules and Administration
Transportation and Infrastructure	Small Business and Entrepreneurship
Veterans' Affairs	Veterans' Affairs
Select, Special, or Other Committees	**Select, Special, or Other Committees**
Select Intelligence	Select Intelligence
Standards of Official Conduct	Select Ethics
	Special Aging
	Indian Affairs

Member staffs serve the individual members in their offices, whereas committee staffs are hired by the committees and assist the members with their committee work. The numbers of both member staffs and committee staffs grew substantially during the latter half of the twentieth century, though they have remained steady in the Senate and fallen modestly in the House since the mid-1980s.

Congress also maintains three nonpartisan agencies that provide research and analysis. The Congressional Research Service (CRS) was created in 1914 to provide research support to the committees and members of Congress. The General Accounting Office (GAO), renamed the Government Accountability

Office in 2004, was created in 1921 to give the Congress analytic and investigatory capabilities. And in 1974, the Congress created the Congressional Budget Office (CBO) to provide it with independent information and analysis on budget options and choices. In all three cases, Congress was interested in assuring that it had analytical talent equal to that in the agencies of the executive branch and the offices of interest groups.

THE LEGISLATIVE PROCESS

House committees and their chairs are less powerful now than they were in the 1950s and 1960s, whereas the chamber leaders are more powerful. Although committee leaders are still influential in their committees, the chamber leaders control the floor. Increasingly, House leaders have been willing to bypass normal House procedures, often referred to as the "regular order," if that seems necessary to accomplish the majority party's goals. The legislative process in the Senate, on the other hand, is increasingly complex and cumbersome, making the regular order little more than a fading memory. Senators have always had the right of unlimited debate and the right to offer any amendment to any bill, but in recent years they have exercised these rights with greater frequency and on less obviously consequential matters. Hence, as political scientist Barbara Sinclair has noted, Senate leadership has "become

Q3 What are the stages of consideration through which most legislation must pass to become a law?

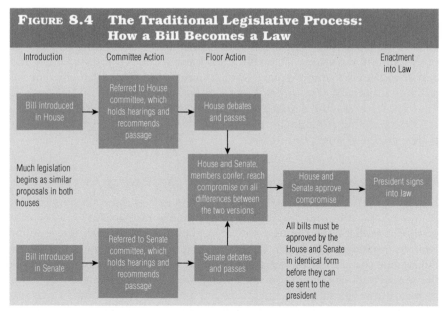

FIGURE 8.4   The Traditional Legislative Process: How a Bill Becomes a Law

Introduction   Committee Action   Floor Action   Enactment into Law

Bill introduced in House → Referred to House committee, which holds hearings and recommends passage → House debates and passes

Much legislation begins as similar proposals in both houses

House and Senate, members confer, reach compromise on all differences between the two versions → House and Senate approve compromise → President signs into law

Bill introduced in Senate → Referred to Senate committee, which holds hearings and recommends passage → Senate debates and passes

All bills must be approved by the House and Senate in identical form before they can be sent to the president

Source: Roger H. Davidson, Walter J. Oleszek, Francis E. Lee, and Eric Schickler, *Congress and Its Members*, 14th ed. (Washington, D.C.: Congressional Quarterly Press, 2014), 207. See also Walter J. Oleszek, *Congressional Procedures and the Policy Process*, 9th ed. (Washington, D.C.: CQ Press, 2014), 14–15 for a good description of the differences between conventional and unconventional law making.

an exercise in accommodating all interested parties."[20] The traditional legislative process (see Figure 8.4, shown here in a highly simplified version), requires levels of patience and restraint that recent legislative majorities have been incapable of showing.[21]

Introduction and Assignment

Only a member of the House or Senate can introduce a bill, and then that member is the bill's sponsor. When a bill is introduced in the House or Senate, it is given a bill number (HR 1, for example, would be House Resolution 1, whereas S 1 would be Senate Bill 1) and assigned to the committee of appropriate jurisdiction for initial consideration. Whereas Senate traditions still largely require that bills be assigned to one committee, House rules permit simple referral and two kinds of complex referral: sequential referral and split referral.

referral The process by which a bill is referred or assigned to a standing committee for initial consideration.

Simple **referral** is the traditional practice of referring a bill to the single committee within whose jurisdiction it most nearly fits. The two forms of complex referral used in the House are intended to recognize and account for the fact that many bills contain subject matter of interest to more than one committee. Sequential referral occurs when a bill is sent first to one committee and then to another. Split referral is when a bill is actually split, and relevant sections are sent to different committees. When employing complex referral, the Speaker designates one of the committees as primary. When the primary committee reports, the Speaker sets deadlines for the other committees to complete their work.

Increasingly, key bills, often the most important bills of the session, and usually the top priorities of the majority party, are removed from some or all of the committee process. These bills, for example the Republican House and Senate bills to revise and replace Obamacare in 2017, are assigned to special working groups or task forces appointed by the majority party leadership. The task force may be drawn at least partially from the membership of the relevant standing committees, but they are led by the leaders themselves or by leadership loyalists, throughout.[22]

Committee and Subcommittee Deliberation

Bills assigned to one or more standing committees for review can be treated at the level of the full committee or assigned to a subcommittee for initial consideration. At either level, the stages of consideration are essentially three: public hearings, markup, and report. Public hearings reflect the open, participatory, democratic character of the legislative process. They create a public record of a broad spectrum of opinion on the issues involved and give interested parties a chance to weigh in before final decisions are made. If a bill receives its initial consideration in subcommittee, full committee consideration will often go right to markup and forgo a second set of public hearings.

After hearings have been held, committee members move to the markup or bill-rewriting stage of the process. Here committee members go through the bill paragraph by paragraph, line by line, and word by word, and rewrite the text until it satisfies a majority of them that it is the best treatment of the issues in the bill that is then possible.

Finally, after the bill has proceeded through subcommittee and committee markup and has been approved by a majority vote of the full committee, the committee staff prepares a report that describes the intent of the bill, its major provisions, and the cost of implementation. This report, once approved by committee, is attached to the bill as it is sent to the floor for debate and final passage. The report is important because it is often the only thing that other members read before deciding whether or not to support the bill.

In the modern Congress, with its increasingly fluid and leadership-driven legislative process, bills frequently are changed, usually after a discussion between committee and chamber leaders, to improve the bill's prospects on the floor. Post-committee changes to bills are particularly common on key majority party bills where the pressure to assure passage is great.[23]

Agenda Setting and the Legislative Calendar

Key leadership bills are scheduled for floor consideration at the most advantageous time, while bills reported from the regular standing committees are listed in chronological order on one of several calendars. Calendars are lists of bills awaiting action. Although bills in both the House and Senate go onto the appropriate calendars in the order in which they come from the committees, they do not go to the floor in that order. In the Senate, the majority and minority leaders determine through discussion and negotiation which bills will come up in which order and how they will be discussed. The leaders produce a unanimous consent agreement that describes the way a particular bill will be handled on the floor. Because any senator can block a unanimous consent agreement merely by objecting to it, most divisive issues are bargained out before floor debate even begins.

The House process, again, is more formal, detailed, and rigid. The House Rules Committee shuffles the calendars to put the most important bills up for consideration on the floor in the order and under circumstances most likely to lead to majority party success. The **Rules Committee** sets the conditions for debate and amendment of bills on the floor through a formal rule or special order. The rule lays out when the bill will come up for floor consideration, how long debate on the bill will run, and what kinds of amendments, if any, will be permitted.

Rules Committee Committee that writes rules or special orders that set the conditions for debate and amendment of legislation on the floor of the House.

In general, the Rules Committee produces three kinds of rules or special orders: open rules, closed rules, and modified closed rules, also called structured rules. An open rule permits amendments to be offered to any part of the bill. A closed rule forbids amendments to the bill, thereby requiring an up or down vote on the bill as it stands. A modified closed rule prohibits amendments to some sections of the bill and allows them to others. In the contemporary Congress, open rules are rare. About two-thirds of bills are brought up under modified closed or structured rules and one-third under closed rules.

Special devices exist for bringing minor bills to the floor quickly. Most importantly, the suspension of the rules procedure is in order every Monday and Tuesday. Suspension of the rules permits forty minutes of debate, no amendments, and requires a two-thirds vote to pass. In recent years, nearly three-quarters of all bills came to the floor under suspension of the rules.

Floor Debate and Amendment

Floor debate in the House proceeds through a highly structured series of steps to a vote on final passage. House rules empower the Speaker and allow the majority party to work its will with relative ease. In the House, the process of floor debate begins with adoption of the rule describing the way the bill will be handled on the floor. After the appropriate rule has been adopted, the House dissolves itself into a parliamentary form known as the Committee of the Whole House on the State of the Union.

Committee of the Whole
House convened under a set of rules that allows limitations on debate and amendment and lowers the quorum required to do business from 218 to 100 to facilitate speedier action.

The **Committee of the Whole** is simply the House and all of its members operating under a set of rules that is less restrictive than the formal rules of the House. The key rules that apply in Committee of the Whole are that the quorum required to do business is 100, as opposed to 218 under the regular House rules, debate can be limited, and amendments, if allowed, are considered under a "five minute" rule rather than the hour required under regular House rules.

The main stages of floor consideration are general debate, amending, and a vote on final passage by the House. The time allotted for general debate is defined in the relevant rule and is evenly divided between those who favor and those who oppose the bill. Floor managers, usually the bill's sponsor or a senior member from the committee that handled the bill, manage the time available to both sides and parcel it out to members who want to speak to the general merits or demerits of the bill. Floor debate serves to educate uninformed members about the nature and contents of the bill and to surface the strongest arguments in its favor and the most telling points that its opponents have to make.

After general debate, and assuming that the rule under which the bill is being considered allows amendments, the bill is read for amendment. After a particular section is read, any member can offer an amendment (a proposal to change the language of the section) and have five minutes to explain it and argue in its favor. A member opposing the amendment then gets five minutes to explain the basis for his or her opposition. After voting on amendments, the Committee of the Whole "rises" and reports the amended bill back to the full House for a vote on final passage.

filibuster Senators enjoy the right of unlimited debate. Use of unlimited debate by a senator to stall or block passage of legislation is called a filibuster.

The process of floor debate in the Senate is more fluid than in the House. Each senator enjoys the right of unlimited debate, or **filibuster,** and can block a bill from coming to the floor merely by placing an informal "hold" on it until her or his reservations about the bill are addressed. Because each senator has numerous ways to stop action—filibuster, hold, and denial of unanimous consent being only the most obvious—the Senate moves slowly and by negotiation, rather than in accord with formal rules and procedures as the House does.

TABLE 8.3	Senate Action on Cloture Motions, 1950–Present		
Years	**Motions Filed**	**Votes on Cloture**	**Cloture Invoked**
1951–1960	2	2	0
1961–1970	28	26	4
1971–1980	159	111	44
1981–1990	202	139	54
1991–2000	361	254	82
2001–2010	477	367	204
2011–2017	573	487	360

Source: http://www.senate.gov/pagelayout/reference/cloture_motions/clotureCounts.htm.

Many observers now consider the Senate to be very nearly dysfunctional. While filibusters were once employed only on critical issues—like southern senators standing against civil rights bills in the 1960s—now they are employed with regularity. To stop a filibuster, 60 votes in favor of **cloture** are required. Cloture stops debate and moves, eventually, to a vote on final passage. Gerald Seib, the *Wall Street Journal*'s congressional correspondent, recently argued that filibusters and cloture votes were symptoms of the wider disease of excessive partisanship. Robert Dole, a former senator from Kansas and Republican leader, said "The bottom line is today it's become a 60-vote not a 50-vote Senate" (see Table 8.3).[24]

cloture A cloture vote, requiring a 60-vote majority, is the only way to halt a filibuster in the Senate.

In 2013, the Senate's majority leader, Democrat Harry Reid of Nevada, moved several times to limit without destroying the filibuster. Reid finally resorted to what both sides called the "nuclear option," a simple majority vote approving the most important Senate rules change in decades. By a 52–48 vote, Democrats declared that filibusters would be out of order on executive and judicial nominees, though not on Supreme Court nominees and not on legislation. Democrats then moved a series of previously stalled nominations while Republicans warned of retaliation when they regained control of the Senate and the White House.[25] Republicans did regain control of the Senate in 2015 but waited until the debate over President Trump's nomination of Neil Gorsuch to the U.S. Supreme Court, which Democrats threatened to block, to extend the rule change to Supreme Court nominations. Now the filibuster exists only on legislation and many wonder how long that will last.

House/Senate Conference Committees

Bills cannot be sent from the Congress to the president for approval until they have been passed in identical form by both the House and the Senate. However, given the committee and floor consideration processes described earlier, it should not be surprising that many bills pass the House and Senate in somewhat different versions. These differences have to be resolved to the satisfaction of both houses so that they can then agree to identical versions of the bill that can be forwarded to the president.

About 10 percent of bills, including many of the most important bills each year, go to conference committees. Conferees are named from the House by the Speaker and from the Senate by the majority leader. Conferees are usually leading members of the committee or committees of jurisdiction and include each chamber's most knowledgeable members. Traditionally, conference committees resolve the differences before them by horse-trading over the sections most important to each chamber and by splitting the difference where that is possible. In some instances, usually on minor bills and when time is short, one house may just adopt the version of the bill passed by the other house. In other instances, differences are resolved in informal negotiations between leaders of the majority party in the House and Senate.

CONGRESSIONAL DECISION MAKING

Q4 What pressures operate on a member of Congress as he or she prepares to make an important legislative decision?

Members of Congress are expected to be aware of and open to outside influence as they make the many decisions and choices confronting them. Members must pay attention to the views of their constituents, their staffs, partisan colleagues and leaders, interest groups and their lobbyists, and the president and his representatives in the executive branch. Moreover, members are expected to use their own judgment because they have knowledge and access to information that is available to few others.[26]

Constituents

A member's constituents, the voters in his or her district, are the only people who can decide whether that member keeps her or his job. Interest groups, party leaders, even the president, can favor or oppose a particular member's reelection, but only the voters in the district can vote them in or out. Naturally, members of Congress pay close attention to opinion in their district. Yet, members have a difficult time deciphering district opinion on many issues. Most states, and even most districts, are diverse, containing voters and groups of voters who hold a wide range of opinions and views.[27] These diverse groups are likely to see issues from several different perspectives.

Members working to secure reelection have several tools to use in earning the appreciation of their constituents. The surest route to constituent approval is through what we call casework. **Casework** is active and direct problem-solving on behalf of constituents. Traditionally, the service that a member of Congress has been most likely to perform for a constituent has been to intervene on her or his behalf with some recalcitrant or unresponsive federal agency. The member's leverage with the bureaucracy comes from Congress's control over the funding, personnel, and programs of the agencies of the executive branch. The member's reward for his or her good services comes in the form of constituent gratitude and votes on election day.[28]

Many in Congress also look to new online communication tools to stay in touch with their constituents. Members use televised town hall meetings,

casework Casework refers to the direct assistance that members of Congress or their staff provide to constituents who need something from a federal agency or department.

satellite press conferences, cable news appearances posted to YouTube, and blogs to stay in touch with constituents. Other more personal tools, including Facebook, Twitter, Instagram, Tumblr, and Pinterest, allow Members of Congress to show a more personal and casual side to constituents and voters.[29]

Staff, Colleagues, and Party Leaders

Members of Congress not driven to a particular decision by well-formed constituency opinion often look to their staffs, colleagues, and party leaders for clues on how to vote. Members are too busy to study every issue closely, so they look for guidance to staff members who have been assigned to monitor the relevant issue area. They also look to relevant committee leaders, acknowledged substantive experts, and individual members with whom they most frequently agree. On a few issues, party leaders will demand that members support the party position and members will be under great pressure to do so.[30]

Interest Groups and Lobbyists

When members look past their staffs and colleagues in search of cues about how to vote on a particular issue, they run quickly into interest groups and their lobbyist representatives. Members value interest groups and lobbyists (many of whom are former members of Congress) for the knowledge and information that they can bring to the process. But by the time a bill reaches the floor and members are required to make a final decision on it, they are not looking for detailed information so much as for a clear signal on whether to support or oppose it. Members without strong feelings on a bill may trade their support or opposition for future consideration, such as during the next election campaign, from the lobbyist.[31]

The President and the Bureaucracy

Article I, section 3, of the Constitution requires that the president "give to the Congress Information of the State of the Union and recommend to their Consideration such Measures as he shall judge necessary and expedient." The president follows his State of the Union message each year with a set of administration bills for the consideration of Congress. At the end of the legislative process, the president is empowered to consider each law passed by Congress and decide whether to approve or veto it. Knowing that the president possesses this power leads Congress to take his views into account and even to actively bargain with him while bills are being crafted. Finally, Congress requires the president to report and recommend initiatives in such specific substantive areas as the economy and the environment, and, of course, the president submits an annual budget to Congress each year. How Congress and the president cooperate—or don't—to produce the budget highlights the separation of powers and checks and balances at the heart of our constitutional democracy.

FISCAL DECISION MAKING: BUDGETS, TAXES, AND SPENDING

Fundamentally, the budgetary process sets the government's priorities by making explicit decisions about revenues and expenditures. On the revenue side, the basic questions are how much money is to be raised, through what kinds of taxes and fees, and on whom will they be levied? On the expenditure side, the basic questions are how much money will be spent, on which programs, and for whose benefit? The budget for the 2018 fiscal year called for a record $4.1 trillion in spending. Not surprisingly, extended battles occur each year between the president and Congress over how the necessary revenue will be raised and how it will be distributed across the government's various programs, obligations, and responsibilities.

Budget Preparation

As shown in Table 8.4, the federal budget is prepared in two major phases: the first occurs in the executive branch, the second in the legislative branch. Preparation of the fiscal year (FY) 2018 budget began in the executive branch in the spring of 2016 so that it could be delivered to Congress for consideration early in 2017. Congress's consideration of the budget is supposed to be finished by summer 2017 so that FY 2018 can begin on October 1, 2017.

Jim Wallis, a leader of Sojourners, a Christian social justice group, opposes spending cuts, arguing that "budgets are moral documents."

The process seldom runs smoothly and frequently produces great conflict between the president and Congress.[32]

The process of budget preparation within the executive branch occurs as a set of structured discussions and negotiations among the president, the Office of Management and Budget (OMB), and the departments of the executive branch. The process begins in April each year. OMB presents the president with an analysis of the state of the economy and projections of economic performance for the coming year. On the basis of broad presidential guidance, the OMB formulates guidelines to the agencies, and the agencies respond by analyzing their current programs and outlining their budgetary needs for the coming year. The OMB analyzes the agency input and advises the president on how to respond to it, and the president establishes more detailed guidelines and targets for the agencies to follow.

During the summer, agencies refine their budgetary requests. In the fall, agencies submit their formal budget proposals along with analysis and arguments required to support budget allocations beyond those initially proposed by the president and OMB. OMB reviews the requests, holds hearings on each agency's request, and makes recommendations to the president who then sets each agency's budget allocation. OMB informs the agencies of the president's decisions.

During the winter OMB prepares the president's budget message to Congress and the budget document itself. The president reviews the latest economic data and projections, makes final adjustments in the budget and the budget message to Congress, and submits both to Congress by the first Monday in February.

During the entire time that the president's budget is in preparation, the Congressional Budget Office (CBO) is anticipating it, analyzing what it thinks will be in it, and developing a congressional alternative if that seems necessary. The CBO is required to submit an analysis of the president's budget to the House and Senate Budget Committees by February 15, and by February 25 the standing committees of both houses must submit their projections on revenues and expenditures to their respective budget committees.

On the basis of this information, the Budget Committees must produce a concurrent resolution on the budget by April 1. The concurrent resolution sets overall expenditure levels, estimates outlays for major budgetary categories, and makes a recommendation on revenue levels. Congress must complete action on the concurrent resolution and adopt it by April 15.

Between April 15 and June 10, the House Appropriations Committee produces thirteen appropriations bills that authorize spending in major budgetary categories for the coming fiscal year. If the spending totals in the appropriations bills breach the spending targets in the concurrent resolution, a process called **reconciliation** occurs to bring budgetary totals into conformity with mandated ceilings. Reconciliation is to be complete by June 15, and work on the budget as a whole is to be complete by June 30. Assuming that agreement by the Senate and the president is secured, the budget goes into effect on October 1. Difficulties abound, and the process is rarely completed on time.

reconciliation Congressional process to resolve differences if appropriations bills approve more spending than the spending targets permit.

TABLE 8.4	Major Steps in Preparation of the Fiscal Year 2018 Budget
Executive Branch Preparation	
2016	
April–May	Budgetary framework set. The president and the OMB set broad budgetary parameters and communicate them to the agencies.
June–August	Agency budget preparation. Agencies build their budgets in light of presidential and OMB instructions.
September–November	OMB review. OMB reviews agency budgets, holds hearings, and makes recommendations to the president. The president makes final decisions on agency budgets.
December–January	Final budget preparation. Final economic reviews are conducted and adjustments are made, and the final budget is prepared for submission to Congress.
Congressional Preparation	
2017	
First Monday in February	Congress receives the president's budget.
February 15	CBO reports to the Budget Committee on the fiscal outlook, budget priorities, and how they relate to the president's budget.
February 25	Congressional committees submit to the Budget Committee estimates on revenues and spending.
April 1	Budget Committee reports concurrent resolution on the budget to each house.
April 15	Both houses complete action on the concurrent resolution.
May 15–June 10	House Appropriations Committee must complete consideration on all thirteen appropriations bills.
June 15	Congress must pass a reconciliation bill, which brings budget totals in line with approved ceilings.
June 30	House completes action on all appropriations bills.
October 1	Fiscal year 2018 begins.

Congress frequently gets the blame when the budget does not pass on time, when a government shutdown looms because an increase in the debt ceiling has not passed, or when the push to repeal and replace Obamacare falls short in the Senate. But Congress was designed to move slowly and to make it much easier to stop things from happening than to make them happen. Separation of powers, checks and balances, and bicameralism are just the biggest roadblocks to rapid action, not the only ones. Dozens of smaller potholes, many lodged in House and Senate rules, slow down legislative traffic.

PUBLIC DISAPPROVAL AND CONGRESSIONAL REFORM

Congress never stands very high in the public mind; hence, waves of reform regularly roil the congressional waters. Reform waves usually are driven by a combination of public and member concern about the efficiency, representativeness, and morality of the institution and its members. The modern Congress was shaped by post–World War II responses to the growth of presidential power. The Legislative Reorganization Act of 1946 sought to enhance the efficiency and effectiveness of the Congress by reducing the number of standing committees in the House and Senate, providing them with permanent professional and clerical support, and reasserting Congress's role in the budgetary process (see Figure 8.5).

The Legislative Reform Act of 1970 was designed to open Congress to greater public scrutiny, enhance its decision-making capabilities in key areas such as legislative management and budgeting, and empower the majority party in Congress. But empowered majorities tend to limit the rights of minorities and to tighten those limits over time as they seek to enact their agenda. This is particularly true of the House where the rules allow for majority party dominance.

House scandals in the early 1990s, including those surrounding the House bank and post office, led to a new wave of congressional reform. In the wake of stunning victories in 1994, House Republicans promised a more open, fair, and accountable Congress. They swore they would not run roughshod over the Democratic minority as it, they claimed, had run roughshod over them.

Q5 How serious has Congress been in its recent reform efforts?

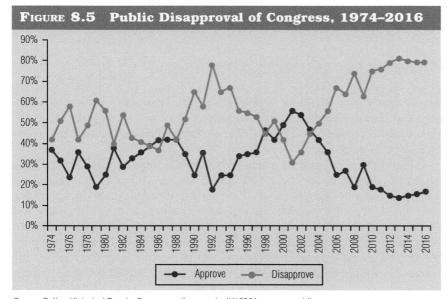

FIGURE 8.5 Public Disapproval of Congress, 1974–2016

Source: Gallup Historical Trends. See www.gallup.com/poll/1600/congress-public.aspx.

But power is difficult not to wield and opposition soon comes to seem like obstruction. The Republican leadership used closed rules, extended votes, arm twisting, and a proliferation of pork barrel spending to move their agenda through the Congress. After 2003, a series of scandals, many tying back to Majority Leader Tom DeLay (R-TX), and the war in Iraq turned public opinion against the Republican majority.

Democrats claimed that Republicans had fostered a "culture of corruption" in Washington that needed to be replaced. They promised to end gridlock by limiting partisanship and restoring comity in Congress. They also promised to restore the regular order, allow the minority more opportunity to participate in debate and offer amendments, and open conferences to the public. Democrats soon backed off these procedural promises, deciding it was more important to pass bills than to worry unduly about whether the Republicans were on board. Similarly, President Trump, with Republican majorities in both houses of Congress, promised to "drain the swamp" in Washington and make the city work for the American people. Speaker Ryan promised to demonstrate that Republicans could govern by passing Obamacare reform, tax reform, and a major infrastructure bill early in the Trump administration. Mitch McConnell, Republican majority leader in Senate, was quieter because he knew Senate rules gave every member the power to slow if not to halt action on important bills.

Institutional reform is a continuous process in Congress, as it is in most major social institutions. The public expects responsiveness (these are the representatives of the people, after all), efficiency (the ability to identify and effectively address important issues and problems), and morality (basic honesty) from the Congress. These expectations are rarely fulfilled. Despite their reform efforts, public approval of Congress sank to all-time lows, touching just 14 percent approval in late 2013. By 2016 it had soared to 17 percent.

Chapter Summary

Americans of the founding period knew both that government is necessary and that the powers awarded to government can be misused. The U.S. Constitution envisioned a powerful national government with a bicameral legislature at its center.

Initially, the new Congress conducted most of its important business in open discussion on the floors of the House and Senate. Only as the membership and workload of Congress grew did leadership powers expand and standing committees become central to the legislative business of both the House and the Senate. The standing committee system in Congress was built around fixed committee jurisdictions that promoted member expertise. The seniority norm, which held that the member of the majority party with longest service on the committee should be the committee chair, further promoted the development of expertise.

The most important committees in the Congress are the standing committees. They have fixed jurisdictions and continue from one Congress to the next. When a bill is introduced into the House or the Senate, it is assigned to the appropriate standing committee. The committee consideration process typically involves public hearings, markup, and drafting a report that describes the major provisions of the bill. Floor consideration of bills reported out of committee typically involves general debate, amendment, and a vote on final passage. If the House version and Senate version of a bill differ, a conference committee of members drawn from both chambers is appointed to resolve the difference between the House version and Senate version of the bill. The bill can then be sent on for the president's consideration.

The president is involved in Congress' work from his State of the Union address to his decision to sign or veto every bill that comes from the Congress. The interplay between the president and Congress is particularly clear on the preparation of the national budget. Though the president prepares and submits a budget to Congress each year, Congress, and especially the House, knows that "the power of the purse" rests with them. Power is only power if you control and use it—so the Congress controls the budgetary process.

Although the legislative process seems clear enough, the Congress at work always looks slightly out of control. Majorities seem unable to develop and adopt credible programs and often seem unable to hold their members together even on critical votes; minorities seem negative and shrill, accusing the majority of wanting to do hurtful things in ways that will be fraught with waste, fraud, and corruption. Members seem to be pulled to and fro by constituents, party leaders, lobbyists, and representatives of the administration. Naturally, citizens come to think ill of those who seem incapable of solving the nation's problems or even of discussing them sensibly and civilly.

Key Terms

appropriations committees	popular sovereignty
authorizing committees	reciprocity norm
casework	reconciliation
cloture	redistricting
Committee of the Whole	referral
conference committees	Rules Committee
delegate	select committees
filibuster	seniority norm
gerrymander	specialization norm
joint committees	standing committees
legislative supremacy	trustee
politico	unanimous consent

Suggested Readings

Davidson, Roger H., Walter J. Oleszek, Francis E. Lee, and Eric Schickler. *Congress and Its Members*, 15th ed. Washington, D.C.: Congressional Quarterly Press, 2015. This textbook highlights the effect on the institution of the fact that members must perform effectively both in Washington and back in their districts.

Dodd, Lawrence C., and Bruce I. Oppenheimer, *Congress Reconsidered.* Washington, D.C.: CQ Press, 2016. Leading congressional scholars assess the performance of the modern congress and reforms that might be undertaken to improve that performance.

Mayhew, David R. *The Imprint of Congress.* New Haven, CT: Yale University Press, 2017. A leading congressional scholar describes the distinctive imprint congress on our national politics and policy.

Sinclair, Barbara. *Unorthodox Lawmaking: New Legislative Processes in the U.S. Congress*, 4th ed. Washington, D.C.: Congressional Quarterly Press, 2012. This book describes the contemporary legislative process with a particular focus on recent changes in it.

Smith, Steven S., Jason M. Roberts, and Ryan J. Vander Wielen. *The American Congress*, 8th ed. New York: Cambridge University Press, 2013. Classic textbook on the changing place and role of Congress in American politics.

Web Resources

1 www.thehill.com
   An online newspaper that covers all things Congress.

2 thomas.loc.gov
   The Thomas home page provides links to the *Congressional Record*, the texts of bills and reports on their status, committee information, and documents on the legislative process and on congressional history.

3 www.house.gov
   Official website of the United States House of Representatives. This site includes up-to-date information of legislative activity, votes of members, member biographies, and contact information.

4 www.senate.gov
   Official website of the United States Senate. Resources of interest include a virtual tour, legislative news, committee assignments, biographies of members, and an archive searchable by keyword.

5 www.rollcall.com
   An online periodical that specializes in covering daily events on Capitol Hill.

Notes

1 Adam Liptak, "When Does Gerrymandering Cross a Line," *New York Times*, May 16, 2017, A18.

2 Barbara Sinclair, *Unorthodox Lawmaking: New Legislative Processes in the U.S. Congress*, 4th ed. (Washington, D.C.: Congressional Quarterly Press, 2011).

3 John Locke, *Second Treatise*, chap. 13, no. 150 (New York: Cambridge University Press, 1960), 413–414.

4 Raymond A. Smith, *The American Anomaly*, 2nd ed. (New York: Routledge, 2011), 76, 84.

5 Roger H. Davidson, Walter J. Oleszek, Frances E. Lee, and Eric Schickler, *Congress and Its Members*, 15th ed. (Washington, D.C.: Congressional Quarterly Press, 2016), 6.

6 Katelin P. Isaacs, Congressional Research Service, "Retirement Benefits for Members of Congress," November 11, 2016.

7 Andrew Katz, "Congress Now Mostly a Millionaire's Club," *Time*, January 9, 2014.

8 John R. Hibbing, *Congressional Careers: Contours of Life in the U.S. House of Representatives* (Chapel Hill, NC: University of North Carolina Press, 1991), 2.

9 Davidson, et al., *Congress and Its Members*, 60.

10 Walter J. Oleszek, *Congressional Procedures and the Policy Process*. 9th ed. (Washington, D.C.: CQ Press, 2014), 27.

11 Randall B. Ripley, *Party Leaders in the House of Representatives* (Washington, D.C.: Brookings Institution, 1967), 54; Davidson, Oleszek, and Lee, *Congress and Its Members*, 157–159, 170–173.

12 Ripley, *Party Leaders in the House of Representatives*, 6–8.

13 Carl Hulse and David M. Herszenhorn, "After Boehner, House Hard-Liners Aim to Weaken Speakership Itself," *New York Times*, October 11, 2015, A21.

14 David W. Rohde, *Parties and Leaders in the Postreform House* (Chicago: University of Chicago Press, 1991), 83–88.

15 Phil Duncan, "Senate Leader's Role a Recent One," *Congressional Quarterly Weekly Report*, May 18, 1996, 1368–1369.

16 Christopher J. Deering and Steven S. Smith, *Committees in Congress*, 3rd ed. (Washington, D.C.: Congressional Quarterly Press, 1997), 26.

17 John Hibbing, *Congressional Careers*, 126.

18 Barbara Sinclair, *The Transformation of the United States Senate* (Baltimore, MD: Johns Hopkins University Press, 1989), 145. See also Sinclair, *Unorthodox Lawmaking*, 82–86.

19 Ida R. Brudnick, "Congressional Salaries and Allowances," Congressional Research Service, January 7, 2014.

20 Sinclair, *The Transformation of the U.S. Senate*, 131.

21 David Hawkings, "How Bad Political Manners Fomented the Health Care Mess," *Roll-Call*, July 4, 2017..

22 Sinclair, *Unorthodox Lawmaking*, 18, 54, 147.

23 Sinclair, *Unorthodox Lawmaking*, 21.

24 Gerald F. Seib, "Senate Woes Flag Wider Disease," *Wall Street Journal*, February 15, 2010, A2.

25 Jeremy W. Peters, "Senate Vote Curbs Filibuster Power to Stall Nominees," *New York Times*, November 22, 2013, A1, A16.

26 Rohde, *Parties and Leaders in the Post-reform House*, 41; Davidson, Oleszek, Lee, and Schickler, *Congress and Its Members*, 259–263.

27 Richard Fenno, *Home Style: House Members in Their Districts* (Boston, MA: Little, Brown, 1978), 1–30.

28 Morris P. Fiorina, *Congress: Keystone of the Washington Establishment* (New Haven, CT: Yale University Press, 1977), 42–43.

29 Janie Velencia, "Members Get Personal on Instagram, Tumblr and Pinterest," *Roll Call*, January, 22, 2014.

30 Steven S. Smith, *Party Influence in Congress* (New York: Cambridge University Press, 2007).

31 Steven Brill, "On Sale: Your Government," *Time*, July 12, 2012, 28–35.

32 Center for Budget and Policy Priorities, "Policy Basics: Introduction to the Federal Budget Process," April 20, 2015.

Chapter 9

THE EXECUTIVE BRANCH
The President, the Bureaucracy, and Executive Power

Focus Questions: from reading to thinking

Q1 How did the Founders limit the powers that they placed with the president?

Q2 What forces account for the growth of executive power over the course of American political history?

Q3 Why does the president have an easier time in shaping and implementing foreign policy than he does domestic policy?

Q4 How does the president relate to the executive branch?

Q5 Should we be concerned that White House staff members have replaced members of the cabinet as the president's closest advisers?

The Constitution TODAY

THE UNITARY EXECUTIVE THEORY OF PRESIDENTIAL AUTHORITY

Article II, section 1: "The executive power shall be vested in a President of the United States of America."

While the constitutional origins of presidential authority are clear, centering on the clause above, the scope and limits of that authority are hotly contested. Scholars have long noted that while the powers explicitly enumerated in the Constitution's Article II are few—commander-in-chief, pardon power, and, with the advice and consent of the Senate, broad appointment powers—the president has additional unenumerated powers.

Moreover, students of executive power all the way back to John Locke (1632–1704) have argued that kings and presidents may have to act outside the law or even in contravention of the law when great dangers threaten. The "inherent powers" of the executive, they argue, may require bold action, even action that would be illegal under normal circumstances, to confront dire threats. Officials of the George W. Bush administration argued for an even broader "unitary executive" theory of presidential authority. The **unitary executive theory** holds that the president is the sole authority in the executive branch and any attempt to limit that authority is unconstitutional.

unitary executive theory
Strong presidency theory holding that the president embodies executive authority and is the sole judge, particularly in wartime, of what is required to protect the nation and its people.

While the Bush administration's view of untrammeled executive authority was distinctive, it was not unprecedented. Presidents, congressmen, Supreme Court justices, and scholars have been wrestling with these issues since the founding period. The key issue is whether presidential authority claims are to be seen within a separation of powers context or a unitary executive authority context.

The Bush administration's "War on Terror" in the wake of the 9/11 attacks raised these issues anew. Though Congress authorized the administration to "use all necessary and appropriate force against those nations, organizations, or persons he determines planned, authorized, committed, or aided the terrorist attacks," administration lawyers led by John Yoo claimed the authorization was unnecessary. Yoo wrote that "the power to initiate military hostilities, particularly in response to the threat of an armed attack, rests exclusively with the president." Moreover, Bush administration lawyers claimed that the president's commander-in-chief powers gave him exclusive control over decisions about how to wage the war against terror.

Initially, a public in deep shock after 9/11 and Republican majorities in both houses of Congress did not resist expansive presidential authority claims. But as the emergency receded in the public mind, the Afghan and Iraq wars soured, and more information about administration policies emerged, opposition built in public opinion, the courts, and finally in the Congress.

The Bush administration's unitary executive theory came under Supreme Court review in *Hamdan v. Rumsfeld* (2006). The Bush administration claimed the right to employ military tribunals to try Guantanamo detainees. Writing for the majority, Justice John Paul Stevens declared, "Whether or not the president has independent power, absent congressional authorization, to convene military commissions, he may not disregard limitations that Congress has, in proper exercise of its own war powers, placed on his powers." When presidents claim unitary executive power, Congress and the courts respond with separation of powers.

Not surprisingly, presidents operating in peacetime, or even after the initial shock of war has passed, are more constrained. While the Obama administrative did not advance the unitary executive argument championed by the Bush administration, it regularly asserted broad executive powers. When Obama tried to change immigration policy, the courts checked him; when he sought an opening with Cuba, Congress refused to lift the long-standing embargo on most trade; and Obama claimed executive authority to join the Paris climate change accords largely because he knew that the Republican controlled Senate would not ratify a treaty on the topic. President Trump moved systematically to roll back Obama's executive orders on immigration, Cuba, and climate change, but saw his own travel ban blocked by the courts in the first months of his administration. The Founders, architects of our system of limited government, separation of powers, and checks and balances, would have recognized the process.

⬥✦⬥

THE PRESIDENT OF THE UNITED STATES

Popular expectations surrounding the presidency spring from a civics book image of the president as being in charge of the national government. The reality is somewhat different. Constitutional authority and political resources are shared by the president, Congress, and the courts.[1] The resulting dilemma was nicely stated by Stephen Skowronek. In describing the mismatch between popular understanding of the president in the American political system and the office's constitutional authority, Skowronek writes, "Formally, there is no central authority. Governing responsibilities are shared, and assertions of power are contentious. Practically, however, it is the presidency that stands out as the chief point of reference ... it is the executive office that focuses the eyes and draws out the attachments of the people."[2]

Article II of the Constitution outlines the powers of the presidency and its relationships to the other branches only in broad terms. Edward S. Corwin, the leading mid-twentieth-century student of the presidency, warned that the Constitution's broad language concerning the war powers (Congress declares war, the president is commander in chief) was "an invitation to struggle."[3] That struggle ebbs and flows over time.

George W. Bush and Dick Cheney, convinced that presidents weakened by Vietnam and Watergate had allowed Congress and the courts to encroach upon the executive's rightful prerogatives, were determined to restore them. During Bush's first term, and especially after 9/11, the administration advocated the unitary executive theory of presidential power. Barack Obama entered the presidency facing unprecedented problems: two wars with which the public had grown impatient and national and global economies in deep distress. Big problems require big powers, but not necessarily powers exercised unilaterally. Donald Trump entered the presidency with the nation in a different kind of distress—political and emotional distress following one of the most raucous and negative campaigns in modern American history. Each new president, some consciously and some unconsciously, adopt a theory of the presidency and a style of being president. For most, the style is familiar and reassuring, for some, less so.

In this chapter, we analyze the range of foreign and domestic policy responsibilities of the modern president. We ask how the presidential establishment—the White House staff, the Executive Office of the President, the cabinet, and the office of the vice president—is organized to assist the president in stretching his powers to meet his responsibilities. We ask how the president presides over, even if he does not exactly manage, the executive branch or bureaucracy. We conclude with a discussion of concerns about the presidency and reforms that might be undertaken to address them.

THE CONSTITUTIONAL BASES OF PRESIDENTIAL AUTHORITY

Q1 How did the Founders limit the powers that they placed with the president?

Most of the delegates arriving in Philadelphia in the summer of 1787 for the Constitutional Convention were convinced that executive power had to be both enhanced and restrained simultaneously. No one quite knew how to do that, much less how to describe the result to a skeptical public.

The Founders had little difficulty establishing the eligibility criteria for the new office. The president would have to be at least thirty-five years of age, fourteen years a resident, and a natural-born citizen of the United States. Other questions were more difficult: who would choose the president and by what means, how long would he serve, and would he be eligible to serve two or more terms successively? The convention struggled over these questions until within days of final adjournment.[4]

Executive Authority in the Constitution

Article II of the Constitution begins boldly, stating: "The executive Power shall be vested in a President of the United States of America." But what did the Founders intend to be included in executive power? In the monarchies of Europe, the executive power was broad indeed, extending to the right to conduct foreign affairs (including war), grant reprieves and pardons, create administrative offices and appoint persons to them, direct the bureaucracy, veto legislation, and call and disband legislatures.

The Founders had a narrower view of executive power. Most of the president's executive powers, both in domestic legislative and administrative affairs and in foreign and military affairs, were hedged about with legislative and judicial checks. Moreover, the Founders were intent on focusing future presidents on the Constitution as the source of their authority and of limits on that authority. The final paragraph of Article II, section 1, of the Constitution is an oath of office, the only one in the Constitution, which reads, "I do solemnly swear (or affirm) that I will faithfully execute the office of President of the United States, and will to the best of my ability, preserve, protect and defend the Constitution of the United States."

Nonetheless, the Founders knew that they could see the future only dimly, so they constructed the executive power loosely. As the nation has grown, expanded, and matured, the formal or constitutional powers of the presidency have been supplemented by informal powers that have grown up around them.

The Pardon Power.   Article II, section 2, gives the president the right "to grant reprieves and pardons for offenses against the United States except in cases of impeachment." A **reprieve** is a temporary postponement of the effect of a judicial decision to give the executive time to consider a request for a pardon.

George Washington (seated) meets with members of his cabinet: From left, Secretary of State Thomas Jefferson, Secretary of the Treasury Alexander Hamilton, Secretary of War Henry Knox, and Attorney General Edmund Randolph (background).

North Wind Picture Archives

A **pardon**, whether awarded before or after a formal judicial finding, wipes the slate clean and makes the recipient of the pardon a "new person" in the eyes of the law.

reprieve A temporary postponement of the effect of a judicial decision to give the executive time to consider a request for a pardon.

pardon A pardon makes the recipient a new person in the eyes of the law as if no offense had ever been committed.

The Power to Propose and the Power to Veto.   Article II, section 3, gives the president the right to propose legislation to the Congress for its consideration. It states: "He shall from time to time give to the Congress Information of the State of the Union, and recommend to their Consideration such Measures as he shall judge necessary and expedient." This provision of the Constitution legitimates the president's participation in the early or agenda-setting stage of legislative activity in the Congress.

veto power The president has the right to veto acts of Congress. The act can still become law if both houses pass the bill again by a two-thirds vote.

The president's **veto power** (veto is Latin for "I forbid") appears in Article I, section 7, of the Constitution. This provision requires that every bill passed by Congress be presented to the president for his evaluation. If he approves, he signs it, and it becomes law. If he disapproves, he sends the bill back to Congress with his objections. After considering the president's objections, Congress can either repass the original bill by a two-thirds vote in each house, in which case it becomes a law over the president's objections, or it can revise the bill to try to win the president's approval.

Overriding a president's veto is difficult. Therefore, the veto is as important as a threat as it is in actual use. Members of Congress who know that the president is opposed to certain provisions of a bill are likely to think about revising those provisions in order to avoid a veto. The veto threat allows the president and his representatives to be involved throughout the legislative process rather than simply at the very beginning and the very end.

The "Take Care" Clause. Article II, section 3, states that "the president shall take Care that the Laws be faithfully executed." Under normal circumstances, the "take care" clause simply requires that the president efficiently administer the laws that Congress has passed. However, under extraordinary circumstances, such as those that faced President Lincoln as the Civil War approached, presidents have argued that extraordinary actions, even actions outside the law, may be required to save the nation. Not surprisingly, presidents sometimes see extraordinary circumstances where others do not.

The Appointment Power. Presidents argue that if they are responsible to "take care" that the laws be faithfully executed, they must have the power to appoint and remove officials acting on their behalf. The Founders agreed in part. Article II, section 2, split the **appointment power** as follows: "he shall nominate, and by and with the Advice and Consent of the Senate, shall appoint Ambassadors, other public Ministers and Consuls, Judges of the Supreme Court, and all other Officers of the United States, whose Appointments are not herein otherwise provided for, and which shall be established by Law." The president shares the power of appointing senior officials with the Senate and can appoint officers only to positions previously created by the Congress.

appointment power Article II, section 2, of the Constitution empowers the president, often with the advice and consent of the Senate, to appoint many senior government officials.

treaty-making power Article II, section 2, of the Constitution gives the president, with the advice and consent of the Senate, the power to make treaties with foreign nations.

Treaty Making and Foreign Affairs. The Founders also sought to involve both the Congress and the president in foreign affairs. Article II, section 2, says the president "shall receive Ambassadors and other public Ministers." This right to receive the envoys of foreign nations has evolved into the important right to recognize and initiate formal relations with the nations of the world.

Article II, section 2, also provides that the president "shall have power, by and with the advice and consent of the Senate, to make treaties, provided two-thirds of the Senators present concur." Presidents have liberally supplemented their **treaty-making power** with **executive agreements**. Executive agreements are negotiated between the president and foreign nations and have the same legal status as treaties but do not require Senate confirmation. On the other

executive agreements Agreements negotiated between the president and foreign governments. Executive agreements have the same legal force as treaties but do not require confirmation by the Senate.

hand, they remain in force only during that president's term, unless confirmed or renewed by his or her successor.

Commander in Chief. Finally, Article II, section 2, provides that "The President shall be commander in chief of the Army and Navy of the United States, and the Militia of the several States, when called into the actual Service of the United States." The Congress was given the responsibility and power to "raise and support" armies and navies and to "declare war." The Founders were quite clear that the choice of peace and war that had rested with the monarchs of Europe would not be given to the president. The president would be in charge after the armed forces were committed to battle, but the decision of whether or not to commit them would rest with the Congress.[5] As we shall see below, the modern world has rewritten the Founders clear intent on war-making.

The Impeachment Process. The national executives with whom the Founders were most familiar were the crowned heads of Europe. But the Founders rejected monarchy; instead, they wanted a strong executive that could be checked by a watchful Congress. **Impeachment** is the process by which Congress can remove officers of the national government, including the president. Article I, section 2, places "the sole Power of Impeachment," that is, formulating the statement of charges of wrongdoing, in the House of Representatives. Article I, section 3, declares that "The Senate shall have the sole Power to try all impeachments" and that "When the President of the United States is tried, the Chief Justice shall preside." Article II, section 4, defines the charges for which impeachment might be levied as "treason, bribery, or other high crimes and misdemeanours."

impeachment The process of removing national government officials from office. The House votes a statement of particulars or charges, and a trial is conducted in the Senate.

Impeachment begins when the House votes a set of charges and proceeds to a trial on the charges conducted in the Senate. A two-thirds vote among senators present is required to convict, and punishment extends only to removal from office and a prohibition against further national government service. Offenders are, however, subject to additional action in the state and federal courts. Only nineteen officers of the national government, including Presidents Andrew Johnson and Bill Clinton, one senator, one cabinet officer, and fifteen federal judges, have been impeached by the House, and only eight federal judges have actually been convicted in the Senate.

Opposition party talk of presidential impeachment is not uncommon, but such talk regarding Donald Trump began early and did not abate. But getting beyond "talk" of impeachment is hard. Only two presidents, Andrew Johnson after the Civil War and Bill Clinton in the late 1990s, were successfully impeached by the House, but the Senate failed to convict either one. Neither were charged with treason or bribery, fairly well-defined crimes, but with other activities argued to be "high crimes and misdemeanours." This highlights the fact that the decision to impeach, let alone to convict, is as much a political as a legal judgment. Hence, a president, whether Trump or any other, whose party controls either house of Congress, let alone both, is unlikely to be impeached and highly unlikely to be impeached and convicted. However, a president facing a Congress controlled by the other party must be wary. Elections matter!

THE GROWTH OF PRESIDENTIAL POWER

Q2 What forces account for the growth of executive power over the course of American political history?

The Founders were both determined that the president provide energy, focus, and direction to the government and concerned that he work with the Congress and the courts within a framework of law. Therefore, they required the president to share most of his powers and authority with the Congress. Nonetheless, many of the Founders feared that executive power would expand and grow over time and would in the end become overbearing.

In fact, presidential power remained largely within its constitutional bounds during the nineteenth century.[6] However, the twentieth century brought domestic and international crises that demanded bold and concerted actions for which the executive seemed best fitted. Modern presidents in wartime including Franklin Roosevelt, Harry Truman, Lyndon Johnson, Richard Nixon, and George W. Bush have been accused of harboring imperial aspirations. A quick look at Figure 9.1 suggests that greatness requires a great challenge—revolution, civil war, depression, and world war—for a president to meet and overcome. Presidential failure comes from facing great challenges ineffectually.

The Modern Presidency

As the twentieth century dawned, the United States was becoming an industrial power with international political and economic interests, but it was not yet a significant military power. The first third of the twentieth century brought

Every president hopes to be remembered among the greats. Only a few are, but the image-makers never stop trying. Here President Bush was carefully positioned at Mount Rushmore to suggest how well he would fit there. History had other ideas.

Getty Images/AFP/Paul J. Richards

FIGURE 9.1 Ranking the Performance of U.S. Presidents

Great	Average	Below Average
1. Washington	14. McKinley	26. Arthur
2. Lincoln	15. Madison	
3. F. Roosevelt	16. Monroe	**Below Average**
	17. L. Johnson	27. B. Harrison
Near great	18. Kennedy	28. Ford
4. Jefferson		29. Hoover
5. T. Roosevelt	Where to put Barack Obama?	30. Carter
6. Jackson		31. Taylor
7. Truman		32. Grant
8. Reagan		33. Nixon
9. Eisenhower	**Average**	34. Tyler
10. Polk	19. Taft	35. George W. Bush
11. Wilson	20. John Q. Adams	36. Fillmore
	21. George H.W. Bush	
Above Average	22. Hayes	**Failure**
12. Cleveland	23. Van Buren	37. A. Johnson
13. John Adams	24. Clinton	38. Pierce
	25. Coolidge	39. Harding
		40. Buchanan

Source: Harold W. Stanley and Richard G. Niemi, *Vital Statistics on American Politics, 2015–2016* (Washington, D.C.: CQ Press, 2015), Table 6.2, 243–245. See also Brandon Rottinghaus and Justin Vaughn, "Expert Survey of Presidential Greatness," 2015, www.polsci.uh.edu/faculty/rottinghaus.htm.

threats, both at home and abroad, that demanded immediate and decisive action. Presidents like Theodore Roosevelt, Woodrow Wilson, and Franklin Roosevelt drew power to themselves when Congress was slow to respond.

Theodore Roosevelt is generally credited with expanding presidential power both by how he acted in office, "speak softly [which he did not do] but carry a big stick [which he did do]," as well as how he understood the office. TR articulated what has come to be known as the "stewardship theory" of the presidency. In this view, the president is the nation's elected leader and steward of its security and its future prospects and promise. Woodrow Wilson agreed with TR, declaring that the president "is at liberty, both in law and conscience, to be as big a man as he can. His capacity will set the limit." TR and Wilson were heralding the new plebiscitary presidency of the twentieth century.

The greater visibility and broader responsibilities of the president seemed to call for institutional reform. Presidents found that they needed help to lead, so Congress approved the Reorganization Act of 1939 that established the Executive Office of the President (EOP) and provided additional staff assistance to the president.[7]

The modern presidency was largely defined by FDR's dramatic responses to the Depression and World War II. In domestic politics, Roosevelt pushed the Congress and courts into approving his legislation, but they did, in fact, approve it. In foreign affairs, Roosevelt took a number of actions between 1939 and American entry into the war late in 1941 that were constitutionally dubious. His shoot-on-sight order to American naval forces convoying supplies to Great Britain moved the United States to the brink of war. Even more starkly, President Truman's order in 1950 to American air and naval forces to assist the South Koreans against the invading North Koreans was taken unilaterally.[8] Both Roosevelt and Truman informed congressional leaders of what they intended to do, but neither sought congressional advice and counsel before acting.

Where Was the Expanded Authority Found?

Where have the vast new executive powers that have arisen since World War II been found? Generally they have been found outside the Constitution, in **inherent powers** associated with sovereignty and nationhood, in congressional acts and judicial interpretations, and in enlarged public expectations.

Presidents, most prominently Lincoln, FDR, and George W. Bush, have argued that sovereign nations under great threat or operating in the international system have broad rights of self-defense. Inherent powers allow the president to take actions required to protect and defend the nation, whether those actions are explicitly sanctioned by existing law or not. The logic is that it makes no sense to scrupulously adhere to law and procedure if the nation is gravely harmed or destroyed in the process.

In foreign and military affairs, Congress's broad authorization of presidential initiative in the Gulf of Tonkin Resolution to carry out the Vietnam War seemed to expand executive authority still further. By the 1970s scholars, politicians, and citizens were warning of an "imperial presidency."[9] Congress's joint resolution of September 14, 2001, broadly authorizing President Bush to "use all necessary and appropriate force" against threats posed by international terrorism raised these questions anew.[10]

But presidential power has grown in domestic politics as well. Since 1937, the Supreme Court has been willing to sanction extensive government regulation of the economy and of social life. In response to the court's newly permissive view, Congress passed, for example, the Employment Act of 1946 charged the president to "foster and promote free competitive enterprise, to avoid economic fluctuations or to diminish the effects thereof, and to maintain employment, production, and purchasing power."

Should we be concerned that modern presidential power has expanded in the absence of formal constitutional amendments. It does seem, after all, that the whole point of a written constitution was to specify the powers granted to Congress, the president, and the courts unambiguously. On the other hand, if Congress, the courts, and the public agree on the modern need for expanded presidential powers, that has weight too. What do you think?

inherent powers Powers accruing to all sovereign nations, whether or not specified in the Constitution, allowing executives to take actions required to defend the nation and protect its interests.

THE RANGE OF PRESIDENTIAL RESPONSIBILITIES

The range of presidential responsibility today is very broad. In foreign affairs, the president acts as commander in chief, chief diplomat, and chief trade negotiator. In domestic affairs, the president acts as chief executive, chief legislator, party leader, and leader of the nation. In a few of these areas, the president has formal constitutional and legal powers that give him a strong position from which to act. However, in most cases, especially in domestic affairs, he has only informal powers that give him the right, sometimes merely the opportunity, to be involved and the leverage to affect outcomes but leave him far short of being able to dictate or control events.

Q3 Why does the president have an easier time in shaping and implementing foreign policy than he does domestic policy?

Aaron Wildavsky's famous essay entitled "The Two Presidencies" pointed out that presidents find it easier to lead in foreign policy than in domestic policy.[11] In foreign policy, the president is usually thought to have more current and often more relevant information than either the Congress or the public. The interest group structure involved in foreign affairs is much thinner than that involved in domestic affairs, and most foreign policy conflicts are interpreted as us-against-them events to which citizens respond with a rally-round-the-flag reaction of automatic support for the U.S. position. The relatively free hand that President George W. Bush had in preparing for and conducting the early stages of the wars in Afghanistan and Iraq or that Donald Trump had in confronting North Korea over its nuclear weapons program are excellent examples of this phenomenon.

The exercise of presidential authority in domestic affairs is more complex and is often challenged. Public opinion, to say nothing of congressional opinion, is commonly split in regard to domestic policy issues. Most things that a president might propose to do with taxes, social security, health care, or environmental policy will generate support from some and opposition from others. Moreover, many interest groups and both major parties have established positions on most of the domestic policy issues of moment, so a fight is virtually guaranteed.

The Foreign Policy Presidency

Presidents have argued and Congress generally agreed that the heightened global dangers of the modern world, the president's ability to act quickly, and his superior sources of information and access to expertise make him the dominant force in U.S. foreign policy. Every president since Truman has deployed U.S. forces around the world and even moved them toward and into conflict situations on his own authority.[12]

Commander in Chief. The president commands U.S. armed forces during war and peace. He commissions the officer corps and nominates its members for promotion; deploys troops, ships, and other military assets as seems most

Struggling Toward Democracy

Congress has not declared war since 1941 in the wake of the Japanese attack on Pearl Harbor. Yet we have engaged in a lot of conflict and several major wars—Korea, Vietnam, Iraq, Afghanistan—since 1941.

What do you think?

- Is the American way of going to war broken?
- If so, is there a democratic way of going to war in the modern world?

War Powers Resolution
Passed in Congress in 1973 requiring the president to consult with Congress on the use of force and to withdraw U.S. forces from conflict should congressional approval not be forthcoming.

reasonable; and participates in setting overall military and defense strategy. However, the Constitution gives to Congress the right "to declare war" and the power to regulate all of the president's activities through the power of the purse. Hence, the president and Congress have struggled over the meaning and boundaries of the president's role as commander in chief.

Two key aspects of the post–World War II period led to broad changes in the constitutional positions of Congress and the president in regard to war-making. First, in the wake of World War II, presidents negotiated and Congresses approved and provided funds for a worldwide network of defense treaties including NATO, SEATO, CENTO, ANZUS, and the Rio Pact that obligated the United States to come to the aid of member nations if they were attacked.

Second, the U.S. policy of "containment" directed against the Soviet Union, China, and communism in general was central to our Cold War strategy. Opinion leaders in and out of government as well as the general public were convinced that the United States was engaged in a worldwide struggle against communism (today you could substitute radical Islam for communism). Presidents were thought to be acting responsibly as they moved American military assets around the world to have them always in position where they might be most needed. Increasingly, presidents came to argue that their powers as commanders in chief gave them the constitutional right to initiate hostilities and to determine their scope and duration. Congress's reaction to the implications of presidential war-making in Vietnam was to pass the **War Powers Resolution** in 1973. Nonetheless, a workable balance between legislative and executive influence over war-making has been elusive (see Pro and Con box).

President George W. Bush went to Congress and the United Nations prior to the 2003 Iraq war. A compliant Congress, with most Democrats joining all of the Republicans in both the House and Senate, gave the president authority to use force if he deemed it necessary to control the dangers posed by Saddam Hussein. Failing to receive the full support of the United Nations Security Council, Bush declared Iraq to be a gathering danger and launched the war in March 2003.

Although the Republican Congress initially was reluctant to set limits on President Bush's claims to broad powers as commander in chief in wartime, the Supreme Court rejected some of his claims. Throughout the Afghan and Iraq wars, the Bush administration claimed that the president as commander in chief could hold "enemy combatants" including American citizens for the duration of the conflict, with no access to lawyers or courts, and try them in military tribunals as he thought best. In a series of cases in 2004, the Supreme Court reminded the Bush administration that "a state of war is not a blank check for the president when it comes to the rights of the nation's citizens."[13]

In 2006, the Supreme Court rejected the Bush administration's plan to try Guantanamo detainees before military commissions. The court found that the proposed commissions were not authorized by Congress and rejected the

Pro & Con

Must Presidents Have the Initiative in War-Making?

Article I, section 8, declares that "the Congress shall have Power . . . to declare War," whereas Article II, section 2, says that "the President shall be Commander in Chief of the Army and Navy." The president is, of course, empowered to respond to attacks on the United States because an attack would initiate a state of war and render Congress's "declaration" unnecessary.

That logic seemed to work through the middle of the twentieth century. But every president of the past seventy years has argued that U.S. involvement in international collective security organizations like the UN and NATO, along with the stationing of U.S. military forces on bases and at sea around the world, means that U.S. interests, territory, and sovereignty are exposed and in essence constantly engaged. Presidents also contend that they have the right to move American troops, planes, ships, and equipment around the world to where they are most likely to be needed. Finally, they contend that an attack on an American treaty ally or on American forces, citizens, or interests anywhere in the world is an attack on the United States and permits action by the president as commander in chief.

What room is left for Congress in decisions about going to war? Congress tried to answer that question in 1973 by passing, over President Nixon's veto, the **War Powers Resolution**. Effectively, Congress offered to give up its right to declare war to gain some leverage over how long presidential uses of force could be sustained without congressional approval.

The War Powers Resolution contains three key provisions:

1. Section 3 requires that "The President in every possible instance shall consult with Congress before introducing United States Armed Forces into hostilities or into situations where imminent involvement in hostilities is clearly indicated."
2. Section 4 requires that when U.S. forces are engaged, "the President shall submit within 48 hours" to the Congress information concerning "the circumstances necessitating the introduction; . . . the constitutional and legislative authority under which such introduction took place; . . . the estimated scope and duration of the hostilities or involvement."
3. Section 5 requires that "within 60 calendar days" of the submission of the report mentioned in point 2, "the President shall terminate any use of United States Armed Forces . . . unless the Congress" agrees.

No president has ever acknowledged the constitutionality of the War Powers Resolution. Each has argued that his powers as commander in chief are sufficient to deploy U.S. armed forces around the world and that participation in congressionally approved collective security regimes like the United Nations permits presidents to use force in defense of U.S. interests and those of our allies.

What do you think?
- What should the respective roles of Congress and the president be in determining the use of U.S. military force in the world?
- Is Congress too addled, divided, and slow to play a credible role in decisions on such critical matters?
- After the performances of Presidents Johnson and Nixon in regard to Vietnam and Bush in regard to Iraq, how can we be confident that presidents will use good judgment?

PRO	CON
Modern conflicts happen too fast for debate	The constitution says congress shall declare war
U.S. Interests are engaged globally	Conflict rarely breaks out without warning
International agreements contain security commitments	Consultation with congress is still required

administration's contention that the federal courts had no jurisdiction to hear the case. Justice John Paul Stevens, writing for the court's majority, declared, "The executive is bound to comply with the rule of law that prevails in this jurisdiction [i.e., nation]."[14] In 2008 the court affirmed the right of detainees to have access to U.S. courts, but Congress blocked the Obama administration from bringing detainees to trial in U.S. federal courts.

President Donald Trump's blustery confidence and aggression, admired by many of his supporters, worried most Democrats and some Republicans in and out of Congress. The 2017 long-distance shouting match between Donald Trump and the North Korean dictator Kim Jong-un, with his growing nuclear arsenal, unnerved many. Scholars have proposed that presidents' unilateral control over the U.S. nuclear arsenal be revised to require broader consultation, with the defense secretary, joint chiefs, and congressional leaders except in the case of surprise attack. In late 2017, Senator Bob Corker (R-TN), Chairman of the Senate Foreign Relations Committee, held the first hearing in four decades on control of nuclear weapons. Some witnesses favored legislative action while others warned against constraining presidential authority in wartime. Do you think a single person should command the U.S. nuclear arsenal?

Chief Diplomat.   The president and Congress share control of our relations with other nations. The president has the initiative in nominating U.S. ambassadors to other nations as well as the leading members of the policymaking teams at the Departments of State and Defense and the National Security Council and in negotiating treaties and multilateral agreements with other nations. The Senate must confirm or reject the president's nominations and actions, and the House and Senate both must agree to provide necessary funds.

Congress can also make policy on a whole range of matters including foreign aid, trade, immigration, and intellectual property that affect our relations with the rest of the world. Alternatively, the president can use executive agreements instead of treaties to bypass Congress on issues when he thinks they are important but anticipates trouble with Congress. Not surprisingly, presidents prefer executive agreements to formal treaties (see Table 9.1).

Chief Trade Negotiator.   As markets and trade have become global, the president's role as chief trade negotiator has become more important. Most economists agree that global free trade benefits consumers by providing them access to high-quality goods at competitive prices. However, imports challenge domestic goods and the businesses and workers that produce them. Decline in the U.S. share of the world market in sectors like steel, autos, and electronics in recent decades highlighted some of the negative impacts of free trade. Public opinion generally favors protection of U.S. markets and interests, and Congress gave the president new powers to punish unfair international trade practices.

The United States has pursued a two-track international trade strategy. One track has been to pursue multilateral trade agreements that lower trade barriers either regionally or globally. A second track has been to pursue bilateral negotiations with nations such as Taiwan, Japan, and China with which the

Table **9.1** Treaties and Executive Agreements, 1789–2017		
Period	**Number of Treaties**	**Number of Executive Agreements**
1789–1839	60	27
1839–1889	215	238
1889–1932	431	804
1933–1944 (F. Roosevelt)	131	369
1945–1952 (Truman)	132	1,324
1953–1960 (Eisenhower)	89	1,834
1961–1963 (Kennedy)	36	813
1964–1968 (Johnson)	67	1,083
1969–1974 (Nixon)	93	1,317
1975–1976 (Ford)	26	666
1977–1980 (Carter)	79	1,476
1981–1988 (Reagan)	125	2,840
1989–1992 (Bush 41)	67	1,350
1993–2000 (Clinton)	209	2,048
2001–2008 (Bush 43)	147	1,990
2009–2016 (Obama)	28	1,414
2017–2021 (Trump)		

Sources: Harold W. Stanley and Richard G. Niemi, *Vital Statistics on American Politics, 2015–2016* (Washington, D.C.: Congressional Quarterly Press, 2015), Table 9.1, 326; Office of the Assistant Legal Adviser for Treaty Affairs, U.S. Department of State, Washington, D.C.

United States has a significant trade deficit to ensure that their markets are as open to U.S. goods as our markets are to their goods. President Trump favors the bilateral track. He appealed to anti-free trade sentiment in the 2016 campaign by threatening to withdraw from NAFTA and the Trans-Pacific Partnership (TPP). He did withdraw from the TPP and moved to renegotiate NAFTA.

The Domestic Policy Presidency

Winning the presidential election opens a window of opportunity to act as national leader, to claim a popular mandate and to govern. The popular mandate of national leader may be extended to early legislative leadership if the new president hits the ground running and is in position to move his program quickly into and through the Congress. Yet, none of this is automatic. The journalist Joshua Green recently declared "a fundamental truth of the modern presidency: that the president needs the Congress more than Congress needs the president."[15] An old adage has long had it that the president proposes and the Congress disposes.

The modern president's legislative leadership hinges on the fact that each year he prepares a budget and a legislative program and submits them to Congress for consideration. Presidents have more legislative success early in their terms than they do later. Political scientist Paul Light found that new presidents since 1960 have enjoyed 72 percent success rates on bills sent to Congress between January and March of their first year, 39 percent on bills sent between April and June, and 25 percent on bills sent between July and December.[16] Light also showed that a new president's prospects are enhanced not only by acting quickly but also by having a clear substantive focus and message.

In 2001, for example, newly elected President George W. Bush won an extensive package of tax cuts and his No Child Left Behind education bill. President Obama pursued health care reform to completion in his first year in office. President Trump's first priority was to repeal and replace Obamacare, and then to move quickly to tax reform and a major infrastructure program. When Trump's Obamacare repeal and replace legislation twice collapsed in Congress, even though Republicans controlled both the House and the Senate, the president's entire first-year agenda was threatened. He did recover by passing a major tax reform bill just before Christmas, but it was a rough first year.

Each new president knows that he must strike quickly because his clout is likely to decline over time. He knows that nearly half, sometimes more than half, of the members of Congress stand in determined partisan opposition to

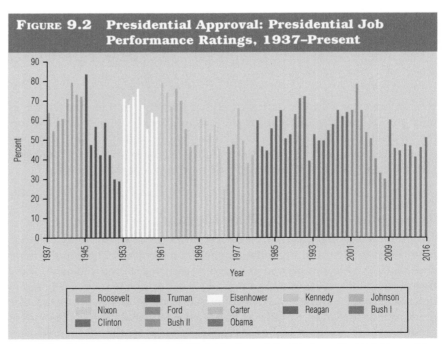

FIGURE 9.2   Presidential Approval: Presidential Job Performance Ratings, 1937–Present

Source: Gallup data from the Roper Center for Public Opinion Research. See Data Access, Presidential Approval. See also UCSB, The American Presidency Project, "Job Approval."

his program and that many members of his own party have reservations about his ideas and have their own interests to protect and pursue. And finally, the president knows that most of the 2.7 million civilian employees of the federal government are going to do pretty much the same thing the day after he takes office as they did the day before he took office (see Figure 9.2).

Nonetheless, modern presidents have tools for keeping in touch with the public that earlier presidents simply did not have. Franklin Roosevelt made excellent use of the new radio technology in the 1930s and John Kennedy did the same with television in the 1960s. Today's technology gives presidents many new channels for communication with the public. President Trump's affinity for Twitter is well known.

National Leader. A president's most important relationship is with the American people. Their votes put him in office, their votes can return him to office, and their approval gives him the momentum and confidence to govern. A president who is riding high in the polls is more likely to hold news conferences, make major speeches around the country and to the Congress, and generally try to set the tone for national politics.

However, the strength that presidents derive from opinion polls is often fleeting. Most presidents enter office with job approval ratings at or above 60 percent, but in the last 70 years only five presidents, Franklin Roosevelt, Dwight Eisenhower, Ronald Reagan, Bill Clinton, and Barack Obama, left office with approval ratings over 50 percent. Only Bill Clinton left office with higher ratings than he had in his first year. Donald Trump's early job approval ratings were the lowest in modern times, languishing near and often below 40, but Republicans in Congress knew that if he failed—they failed too.[17]

Party Leader. The president is the titular leader of his party and does have some influence over its activities. He gets to select the party's national leaders including the national party chairman and he can affect though often he cannot absolutely determine the positions taken by the national party in its platform and other statements. However, the president does not control his party members in Congress; they select their own leaders, take positions determined in their own caucuses, and control their own campaign resources. The president exercises even less control over his party at the state and local levels; they recruit their own candidates and design and run their own campaigns. The president makes no attempt to control his party below the level of the national apparatus.

Chief Legislator. The idea that the president should be the nation's chief legislator is a new one. Until 1921, the executive departments and agencies submitted their own budgetary requests and legislative proposals to the Congress. Creation of the Bureau of the Budget in 1921 gave the president the institutional tools to exercise better control over budgeting and policy development.

Presidents depend on their legislative liaison staffs to keep them in touch with Congress and to structure the trades, bargains, and compromises necessary to nudge their bills through the process. Still, presidents frequently are reduced to bargaining behind the threat or actual use of their veto power. Some presidents have depended on the veto much more heavily than others, but for all presidents it represents significant leverage in their dealings with Congress (see Table 9.2).

President Bush took a different tack. He cast his first veto on a bill designed to broaden access for federal funds for stem cell research on July 19, 2006, nearly six years into his presidency. By the time he cast his first veto, he had bargained behind the threat of a veto at least 135 times. More importantly, he issued signing statements challenging 1,200 sections of bills passed by Congress, more than all previous administrations combined.[18] Previous presidents used signing statements to claim credit for the passage of a law or to provide their sense of the law's meaning and import. The Bush administration used signing statements to declare that provisions that it believed intruded on executive authority were not binding on the president. Michelle Broadman of the Justice Department's Office of Legal Counsel said, "The president must execute the laws faithfully, but the Constitution is the highest law of the land. If the Constitution and the law conflict, the president must choose."[19]

Critics contend that signing statements impinge on Congress's lawmaking power and on the federal courts' right to declare what is and is not constitutional. In July 2006, an American Bar Association panel declared signing statements to be "contrary to the rule of law and our constitutional system of separation of powers . . . . The President's constitutional duty is to enforce laws

TABLE 9.2 Presidential Vetoes and Overrides, 1933–2016			
President	**Number of Bills Vetoed**	**Number of Vetoes Overridden**	**Percent of Vetoes Overridden**
Roosevelt	635	9	1.4
Truman	250	12	4.8
Eisenhower	181	2	1.1
Kennedy	21	0	0
Johnson	30	0	0
Nixon	43	7	16.3
Ford	66	12	18.2
Carter	31	2	.5
Reagan	78	9	11.5
Bush	46	1	2.2
Clinton	37	2	6.0
Bush	12	4	33
Obama	12	1	8.3
Trump	0	0	0

Source: Harold W. Stanley and Richard W. Niemi, *Vital Statistics on American Politics, 2015–2016* (Washington, D.C.: Congressional Quarterly, 2015), Table 6.9, 257–258. See also http://www.presidency.ucsb.edu/data/vetoes.php.

he has signed into being unless and until they are held unconstitutional by the Supreme Court . . . . The Constitution is not what the President says it is."[20] As a former constitutional law professor and a new president, Obama said he would use signing statements with "restraint" and only in cases where he had "well-founded constitutional objections." In fact, President Obama did employ signing statements but only about one-fifth as often as President Bush did.[21]

Chief Executive. The civics book view of the president is that he supervises the work of the departments and agencies of the executive branch of the national government. His supervision of the executive branch is grounded in the right to appoint, with the advice and consent of the Senate, the leaders of the departments and agencies, propose policies and programs, and oversee their implementation after they are passed into law.

The executive branch of the national government employs civilian workers in offices scattered all over the country. These civilian employees of the national government work for fifteen major departments and 140 separate agencies. The departments range in size from 740,100 in the Department of Defense to 4,000 in the Department of Education. The departments cover such diverse fields as homeland security, foreign policy, health care, and management of the nation's public lands.

The president's management of this massive and far-flung bureaucracy hinges on his right to control the appointments and subsequent conduct in

AP Photo/Rex Features

Presidents highlight their political commitments by where they go and with whom they meet. Here, President Trump meets with coal miners to push his energy and jobs agendas.

office of 3,400 senior policymakers. About 1,100 of these positions require Senate confirmation. These political appointees serve at the pleasure of the president and are subject to removal at his discretion. The president also has the right to move within or between agencies about 8,500 members (grades 16 through 18) of the Senior Executive Service.

One of the most frequent criticisms of the early Trump administration was that it was painfully slow in filling senior administrative positions in the government. Few expected Donald Trump to win the presidency, so his transition preparations were limited. When he did win, he wondered publicly whether all the empty positions awaiting new Republican appointees were even necessary. The departments of State, Defense, Treasury, Commerce, and others remained understaffed through the first year. But it soon became evident that advancing new policies in national security, health care, immigration, and taxation required experienced leadership in the government's departments.[22]

THE FEDERAL BUREAUCRACY

Q4 How does the president relate to the executive branch?

When we think of the federal government, we usually think of the president and Congress. Their elections, their policy battles, their triumphs and scandals are the stuff of our evening news. But there is another federal government, the permanent government of departments and agencies with their 2.7 million civilian employees, commonly referred to as the bureaucracy, that we think about less frequently. While governments throughout time have had their officials and functionaries, the term **bureaucracy** suggests modern systems of organization, communication, and control. It refers to a hierarchical organization in which offices have specific missions and employees are assigned specific responsibilities based on merit, knowledge, and experience.

bureaucracy A hierarchical organization in which offices have specified missions and employees are assigned responsibilities based on merit, knowledge, and experience.

The president, Congress, and the courts all have important constitutional and legal roles in organizing and monitoring the bureaucracy; yet, none has the exclusive right to control and direct it. The place of the bureaucracy in the American separation of powers system is complex. This creates ambiguity and invites a continuous struggle for influence over what the bureaucracy does and how it does it. Scholars have expressed this insight in a number of interesting ways. Herbert Simon and his colleagues note that "the separation of powers ... somewhat beclouds the right of the chief executive to control administration." Richard E. Neustadt describes the design and structure of the U.S. political system as "separated institutions *sharing* power."[23]

Unlike officials elected or appointed to fixed terms of office, bureaucrats often make careers of public employment. These government employees do every kind of work imaginable, from mopping floors to tending to the national forests to doing cancer research. Hence, the bureaucracy, particularly at the federal level, has become an increasingly accurate reflection of the society it serves. The proportions of the federal bureaucracy made up of blacks, Hispanics, and women have all nearly doubled during the post–World War II period (see Table 9.3).

TABLE 9.3 Demographic Characteristics of the Federal Bureaucracy			
	Percent Blacks	**Percent Hispanics**	**Percent Women**
1950	9.3		24.0
1960	11.7		25.0
1970	15.0	3.3	27.0
1980	15.5	4.1	35.1
1990	16.6	5.3	42.7
2000	17.9	6.6	45.0
2010	17.9	7.8	43.0
2015	18.4	8.5	42.5

Source: Office of Personnel Management, *The Fact Book, 2008* (Washington, D.C.: U.S. Government Printing Office, 2010), 10–11. OPM, Common Characteristics of the Government (CCOG), June 2016. Tables 9, 11.

THE STRUCTURE OF THE NATIONAL BUREAUCRACY

The most important components of the federal bureaucracy are the fifteen cabinet departments, each headed by a secretary nominated by the president and approved by the Senate (see Table 9.4). Cabinet secretaries made $207,800 in 2017. The deputy secretary is usually the day-to-day manager of the department ($187,000). Staff offices provide financial, legal, communications, and other services to the secretary. Each line office, under which the major substantive programs of the department fall, is headed by an undersecretary ($172,100). Each undersecretary administers related programs that deliver benefits and services to the department's clients. The bureau or service is the basic organizational unit of the federal government. In addition to the departments are dozens of regulatory commissions and agencies and literally hundreds of government corporations, institutes, and advisory panels and boards.

Cabinet Departments

The departments of the federal government are of three broad types and have appeared in three broad waves. The initial federal establishment consisted of the attorney general and three departments assigned the basic tasks of government. A second wave of departments, most charged with serving the needs of specific clientele groups, was added between the mid-nineteenth and the early twentieth centuries. A third wave of general social service departments was added after World War II, mostly in the 1960s and 1970s. The Department of Homeland Security was established in 2003.

The departments of the federal government employ most of the federal workforce and administer most of the federal government's programs.

They manage our foreign affairs, see to our defense, administer the federal parks and forests, and run our welfare, urban renewal, and transportation programs. In general, these are large organizations structured in the classic bureaucratic fashion. They are multilayered, hierarchical organizations in which lines of authority run from the secretary to the bureau chief and his or her operational subordinates.

Cabinet members well know that they have been appointed to their positions by the president and can be removed by him if he becomes dissatisfied with their work. Cabinet members know just as well that they have been confirmed in their positions by the Senate and are dependent on Congress for approval of their programs and budgets and that they remain subject to congressional scrutiny and investigation.

Cabinet secretaries also find that the career bureaucrats in their departments have their own ideas and interests, some of which conflict with the president's. Moreover, each department has ties to organized interests that care deeply

TABLE 9.4 Cabinet Departments of the U.S. Government		
Departments	**Founded**	**Employees**
Original Departments		
Department of State	1789	32,400
Department of the Treasury	1789	87,300
Department of War (renamed Defense in 1947)	1789	740,100
Attorney General (Department of Justice established in 1870)	1789	116,200
Clientele Departments		
Department of Interior	1849	60,000
Department of Agriculture	1862	83,800
Department of Commerce	1903	42,600
Department of Labor	1903	13,900
Department of Veterans Affairs	1989	364,100
Service Departments		
Department of Health, Education, and Welfare (renamed Department of Health and Human Services in 1979)	1953	75,100
Department of Housing and Urban Development	1965	7,700
Department of Transportation	1966	55,300
Department of Energy	1977	15,200
Department of Education	1979	4,000
Department of Homeland Security	2003	189,300

Source: Budget of the United States Government: Analytical Perspectives, Fiscal Year 2018 (Washington, D.C.: U.S. Government Printing Office, 2017), Table 7.1, 61. All numbers are 2018 estimates.

about the programs administered by the department and work closely with the career bureaucrats in the department to protect and enhance them.

Effective department secretaries must find a way to work with all of the constituencies in and around their departments. On occasion, this will mean that they will have to stand up to the president on behalf of their departments, their programs, and the interests they serve. Presidents understand this, but they do not like it. Hence, cabinet secretaries usually come to be seen as friendly emissaries to their departments and the interests they serve rather than as fully integrated and completely trustworthy members of the president's inner policy circle.

Regulatory Commissions and Agencies

Today there are twelve independent regulatory commissions (see Table 9.5). Several of the more prominent are the Securities and Exchange Commission (SEC), the Federal Reserve (Fed), the Consumer Product Safety Commission (CPSC), the Federal Trade Commission (FTC), and the Federal Communications Commission (FCC). **Regulatory commissions** are headed by boards rather than single executives. Commissioners are appointed by the president with the advice and consent of the Senate. The boards must be bipartisan, with relatively long and overlapping terms. Commissioners can be dismissed only for "inefficiency, neglect of duty, or malfeasance."

The regulatory commissions direct and monitor critical parts of our national life. For example, the Federal Reserve monitors the banking system and adjusts money and credit markets to produce steady economic growth.

regulatory commissions
Commissions headed by bipartisan boards charged with developing, implementing, and adjudicating policy in their area of responsibility.

TABLE 9.5	Membership, Terms, and Partisan Balance of Major Federal Regulatory Agencies		
Agency	**Number of Members**	**Term in Years**	**Partisan Balance**
Consumer Product Safety Commission	5	7	No more than three from one party
Federal Communications Commission	5	5	No more than three from one party
Federal Election Commission	6	6	No more than three from one party
Federal Energy Regulatory Commission	5	4	No more than three from one party
Federal Maritime Commission	5	5	No more than three from one party
Federal Reserve Board	7	14	No partisan limits
Federal Trade Commission	5	7	No more than three from one party
National Labor Relations Board	5	5	No partisan limits
National Mediation Board	3	3	No more than two from one party
National Transportation Safety Board	5	5	No more than three from one party
Nuclear Regulatory Commission	5	5	No more than three from one party
Securities and Exchange Commission	5	5	No more than three from one party

Source: Robert E. DiClerico, *The American President,* 4th ed. (Englewood Cliffs, NJ: Prentice-Hall, 1995), 168. Revised and updated by the author.

The Federal Reserve (The Fed) is the most high profile Independent Regulatory Commission. Here, Fed Chairman nominee Jerome Powell testifies before the Senate Committee on Banking, Housing, and Urban Affairs.

The Federal Communications Commission regulates the nation's airwaves, and the Consumer Product Safety Commission tests and licenses many of the products that we use every day.

The 2017–2018 *United States Government Manual* listed four dozen more major agencies, boards, and institutes. These include such familiar names as the Environmental Protection Agency (EPA), the National Transportation Safety Board (NTSB), and the National Institutes of Health (NIH). You hear about the EPA whenever an environmental hazard like an oil spill occurs, about the NTSB following a plane crash, and about NIH during a health crisis. These entities are of various designs and, because they are more technical than political, they generally lack the explicit partisan balance of independent regulatory commissions.

Presidential Control of the Bureaucracy

Most citizens assume that the president is "in charge" of the executive branch in some direct and unambiguous sense. In fact, the president and the Congress struggle to control the bureaucracy while the courts act as arbiters to ensure that the struggle takes place on the basis of the legal authorities of both branches.[24]

In our constitutional system of separation of powers and checks and balances, the bureaucracy takes direction from many sources.[25] The president exercises the most day-to-day influence over the bureaucracy through his power of appointment, his power to propose new programs and budgets, and his power to restructure and reorganize. The legislature grants or refuses new programs and funding, confirms nominees, and engages in oversight and investigation. The judiciary intervenes to resolve disputes over interpretation of statutes and to monitor due process and fairness. These constitute powerful limits on bureaucratic discretion and make the bureaucracy more responsive to its several masters than is commonly realized.[26]

The president has three main sources of control over the bureaucracy. Together these sources of control have the potential to enhance coordination and accountability in government. First, the president can use his power of appointment and removal to place loyal and competent executives in the top layers of the bureaucracy. Second, the president can alter administrative procedures and reorganize agencies and departments to better achieve his purposes. Third, the president can centralize decision-making authority over personnel, programs, and budgets in the Office of Personnel Management (OPM), the Office of Management and Budget (OMB), and his various policy councils.[27]

Presidents select, often subject to Senate confirmation, the officials who serve at the top levels of the bureaucracy. These officials serve as the president's representatives in and to their departments and agencies. Presidents try in numerous ways—through the heavy hand of the OMB, through participation in policy councils and other decision-making groups, and through personal meetings and communication with senior White House officials—to keep their appointees committed to their programs.

Some presidents, often Republican presidents, use their leverage over the bureaucracy to limit its intrusion into the private sector. Conservatives tend to think that compliance with bureaucratic rules and regulations constrains competitiveness and drives unnecessary costs into business. Some presidents, often Democratic presidents, empower the bureaucracy to insure that federal laws and regulations are closely followed. For example, the Obama administration blamed lax regulation of the financial industry for permitting the great recession of 2008 and 2009. They proposed a council of regulators to monitor systemic risk and a new consumer financial protection agency to insure that consumers understood the financial products they used. Many Republicans argued that increased bureaucracy would stifle financial innovation and limit consumer choice. Is increased financial regulation a good idea or not?

Every president seeks—some at the margins, some more thoroughly—to reorganize the bureaucracy. Political reform often is simply an attempt to upgrade communications, personnel, and financial systems—to bring the "best practices" of the private sector into the public sector. Sometimes broader attempts are made to reorganize the departments, agencies, and bureaus of the federal government. Since World War II, several new cabinet-level departments have been added to the federal bureaucracy. President Truman reorganized the national security bureaucracy. President Johnson divided the Department of Health, Education, and Welfare into the Department of Health and Human Services and the Department of Education. President Carter added the Department of Energy, President Reagan added the Department of Veterans Affairs, and President Bush added the Department of Homeland Security.

The president's fiscal powers also provide the means for centralizing control over the bureaucracy. Presidents use their power to propose budgets to set the priorities of their administrations. Departments and agencies are required to submit legislative proposals and new rules and regulations to the Office of Management and Budget in the Executive Office of the President for approval before submitting them to Congress or putting them into effect. This gives the White House an opportunity to assure that all new proposals coming from the executive branch comport with the president's program.

THE PRESIDENTIAL ESTABLISHMENT

Presidents organize their White House offices and staff support to ensure that they get the advice and information they need to make all of the choices and decisions that come before them. Most presidents come into office promising

cabinet The secretaries of the fifteen executive departments and other officials designated by the president. The cabinet is available to consult with the president.

"cabinet government," that is, that they will look to members of their **cabinet** as their most prominent sources of advice. However, it does not take long for presidents to realize that they do not know or trust their cabinet secretaries nearly as much as they do their senior White House aides. Therefore, most presidents leave office having abandoned any pretense of cabinet government in favor of a tight circle of senior advisers from the White House staff. President Trump made no early pretense of cabinet government, depending instead on his White House staff from the beginning.[28]

The Executive Office of the President

Executive Office of the President (EOP) Established in 1939, the EOP houses the professional support personnel working for the president.

The Executive Office of the President (EOP) was established in 1939 as part of an attempt to ensure that the president had adequate staff support. Today the EOP consists of nearly 1,700 professionals who assist the president in his relations with the bureaucracy, the Congress, interest groups, the media, and the public. Figure 9.3 illustrates the EOP.

Organizationally, the White House staff falls within the EOP and is its nerve center. Other key offices in the EOP are the Office of Management and Budget (OMB) and the National Security Council (NSC).

The White House Staff. Although each president organizes his staff as he thinks appropriate, there have been two broad approaches to staff organization at least since Franklin Roosevelt. Roosevelt organized his staff on the model of a wheel on which each spoke, each key staffer, led directly to the president. Roosevelt even assigned overlapping responsibilities to his aides so that he would never be dependent on information and advice from a single source. Truman, Kennedy, Johnson, Carter, and Clinton followed similar designs.

Q5 Should we be concerned that White House staff members have replaced members of the cabinet as the president's closest advisers?

Eisenhower used a hierarchical staff design, familiar from his military experience, in which lines of authority and reporting were clear, with a dominant chief of staff who served as gatekeeper to the president. Nixon followed an even more rigidly hierarchical system, whereas Reagan initially employed the "troika" of James Baker, Edwin Meese, and Michael Deaver in place of a single chief of staff.

President George W. Bush named a seasoned and influential cabinet including Colin Powell at State and Donald Rumsfeld at Defense, and sought to lean on them for advice and counsel. Bush's White House staff revolved around the efficient and discrete chief of staff, Andrew Card, and Karl Rove, the president's long-time political adviser and strategist. What made the Bush first term distinctive was the outsized role, often behind the scenes, but still unmistakable, of Vice President Dick Cheney.

The Obama cabinet looked a lot like George W. Bush's first term cabinet. Similarities to the Bush cabinet included powerful figures like Hillary Clinton at State, and the Republican holdover Robert Gates at Defense. In 2011, Gates retired and was replaced by an equally experienced Washington hand in the person of Leon Panetta. In early 2013, Massachusetts senator John Kerry, an

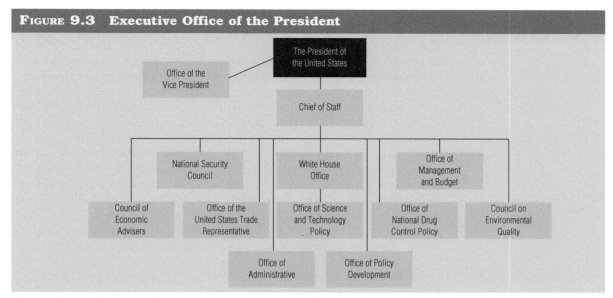

FIGURE 9.3 Executive Office of the President

Note: There is no formal or legal hierarchy among the offices within the Executive Office of the President, but there are patterns of greater and lesser influence. The top tier of offices is generally more influential than the lower tiers. Nonetheless, even among the top officials including the vice president, chief of staff, National Security adviser, and Office of Management and Budget director, much depends upon the ease and frequency of access to the President.

Source: U.S. Government Manual, 2013 (Washington, D.C.: U.S. Government Printing Office, 2013), 21.

early endorser of Obama's first presidential campaign, replaced Hillary Clinton at the State Department. On the White House staff were long-time counselor and policy aide Valerie Jarrett, and David Axelrod, the political strategist from the 2008 campaign. President Obama's first chief of staff was the gruff, demanding, and sometimes profane Rahm Emanuel, a former Clinton White House staffer, and top House leader. Vice President Joe Biden, former five-term senator from Delaware and a foreign and domestic policy expert, played the role of senior adviser and counselor, rather than the independent power center and policy shop that Dick Cheney had made of his office.

President Donald Trump's outsider candidacy, during which he was rejected by much of the traditional Republican Party leadership, especially in its foreign policy wing, left him with a delicate task. The traditional balancing of cabinet positions by gender, race, ethnicity, and region took a backseat to early support and loyalty. Trump's initial cabinet was heavy with older, white, male, businessmen and generals, most of whom had not previously worked in the civilian side of government. Rex Tillerson, former Exxon-Mobil CEO, was secretary of state, former general James Mattis was secretary of defense, and former general John Kelly was secretary of Homeland Security. The senior White House staff included Ivanka Trump, Jared Kushner, Donald Trump's son-in-law and Ivanka Trump's husband, former Breitbart executive and chief strategist Steve Bannon, and, after the brief tenure of former general Michael Flynn, General

H.R. McMaster served as National Security advisor. Trump's initial instinct was to allow many senior advisers easy access to the oval office. Soon General John Kelly was moved from Homeland Security to White House chief of staff to try to instill some order. Soon, Bannon was exiled back to Breitbart, but Kelly struggled to manage a White House staff serving the disrupter-in-chief—Donald Trump.

No matter how the White House staff is organized, its job is to get the right people and information to the president in a timely fashion and in the right amounts to permit him to make his decisions. The president must know the issues that he is being asked to decide, the options that are available to him, the opinions of his senior staff and cabinet advisers especially if they differ, and how the decision is likely to be received by key interests and the public. Finally, the staff must assist in transmitting the president's decisions and the reasons for them to the departments and agencies, Congress, the media, opinion leaders, and the public. If none of this sounds particularly like what goes on in the Trump White House, that may be the source of at least some of the problems.

Office of Management and Budget (OMB) Part of the Executive Office of the President that provides budgetary expertise, central legislative clearance, and management assistance to the president.

Office of Management and Budget (OMB).   The history of OMB dates back to 1921 when the Bureau of the Budget was created within the Department of the Treasury. The Bureau of the Budget was moved from Treasury into the Executive Office of the President in 1939, and in 1970 it was renamed the **Office of Management and Budget** to highlight its management tasks as well as its more obvious budgetary responsibilities.

The main responsibilities of the OMB include assisting the president in preparing the annual budget, performing the central legislative clearance function to ensure that the legislative priorities of the departments and agencies of the executive branch comport with the president's program, and monitoring the implementation of programs to ensure that they are both effective and cost-efficient. Fundamentally, the OMB is responsible for ensuring that the rest of the federal government reflects both the programmatic and budgetary goals of the administration.

National Security Council (NSC) Part of the Executive Office of the President, established in 1947, that coordinates advice and policy for the president on national security issues.

National Security Council (NSC).   Although the importance of the **National Security Council**, established in 1947, has varied from administration to administration, it is the EOP entity responsible for coordinating advice and policy for the president on national security. The statutory members of the NSC include the president, vice president, and the secretaries of state and defense. Statutory advisers to the NSC include the chairman of the Joint Chiefs of Staff and the directors of the Central Intelligence Agency and the Arms Control and Disarmament Agency.

The Vice President

The Constitution says simply, "The Vice President of the United States shall be President of the Senate, but shall have no Vote, unless they be equally divided." The vice president has no other duty but to preside in the Senate unless specifically assigned other duties by the president. Typically, vice presidents have languished, restricted largely to representing the president to groups of secondary importance and, with the advent of jet travel, attending funerals of foreign dignitaries.

But the stature of the office has risen in recent decades. President Jimmy Carter, with no Washington experience before the presidency, leaned heavily on Vice President Walter Mondale, a Washington insider and long-time senator from Minnesota. Mondale gave candid advice, always confidentially and often in private, and Carter included him in all major discussions and decisions. George Bush, vice president during the Reagan years, was involved in many important decisions but never fully trusted by the Reagan insiders. Bill Clinton made Al Gore an integral part of his policy team. Gore set his daily and weekly schedule after the president set his so that he could select which of the president's meetings he wished to attend.

Dick Cheney was clearly the most influential vice president in American history. Like Carter, Reagan, and Clinton, President George W. Bush came to office with no previous Washington experience. Cheney had previously served in the House leadership, as chief of staff in Gerald Ford's administration, and as secretary of defense in the first president George Bush's administration. Vice President Cheney became the senior day-to-day manager in the Bush administration.

President Obama undoubtedly wanted Vice President Biden to help him shoulder the burdens of office, but both saw the Cheney model as a step too far. The vice president's role is always somewhat awkward, but Biden consistently acted as a senior advisor to President Obama and a problem-solver when critical issues arise domestically or internationally.

President Donald Trump's larger-than-life personality eclipsed Vice President Mike Pence during the 2016 campaign. But as the focus turned from campaigning to governing, Vice President Pence emerged as a more consequential figure. His experience in Congress and as governor of Indiana gave him knowledge that Trump simply did not have. Nonetheless, Trump's penchant for turmoil often overwhelmed Pence's preference for careful planning and execution.

The president's job is intensely demanding, and every holder of it recognizes the value of having a second seasoned and successful politician of independent national stature with whom to discuss the central issues of the day. This makes the choice of vice president as important as any choice a presidential hopeful will make. The vice president not only steps in if the president should die or otherwise be incapacitated but, if the choice is well made, serves as a valuable resource and partner day-to-day.[29]

PRESIDENTIAL REFORM TODAY

Demands on the modern presidency are many, shortcomings are evident, and talk of reform is effectively continuous. Americans watch hopefully as each new president struggles to turn campaign promises into political and policy accomplishments. What lessons might presidents learn from their predecessors and what reforms to the presidency seem most pressing?

First, American presidents must recognize and acknowledge that they are one participant, though a leading participant, in a system of shared powers and legal limits. The view held by President Bush and Vice President Cheney, that the presidency in wartime is an office essentially without limits in domestic and international law, is historically implausible and proved to be politically untenable. Similarly, Donald Trump's populist instincts rebelled at judicial challenges to his travel ban, Congress's slow struggle to repeal and replace Obamacare, and unfavourable media coverage. Better to sacrifice sole control and early speed for broader support in Congress, the courts, and the public.

Second, many worry that how the nation goes to war is dangerously murky. The Founders believed that no question was more critical to a free society. War empowers government, so the Constitution requires that the people's representatives in Congress declare war before the president is authorized to conduct it. But Congress has not declared war since the Japanese attacked Pearl Harbor in December 1941. Rather, in Korea in the 1950s, Vietnam in the 1960s, and Afghanistan and Iraq in the wake of 9/11, often in conditions of fear, confusion, and apparent danger, Congress has hurried to give the president a bipartisan blank check. Discussion might center on reform of the War Powers Act, but it might well require that the U.S. Supreme Court affirm the War Powers Act and define what counts as a declaration of war in the twenty-first century.

Finally, thinking clearly about the roles of the vice president, cabinet, and White House staff seems critical. Presidents have massive responsibilities and need a lot of help in fulfilling them. But if the helpers are out of position they do the president—who let them get and stay out of position—harm. An outsized vice president undercuts the president by raising doubts about who is in charge. Presidents need vice presidential partners, but vice presidents should act as senior advisers, not as gate-keepers or alternative points of decision.

Despite the almost universal sense that the complexities confronting the modern president require a well-organized, generally hierarchical White House staff, with a clearly designated and empowered chief of staff, complaints about the White House staff abound. Critics call for staffers to act as honest brokers, facilitators, and process managers, rather than as policy advocates and program managers. And finally, critics point out that the president's interest and the public's interest are not the same and that the White House staff too frequently mistakes the former for the latter. This seems particularly likely when the president's family members play senior White House roles.

Chapter Summary

Most of the powers awarded to the executive in the Constitution are to be shared with the legislature. The president alone wields pardon power, but his appointment power, treaty-making power, and war-making power all require advice and consent of the Senate or prior action by the whole Congress. On the other hand, the president is expressly invited into the legislative process by his proposal and veto powers. The Founders produced a system of shared powers in which the president simply cannot succeed without the ongoing cooperation—sometimes grudging, to be sure—of both Congress and the courts.

The presidency reached its full stature in the middle of the twentieth century just as the United States emerged as a dominant world power. The presidency that we know today was created by Franklin Roosevelt, reached the height of its power under Truman and Kennedy, and began to come apart under Johnson and Nixon. Presidents from Jimmy Carter, through Ronald Reagan and George H. W. Bush, to Bill Clinton sought to maintain the U.S. position in the world while recognizing that U.S. resources are limited. George W. Bush reached further, fell, and future presidents will be sobered by his example. Barack Obama, determined not to repeat Bush's aggressive foreign policy, left problems with North Korea, Russia, and the Middle East unresolved. What lessons Donald Trump has learned from his predecessors remain to be seen.

The term *bureaucracy* refers to a large, complex, hierarchical organization, whether public or private, in which offices have specific missions and employees have specific responsibilities based on merit. The federal bureaucracy is divided into fifteen major cabinet departments, more than a dozen independent regulatory commissions, fifty-four major agencies, boards, and services, and literally hundreds of advisory committees and panels. The cabinet departments are organized hierarchically. Below the cabinet secretary are several layers of undersecretaries and assistant secretaries before one gets to the level of the bureau or service where the actual administration of programs and delivery of services take place. Program implementation is made difficult by the presence of imprecise and contradictory goals, fragmentation and faulty coordination, and imprecise measures of success.

Key Terms

appointment power

bureaucracy

cabinet

executive agreements

Executive Office of the President (EOP)

impeachment

inherent powers

National Security Council (NSC)

Office of Management and Budget (OMB)

pardon

regulatory commission

reprieve

treaty-making power

unitary executive theory

veto power

War Powers Resolution

Suggested Readings

Baker, Peter. *Obama: The Call of History*. New York: New York Times/Callaway, 2017. Baker, a White House reporter, explores Obama's accomplishments and disappointments and asks how the balance will be viewed in history.

Edwards, George C. III, *Overreach: Leadership in the Obama Presidency*. Princeton, NJ: Princeton University Press, 2015. Edwards argues that presidents, and not just Obama, overreach when they embrace policies whose success requires the president to change public opinion.

Ellis, Richard J. *The Development of the American Presidency*. 3rd ed. New York: Routledge, 2018. Ellis provides a deep history of the American presidency and how its roles and powers have evolved over time.

Fisher, Louis. *Presidential War Power*, 3rd ed. revised. Lawrence: University Press of Kansas, 2013. Fisher's thesis is that although the decision to use force was given by the Founders to Congress, presidents have usurped it in the twentieth century.

Goodsell, Charles T. *The New Case for Bureaucracy*, 5th ed. Washington, D.C.: CQ Press, 2014. The bureaucracy is subject to a great deal of criticism. Goodsell draws on a wide range of argument and information to make a strongly positive case for the bureaucracy.

Han, Lori Cox, ed. *New Directions in the American Presidency*. 2nd ed. New York: Routledge, 2018. Leading scholars of the U.S. presidency and the executive branch explore how the Office of the President and related institutions have evolved and changed in recent decades and over the course of the nation's history.

Holzer, Marc and Richard W. Schwester. *Public Administration: An Introduction*, 2nd ed. New York: Routledge, 2016. An excellent overview of public administration in the modern era.

Web Resources

1   www.ipl.org/div/potus/
    The Internet Public Library includes a POTUS (Presidents of the United States) site that provides excellent information and links for each president.

2   www.whitehouse.gov
    Official site of the president; includes a White House history, virtual tour, press releases, documents, and photographs.

3   loc.gov
    The Library of Congress site provides links to all federal websites. You can find access points to any agency within the executive branch and learn about the president's relationships with these groups.

4   www.presidency.ucsb.edu
    The American Presidency Project at the University of California, Santa Barbara, provides a treasure trove of information and data about presidents from Washington forward.

5 www.usajobs.gov
The federal government's official site for those interested in jobs. The site is run by the Office of Personnel Management.

Notes

1 Charles O. Jones, *The Presidency in a Separated System*, 2nd ed. (Washington, D.C.: Brookings Institution, 2005), 1–3.

2 Stephen Skowronek, *The Politics Presidents Make: Leadership from John Adams to George Bush* (Cambridge, MA: Harvard University Press, 1993), 20.

3 Edward S. Corwin, *The President: Office and Powers, 1787–1957* (New York: New York University Press, 1957, originally published, 1940), 3, 171.

4 Calvin Jillson, "The Executive in Republican Government: The Case of the American Founding," *Presidential Studies Quarterly* (Fall 1979): 386–402.

5 Louis Fisher, *Presidential War Power*, 2nd ed. (Lawrence, KS: University Press of Kansas, 2004), 3–16.

6 Stephen Skowronek, *Building a New American State: The Expansion of National Administrative Capacities, 1877–1920* (New York: Cambridge University Press, 1982).

7 John Hart, *The Presidential Branch: Executive Office of the President from Washington to Clinton*, 2nd ed. (Chatham, NJ: Chatham House, 1995), 4.

8 Robert E. DiClerico, *The American President*, 5th ed. (Upper Saddle River, NJ: Prentice-Hall, 2005), 34.

9 Arthur Schlesinger Jr., *The Imperial Presidency* (Boston, MA: Houghton Mifflin, 1973).

10 Matthew Crenson and Benjamin Ginsberg, *Presidential Power: Unchecked and Unbalanced* (New York: W.W. Norton, 2007).

11 Aaron Wildavsky, "The Two Presidencies," in Aaron Wildavsky, *The Presidency* (Boston, MA: Little, Brown, 1969), 230–243. More recently, see Bryan W. Marshall and Richard L. Pacelle, "Revisiting the Two Presidencies," *American Politics Review*, vol. 33, no. 1 (January 2005): 81–105.

12 Fisher, *Presidential War Power*, 69, 75, 81.

13 Quoted in Anthony Lewis, "License to Torture," *New York Times*, October 15, 2005, A35.

14 Linda Greenhouse, "Justices, 5–3, Broadly Reject Bush Plan to Try Detainees," *New York Times*, June 30, 2006, A1, A18.

15 Joshua Green, *Devil's Bargain: Steve Bannon, Donald Trump, and the Storming of the Presidency* (New York: Penguin Books, 2017), 239.

16 Paul Light, *The President's Agenda*, 3rd ed. (Baltimore, MD: Johns Hopkins University Press, 1999), 45. See also, Jeffrey S. Peake, "Presidential Agenda-Setting in Foreign Policy," *Political Research Quarterly*, vol. 54, no. 1 (March 2001): 69–86.

17 Jones, *The Presidency in a Separated System*, 133–145. See also, Matt Flegenheimer, "For Better or Worse, Lawmakers Find Themselves Bound to Trump," *New York Times*, August 18, 2017, A16.

18 John T. Woolley and Gerhard Peters, *The American Presidency Project*, University of California, Santa Barbara, see http://www.presidency.vcsb.edu/signingstatements.php

19 Charlie Savage, "Obama's Embrace of Bush Tactic Criticized by Lawmakers of Both Parties," *New York Times*, August 9, 2009, Y18.

20 Michael Abramowitz, "Bush's Tactic of Refusing Laws Is Probed," *Washington Post*, July 24, 2006, A5.

21 The American Presidency Project, Signing Statements, http://www.presidency.ucsb.edu/data.php.

22 David Lewis, "Trump's Slow Pace of Appointments Is Hurting Government—And His Own Agenda," Monkey Cage, *Washington Post*, August 3, 2017. See also the *Washington Post's* executive appointments tracker at: https://ourpublicservice.org/issues/presidential-transition/political-apointee-tracker.php.

23 Joel D. Aberbach, *Keeping a Watchful Eye: The Politics of Congressional Oversight* (Washington, D.C.: Brookings Institution, 1990), 3 (both quotations).

24 Mark Rozell, *Executive Privilege: Presidential Power, Secrecy, and Accountability*, 2nd ed., revised (Lawrence: University Press of Kansas, 2002).

25 Francis E. Rourke, "Whose Bureaucracy Is This Anyway? Congress, the President and Public Administration," the 1993 John Gaus Lecture, *PS: Political Science & Politics*, December 1993, 687–691.

26 B. Dan Wood and Richard W. Waterman, *Bureaucratic Dynamics: The Role of Bureaucracy in a Democracy* (Boulder, CO: Westview Press, 1994), 1.

27 Paul C. Light, *A Government Ill-Executed* (Cambridge, MA: Harvard University Press, 2009), 163–188.

28 Richard A. Smith, "Make the Cabinet More Effective," *New York Times*, Op-Ed, January 11, 2013, A21.

29 Mark Landler, "Obama's Growing Trust in Biden Is Reflected in His Call on Troops," *New York Times*, June 25, 2011, A4, A9.

Chapter **10**

THE FEDERAL COURTS
Originalism versus Living Constitutionalism

Focus Questions: from reading to thinking

Q1 What is the common law tradition?

Q2 How did the theory and practice of judicial review arise in the United States?

Q3 What is the place of the Supreme Court in the judicial system of the United States?

Q4 How have the climate and tone surrounding the process of nomination and confirmation to judicial posts changed since the mid-1950s?

Q5 Is judicial activism necessary because some issues are just too difficult for the political branches of the government to confront?

DOES THE CONSTITUTION ENVISION JUDICIAL REVIEW?

Article III, sections 1 and 2 (in part): "The judicial power of the United States . . . shall extend to all cases, . . . arising under this Constitution, the laws of the United States, and treaties made, . . . under their authority."

During the 2016 campaign, Donald Trump called for a "complete and total ban on Muslims coming to this country." During his first week in office, he signed an executive order sharply limiting access to the U.S. to citizens of seven, later six, majority Muslim countries. When several federal courts found the orders potentially discriminatory and suspended their implementation pending further hearings, President Trump declared that any subsequent terror attacks would be the fault of the courts. Since the president considered the threat of terror attacks so dire, could he have simply looked at the court orders and said "I disagree," and ordered the Department of Homeland Security to continue implementing the travel ban? No, but this is not the first time the question had come up.

One of the most consequential fights in American political history occurred in Thomas Jefferson's first term as president. The federal government was still relatively new and the relationships between the executive, legislative, and judicial branches were not yet set. The judiciary was an independent branch of government, but as Alexander Hamilton famously wrote in *Federalist* No. 78, it was considered the "least dangerous branch." The president commanded the power of the sword; the Congress commanded the power of the purse; but what power did the courts command?

Judicial review, the power to declare federal and state laws null and void, became the foundation of judicial power. The basic storyline behind the Supreme Court's first use of judicial review in *Marbury v. Madison* (1803) is well known. Thomas Jefferson and his Jeffersonian Republicans won the election of 1800, displacing Federalist President John Adams and the Federalist majorities in Congress. Before the new administration took power, President Adams and the Federalists in Congress created new courts and filled them with dependable Federalist judges. Jefferson dismantled the new courts and refused to seat most of their judges. The issue was carried into the courts, setting up a confrontation between Chief Justice John Marshall and President Thomas Jefferson.

Marshall knew that he was playing the weaker political hand. He could order Jefferson to deliver Marbury's judicial appointment papers. But Jefferson could simply ignore the order, thus highlighting and perhaps permanently establishing the weakness of the court. Instead, Marshall deftly masked the court's present weakness to lay the foundation for its future strength. Marshall declared that while Marbury deserved his judicial appointment, the court could not order its delivery because the law by which the previous Federalist Congress and president had created the new courts was unconstitutional. Marshall both avoided issuing an order that Jefferson might ignore and employed a power, judicial review, that the Supreme Court had not previously exercised. Marshall made two critical points: one, that laws which contravene the Constitution are void, and, two, that it is the court's particular duty to declare them so. Marshall wrote that the very logic of written constitutions and limited government "must be, that an act of the legislature repugnant to the constitution is void." He then added that, "it is emphatically the province and duty of the judicial department to say what the law is."

Jefferson and most observers agreed with Marshall's first point, a law that contravenes the Constitution is void, but many, including Jefferson, disagreed with his second point, that it is distinctively the court's role to say which acts of government are constitutional and which are not. Jefferson believed that each department of government, the executive, legislative, and judicial was entitled to interpret the Constitution in regard to its own powers and responsibilities. Jefferson laid out his "departmental" view of constitutional interpretation in a letter to Abigail Adams, former President Adams' wife, concerning pardons that he had issued to journalists convicted under the Alien and Sedition Acts. He wrote that the executive and judicial branches "are equally independent in the sphere of action assigned to them. The judges, believing the law constitutional, had a right to pass a sentence of fine and imprisonment, because that power was placed in their hands by the constitution. But the executive, believing the law to be unconstitutional, was bound to remit the execution of it; because that power has been confided to him by the constitution." Jefferson held to his "departmental" view of constitutional interpretation throughout his life.

THE FEDERAL COURTS

L aw and the courts play a larger and more powerful role in the United States than in any other country in the world. In most countries, the courts simply apply current law. In the United States, courts judge current law and policy in light of the more fundamental law of the U.S. Constitution. Because they decide so many critical issues, the temperature around our judges and courts has risen in recent decades.

Political scientist Herbert Jacob defines **law** very simply as "authoritative rules made by government."[1] Another student of the American judicial system, Henry Abraham, offers a similar but somewhat more descriptive definition. Abraham says that "law, broadly speaking, represents the rules of conduct that pertain to a given political order of society, rules that are backed by the organized force of the community."[2] Although all law is backed by the legitimate authority of the community, there is a hierarchy in U.S. law based on the source from which it flows. The Constitution is the most fundamental source of law; legislation is next; and executive orders and agency rules and regulations are the lowest. To be legally binding, agency rules must implement valid statutes, and statutes to be valid must fall within the range of legislative authority granted in the Constitution. Disagreements about what law requires, permits, or prohibits are taken before courts for resolution.

law Authoritative rules made by government and backed by the organized force of the community.

AP Photo/Susan Walsh

Chief Justice John G. Roberts Jr. was sworn in on September 29, 2005, by Justice John Paul Stevens as President Bush and Jane Sullivan Roberts watched.

In this chapter we describe the origins, development, structure, and role of the U.S. federal courts. First, we describe the English common law background of American law and the formal origins of U.S. courts in Article III of the Constitution. Second, we describe the three-tier structure of the federal courts, rising from the district courts, through a layer of appellate courts, to the United States Supreme Court. We conclude the chapter by dealing with two volatile issues—judicial selection and judicial philosophy. Judicial selection involves the process and politics of selecting federal judges. Judicial philosophy involves the disputed role of judges in our democracy. Should judges merely apply the law or should they interpret and expand the law to fit new cases and address pressing social issues?

Q1 What is the common law tradition?

THE COMMON LAW ORIGINS OF THE AMERICAN LEGAL SYSTEM

The legal traditions of the United States derive from those of England and were deeply embedded in the American mind well before national independence. The English **common law** tradition involved the slow and incremental accumulation of judicial decisions over time. The phrase *common law* refers to the law as announced by the king's judges and therefore common to the whole realm as opposed to the customs and traditions of one local community or region. Over the centuries this judge-made common law expanded into a "broad jurisprudence of right and remedy" that colonial Americans

common law Law developed over time as judges decide particular legal disputes and then future judges cite earlier decisions in resolving cases with similar issues and facts.

identified as a principal defense of their liberties.[3] The common law limited the power of government and constrained the ways in which power might assert itself against individual citizens.

Two statements by England's most famous jurist, Sir Edward Coke, chief justice of the King's Bench during the early seventeenth century, describe the role of the common law and the courts in limiting political power. On November 13, 1608, in response to the king's assertion that he could decide legal disputes on his own royal authority, Chief Justice Coke responded that "the King in his own person cannot adjudge any case . . . but that this ought to be determined and adjudged in some Court of Justice, according to the law and custom of England."

Two years later, in **Bonham's Case** (1610), Coke noted that "It appears in our books, that . . . when an Act of Parliament is against common right and reason . . . the common law will controul it, and adjudge such Act to be void."[4] During the colonial and early national periods American jurists developed the idea that political power is constrained by law and that some acts of the political authorities are null, void, and unenforceable because they conflict with the fundamental traditions of the community as articulated initially in its common law, and later in its written constitution.

Two judicial principles, precedent and *stare decisis*, help explain the nature and development of the common law. The common law is a body of legal traditions and principles developed over time as judges consider and solve particular legal problems and disputes. Judges cite these earlier decisions as **precedents** or controlling examples in resolving later cases that involve similar issues. The judicial principle of **stare decisis**, which is Latin meaning "let the decision stand," is the injunction to depend on earlier cases or precedents to decide later cases of a similar nature.

British colonists brought the common law with them when they emigrated, but in the intervening four centuries American legislatures have refined and specified common law principles in state and federal statutes. While the principles of the common law—the key role of judges, case law, and precedents—are still clearly visible in American law, specific rights and responsibilities are ensconced in statutes.

> **Bonham's Case** (1610) British case in which Sir Edward Coke, chief justice of the King's Bench, laid the foundation for judicial review.

> **precedent** A judicial decision that serves as a rule or guide for deciding later cases of a similar nature.

> **stare decisis** The judicial principle of relying on past decisions or precedents to devise rulings in later cases.

THE CRIMINAL LAW AND THE CIVIL LAW

Within the common law tradition there is a distinction between two general types of statutory law. **Criminal law** prohibits certain actions and prescribes penalties for those who engage in the prohibited conduct. Murder, rape, and burglary are violations of the criminal law. Criminal charges are brought by government against an individual or individuals, and convictions can result in jail time or even in the death penalty in jurisdictions that permit it. The **civil law** deals primarily with relations between private persons or organizations as in marriage and family law, contracts, and the buying and selling of property. Civil charges are brought by one individual against another, and violations result more in judgments and fines than in incarceration or physical punishment.

> **criminal law** Criminal law prohibits certain actions and prescribes penalties for those who engage in the prohibited conduct.

> **civil law** Civil law deals primarily with relations between individuals and organizations, as in marriage and family law, contracts, and property. Violations result more in judgments and fines than punishment as such.

CASES AND THE LAW

The American legal system is set in motion only when a case or controversy brings parties, one of which may be a governmental entity, who are directly involved in a dispute before an appropriate court. Henry Abraham notes that "the presence of the following four conditions: (1) an adversary process, (2) a justiciable issue, (3) ripeness for judicial determination, and (4) an actual disposition" are required in disputes that come before the American judiciary for resolution.[5]

American courts deal in real cases and controversies; they do not give advisory opinions or respond to hypothetical or "what if?" queries from individuals or from public officials. The adversary process involves a complainant who alleges a specific wrong act and a respondent who denies that the act was wrong or denies that he or she committed the act if it was wrong. Courts judge whether an individual has standing or eligibility to come before the court by whether he or she is suffering or threatened with real harm from the act complained of.

justiciability Legal term indicating that an issue or dispute is appropriate for or subject to judicial resolution.

Second, a court must determine whether the controversy brought before it is justiciable. **Justiciability** simply means subject to judicial resolution. Some issues are thought to require political rather than judicial resolution, and the courts have traditionally declined to enter what has been referred to as the "political thicket."

Third, courts consider whether an issue is ripe for judicial resolution. Ripeness involves the questions of timeliness and necessity. For example, a legislative action like the passage of term limits that threaten harm somewhere down the road but have not yet produced harm by displacing a public official would be avoided. Courts do not act until someone has been harmed or harm is clearly imminent. Finally, courts treat only cases in which their findings will, at least potentially, resolve or dispose of the issue. U.S. courts, for example, will dismiss cases in which there is insufficient evidence to convict or in which evidence has been illegally obtained.

THE BIRTH OF THE AMERICAN LEGAL SYSTEM

The federal Constitution provided for a national government with separated, defined, and limited powers. Article III, section 1, of the Constitution declared: "The judicial power of the United States, shall be vested in one Supreme Court, and in such inferior courts as the Congress may from time to time ordain and establish." Although the foundation of judicial power was laid in the Constitution, the structure of judicial authority remained to be built. That construction occurred during the new nation's early history.

As President Washington and the first Congress took office, it remained unclear what role the judiciary would play in American political life, how much influence it would really have, and how it would defend itself and check its competitors in Congress and the executive branch. The checks and balances that were to hold the executive and legislative powers in place seemed clear; but how the judiciary would defend itself was much less clear.

Yet ideas and practices were at large that suggested an important role for American courts. Alexander Hamilton had explained in *Federalist* No. 78 that "the courts were designed to be an intermediate body between the people and the legislature, in order among other things, to keep the latter within the limits assigned to their authority." Hamilton reasoned that if the limits on government embedded in the Constitution were to be meaningful, "the courts of justice . . . must . . . declare all acts contrary to the manifest tenor of the Constitution void. Without this, all the reservations of particular rights or privileges would amount to nothing." Hamilton was right. Nonetheless, the judiciary had to fight to establish its place and power in the new government.

The Judiciary Act of 1789 and the Origins of Judicial Review

The first Congress under the new Constitution turned immediately to organizing the federal judiciary. The **Judiciary Act of 1789** constituted the Supreme Court with six justices and created a two-tiered system of lower federal courts. Moreover, section 25 charged the federal courts to review acts and decisions of the state governments for compatibility with the Constitution and with federal statutes. The Judiciary Act of 1789 is still the basic law governing the federal courts though, of course, it has been amended many times.

Judiciary Act of 1789 Originating act for the federal judiciary passed by the first Congress.

The Judiciary Act of 1789 defined the structure and basic procedures of the federal courts. Each state was given a federal district court to exercise trial jurisdiction, and there were three circuit or appellate courts—the eastern, the middle, and the southern districts. The circuit courts were composed of two Supreme Court justices (one after 1793) and the local district judges "riding circuit" throughout their territory. The United States Supreme Court capped the new nation's judicial system.

Q2 How did the theory and practice of judicial review arise in the United States?

Judicial Review

Virginia's John Marshall served as chief justice of the U.S. Supreme Court for thirty-four years, from 1801 to 1835. During that time, Marshall took a court whose power and position in the new government were unclear and established it as an equal and coordinate branch of the national government. In addition to establishing its own place and power in the national government, the Marshall Court also gave content and weight to the supremacy clause.

In the famous case of *Marbury v. Madison* (1803), Marshall declared **judicial review** to be the prerogative of the courts. He wrote, on behalf of a unanimous Supreme Court, that "it is, emphatically, the province and duty of the judicial department, to say what the law is. . . . So, if a law be in opposition to the constitution; the court must . . . decide that case . . . conformable to the constitution, disregarding the law."

judicial review Power of any federal court to hold any law or official act based on law to be unenforceable because it is in conflict with the Constitution.

Marshall's goal of securing the position and importance of the judiciary in the new national government did not go unopposed. Years later, President Jefferson was still arguing that Marshall's expansive reading of the judiciary's role violated separation of powers. Jefferson argued to Virginia Judge Spencer Roane in a letter of September 6, 1819, that each of the three branches of government "has an equal right to decide for itself the meaning of the Constitution in the cases submitted to its action . . . and that the Court is neither more learned nor more objective than the political branches of the government." Nor was Jefferson alone in his resistance to the dominant role that John Marshall claimed for the federal courts in constitutional interpretation. In 1832 President Andrew Jackson claimed that "the Supreme Court . . . ought not to control the coordinate authorities of the Government. The Congress, the Executive, and the Court must each for itself be guided by its own opinion of the Constitution."[6] Nonetheless, Marshall's view, firmly pressed over his three and one-half decades as chief justice, prevailed.[7]

Judicial Review of Congressional Legislation.   Although the exercise of judicial review is usually thought of as striking down acts of the president and Congress, this has in fact been fairly uncommon (see Table 10.1). On only two occasions before the Civil War, the landmark cases of *Marbury v. Madison* (1803) and *Dred Scott v. Sandford* (1857), did the Supreme Court strike down

TABLE 10.1	Number of Federal Statutes Held Unconstitutional by the Supreme Court, 1790–2014		
Period	**Number**	**Period**	**Number**
1790–1799	0	1900–1909	9
1800–1809	1	1910–1919	6
1810–1819	0	1920–1929	15
1820–1829	0	1930–1939	13
1830–1839	0	1940–1949	2
1840–1849	0	1950–1959	4
1850–1859	1	1960–1969	18
1860–1869	4	1970–1979	19
1870–1879	7	1980–1989	16
1880–1889	4	1990–1999	24
1890–1899	5	2000–2009	16
		2010–2014	13
		Total	177

Source: Lawrence Baum, *The Supreme Court,* 12th ed. (Washington, D.C.: Congressional Quarterly Press, 2015), 168; see also Harold W. Stanley and Richard G. Niemi, *Vital Statistics on American Politics, 2015–2016* (Washington, D.C.: Congressional Quarterly Press, 2015), 289.

acts of Congress. Judicial review became more frequent after the Civil War and more frequent still after 1960. Its rate of use increased again in the mid-1990s. Still, only 177 acts of Congress have been declared unconstitutional over the entire history of the country.

Judicial Review of State Legislation.   One of the main reasons for replacing the Articles of Confederation with the stronger federal Constitution was so some national government entity could monitor the activities of the several state governments. Many people, including Madison, argued for a mandatory national review of all state laws before they went into effect. Although this requirement, referred to in the Constitutional Convention as the "universal negative," was not included in the Constitution, the supremacy clause did allow review of state actions that appeared to conflict with the national Constitution. Not surprisingly, the federal courts have employed judicial review more frequently against the states than against Congress and the president (see Table 10.2).

About 1,300 state laws and provisions of state constitutions have been declared unconstitutional since 1790. Judicial review of the acts of the states was used with increasing frequency until the late 1980s. Since then, the high court's increasing respect for the rights and autonomy of the states led to a precipitous drop in those numbers.

TABLE 10.2	Number of State Laws and Local Ordinances Held Unconstitutional by the Supreme Court, 1790–2014		
Period	**Number**	**Period**	**Number**
1790–1799	0	1900–1909	40
1800–1809	1	1910–1919	119
1810–1819	7	1920–1929	139
1820–1829	8	1930–1939	92
1830–1839	3	1940–1949	61
1840–1849	10	1950–1959	66
1850–1859	7	1960–1969	151
1860–1869	24	1970–1979	195
1870–1879	36	1980–1989	164
1880–1889	46	1990–1999	62
1890–1899	36	2000–2009	38
		2010–2014	16
		Total	1,321

Source: Lawrence Baum, *The Supreme Court,* 12th ed. (Washington, D.C.: Congressional Quarterly Press, 2015), 163; see also Harold W. Stanley and Richard G. Niemi, *Vital Statistics on American Politics, 2015–2016* (Washington, D.C.: Congressional Quarterly Press, 2015), 289.

Judicial Review of Lower Court Action.   The Supreme Court exercises a particularly intensive form of judicial review over the lower courts of the federal system. As the vast majority of cases that the Supreme Court hears come as part of its discretionary jurisdiction, as opposed to the mandatory cases that it must hear, only cases that are important and might have been wrongly decided by the lower courts are chosen for hearing and decision. Hence, fully two-thirds of the cases reviewed by the Supreme Court result in reversal of the lower court in whole or in part.[8]

THE STRUCTURE OF THE FEDERAL JUDICIAL SYSTEM

Article III, section 1, of the Constitution outlines the structure and powers of the federal judiciary. It provides, as noted above, that "The judicial Power of the United States, shall be vested in one supreme Court, and in such inferior Courts as the Congress may from time to time ordain and establish." This provision clearly assumed that Congress would specify the makeup of the Supreme Court and would establish a system of inferior courts as the needs of the nation developed over time. The federal court system now consists of three layers with the U.S. district courts at the base, the U.S. courts of appeals in the middle, and the U.S. Supreme Court at the top.

Article III, section 2, provides that the judicial power of the federal courts "shall extend to all Cases, in law and equity, arising under this Constitution, the Laws of the United States, and Treaties made, or which shall be made, under their Authority." Most cases that arise in the federal courts fall into three categories. Political scientist Lawrence Baum describes these categories as follows: "First are the criminal and civil cases that arise under federal laws, including the Constitution. . . . Second are cases to which the U.S. government is a party. . . . Third are civil cases involving citizens of different states if the amount in question is at least $75,000."[9]

Q3 What is the place of the Supreme Court in the judicial system of the United States?

The Lower Federal Courts

The lower courts of the federal system are composed of the U.S. district courts and a number of special courts of limited jurisdiction. The **district courts** are the primary trial courts of the federal system. The special courts hear cases within defined subject matter jurisdictions like taxation, bankruptcy, or military law.

district courts The ninety-four general trial courts of the federal judicial system.

District Courts.   The district courts have authority to try most cases within the federal court system. Twenty-six states have a single district court, whereas some of the larger and more populous states have as many as four district courts. There are ninety-four U.S. district courts in the fifty states, the District of Columbia, and the U.S. territories. In the 2016 term, the district courts processed about 291,851 civil cases and 77,357 criminal cases.[10] Bankruptcy court filings fell dramatically following Congress's 2005 passage of bankruptcy reform, from

1.2 million cases in 2005 as people sought to beat the deadline, to 600,000 in 2006. After a modest increase in 2007, the 2008–09 recession produced 1 to 1.5 million bankruptcies annually through 2012. As the economic recovery took hold, bankruptcies fell to 805,580 in 2016.

Most cases in the district courts are tried before a single judge. Each district has at least two judges, and some have up to twenty-eight. There are 673 federal district court judges in the ninety-four districts. An additional 500 retired or senior judges, eligible to retire at full pay, continue to work full or part time. A very few cases, usually cases that are important and require expedited treatment, are tried before special three-judge panels composed of two district court judges and one court of appeals judge. District court judges make $205,100.

Special Courts. Congress is empowered in Article I, section 8, of the Constitution to "constitute tribunals inferior to the Supreme Court." These legislative courts include the U.S. Tax Court, the U.S. Court of Military Appeals, territorial courts, and the U.S. Court of Veterans Appeals. In addition, each district court employs special legislative judges, called bankruptcy judges and magistrate judges. Bankruptcy judges handle the specialized workload in their area. Magistrate judges are appointed by district judges to assist with pretrial motions, rule on routine matters, and try and decide minor civil and criminal cases.

Courts of Appeals

There are thirteen U.S. **courts of appeals**. Twelve have jurisdiction over certain regions of the country. The thirteenth is the U.S. Court of Appeals for the Federal Circuit that has jurisdiction over tax, patent, and international trade cases (see Figure 10.1). Each court of appeals has six to twenty-eight judges, depending on the workload, with a total of 179 appeals court judgeships authorized in 2016. Usually judges sit in groups of three, with two constituting a quorum, to decide cases. Occasionally, in critical cases, all of the judges assigned to the appeals court will sit as a single panel. Appeals court judges make $217,600.

courts of appeals Thirteen courts that form the intermediate level of the federal judicial system and hear appeals of cases tried in the federal district courts.

The purpose of the courts of appeals is to provide a forum for review of decisions made by the district courts. Appeals usually deal with questions of procedure and of the application of rules of law rather than of facts or interpretation of facts, although questions of law and fact are sometimes difficult to disentangle. The courts of appeals also hear appeals of decisions of the Tax Court, Court of Federal Claims, Court of Veterans Appeals, and certain federal agencies. The courts of appeals handled 60,357 cases in 2016.

The U.S. Supreme Court

The U.S. **Supreme Court** is the most powerful judicial tribunal in the world. Over the course of its history it has addressed, sometimes successfully, sometimes not, the most important and often the most contentious issues facing our society. In the past half century, the Supreme Court has determined policy in

Supreme Court The high court or court of last resort in the American judicial system.

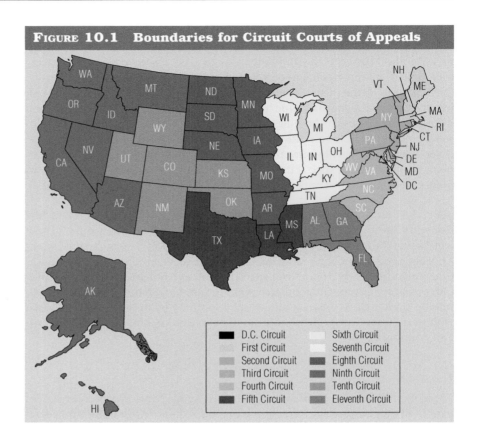

FIGURE 10.1 Boundaries for Circuit Courts of Appeals

regard to civil rights, voting rights, flag burning, abortion, and a host of equally contentious issues. In the hotly disputed 2000 presidential election, the Supreme Court ultimately stepped in to decide the contest, some would say directly, others indirectly, in favor of George W. Bush. In the 2015 term, litigants brought about 6,475 cases and applications to the Supreme Court. Of these, the court heard arguments and wrote full opinions in only 62. Associate Justices of the Supreme Court make $251,800 and the Chief Justice makes $263,300.

Federal judges can supplement their income modestly through teaching, speaking, and book royalties. Supreme Court justices are allowed about $25,000 a year for teaching, usually a summer law school class, and honoraria for speeches. Book royalties are not limited and some federal judges and justices make significant income from them.

The Supreme Court has both original and appellate jurisdiction. However, the court exercises the **original jurisdiction** outlined in Article III, section 2, of the Constitution less than once a year, or just about 200 times since 1789. The **appellate jurisdiction** of the Supreme Court derives from its responsibility to oversee and review the decisions of the U.S. courts of appeals, the U.S. district courts, the special legislative courts, the territorial courts, and the state courts of last resort when a federal question is at issue (see Figure 10.2).

original jurisdiction Mandatory jurisdiction of the Supreme Court as laid out in Article III of the Constitution.

appellate jurisdiction Substantive area in which a higher court may hear cases appealed from a lower court.

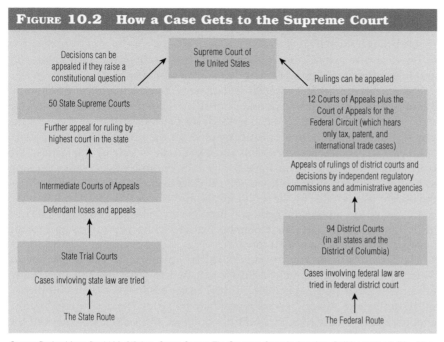

FIGURE 10.2 How a Case Gets to the Supreme Court

Supreme Court of the United States

Decisions can be appealed if they raise a constitutional question

Rulings can be appealed

50 State Supreme Courts

12 Courts of Appeals plus the Court of Appeals for the Federal Circuit (which hears only tax, patent, and international trade cases)

Further appeal for ruling by highest court in the state

Appeals of rulings of district courts and decisions by independent regulatory commissions and administrative agencies

Intermediate Courts of Appeals

Defendant loses and appeals

94 District Courts (in all states and the District of Columbia)

State Trial Courts

Cases invloving state law are tried

Cases involving federal law are tried in federal district court

The State Route

The Federal Route

Source: Derived from David M. O'Brien, *Storm Center: The Supreme Court in American Politics,* 11th ed. (New York: Norton, 2017), 169.

The Supreme Court has almost complete discretion over the cases that it chooses to hear. Observers complain that the court has used this discretion to dramatically cut its workload. In 1985 the court produced 146 signed opinions. By 2000 the number of signed opinions was down to the mid-70s. In the 2015 term it fell to just 62 signed opinions.

The Supreme Court chooses to hear particular cases primarily when differences of interpretation have arisen among the courts of appeals. Most cases come to the Supreme Court by a **writ of certiorari**—an order to a lower court to produce a case for review. The justices' law clerks review the thousands of "cert" requests that come to the court each term and advise the justices on which cases raise interesting and important federal and constitutional issues. The **rule of four** requires that four justices agree before a writ of certiorari will be granted and a case heard before the Supreme Court.

The U.S. Supreme Court holds one term each year beginning on the first Monday in October. The term is divided into a series of sittings of about two weeks, during which the court meets to hear oral arguments and decide cases, and recesses of two weeks or more during which the justices do their legal research and writing. The justices meet in conference during their sittings and less frequently during recesses to discuss the cases before them. After mid-May, the court hears no more new cases and holds formal sessions only to announce decisions.

During sittings, arguments are heard Monday through Wednesday from 10 a.m. to 3 p.m. with an hour off for lunch. Each case usually receives one hour, with

writ of certiorari Judicial instrument that makes a formal request that a case be reviewed by a higher court.

rule of four Four justices must approve a writ of certiorari before a case will be heard on appeal before the Supreme Court.

oral argument The opportunity in a case before the Supreme Court for the opposing lawyers to present their legal arguments orally.

briefs Written arguments prepared by lawyers in a case outlining their view of the relevant law and the decision that should be rendered based on the law.

amicus curiae brief An argument filed with the court by a party interested in a case but not directly involved in it as a contending party. *Amicus curiae* is Latin for "friend of the court."

opinion Written finding or decision of a court.

the time equally divided between the two sides. Prior to **oral argument** the justices read the **briefs** or written arguments of the disputants and any **amicus curiae briefs** written by interested persons or groups who are not formal parties to the case. The justices then question the lawyers about the legal arguments and logic offered in their written and oral presentations.

Each week the justices meet in a conference or closed session from about 3 p.m. to 6 p.m. on Wednesdays and from 10 a.m. to 6 p.m. on Fridays to discuss the cases heard that week. The chief justice leads these discussions and can, by the way he frames the questions at issue, try to shape the results of the discussions. Following the conference discussion and a preliminary vote by the justices, the chief justice, if he is in the majority, assigns the drafting of the court's decision to himself or to one of his colleagues. If the chief justice is not with the majority, the assignment is made by the senior justice in the majority. Distribution of the court's workload among the justices is usually very balanced although the chief justice and some of the senior members close to him get a disproportionate number of the most important cases.

The Supreme Court's decision is called an **opinion.** Each justice writes six to ten opinions each term. The justice assigned to write the court's opinion produces a draft that is circulated to the other justices for their comments, suggestions, and advice. Several drafts may be written and circulated before enough justices are willing to adopt the opinion as the final statement of the

AP Photo/J. Scott Applewhite

Justices of the Supreme Court of the United States. Standing from left to right are Justice Elena Kagan, Justice Samuel Alito, Justice Sonia Sotomayor, and Justice Neil Gorsuch. Seated from left to right are Justice Ruth Bader Ginsburg, Justice Anthony Kennedy, Chief Justice John Roberts, Justice Clarence Thomas, and Justice Stephen Breyer.

court in the case at hand. A decision of the court may receive various levels and kinds of support or opposition from the nine justices.

Each justice assigned to draft an opinion for the court hopes to produce a unanimous opinion—that is, an opinion that each justice will approve and sign. However, this is not always possible. A majority opinion is an opinion that a majority of the court, although not every member, has approved and signed. A minority opinion is one that several members, but not enough to constitute a majority, produce as preferable to the majority opinion. Finally, individual justices may produce opinions that vary in some large or small way from the view that any other justice is willing to adopt. A concurring opinion is produced by a justice who concurs with or accepts the basic thrust of the court's majority opinion but wishes to provide a somewhat different rationale for the result. A dissenting opinion is produced by a justice who disagrees with the court's finding as stated in the majority opinion and wishes to explain why.

The result of the Supreme Court's deliberations is usually to affirm the lower court, reverse the lower court, or remand the case back to the lower court for further consideration. If the Supreme Court agrees with the ruling made by the lower court, it is said to **affirm** the lower court. If the justices **reverse** the lower court, this means that they disagree in whole or in part with the result at that level and they explain why. Finally, they may **remand** the case back to the lower court to consider certain issues or to focus on certain specific questions.

affirm Action by a higher court supporting the decision of a lower court.

reverse Action by a higher court to overturn the decision of a lower court.

remand To send a case back to a lower court for further consideration.

JUDICIAL NOMINATION AND APPOINTMENT

The formal process for selecting federal judges used to be very straightforward. Each of the approximately 1,000 active federal judges was nominated by the president and confirmed by a majority of U.S. senators present and voting on the nomination. Once confirmed, federal judges hold their positions "during good behavior," which essentially means for life, because they can be removed from office only by the difficult and cumbersome process of impeachment by the House of Representatives and conviction by the Senate.[11]

04 How have the climate and tone surrounding the process of nomination and confirmation to judicial posts changed since the mid-1950s?

Backgrounds of Members of the Federal Judiciary

Historically, more than 90 percent of the nominees to the federal bench have shared partisan affiliation with the presidents who nominated them and two-thirds have been prominent political activists.[12] Half have had experience as judges, and nearly half were sitting judges on state benches when nominated to the federal bench. Almost 90 percent have been male, and almost 90 percent have been white, although both of those number are slowly coming down.

Most presidential nominations to the judiciary are approved by the Senate. About forty-five to fifty judges a year are nominated and confirmed to the federal bench. Political scientists Deborah Barrow, Gary Zuk, and Gerald

Gryski have shown that "modern presidents . . . change anywhere from 35 to 60 percent of the membership on the lower federal courts during their stay in office."[13] As a result, partisan change in the White House can lead to substantial change in the ideological coloration of the judiciary in a relatively few years. No modern president had a greater impact on the make-up of the federal courts in their first year than Donald Trump.

When Franklin Roosevelt assumed the presidency early in 1933, after many years of Republican rule, only 22 percent of federal judges were Democrats. FDR achieved a Democratic majority among federal judges by 1940, and the Democratic ascendancy peaked during the presidency of Lyndon Johnson, when 70.5 percent of federal judges were Democrats. Ronald Reagan reversed these numbers in the 1980s. During eight years as president, Reagan appointed 48.9 percent of all federal judges, and at the end of the first President Bush's term in 1992 over 70 percent of federal judges were Republican. President Clinton appointed 46.6 percent of the federal judiciary and at the end of his eight years in office (1993–2001), 53.4 percent of federal judges were Democrats. President George W. Bush appointed 37 percent of sitting federal judges by the end of 2008. At that time, about 60 percent of sitting federal judges and six of nine Supreme Court justices were appointed by Republican presidents (see Table 10.3).[14]

President Barack Obama had 329 judicial appointments approved by the Senate. Obama's appointments constituted about one-third of the federal judiciary and brought the balance between judges appointed by Democrats back above 50 percent. Moreover, following the Sotomayor and Kagan appointments, four of nine justices had been named by Democratic presidents, the most since the Nixon years.

TABLE 10.3	Demographic Characteristics of Federal Judicial Appointments, Presidents Johnson through Obama					
President	Party	% White	% Black	% Hispanic	% Asian	% Female
Johnson	Dem.	93.4	4.1	2.5	.0	1.6
Nixon	Rep.	95.5	3.4	1.1	.0	.6
Ford	Rep.	88.5	5.8	1.9	3.9	1.9
Carter	Dem.	78.2	13.9	6.9	.5	14.4
Reagan	Rep.	92.2	2.1	4.8	.7	8.3
Bush I	Rep.	89.2	6.8	4.0	.0	19.6
Clinton	Dem.	75.1	17.4	5.9	1.3	28.5
Bush II	Rep.	81.2	6.9	10.3	1.5	20.7
Obama	Dem.	64.0	18.4	10.8	6.4	41.2

Source: Harold W. Stanley and Richard G. Niemi, *Vital Statistics on American Politics, 2015–2016*, Washington, D.C.: CQ Press, 2015, 280–281. See also Alliance for Justice, "Judicial Selection Snapshot," 2017.

The Supreme Court and American politics more generally were deeply shaken by the unexpected death of Associate Justice Antonin Scalia on February 13, 2016. Scalia, appointed to the Supreme Court in 1986 by President Ronald Reagan, had long been the intellectual leader of the conservative majority on the court. Brilliant and combative, willing to turn his wit and scorn on his allies and opponents alike, including Chief Justice John Roberts, Scalia was better at laying out conservative judicial doctrine and theory than at building court majorities. Scalia's death elicited generous praise and real sadness. It also elicited almost immediate political calculation. Within hours of the announcement of Scalia's death, Mitch McConnell, the Republican majority leader in the Senate, announced that the Senate would not consider any nomination that Obama might make. When Donald Trump won, Senate Republicans sunnily looked forward to a presidential nomination. Clearly, the Supreme Court nomination process has come under great pressure. Let's look at that process as it has worked historically.

The Nomination Process

Presidents follow different nomination processes in regard to the lower federal courts than they do in regard to the Supreme Court. A nomination to a U.S. district court is cleared with the U.S. senators, a process called **senatorial courtesy,** and other political figures of the president's party from the state in which the nominee will serve. Senators and state political figures play a smaller role in nominations to the U.S. circuit courts of appeals because the circuits include several states. Moreover, judges are usually elevated from the district court bench, so the Senate has already approved them once and their judicial records and performance are more clearly established.

senatorial courtesy Expectation that the president will clear federal district court judgeship appointments with senators of his party from the state in which the judge will serve.

Beginning with the Eisenhower administration (1953–1961), the Standing Committee on the Federal Judiciary of the American Bar Association (ABA) was given early notice of judicial nominations. The ABA's committee studied the nominees' legal and judicial record and declared the candidate "well qualified," "not opposed," or "not qualified." The Bush administration (2001–2009) suspended the ABA's traditional role, arguing that the committee had a liberal bias, but the Obama administration (2009–2017) brought them back into the process as soon as it took office. The Trump administration suspended them again.

Nominations to the Supreme Court are so important that presidents and their close advisers hold these nominations for themselves even though they are inundated with advice from others.[15] As soon as a nomination is made, the White House appoints a team of experienced confirmation managers, former senators or White House operatives, to help the nominee navigate the process successfully. Nominees are ushered through a series of meetings with senators, beginning with members of the leadership and the Judiciary Committee. The managers also organize a series of twelve to fifteen "murder boards" to prepare the nominees for the questions they might expect from members of the Judiciary Committee.[16]

Struggling Toward Democracy

Over the course of American history, Supreme Court justices have served an average of 15.65 years each.

What do you think?

- Does the fact that federal judges have lifetime appointments make them better servants of our democracy or somehow undemocratic?

Coalitions of interest groups favoring and opposing the nomination seek to make their case to the public and to the senators who will vote on the nomination. Tens of millions of dollars are spent by both sides. As the spending and the rhetoric ratchet steadily higher, senators, dependent on these same interest groups for political and campaign support, are caught in the middle. In 2005, the judicial nomination and confirmation process in the Senate nearly exploded as Senate Democrats threatened to filibuster conservative nominees including Roberts and Alito and Republicans threatened the "nuclear option" of changing Senate rules to allow approval of judicial nominees by simple majority—50 votes instead of 60. Negotiations resolved the standoff.

Nonetheless, partisan tensions continued to build. In late 2013, the Senate Democratic Leader, Harry Reid of Nevada, pushed through a change in Senate rules to allow approval of most presidential nominees, though not Supreme Court nominees, with 50 votes. In 2017, as Democrats, now in the minority, filibustered the nomination of Neil Gorsuch to the Supreme Court, Republican Majority Leader, Mitch McConnell of Kentucky, changed the rules again to allow approval of Supreme Court nominees by simple majority. Both sides acknowledged that these rules changes would make the Senate even more partisan and conflictual but each blamed the other for leaving them no choice.

The Confirmation Process

The Senate takes very seriously its responsibility to advise and consent on presidential nominations to the Supreme Court. Of the 162 Supreme Court nominations forwarded to the Senate by presidents during the country's history, 125 were approved. Seven of the men confirmed to the Supreme Court, mostly early in the nation's history, declined to serve—so 118 men and women have sat on the high court. The Senate took no action on eleven nominees, postponed three, rejected twelve, and eleven were withdrawn.[17]

Brown v. Board of Education (1954) This landmark case overturned *Plessy* and declared that racial segregation in public schools was unconstitutional.

Nonetheless, the climate of confirmation politics began to change after the *Brown v. Board of Education* desegregation decision in 1954 and certainly after the Great Society initiatives of the mid-1960s raised the temperature of our social life. Ten of the twenty-four nominees since 1968 have received twenty-five or more negative votes in the Senate and six have been rejected or withdrawn. Mark Silverstein points out that "powerful groups from all points along the ideological spectrum now consider a sympathetic judiciary essential to the development and achievement of important policy goals."[18]

confirmation hearing
Nominees for federal judicial posts appear before the Senate Judiciary Committee to respond to questions from the members.

The most intensely public forum in which the scrutiny of a judicial nominee occurs is the **confirmation hearing** held by the Senate Judiciary Committee. Committee staff members gather extensive information about the nominee and investigate questions and issues that arise. After the preparation and inquiry are complete, public hearings are scheduled in which the nominee is questioned at length, often over the course of several days, and others, both those favoring and those opposing the nomination, provide their views to the committee.

Judge Neil Gorsuch at the first day of his confirmation hearings in Washington. Judge Gorsuch spoke of his background, the people and principles that had the greatest influence on him, and the need for independent-minded jurists. March 20, 2017.

Senators ask questions that they hope will suggest how a nominee might think about, if not how he or she might vote, on the key social and political issues likely to come before the court. Nominees invariably decline to respond in ways that would suggest that they have prejudged important and controversial issues that might later come before them. The confirmation hearing is a frustrating exercise for all concerned.

Following the public hearing, the members of the Judiciary Committee vote on whether to report the nomination to the full Senate with a positive or negative recommendation. The full Senate then debates the nomination and a confirmation vote is taken. Most senators agree that judicial nominees should be judged on qualifications, experience, character, and temperament. More recently, senators have begun to argue that it is appropriate to take ideology into account as well.[19]

THE SUPREME COURT AND THE EXPANSION OF INDIVIDUAL RIGHTS

The appointment of Earl Warren as chief justice of the Supreme Court in 1953 marked a new era. Warren was an accomplished political leader and former governor of California rather than a judicial scholar or sitting judge. He moved the court from the New Deal posture of judicial restraint and deference to the political branches of the government to the posture of an assertive, even demanding, advocate of individual rights and liberties.[20]

The Warren Court made a long series of dramatic rulings expanding individual rights in such diverse areas as freedom of speech, press, and religion, the rights of minorities to equal political rights and economic opportunities, the rights of accused persons to counsel and to fair and speedy trials, and the rights of citizens to due process before legislative and administration committees and boards. Many citizens came to feel that the Warren Court was moving too far too fast in areas such as civil rights and the rights of the accused.

Earl Warren's 1969 resignation gave President Richard Nixon the opportunity to nominate his replacement. Republicans and southern conservatives, hoping that the new chief justice would lead the court in rolling back some of the Warren Court's more liberal initiatives, were heartened by the nomination and Senate approval of Warren Burger. Burger was a conservative jurist with thirteen years of experience on the District of Columbia Circuit Court of Appeals.

Yet, the Burger Court did more to consolidate than to challenge the legacy of the Warren Court. It upheld affirmative action programs, recognized a woman's right to seek abortion services, and expanded the rights to counsel and against self-incrimination for persons accused of crimes.

Modern Judicial Conservatism Ascendant

William Rehnquist served on the high court for 33 years, the last 18 as chief justice. He was named an associate justice by President Nixon in 1972 and elevated to chief justice by President Reagan in 1986. He died in 2005. The Rehnquist court limited the scope of the federal government while strengthening the role of the judiciary against both Congress and the executive. He led the court to strengthen the role of the police, limit the appellate rights of convicts, allow indirect government funding of religious schools and enhance the role of the states in American federalism.[21]

Roe v. Wade (1973) With this landmark decision, the court struck down a Texas law regulating access to abortion as a violation of a woman's fundamental right to privacy.

Webster v. Reproductive Health Services (1989) The court upheld abortion regulations that did not prohibit a woman from having an abortion, but reasonably furthered the state's interest in encouraging childbirth. The trimester analysis was rejected; *Roe*, however, was not overturned.

The Rehnquist court sought to limit, where it could not overturn, the ban on school prayer, affirmative action, gay rights, and the rights of women seeking abortion services.[22] For example, *Roe v. Wade* (1973), decided in Justice Rehnquist's first year on the court, established a woman's right to choose abortion, especially early in her pregnancy. As the court became more conservative and soon after Rehnquist was elevated to chief justice, *Webster v. Reproductive Health Services* (1989) provided an opportunity to limit access to abortion services. While not overturning *Roe*, the decision in *Webster* upheld the rights of states to regulate abortion clinics and to prevent public money and facilities from being used to perform abortions.

Civil rights provides another good example of the Rehnquist Court trimming but not completely overturning major liberal precedents. In 1973, in *Regents of the University of California v. Bakke*, the court approved the use of race as one criterion although not as the sole criterion in college admissions. In 1995, the Supreme Court ruled that preferences based on race in government decisions and programs such as hiring and awarding contracts and grants were suspect and usually unconstitutional.

While William Rehnquist undoubtedly moved the high court to the right, he was "unable to assemble a majority of justices willing to take the court—and the nation—as far to the right as he wanted to go." As Richard Gannett of the Notre Dame Law School noted, "Chief Justice Rehnquist changed the conversation. He brought back to the table certain ideas about limited government, federalism, and textualism."[23]

The high court's conservative momentum picked up speed once John Roberts became Chief Justice.[24] Roberts graduated from Harvard Law School, clerked for Justice Rehnquist in 1980, and then worked in the Justice Department and the White House Counsel's Office in the Reagan administration. He was in private practice in Washington when President George W. Bush placed him on the D.C. Circuit Court of Appeals in 2003. Roberts was initially nominated to the Supreme Court to replace Associate Justice Sandra Day O'Connor when she resigned in 2005. Just prior to the start of Roberts's confirmation hearings, Chief Justice Rehnquist died of cancer and Roberts's nomination was switched from associate justice to chief justice.

Roberts performed masterfully in his Senate confirmation hearings, arguing that the courts should decide issues narrowly, speak modestly, and act unanimously where possible. Despite objections from a wide range of liberal interest groups and some Democrats, he was confirmed by a Senate vote of 78 to 22 in September 2005. President Bush then nominated Samuel Alito to succeed O'Connor. Alito had spent fifteen years on the Third U.S. Circuit Court of Appeals, so he was very knowledgeable but less smooth and personable than Roberts. Despite a more determined opposition in the Senate and among liberal interest groups, Alito was confirmed 58 to 42 in February 2006.

The Roberts court started slowly but quickly gained momentum. In the 2005–2006 session, most of the early decisions were unanimous, though as the session went along, issues of executive power arose that created divisions, intense argument, and sharp language in the written opinions. The 2006–2007 session dealt with even more divisive issues, including whether to permit or overturn voluntary integration plans in public schools. Chief Justice Roberts, writing for a deeply divided, 5–4, court, declared that school districts could not use race in an attempt to maintain school integration. Roberts reasoned that discrimination, even in an arguably good cause, was no more legal than discrimination in a bad cause. He wrote that, "The way to stop discrimination on the basis of race is to stop discrimination on the basis of race."[25] The 2007–2008 session was highlighted by a case dealing with the right to bear arms. A 5–4 conservative majority led by Justice Antonin Scalia declared for the first time that the Second Amendment right to bear arms is an individual right rather than a collective right tied to militia service.[26]

In the 2008–2009 session, Chief Justice Roberts continued to guide the court to the right in a range of cases dealing with voting rights, employment, and criminal procedure. Even more ominously, at least from the perspective of the liberal minority, Chief Justice Roberts led the court in rescheduling *Citizens United v. Federal Election Commission* for reargument in a special late-summer session. The first big decision of the 2009–2010 session was the

Citizens United case. The court overturned decades of campaign finance law by finding that corporations and unions have the same free speech rights as individuals in campaigns.[27]

Though Chief Justice Roberts has been an impressive jurist, his court is frequently referred to, only half in jest, as the Kennedy court. With four conservative and four moderate to liberal justices, Anthony Kennedy has long been the classic swing vote. Justice Kennedy has been consistently conservative on business issues, careful to balance federal and state power on federalism issues, moderate on affirmative action issues, and consistently liberal on issues of sexual preference. Since his vote often makes a 5–4 majority one way or the other, he can make the court seem somewhat erratic—or at least hard to summarize simply. For example, in the 2012–2013 term, two critical civil rights cases, one affecting blacks most directly and one affecting gays, were decided. Both were decided 5–4 and Kennedy was the only justice to be in the majority in both cases. *Shelby County v. Holder* struck down critical elements of the Voting Rights Act of 1965 subjecting states with a history of voter discrimination to federal oversight. Civil rights groups and the Obama administration took this decision to be a major defeat. In the other case, *United States v. Windsor*, the court struck down the part of the Defense of Marriage Act denying federal benefits to gay couples, even when married in states allowing gay marriage. Gay rights groups and the Obama administration took this decision to be a major victory.

Nonetheless, Justice Kennedy's pivotal role does not mask the court's increasingly partisan polarization.[28] All of the justices, especially Chief Justice John Roberts, are aware that the court's legitimacy and public standing hinge on being seen as above partisanship, so they vigorously deny partisan motives. Just as scholars and the public seemed to be more and more convinced that partisanship was driving the court, the 2014–15 term delivered a string of liberal decisions. A solid bloc of four liberal justices, a divided group of five conservative justices, and Chief Justice Roberts' desire to tamp down charges of partisanship help explain the string of liberal results. In the two most critical cases of the term, *King v. Burwell*, on Obamacare, and *Obergefeld v. Hodges*, on gay marriage, the liberals attracted the votes to prevail. In the second major challenge to the constitutionality of Obamacare, both Chief Justice Roberts and Justice Kennedy joined the liberals and on gay marriage Justice Kennedy did again.[29]

The 2015–16 term was roiled by one event and one process, both deeply disruptive of the court's normal expectations and procedures. The disruptive event was the untimely and unexpected death of Justice Antonin Scalia in early 2016. The disruptive process was the 2016 presidential nomination and election, which, especially after Scalia's death,

Shelby County v. Holder (2013) The court struck down elements of the 1965 Civil Rights Act including the critical "preclearance" provisions. The court argued that the data used to decide which states were covered by the preclearance provisions were outdated.

United States v. Windsor (2013) The court declared that the Defense of Marriage Act, defining marriage as between one man and one woman, was an unconstitutional denial of gay persons' Fifth Amendment protection of equal liberty.

Getty Images/Chip Somodevilla

Associate Justice Anthony Kennedy has often been the swing vote on the nine-person United States Supreme Court.

focused on the court's narrow balance and the effect that a new appointment might have on it. Meanwhile, the court worked through an important series of decisions on high-profile cases dealing with abortion, affirmative action, immigration, voting rights, and the death penalty.

Before Justice Scalia's death, the court's five-member conservative bloc seemed poised to reassert itself. After his death, the two most important cases of the term, both out of Texas, produced major liberal wins. The long-running *Fisher v. University of Texas* affirmative action case, initiated in 2008 and before the Supreme Court for a second time, upheld by a 4 to 3 vote the university's use of race in admissions decisions, effectively preserving *Grutter v. Bollinger*, the Michigan case from 2003. Just as striking, in a 5 to 3 decision, Justice Kennedy joining the liberals, the court struck down Texas abortion law provisions requiring that doctors administering abortions have admitting privileges at nearby hospitals and that abortion facilities meet tough new design standards as an "undue burden" on women's access to abortion services. Neither outcome was widely anticipated at the start of the term.

Short-handed for most of the 2016–17 term, the high court proceeded cautiously. The court talked its way to unanimity more frequently than in any term in the last 70 years and decided a number of cases on narrow grounds to avoid deep divisions. In general, the court leaned left on a number of civil rights cases, by, for example, recognizing systemic bias in housing, and leaned right in business cases, by, for example, limiting access to class action and arbitration actions. However, in a Missouri case, *Trinity Lutheran Church v. Comer*, the court lowered the wall of separation between church and state by holding that states may not discriminate against churches by denying funds, in this case to improve a school playground, just because the applicant was a church or church related.[30]

THE DISPUTED ROLE OF THE FEDERAL JUDICIARY

How do we explain the fact that American courts play a far more formative role in politically sensitive policy areas such as race, the availability of abortion services, the role of religion in political life, and the rights of the accused than do courts in any other nation? The idea that the courts rather than legislative majorities can and do decide fundamental political issues seems on its face to be blatantly undemocratic.

Some argue, as noted earlier, that one of the main roles of American courts is to limit the political branches of the government to their constitutionally mandated responsibilities. Hence, the federal courts must strike down initiatives, even popular initiatives that command legislative majorities and presidential support, if the courts believe that the Constitution forbids them. Since the mid-1990s, the courts have challenged Congress on the scope of its power to regulate interstate commerce, and since 2005 they have challenged the president on the scope of his commander-in-chief powers.[31] This is what they are supposed to

Q5 Is judicial activism necessary because some issues are just too difficult for the political branches of the government to confront?

do, but it does worry some people, mainly populists and conservatives, when appointed judges overrule elected officials.

Others note that the courts never stay for long outside the mainstream of American political life. Judges, like other members of the nation's social and political elite, share in the broad flow of popular opinion concerning the major issues of the day. Moreover, judges know that the few times when the courts have strayed too far from the mainstream—as with Federalist judges in the Jeffersonian era on issues of free speech and press, or conservative judges in the New Deal era on the expansion of federal authority—popular and political pressures have asserted themselves, and the courts have been forced to back down. Courts and judges know that they must maintain the confidence and respect of the public if their rulings are to be obeyed. They generally know not to overplay their hand.[32]

Limits on Judicial Activism

Political scientist Henry Abraham argues that the courts are subject to multiple pressures from other elements of the political system: "First, the Supreme Court's rulings may be effectively reversed by other participants in the processes of government; second, they are almost inevitably responsive to overall policy formulations, sooner or later; third, for enforcement they must look to the executive branch of the government; and fourth; . . . compliance with them is not necessarily automatic."[33]

Presidential Influence.   One of the most obvious constraints on the independence of the courts is that their membership is defined by the political branches of the government. Presidents nominate judges who must gain majority support in the Senate before they can ascend to the bench. Although less commonly noted, it is also true that presidents affect the activities of the courts by the substance of their litigation policy and by the nature of their appointments in the Justice Department.

Presidents also affect the role and status of the federal courts by the kind of support or lack of support they show to Congress and the public for the decisions of the courts. A famous example of the limits on judicial authority derives from an 1832 conflict between Chief Justice John Marshall and President Andrew Jackson. Marshall ruled in the case of *Worcester v. Georgia* that Indian tribes had to be treated as sovereign and autonomous by both the national and state governments. Upon hearing of Marshall's decision, President Jackson is reported to have declared, "John Marshall has made his decision, now let him enforce it." President Eisenhower's cool reception of the Supreme Court's controversial 1954 desegregation ruling in *Brown v. Board of Education* signaled members of Congress and southern politicians that they would not face presidential ire if they resisted the court.

Much more recently, President Obama used the very high profile occasion of his 2010 State of the Union address, delivered before a joint session of Congress, with six of the nine justices arrayed in front of him and 48 million

Americans watching on television, to call the Supreme Court out for its *Citizens United* campaign finance ruling of the previous week. President Obama called on congressional Democrats to find a constitutional way to stem the potential tide of corporate money in elections. President Trump also has been willing to call out judges and courts when he thinks they are obstructing important policy goals.

Legislative Reaction and Court Curbing.   Congress exercises several forms of fairly direct control over the courts. First, every federal judge must pass Senate confirmation. Second, Chief Justice Roberts and his colleagues well know that the budget of the federal courts is considered and approved, with increases and decreases each year, as Congress thinks appropriate. Third, the number of federal judges, the levels of their professional and clerical support, and their salaries are set by Congress. Fourth, the appellate jurisdiction of the courts is set by Congress and some have called for placing sensitive cultural and religious issues beyond the reach of the courts. Fifth, Congress can always pass new legislation or initiate constitutional amendments if it does not like the way the courts are interpreting existing law.

Popular Sentiment.   Popular noncompliance, although always a threat, has occurred irregularly. Respect for the Supreme Court and its decisions is sometimes stretched, as in the contemporary examples of school prayer, desegregation, abortion, and gay marriage, but for the most part, the court enjoys a reservoir of latent support from the American people. More commonly, the dynamic within the American political system has been for the court to adjust its line of decisions to public sentiment rather than to challenge that sentiment directly. Robert McCloskey argued that "the Court, while sometimes checking or at any rate modifying the popular will, is itself in turn checked or modified . . . . In truth the Supreme Court has seldom, if ever, flatly and for very long resisted a really unmistakable wave of public sentiment. It has worked with the premise that constitutional law, like politics itself, is a science of the possible."[35]

JUDICIAL REFORM TODAY

The federal judiciary is badly in need of reform. Three issues—selection, tenure, and compensation—are frequently mentioned. Many argue that judicial selection has turned into a media circus, that lifetime tenure is outmoded, and that top legal talent avoids the judiciary because salaries are too low.

The judicial nomination process has become highly politicized, especially when one party holds the presidency and the other holds the Senate. In two-thirds of the states, voters have a role in selecting Supreme Court justices. Many of these use a process called the Missouri System or merit selection, whereby an expert panel nominates prospective judges and the governor selects among them. Judges serve a term of six years or so and then have to stand in retention elections if they want to remain in office. Voters vote up or down, yes or no, whether to retain the judge. Would something like the Missouri System

Pro & Con

Does the U.S. Political System Need Judicial Activism to Work?

Courts cannot avoid making policy. Every time a court applies an existing law to a new situation or interprets an existing statute in a novel way, it is reshaping and to some extent elaborating the law. Nonetheless, at some stages in American political history the courts have seemed more eager to lead the national policy conversation than at others. These courts—the Marshall Court of the early national period, the laissez faire courts of Fuller, White, and Taft in the late nineteenth and early twentieth centuries, and the Warren Court of the mid-twentieth century are the three most obvious examples—are said to be engaging in **judicial activism,** and their leading members are called activist judges. Activist judges and courts believe that social, economic, and political problems should be addressed and that the courts are one vehicle for doing so. **Judicial restraint** is the less glamorous view that judges are to follow the lead of the political branches of the government and to avoid policymaking of their own.

Judicial activism and restraint have no natural or logical identity with liberalism or conservatism, big government or small government, active government or passive government. The Marshall Court of the early nineteenth century had a big government, pro-business cast. During the late nineteenth century and the first third of the twentieth century—that is, during the era of laissez faire—judicial activism had a decidedly free market, even antigovernment, cast. Judicial restraint during both of these periods was the stance of those who wanted the courts to step aside so that state and national legislatures and executives could legislate to control large and powerful economic entities like corporations, banks, and railroads. In fact, the same court can be activist in regard to some issues, say commercial regulation, and restrained in regard to others, say presidential war powers.

Beginning in the mid-1950s, many would even say with the appointment of Earl Warren as chief justice, judicial activism came more commonly to be understood as aggressive pursuit of equal rights in areas as diverse as civil rights, gender equity, and the rights of the accused.

judicial activism Active policymaking by courts, especially in sensitive cases such as desegregation and abortion.

judicial restraint The idea that courts should avoid policymaking and limit themselves to implementing legislative and executive intent.

work at the federal level? Such changes would, of course, require a constitution amendment, so maybe just expert nomination of three or four potential judges, presidential selection from among them, and Senate confirmation would work better than what we have? What flaws do you see with this idea?

How about judicial tenure? Life expectancy today is about double what it was when the Constitution was written. Do federal judges need lifetime tenure to assure their independence from social and political pressure? Some say yes, others no. Those who say no call for elections, either initially or in a retention election at the end of a six- to ten-year term. Others call for one long term of eighteen to twenty or twenty-five years with no second term. Should federal judges be able to stay on the bench into their eighties or nineties if they wish?

Finally, graduates from top law schools command first-year salaries that are not far behind the salaries earned by federal judges. Top lawyers in mid-career make several times what federal judges make. Congress controls judicial salaries and until recently was reluctant to raise them above their own.[36]

Judicial restraint was generally understood as the courts following the political branches of the government rather than trying to induce political change on their own.

Many contemporary observers including former President Clinton see judicial activism as a device that is sometimes necessary to assist society in addressing a particularly difficult issue. In presenting a Presidential Medal of Freedom to Judge John Minor Wisdom of the U.S. Fifth Circuit Court of Appeals in 1997, President Clinton said that activist judges "did the whole nation and especially the South a signal service by the courage with which they carried out the civil rights revolution from the 1950s through the 1970s, when so many of the elected officials from the region were dragging their feet."[34]

Many others, including former President George W. Bush argue that democracy requires that the judiciary follow the political branches of the government—the Congress, the president, and the executive branch. In this view, it is the responsibility of the elected representatives of the people to make policy by passing statutes that will be binding on all citizens. It is the role of the courts to evaluate charges that the statutes have been breached and to assess penalties if the courts conclude that the charges are true. Judicial restraint involves an explicit commitment by judges to keep their courts out of policymaking and to limit them to implementing legislative and executive intent.

What do you think?
- Which makes most sense to you—judicial activism or judicial restraint?
- Are charges of judicial activism just a way of saying one doesn't agree with the judge's decision?

PRO	CON
Some problems are too hard for politicians to solve	The Constitution gives Congress the lawmaking power
Justice demands an advocate	Politicians can solve hard issues if given time
Constitutional rights cannot be ignored	Courts must not "find" new rights

THE JUDICIAL ROLE IN THE AGE OF TRUMP

As described in "The Constitution Today" vignette that opened this chapter, John Marshall's profound Supreme Court decision in *Marbury v. Madison* (1803) established the federal courts' role as the final arbiter of what the Constitution allows and what it forbids—in fact, what it means. Marshall explained that a written constitution, laying out the national government's political offices and their powers needed an interpreter, a defender, someone to warn the people, distracted by their personal concerns and interests, when elected or appointed officials were acting beyond their rightful authority.

Fifteen years before Marshall first employed federal judicial review in *Marbury*, Alexander Hamilton famously anticipated it in *Federalist* No. 78, calling on the courts to "declare all acts contrary to the manifest tenor of the Constitution void." Think for a moment about the phrase "manifest tenor"; it is not a narrow phrase, it does not mean "precise letter" of the Constitution so much as it means "broad thrust or general import." Hamilton was drawing on the common law reasoning of England's Lord Coke in *Bonham's Case*, noted earlier, when he declared it the duty of courts to void "an act of Parliament . . . against common right and reason."

In the minds of many, though perhaps not in the minds of many Trump diehards, that is precisely what the federal courts did early in the Trump administration. Most memorably, it took the first full year of the Trump administration to get the travel ban even temporarily approved by the courts. Similarly, when the federal courts blocked a presidential executive order to cut funding to cities that limited cooperation with federal immigration authorities, so-called "sanctuary cities," White House officials decried "unelected judges" attempting to make new immigration policy. Pushing back against political authorities until they get it right is precisely the role that Hamilton, Marshall, and the founding generation came to envision for the federal courts.

While President Trump has been frustrated by the federal courts, he has also been working assiduously to recast them. Because Senate Majority Leader Mitch McConnell and his Republican colleagues refused to consider Obama judicial nominees, including his nomination of Merrick Garland to the Supreme Court, President Trump came to office with 100 vacancies on the federal courts. By comparison, Obama came to office with just 39 vacancies awaiting him. Assuming normal judicial turnover in addition to the 100 vacancies he inherited, President Trump likely will nominate more federal judges than any of his recent predecessors.

The Founders knew that strong-willed politicians would place the national political institutions they created under great pressure. They have throughout American history: we think of Andrew Jackson, Abraham Lincoln, both Roosevelts, and George W. Bush. Once again those institutions come under pressure, especially the judiciary, as Donald Trump bridles at and declaims against challenges to his authority. Republicans in Congress stick with the president, hoping he will help promote their agenda, while Democrats in Congress, just months into the administration, call for impeachment—tensions build. We have been here before and come out the other side, but nerves fray.

Chapter Summary

The Constitution prescribed a national judiciary composed of a Supreme Court and such inferior or lower courts as Congress, rather than the courts themselves, should think necessary. The Constitution included a "supremacy clause" declaring the national government supreme over the state governments within the area of national government responsibility and requiring state officers to swear allegiance to the U.S. Constitution and laws.

Nonetheless, the role and stature of the federal courts remained uncertain during the nation's early years. The Supreme Court began to come into its own during John Marshall's long service (1801–1835) as chief justice. No case did more to establish the role and future importance of the court than *Marbury v. Madison,* for which Marshall wrote the opinion in 1803. *Marbury* made the point that one of the Court's primary roles is to safeguard and defend the Constitution. Judicial review is the power of the courts to declare unconstitutional, that is, incompatible with the Constitution, acts of Congress or the president, state or local governments, or the lower courts.

The modern federal court system is organized on three levels. There are ninety-four district courts, thirteen courts of appeals, and one Supreme Court. Virtually all federal cases are tried in the district courts and are subject to review by the appropriate court of appeals. The Supreme Court has broad discretion to hear only the cases that raise important constitutional issues.

Judges who reach the federal bench have been nominated by the president and confirmed by a majority of the senators present and voting on the nomination. Federal judges hold their jobs "during good behavior," which really means for life; their salaries cannot be reduced and they can be removed only by impeachment by the House of Representatives and trial in the Senate. Presidents have the opportunity to replace with new appointments between one-third and one-half of the federal judiciary, and 90 percent of their appointments come from their own parties.

Finally, because the courts are so powerful, the role that they play in addressing major social issues is intensely debated. Some argue that elected politicians are often reluctant to tackle difficult issues and that judges, with their lifetime appointments, might be better positioned to take a leading role. Judicial activism has been a powerful force at some stages in our national history, as with the Marshall and Warren Courts, but judicial restraint is closer to the popular expectation.

Key Terms

affirm	judicial restraint
amicus curiae brief	judicial review
appellate jurisdiction	Judiciary Act of 1789
Bonham's Case	justiciability
briefs	law
Brown v. Board of Education	opinion
civil law	oral argument
common law	original jurisdiction
confirmation hearing	precedent
courts of appeals	remand
criminal law	reverse
district courts	*Roe v. Wade*
judicial activism	rule of four

senatorial courtesy

Shelby County v. Holder

stare decisis

Supreme Court

United States v. Windsor

Webster v. Reproductive Health Services

writ of certiorari

Suggested Readings

Amar, Akhil Reed. *The Law of the Land: A Grand Tour of Our Constitutional Republic*. New York: Basic Books, 2015. Amar discusses a wide range of constitutional issues through the lens of geographical differences and federalism.

Baum, Lawrence. *American Courts: Process and Policy*, 7th ed. Boston, MA: Houghton Mifflin, 2012. Leading textbook highlighting judicial process, policy, and reform.

Corley, Pamela C., Artemus Ward, and Wendy L. Martinek. *American Judicial Process: Myth and Reality in Law and Courts*. New York: Routledge, 2016. A popular text laying out the structure and procedures of the American judicial system.

Pacelle, Richard L. Jr. *The Supreme Court in a Separation of Powers System*. New York: Routledge, 2015. A description of how the U.S. Supreme Court influences and is influenced by other major actors and forces in American politics.

Sunstein, Cass R. *Legal Reasoning and Political Conflict*, 2nd ed. New York: Oxford University Press, 2018. Sunstein offers a smart discussion of how courts should seek to resolve conflicts in a diverse society.

Wilkinson III, J. Harvie. *Cosmic Constitutional Theory: Why Americans Are Losing Their Inalienable Right to Self-Governance*. New York: Oxford University Press, 2012. Wilkinson criticizes theorists of the right and left for encouraging judicial activism at the expense of the people's elected representatives.

Web Resources

1   www.findlaw.com/casecode/supreme.html
    This is Findlaw's searchable database of the Supreme Court decisions since 1893.

2   www.uscourts.gov
    The official website of the federal judiciary, this site provides news, information, publications, and a list of frequently asked questions regarding the federal judiciary.

3 www.oyez.org
   University of Chicago's Kent College of Law's Supreme Court website. Provides all you might want to know on any Supreme Court case.

4 www.loc.gov/law/guide/
   This website contains links to U.S. judicial branch resources.

5 www.library.cornell.edu/libraries/law
   The Law Library of Cornell Law School serves as a fantastic resource for Supreme Court decisions, hypertext versions of U.S. Code, U.S. Constitution, and Federal Rules of Evidence and Procedure, as well as other law-related sites.

Notes

1 Herbert Jacob, *Law and Politics in the United States* (Boston, MA: Little, Brown, 1986), 6–7.

2 Henry J. Abraham, *The Judicial Process*, 7th ed. (New York: Oxford University Press, 1998), 147.

3 Geoffrey C. Hazard Jr. and Michele Taruffo, *American Civil Procedure: An Introduction* (New Haven, CT: Yale University Press, 1993), 11.

4 Bernard Schwartz, *A History of the Supreme Court* (New York: Oxford University Press, 1993), 3–4.

5 Abraham, *Judicial Process*, 147.

6 Barry Friedman, *The Will of the People* (New York: Farrar, Straus, and Giroux, 2009), 94.

7 Richard A. Smith, The *American Anomaly: U.S. Politics and Government in Comparative Perspective*, 2nd ed. (New York: Routledge, 2011), 21.

8 Lawrence Baum, *The Supreme Court*, 12th ed. (Washington, D.C.: CQ Press, 2016), 92.

9 Baum, *The Supreme Court*, 5–6.

10 Chief Justice John Roberts, "2016 Year-End Report on the Federal Judiciary," December 31, 2016. See http://www.supremecourtus.gov.

11 Steven G. Calabresi and James Lindgren, "Term Limits for the Supreme Court: Life Tenure Reconsidered," *Harvard Journal of Law and Public Policy*, vol. 29, no. 3 (2006): 768–877.

12 Mark V. Tushnet, *Why the Constitution Matters* (New Haven, CT: Yale University Press, 2010), 175.

13 Deborah Barrow, Gary Zuk, and Gerald Gryski, *The Federal Judiciary and Institutional Change* (Ann Arbor, MI: University of Michigan Press, 1996), 12.

14 Alliance For Justice, "Judicial Selection During the Bush Administration," October 6, 2008, 2. www.allianceforjustice.org.

15 Lawrence Baum, *American Courts: Process and Policy*, 7th ed. (Boston, MA: Houghton Mifflin, 2012) 94–98.

16 Richard Davis, *Electing Justice: Fixing the Supreme Court Nomination Process* (New York: Oxford University Press, 2005), 19.

17 http://www.senate.gov/pagelayout/reference/nominations/Nominations.htm.

18 Mark Silverstein, *Judicious Choices: The New Politics of Supreme Court Confirmations* (New York: Norton, 1994), 71.

19 "Who Died and Made You Supreme Court Justice?" *Newsweek*, July 20, 2009, 68.

20 Silverstein, *Judicious Choices*, 49.

21 Charles Lane, "Chief Justice Dies at 80," *Washington Post*, September 4, 2005, A1, A4.

22 Schwartz, *A History of the Supreme Court*, 374.

23 Warren Richey, Rehnquist's Unfinished Agenda," *Christian Science Monitor*, September 6, 2005, 1–2.

24 Adam Liptak, "Justices Offer a Receptive Ear to Business Interests," *New York Times*, December 19, 2010, A1, A32.

25 Linda Greenhouse, "Justices 5–4, Limit Use of Race for School Integration Plans," *New York Times*, June 29, 2007, A1, A20. See also Greenhouse, "In Steps Big and Small, Supreme Court Moved Right," *New York Times*, July 1, 2007, A1, A18.

26 David G. Savage, "Justices Affirm Gun Rights," *Los Angeles Times*, June 27, 2008, A1.

27 Adam Liptak, "Stevens' Era, Nearing End, Takes on Edge," *New York Times*, January 26, 2010, A12.

28 Adam Liptak, "The Polarized Court," *New York Times*, May 11, 2014, SR1. See also Liptak, "Compromise at the Court Veils Its Rifts," *New York Times*, July 1, 2014, A1, A17.

29 Adam Liptak, "Right Divided, Disciplined Left Steers Justices," *New York Times*, July 1, 2015, A1, A19.

30 Adam Liptak, "A Cautious Supreme Court Sets a Modern Record for Consensus," *New York Times*, June 28, 2017, A16.

31 Tom Raum, AP, "Court Asserting Its Own Power," *Dallas Morning News*, June 30, 2006, A24.

32 Richard L. Pacelle Jr., *The Supreme Court in a Separation of Powers System* (New York: Routledge, 2015).

33 Abraham, *Judicial Process*, 364.

34 David S. Broder, "It Is the Judges Who Set the South on a New Course," *Dallas Morning News*, December 8, 1993, A17.

35 Robert G. McCloskey and Sanford Levinson, *The American Supreme Court*, 4th ed. (Chicago: University of Chicago Press, 1960, 2005), 14.

36 Tushnet, *Why the Constitution Matters*, 164. See also Roger C. Cramton and Paul D. Carrington, ed., *Reforming the Court: Team Limits for Supreme Court Justices* (Durham, NC: Carolina Academic Press, 2006.)

Appendix A

The Declaration of Independence

IN CONGRESS, July 4, 1776.

The unanimous Declaration of the thirteen united States of America, When in the Course of human events, it becomes necessary for one people to dissolve the political bands which have connected them with another, and to assume among the powers of the earth, the separate and equal station to which the Laws of Nature and of Nature's God entitle them, a decent respect to the opinions of mankind requires that they should declare the causes which impel them to the separation.

We hold these truths to be self-evident, that all men are created equal, that they are endowed by their Creator with certain unalienable Rights, that among these are Life, Liberty and the pursuit of Happiness.—That to secure these rights, Governments are instituted among Men, deriving their just powers from the consent of the governed.—That whenever any Form of Government becomes destructive of these ends, it is the Right of the People to alter or to abolish it, and to institute new Government, laying its foundation on such principles and organizing its powers in such form, as to them shall seem most likely to effect their Safety and Happiness. Prudence, indeed, will dictate that Governments long established should not be changed for light and transient causes; and accordingly all experience hath shewn, that mankind are more disposed to suffer, while evils are sufferable, than to right themselves by abolishing the forms to which they are accustomed. But when a long train of abuses and usurpations, pursuing invariably the same Object evinces a design to reduce them under absolute Despotism, it is their right, it is their duty, to throw off such Government, and to provide new Guards for their future security.—Such has been the patient sufferance of these Colonies; and such is now the necessity which constrains them to alter their former Systems of Government. The history of the present King of Great Britain is a history of repeated injuries and usurpations, all having in direct object the establishment of an absolute Tyranny over these States. To prove this, let Facts be submitted to a candid world.

He has refused his Assent to Laws, the most wholesome and necessary for the public good.

He has forbidden his Governors to pass Laws of immediate and pressing importance, unless suspended in their operation till his Assent should be obtained; and when so suspended, he has utterly neglected to attend to them.

He has refused to pass other Laws for the accommodation of large districts of people, unless those people would relinquish the right of Representation in the Legislature, a right inestimable to them and formidable to tyrants only.

He has called together legislative bodies at places unusual, uncomfortable, and distant from the depository of their public Records, for the sole purpose of fatiguing them into compliance with his measures.

He has dissolved Representative Houses repeatedly, for opposing with manly firmness his invasions on the rights of the people.

He has refused for a long time, after such dissolutions, to cause others to be elected; whereby the Legislative powers, incapable of Annihilation, have returned to the People at large for their exercise; the State remaining in the mean time exposed to all the dangers of invasion from without, and convulsions within.

He has endeavoured to prevent the population of these States; for that purpose obstructing the Laws for

Naturalization of Foreigners; refusing to pass others to encourage their migrations hither, and raising the conditions of new Appropriations of Lands.

He has obstructed the Administration of Justice, by refusing his Assent to Laws for establishing Judiciary powers.

He has made Judges dependent on his Will alone, for the tenure of their offices, and the amount and payment of their salaries.

He has erected a multitude of New Offices, and sent hither swarms of Officers to harrass our people, and eat out their substance.

He has kept among us, in times of peace, Standing Armies without the Consent of our legislatures.

He has affected to render the Military independent of and superior to the Civil power.

He has combined with others to subject us to a jurisdiction foreign to our constitution, and unacknowledged by our laws; giving his Assent to their Acts of pretended Legislation:

For Quartering large bodies of armed troops among us:

For protecting them, by a mock Trial, from punishment for any Murders which they should commit on the Inhabitants of these States:

For cutting off our Trade with all parts of the world:

For imposing Taxes on us without our Consent:

For depriving us in many cases, of the benefits of Trial by Jury:

For transporting us beyond Seas to be tried for pretended offences:

For abolishing the free System of English Laws in a neighbouring Province, establishing therein an Arbitrary government, and enlarging its Boundaries so as to render it at once an example and fit instrument for introducing the same absolute rule into these Colonies:

For taking away our Charters, abolishing our most valuable Laws, and altering fundamentally the Forms of our Governments:

For suspending our own Legislatures, and declaring themselves invested with power to legislate for us in all cases whatsoever.

He has abdicated Government here, by declaring us out of his Protection and waging War against us.

He has plundered our seas, ravaged our Coasts, burnt our towns, and destroyed the lives of our people.

He is at this time transporting large Armies of foreign Mercenaries to compleat the works of death, desolation and tyranny, already begun with circumstances of Cruelty & perfidy scarcely paralleled in the most barbarous ages, and totally unworthy of the Head of a civilized nation.

He has constrained our fellow Citizens taken Captive on the high Seas to bear Arms against their Country, to become the executioners of their friends and Brethren, or to fall themselves by their Hands.

He has excited domestic insurrections amongst us, and has endeavoured to bring on the inhabitants of our frontiers, the merciless Indian Savages, whose known rule of warfare, is an undistinguished destruction of all ages, sexes and conditions.

In every stage of these Oppressions We have Petitioned for Redress in the most humble terms: Our repeated Petitions have been answered only by repeated injury. A Prince whose character is thus marked by every act which may define a Tyrant, is unfit to be the ruler of a free people.

Nor have We been wanting in attentions to our British brethren. We have warned them from time to time of attempts by their legislature to extend an unwarrantable jurisdiction over us. We have reminded them of the circumstances of our emigration and settlement here. We have appealed to their native justice and magnanimity, and we have conjured them by the ties of our common kindred to disavow these usurpations, which, would inevitably interrupt our connections and correspondence. They too have been deaf to the voice of justice and of consanguinity. We must, therefore, acquiesce in the necessity, which denounces our Separation, and hold them, as we hold the rest of mankind, Enemies in War, in Peace Friends.

We, therefore, the Representatives of the united States of America, in General Congress, Assembled, appealing to the Supreme Judge of the world for the rectitude of our intentions, do, in the Name, and by Authority of the good People of these Colonies, solemnly publish and declare, That these United Colonies are, and of Right ought to be Free and Independent States; that they are Absolved from all Allegiance to the British Crown, and that all political connection between them and the State of Great Britain, is and ought to be totally dissolved; and that as Free and Independent States, they have full Power to levy War, conclude Peace, contract Alliances, establish Commerce, and to do all other Acts and Things which Independent States may of right do. And for the support of this Declaration, with a firm reliance on the protection of divine Providence, we mutually pledge to each other our Lives, our Fortunes and our sacred Honor.

Georgia:
Button Gwinnett
Lyman Hall
George Walton
North Carolina:
William Hooper
Joseph Hewes
John Penn
South Carolina:
Edward Rutledge
Thomas Heyward, Jr.
Thomas Lynch, Jr.
Arthur Middleton
Maryland:
Samuel Chase
William Paca
Thomas Stone
Charles Carroll of Carrollton

Virginia:
George Wythe
Richard Henry Lee
Thomas Jefferson
Benjamin Harrison
Thomas Nelson, Jr.
Francis Lightfoot Lee
Carter Braxton
Pennsylvania:
Robert Morris
Benjamin Rush
Benjamin Franklin
John Morton
George Clymer
James Smith
George Taylor
James Wilson
George Ross

Delaware:
Caesar Rodney
George Read
Thomas McKean
New York:
William Floyd
Philip Livingston
Francis Lewis
Lewis Morris
New Jersey:
Richard Stockton
John Witherspoon
Francis Hopkinson
John Hart
Abraham Clark
Rhode Island:
Stephen Hopkins
William Ellery

New Hampshire:
Josiah Bartlett
William Whipple
Matthew Thornton
Massachusetts:
John Hancock
Samuel Adams
John Adams
Robert Treat Paine
Elbridge Gerry
Connecticut:
Roger Sherman
Samuel Huntington
William Williams
Oliver Wolcott

Appendix B

CONSTITUTION OF THE UNITED STATES

WE THE PEOPLE of the United States, in order to form a more perfect union, establish justice, insure domestic tranquility, provide for the common defense, promote the general welfare, and secure the blessings of liberty to ourselves and our posterity, do ordain and establish this Constitution for the United States of America.

ARTICLE I

Section 1. All legislative powers herein granted shall be vested in a Congress of the United States, which shall consist of a Senate and House of Representatives.

Section 2. The House of Representatives shall be composed of members chosen every second year by the people of the several states, and the electors in each state shall have the qualifications requisite for electors of the most numerous branch of the state legislature.

No person shall be a Representative who shall not have attained to the age of twenty five years, and been seven years a citizen of the United States, and who shall not, when elected, be an inhabitant of that state in which he shall be chosen.

Representatives and direct taxes shall be apportioned among the several states which may be included within this union, according to their respective numbers, which shall be determined by adding to the whole number of free persons, including those bound to service for a term of years, and excluding Indians not taxed, three fifths of all other persons. The actual enumeration shall be made within three years after the first meeting of the Congress of the United States, and within every subsequent term of ten years, in such manner as they shall by law direct. The number of Representatives shall not exceed one for every thirty thousand, but each state shall have at least one Representative; and until such enumeration shall be made, the state of New Hampshire shall be entitled to choose three, Massachusetts eight, Rhode Island and Providence Plantations one, Connecticut five, New York six, New Jersey four, Pennsylvania eight, Delaware one, Maryland six, Virginia ten, North Carolina five, South Carolina five, and Georgia three.

When vacancies happen in the representation from any state, the executive authority thereof shall issue writs of election to fill such vacancies.

The House of Representatives shall choose their speaker and other officers; and shall have the sole power of impeachment.

Section 3. The Senate of the United States shall be composed of two Senators from each state, chosen by the legislature thereof, for six years; and each Senator shall have one vote.

Immediately after they shall be assembled in consequence of the first election, they shall be divided as equally as may be into three classes. The seats of the Senators of the first class shall be vacated at the expiration of the second year, of the second class at the expiration of the fourth year, and the third class at the expiration of the sixth year, so that one third may be chosen every second year; and if vacancies happen by resignation, or otherwise, during the recess of the -legislature of any state, the executive thereof may make temporary appointments until the next meeting of the legislature, which shall then fill such vacancies.

No person shall be a Senator who shall not have attained to the age of thirty years, and been nine years a citizen of the United States and who shall not, when elected, be an inhabitant of that state for which he shall be chosen.

The Vice President of the United States shall be President of the Senate, but shall have no vote, unless they be equally divided.

The Senate shall choose their other officers, and also a President pro tempore, in the absence of the Vice President, or when he shall exercise the office of President of the United States.

The Senate shall have the sole power to try all impeachments. When sitting for that purpose, they shall be on oath or affirmation. When the President of the United States is tried, the Chief Justice shall preside: And no person shall be convicted without the concurrence of two thirds of the members present.

Judgment in cases of impeachment shall not extend further than to removal from office, and disqualification to hold and enjoy any office of honor, trust or profit under the United States: but the party convicted shall nevertheless be liable and subject to indictment, trial, judgment and punishment, according to law.

Section 4. The times, places and manner of holding elections for Senators and Representatives, shall be prescribed in each state by the legislature thereof; but the Congress may at any time by law make or alter such regulations, except as to the places of choosing Senators.

The Congress shall assemble at least once in every year, and such meeting shall be on the first Monday in December, unless they shall by law appoint a different day.

Section 5. Each House shall be the judge of the elections, returns and qualifications of its own members, and a majority of each shall constitute a quorum to do business; but a smaller number may adjourn from day to day, and may be authorized to compel the attendance of absent members, in such manner, and under such penalties as each House may provide.

Each House may determine the rules of its proceedings, punish its members for disorderly behavior, and, with the concurrence of two thirds, expel a member.

Each House shall keep a journal of its proceedings, and from time to time publish the same, excepting such parts as may in their judgment require secrecy; and the yeas and nays of the members of either House on any question shall, at the desire of one fifth of those present, be entered on the journal.

Neither House, during the session of Congress, shall, without the consent of the other, adjourn for more than three days, nor to any other place than that in which the two Houses shall be sitting.

Section 6. The Senators and Representatives shall receive a compensation for their services, to be ascertained by law, and paid out of the treasury of the United States. They shall in all cases, except treason, felony and breach of the peace, be privileged from arrest during their attendance at the session of their respective houses, and in going to and returning from the same; and for any speech or debate in either house, they shall not be questioned in any other place.

No Senator or Representative shall, during the time for which he was elected, be appointed to any civil office under the authority of the United States, which shall have been created, or the emoluments whereof shall have been increased during such time: and no person holding any office under the United States, shall be a member of either House during his continuance in office.

Section 7. All bills for raising revenue shall originate in the House of Representatives; but the Senate may propose or concur with amendments as on other Bills.

Every bill which shall have passed the House of Representatives and the Senate, shall, before it become a law, be presented to the President of the United States; if he approve he shall sign it, but if not he shall return it, with his objections to that house in which it shall have originated, who shall enter the objections at large on their journal, and proceed to reconsider it. If after such reconsideration two thirds of that house shall agree to pass the bill, it shall be sent, together with the objections, to the other house, by which it shall -likewise be reconsidered, and if approved by two thirds of that house, it shall become a law. But in all such cases the votes of both houses shall be determined by yeas and nays, and the names of the persons voting for and against the bill shall be entered on the journal of each house respectively. If any bill shall not be returned by the President within ten days (Sundays excepted) after it shall have been presented to him, the same shall be a law, in like manner as if he had signed it, unless the Congress by their adjournment prevent its return, in which case it shall not be a law.

Every order, resolution, or vote to which the concurrence of the Senate and House of Representatives may be necessary (except on a question of adjournment) shall be presented to the President of the United States; and before the same shall take effect, shall be approved by him, or being disapproved by him, shall be repassed by two thirds of the Senate and House of Representatives, according to the rules and limitations prescribed in the case of a bill.

Section 8.   *enumerated powers* The Congress shall have power to lay and collect taxes, duties, imposts and excises, to pay the debts and provide for the common defense and general welfare of the United States; but all duties, imposts and excises shall be uniform throughout the United States;

To borrow money on the credit of the United States;

To regulate commerce with foreign nations, and among the several states, and with the Indian tribes;

To establish a uniform rule of naturalization, and uniform laws on the subject of bankruptcies throughout the United States;

To coin money, regulate the value thereof, and of foreign coin, and fix the standard of weights and measures;

To provide for the punishment of counterfeiting the securities and current coin of the United States;

To establish post offices and post roads;

To promote the progress of science and useful arts, by securing for limited times to authors and inventors the exclusive right to their respective writings and discoveries;

To constitute tribunals inferior to the Supreme Court;

To define and punish piracies and felonies committed on the high seas, and offenses against the law of nations;

To declare war, grant letters of marque and reprisal, and make rules concerning captures on land and water;

To raise and support armies, but no appropriation of money to that use shall be for a longer term than two years;

To provide and maintain a navy;

To make rules for the government and regulation of the land and naval forces;

To provide for calling forth the militia to execute the laws of the union, suppress insurrections and repel invasions;

To provide for organizing, arming, and disciplining, the militia, and for governing such part of them as may be employed in the service of the United States, reserving to the states respectively, the appointment of the officers, and the authority of training the militia according to the discipline prescribed by Congress;

To exercise exclusive legislation in all cases whatsoever, over such District (not exceeding ten miles square) as may, by cession of particular states, and the acceptance of Congress, become the seat of the government of the United States, and to exercise like authority over all places purchased by the consent of the legislature of the state in which the same shall be, for the erection of forts, magazines, arsenals, dockyards, and other needful buildings;—and

To make all laws which shall be necessary and proper for carrying into execution the foregoing powers, and all other powers vested by this Constitution in the government of the United States, or in any department or officer thereof.

Section 9.   The migration or importation of such—persons as any of the states now existing shall think proper to admit, shall not be prohibited by the Congress prior to the year one thousand eight hundred and eight, but a tax or duty may be imposed on such importation, not exceeding ten dollars for each person.

The privilege of the writ of habeas corpus shall not be suspended, unless when in cases of rebellion or invasion the public safety may require it.

No bill of attainder or ex post facto Law shall be passed.

No capitation, or other direct, tax shall be laid, unless in proportion to the census or enumeration herein before directed to be taken.

No tax or duty shall be laid on articles exported from any state.

No preference shall be given by any regulation of commerce or revenue to the ports of one state over those of another: nor shall vessels bound to, or from, one state, be obliged to enter, clear or pay duties in another.

No money shall be drawn from the treasury, but in consequence of appropriations made by law; and a regular statement and account of receipts and expenditures of all public money shall be published from time to time.

No title of nobility shall be granted by the United States: and no person holding any office of profit or trust under them, shall, without the consent of the Congress, accept of any present, emolument, office, or title, of any kind whatever, from any king, prince, or foreign state.

Section 10. No state shall enter into any treaty, alliance, or confederation; grant letters of marque and reprisal; coin money; emit bills of credit; make anything but gold and silver coin a tender in payment of debts; pass any bill of attainder, ex post facto law, or law impairing the obligation of contracts, or grant any title of nobility.

No state shall, without the consent of the Congress, lay any imposts or duties on imports or exports, except what may be absolutely necessary for executing its inspection laws: and the net produce of all duties and imposts, laid by any state on imports or exports, shall be for the use of the treasury of the United States; and all such laws shall be subject to the revision and control of the Congress.

No state shall, without the consent of Congress, lay any duty of tonnage, keep troops, or ships of war in time of peace, enter into any agreement or compact with another state, or with a foreign power, or engage in war, unless actually invaded, or in such imminent danger as will not admit of delay.

ARTICLE II

Section 1. The executive power shall be vested in a President of the United States of America. He shall hold his office during the term of four years, and, together with the Vice President, chosen for the same term, be elected, as follows:

Each state shall appoint, in such manner as the Legislature thereof may direct, a number of electors, equal to the whole number of Senators and Representatives to which the state may be entitled in the Congress: but no Senator or Representative, or person holding an office of trust or profit under the United States, shall be appointed an elector.

The electors shall meet in their respective states, and vote by ballot for two persons, of whom one at least shall not be an inhabitant of the same state with themselves. And they shall make a list of all the persons voted for, and of the number of votes for each; which list they shall sign and certify, and transmit sealed to the seat of the government of the United States, directed to the President of the Senate. The President of the Senate shall, in the presence of the Senate and House of Representatives, open all the certificates, and the votes shall then be counted. The person having the greatest number of votes shall be the President, if such number be a majority of the whole number of electors appointed; and if there be more than one who have such majority, and have an equal number of votes, then the House of Representatives shall immediately choose by ballot one of them for President; and if no person have a majority, then from the five highest on the list the said House shall in like manner choose the President. But in choosing the President, the votes shall be taken by States, the representation from each state having one vote; a quorum for this purpose shall consist of a member or members from two thirds of the states, and a majority of all the states shall be necessary to a choice. In every case, after the choice of the President, the person having the greatest number of votes of the electors shall be the Vice President. But if there should remain two or more who have equal votes, the Senate shall choose from them by ballot the Vice President.

The Congress may determine the time of choosing the electors, and the day on which they shall give their votes; which day shall be the same throughout the United States.

No person except a natural-born citizen, or a citizen of the United States, at the time of the adoption of this Constitution, shall be eligible to the office of President; neither shall any person be eligible to that office who shall not have attained to the age of thirty five years, and been fourteen Years a resident within the United States.

In case of the removal of the President from office, or of his death, resignation, or inability to discharge the powers and duties of the said office, the same shall devolve on the Vice President, and the Congress may by law provide for the case of removal, death, resignation or inability, both of the President and Vice President, declaring what officer shall then act as President, and such officer shall act accordingly, until the disability be removed, or a President shall be elected.

The President shall, at stated times, receive for his services, a compensation, which shall neither be increased nor diminished during the period for which he shall have been elected, and he shall not receive within that period any other emolument from the United States, or any of them.

Before he enter on the execution of his office, he shall take the following oath or affirmation:—"I do solemnly swear (or affirm) that I will faithfully execute the office of President of the United States, and will to the best of my ability, preserve, protect and defend the Constitution of the United States."

Section 2.   The President shall be commander in chief of the Army and Navy of the United States, and of the militia of the several states, when called into the actual service of the United States; he may require the opinion, in writing, of the principal officer in each of the executive departments, upon any subject relating to the duties of their respective offices, and he shall have power to grant reprieves and pardons for offenses against the United States, except in cases of impeachment.

He shall have power, by and with the advice and consent of the Senate, to make treaties, provided two thirds of the Senators present concur; and he shall nominate, and by and with the advice and consent of the Senate, shall appoint ambassadors, other public ministers and consuls, judges of the Supreme Court, and all other officers of the United States, whose appointments are not herein otherwise provided for, and which shall be by law: but the Congress may by law vest the appointment of such inferior officers, as they think proper, in the President alone, in the courts of law, or in the heads of departments.

The President shall have power to fill up all vacancies that may happen during the recess of the Senate, by granting commissions which shall expire at the end of their next session.

Section 3.   He shall from time to time give to the Congress information of the state of the union, and recommend to their consideration such measures as he shall judge necessary and expedient; he may, on extraordinary occasions, convene both Houses, or either of them, and in case of disagreement between them, with respect to the time of adjournment, he may adjourn them to such time as he shall think proper; he shall receive ambassadors and other public ministers; he shall take care that the laws be faithfully executed, and shall commission all the officers of the United States.

Section 4.   The President, Vice President and all civil officers of the United States, shall be removed from office on impeachment for, and conviction of, treason, bribery, or other high crimes and misdemeanors.

ARTICLE III

Section 1.   The judicial power of the United States, shall be vested in one Supreme Court, and in such inferior courts as the Congress may from time to time ordain and establish. The judges, both of the supreme and inferior courts, shall hold their offices during good behaviour, and shall, at stated times, receive for their services, a compensation, which shall not be diminished during their continuance in office.

Section 2.   The judicial power shall extend to all cases, in law and equity, arising under this Constitution, the laws of the United States, and treaties made, or which shall be made, under their authority;—to all cases affecting ambassadors, other public ministers and consuls;—to all cases of admiralty and maritime jurisdiction;—to controversies to which the United States shall be a party;—to controversies between two or more states;—between a state and citizens of another state;—between citizens of different states;—between citizens of the same state claiming lands under grants of different states, and between a state, or the citizens thereof, and foreign states, citizens or subjects.

In all cases affecting ambassadors, other public ministers and consuls, and those in which a state shall be party, the Supreme Court shall have original jurisdiction. In all the other cases before mentioned, the Supreme Court shall have appellate jurisdiction, both as to law and fact, with such exceptions, and under such regulations as the Congress shall make.

The trial of all crimes, except in cases of impeachment, shall be by jury; and such trial shall be held in the state where the said crimes shall have been committed; but when not committed within any state, the trial shall be at such place or places as the -Congress may by law have directed.

Section 3. Treason against the United States, shall consist only in levying war against them, or in adhering to their enemies, giving them aid and comfort. No person shall be convicted of treason unless on the testimony of two witnesses to the same overt act, or on confession in open court.

The Congress shall have power to declare the punishment of treason, but no attainder of treason shall work corruption of blood, or forfeiture except during the life of the person attainted.

ARTICLE IV

Section 1. Full faith and credit shall be given in each state to the public acts, records, and judicial proceedings of every other state. And the Congress may by general laws prescribe the manner in which such acts, records, and proceedings shall be proved, and the effect thereof.

Section 2. The citizens of each state shall be entitled to all privileges and immunities of citizens in the several states.

A person charged in any state with treason, felony, or other crime, who shall flee from justice, and be found in another state, shall on demand of the -executive -authority of the state from which he fled, be delivered up, to be removed to the state having jurisdiction of the crime.

No person held to service or labor in one state, under the laws thereof, escaping into another, shall, in consequence of any law or regulation therein, be discharged from such service or labor, but shall be delivered up on claim of the party to whom such service or labor may be due.

Section 3. New states may be admitted by the Congress into this union; but no new states shall be formed or erected within the jurisdiction of any other state; nor any state be formed by the junction of two or more states, or parts of states, without the consent of the legislatures of the states concerned as well as of the Congress.

The Congress shall have power to dispose of and make all needful rules and regulations respecting the territory or other property belonging to the United States; and nothing in this Constitution shall be so construed as to prejudice any claims of the United States, or of any particular state.

Section 4. The United States shall guarantee to every state in this union a republican form of government, and shall protect each of them against invasion; and on application of the legislature, or of the executive (when the legislature cannot be convened) against domestic violence.

ARTICLE V

The Congress, whenever two thirds of both houses shall deem it necessary, shall propose amendments to this Constitution, or, on the application of the legislatures of two thirds of the several states, shall call a convention for proposing amendments, which, in either case, shall be valid to all intents and purposes, as part of this Constitution, when ratified by the legislatures of three fourths of the several states, or by conventions in three fourths thereof, as the one or the other mode of ratification may be proposed by the Congress; provided that no amendment which may be made prior to the year one thousand eight hundred and eight shall in any manner affect the first and fourth clauses in the ninth section of the first article; and that no state, without its consent, shall be deprived of its equal suffrage in the Senate.

ARTICLE VI

All debts contracted and engagements entered into, before the adoption of this Constitution, shall be as valid against the United States under this Constitution, as under the Confederation.

This Constitution, and the laws of the United States which shall be made in pursuance thereof; and all treaties made, or which shall be made, under the authority of the United States, shall be the supreme law of the land; and the judges in every state shall be bound thereby, anything in the Constitution or laws of any State to the contrary notwithstanding.

The Senators and Representatives before mentioned, and the members of the several state legislatures, and all executive and judicial officers, both of the United States and of the several states, shall be bound by oath or affirmation, to support this Constitution; but no religious test shall ever be required as a qualification to any office or public trust under the United States.

ARTICLE VII

The ratification of the conventions of nine states, shall be sufficient for the establishment of this Constitution between the states so ratifying the same.

Done in convention by the unanimous consent of the states present the seventeenth day of September in the year of our Lord one thousand seven hundred and eighty seven and of the independence of the United States of America the twelfth. In witness whereof we have hereunto subscribed our Names,

Virginia
G. Washington—Presidt. and deputy from Virginia
New Hampshire
John Langdon, Nicholas Gilman
Massachusetts
Nathaniel Gorham, Rufus King
Connecticut
Wm. Saml. Johnson, Roger Sherman
New York
Alexander Hamilton
New Jersey
Wil. Livingston, David Brearly, Wm. Paterson, Jona. Dayton
Pennsylvania
B. Franklin, Thomas Mifflin, Robt. Morris, Geo. Clymer, Thos. FitzSimons, Jared Ingersoll, James Wilson, Gouv Morris

Delaware
Geo. Read, Gunning Bedford jun, John Dickinson, Richard Bassett, Jaco. Broom
Maryland
James McHenry, Dan of St Thos. Jenifer, Danl Carroll
Virginia
John Blair—, James Madison Jr.
North Carolina
Wm. Blount, Richd. Dobbs Spaight, Hu Williamson
South Carolina
J. Rutledge, Charles Cotesworth Pinckney, Charles Pinckney, Pierce Butler
Georgia
William Few, Abr Baldwin

Bill of Rights

Amendments I through X of the Constitution

AMENDMENT I

Congress shall make no law respecting an establishment of religion, or prohibiting the free exercise thereof; or abridging the freedom of speech, or of the press; or the right of the people peaceably to assemble, and to petition the government for a redress of grievances.

AMENDMENT II

A well regulated militia, being necessary to the security of a free state, the right of the people to keep and bear arms, shall not be infringed.

AMENDMENT III

No soldier shall, in time of peace be quartered in any house, without the consent of the owner, nor in time of war, but in a manner to be prescribed by law.

AMENDMENT IV

The right of the people to be secure in their persons, houses, papers, and effects, against unreasonable searches and seizures, shall not be violated, and no warrants shall issue, but upon probable cause, supported by oath or affirmation, and particularly describing the place to be searched, and the persons or things to be seized.

AMENDMENT V

No person shall be held to answer for a capital, or otherwise infamous crime, unless on a presentment or indictment of a grand jury, except in cases arising in the land or naval forces, or in the militia, when in actual service in time of war or public danger; nor shall any person be subject for the same offense to be twice put in jeopardy of life or limb; nor shall be compelled in any criminal case to be a witness against himself, nor be deprived of life, liberty, or property, without due process of law; nor shall private property be taken for public use, without just compensation.

AMENDMENT VI

In all criminal prosecutions, the accused shall enjoy the right to a speedy and public trial, by an impartial jury of the state and district wherein the crime shall have been committed, which district shall have been previously ascertained by law, and to be informed of the nature and cause of the accusation; to be confronted with the witnesses against him; to have compulsory process for

obtaining witnesses in his favor, and to have the assistance of counsel for his defense.

AMENDMENT VII

In suits at common law, where the value in controversy shall exceed twenty dollars, the right of trial by jury shall be preserved, and no fact tried by a jury, shall be otherwise reexamined in any court of the United States, than according to the rules of the common law.

AMENDMENT VIII

Excessive bail shall not be required, nor excessive fines imposed, nor cruel and unusual punishments inflicted.

AMENDMENT IX

The enumeration in the Constitution, of certain rights, shall not be construed to deny or disparage others retained by the people.

AMENDMENT X

The powers not delegated to the United States by the Constitution, nor prohibited by it to the states, are reserved to the states respectively, or to the people.

Additional Amendments

AMENDMENT XI

(1798)

The judicial power of the United States shall not be construed to extend to any suit in law or equity, commenced or prosecuted against one of the United States by citizens of another state, or by citizens or subjects of any foreign state.

AMENDMENT XII

(1804)

The electors shall meet in their respective states and vote by ballot for President and Vice President, one of whom, at least, shall not be an inhabitant of the same

state with themselves; they shall name in their ballots the person voted for as President, and in distinct ballots the person voted for as Vice President, and they shall make distinct lists of all persons voted for as President, and of all persons voted for as Vice President, and of the number of votes for each, which lists they shall sign and certify, and transmit sealed to the seat of the government of the United States, directed to the President of the Senate;—The President of the Senate shall, in the presence of the Senate and House of Representatives, open all the certificates and the votes shall then be counted;—the person having the greatest number of votes for President, shall be the President, if such number be a majority of the whole number of electors appointed; and if no person have such majority, then from the persons having the highest numbers not exceeding three on the list of those voted for as President, the House of Representatives shall choose immediately, by ballot, the President. But in choosing the President, the votes shall be taken by states, the representation from each state having one vote; a quorum for this purpose shall consist of a member or members from two-thirds of the states, and a majority of all the states shall be necessary to a choice. And if the House of Representatives shall not choose a President whenever the right of choice shall devolve upon them, before the fourth day of March next following, then the Vice President shall act as President, as in the case of the death or other constitutional disability of the President. The person having the greatest number of votes as Vice President, shall be the Vice President, if such number be a majority of the whole number of electors appointed, and if no person have a majority, then from the two highest numbers on the list, the Senate shall choose the Vice President; a quorum for the purpose shall consist of two-thirds of the whole number of Senators, and a majority of the whole number shall be necessary to a choice. But no person constitutionally ineligible to the office of President shall be eligible to that of Vice President of the United States.

AMENDMENT XIII

(1865)

Section 1.   Neither slavery nor involuntary servitude, except as a punishment for crime whereof the party shall have been duly convicted, shall exist within the United States, or any place subject to their jurisdiction.

Section 2.   Congress shall have power to enforce this article by appropriate legislation.

AMENDMENT XIV

(1868)

Section 1.   All persons born or naturalized in the United States, and subject to the jurisdiction thereof, are citizens of the United States and of the state wherein they reside. No state shall make or enforce any law which shall abridge the privileges or immunities of citizens of the United States; nor shall any state deprive any person of life, liberty, or property, without due process of law; nor deny to any person within its jurisdiction the equal protection of the laws.

Section 2.   Representatives shall be apportioned among the several states according to their respective numbers, counting the whole number of persons in each state, excluding Indians not taxed. But when the right to vote at any election for the choice of electors for President and Vice President of the United States, Representatives in Congress, the executive and judicial officers of a state, or the members of the legislature thereof, is denied to any of the male inhabitants of such state, being twenty-one years of age, and citizens of the United States, or in any way abridged, except for participation in rebellion, or other crime, the basis of representation therein shall be reduced in the proportion which the number of such male citizens shall bear to the whole number of male citizens twenty-one years of age in such state.

Section 3.   No person shall be a Senator or Representative in Congress, or elector of President and Vice President, or hold any office, civil or military, under the United States, or under any state, who, having previously taken an oath, as a member of Congress, or as an officer of the United States, or as a member of any state legislature, or as an executive or judicial officer of any state, to support the Constitution of the United States, shall have engaged in insurrection or rebellion against the same, or given aid or comfort to the enemies thereof. But Congress may by a vote of two-thirds of each House, remove such disability.

Section 4.   The validity of the public debt of the United States, authorized by law, including debts incurred for payment of pensions and bounties for services in suppressing insurrection or rebellion, shall not be questioned. But neither the United States nor any state shall assume or pay any debt or obligation incurred in aid of insurrection or rebellion against the United States, or any claim for the loss or emancipation of any slave; but all such debts, obligations and claims shall be held illegal and void.

Section 5.   The Congress shall have power to enforce, by appropriate legislation, the provisions of this article.

AMENDMENT XV

(1870)

Section 1. The right of citizens of the United States to vote shall not be denied or abridged by the United States or by any state on account of race, color, or previous condition of servitude.

Section 2. The Congress shall have power to enforce this article by appropriate legislation.

AMENDMENT XVI

(1913)

The Congress shall have power to lay and collect taxes on incomes, from whatever source derived, without apportionment among the several states, and without regard to any census of enumeration.

AMENDMENT XVII

(1913)

The Senate of the United States shall be composed of two Senators from each state, elected by the people thereof, for six years; and each Senator shall have one vote. The electors in each state shall have the qualifications requisite for electors of the most numerous branch of the state legislatures.

When vacancies happen in the representation of any state in the Senate, the executive authority of such state shall issue writs of election to fill such vacancies: Provided, that the legislature of any state may empower the executive thereof to make temporary appointments until the people fill the vacancies by election as the legislature may direct.

This amendment shall not be so construed as to affect the election or term of any Senator chosen before it becomes valid as part of the Constitution.

AMENDMENT XVIII

(1919)

Section 1. After one year from the ratification of this article the manufacture, sale, or transportation of intoxicating liquors within, the importation thereof into, or the exportation thereof from the United States and all territory subject to the jurisdiction thereof for beverage purposes is hereby prohibited.

Section 2. The Congress and the several states shall have concurrent power to enforce this article by appropriate legislation.

Section 3. This article shall be inoperative unless it shall have been ratified as an amendment to the Constitution by the legislatures of the several states, as provided in the Constitution, within seven years from the date of the submission hereof to the states by the Congress.

AMENDMENT XIX

(1920)

The right of citizens of the United States to vote shall not be denied or abridged by the United States or by any state on account of sex.

Congress shall have power to enforce this article by appropriate legislation.

AMENDMENT XX

(1933)

Section 1. The terms of the President and Vice President shall end at noon on the 20th day of January, and the terms of Senators and Representatives at noon on the 3d day of January, of the years in which such terms would have ended if this article had not been ratified; and the terms of their successors shall then begin.

Section 2. The Congress shall assemble at least once in every year, and such meeting shall begin at noon on the 3d day of January, unless they shall by law appoint a different day.

Section 3. If, at the time fixed for the beginning of the term of the President, the President-elect shall have died, the Vice President-elect shall become President. If a President shall not have been chosen before the time fixed for the beginning of his term, or if the -President-elect shall have failed to qualify, then the Vice President-elect shall act as President until a President shall have qualified;

and the Congress may by law provide for the case wherein neither a President elect nor a Vice President-elect shall have qualified, declaring who shall then act as President, or the manner in which one who is to act shall be selected, and such person shall act accordingly until a President or Vice President shall have qualified.

Section 4.   The Congress may by law provide for the case of the death of any of the persons from whom the House of Representatives may choose a President whenever the right of choice shall have devolved upon them, and for the case of the death of any of the persons from whom the Senate may choose a Vice President whenever the right of choice shall have devolved upon them.

Section 5.   Sections 1 and 2 shall take effect on the 15th day of October following the ratification of this article.

Section 6.   This article shall be inoperative unless it shall have been ratified as an amendment to the Constitution by the legislatures of three-fourths of the several states within seven years from the date of its submission.

AMENDMENT XXI

(1933)

Section 1.   The eighteenth article of amendment to the Constitution of the United States is hereby repealed.

Section 2.   The transportation or importation into any state, territory, or possession of the United States for delivery or use therein of intoxicating liquors, in violation of the laws thereof, is hereby prohibited.

Section 3.   This article shall be inoperative unless it shall have been ratified as an amendment to the Constitution by conventions in the several states, as provided in the Constitution, within seven years from the date of the submission hereof to the states by the Congress.

AMENDMENT XXII

(1951)

Section 1.   No person shall be elected to the office of the President more than twice, and no person who has

held the office of President, or acted as President, for more than two years of a term to which some other person was elected President shall be elected to the office of the President more than once. But this article shall not apply to any person holding the office of President when this article was proposed by the Congress, and shall not prevent any person who may be holding the office of President, or acting as President, during the term within which this article becomes operative from holding the office of President or acting as President during the remainder of such term.

Section 2.   This article shall be inoperative unless it shall have been ratified as an amendment to the Constitution by the legislatures of three-fourths of the several states within seven years from the date of its submission to the states by the Congress.

AMENDMENT XXIII

(1961)

Section 1.   The District constituting the seat of government of the United States shall appoint in such manner as the Congress may direct:

A number of electors of President and Vice President equal to the whole number of Senators and Representatives in Congress to which the District would be entitled if it were a state, but in no event more than the least populous state; they shall be in addition to those appointed by the states, but they shall be considered, for the purposes of the election of President and Vice President, to be electors appointed by a state; and they shall meet in the District and perform such duties as provided by the twelfth article of amendment.

Section 2.   The Congress shall have power to enforce this article by appropriate legislation.

AMENDMENT XXIV

(1964)

Section 1.   The right of citizens of the United States to vote in any primary or other election for President or Vice President, for electors for President or Vice President, or for Senator or Representative in Congress, shall not be denied or abridged by the United States or any state by reason of failure to pay any poll tax or other tax.

Section 2. The Congress shall have power to enforce this article by appropriate legislation.

AMENDMENT XXV

(1967)

Section 1. In case of the removal of the President from office or of his death or resignation, the Vice President shall become President.

Section 2. Whenever there is a vacancy in the office of the Vice President, the President shall nominate a Vice President who shall take office upon confirmation by a majority vote of both Houses of Congress.

Section 3. Whenever the President transmits to the President pro tempore of the Senate and the Speaker of the House of Representatives his written declaration that he is unable to discharge the powers and duties of his office, and until he transmits to them a written declaration to the contrary, such powers and duties shall be discharged by the Vice President as Acting President.

Section 4. Whenever the Vice President and a majority of either the principal officers of the executive departments or of such other body as Congress may by law provide, transmit to the President pro tempore of the Senate and the Speaker of the House of Representatives their written declaration that the President is unable to discharge the powers and duties of his office, the Vice President shall immediately assume the powers and duties of the office as Acting President.

Thereafter, when the President transmits to the President pro tempore of the Senate and the Speaker

of the House of Representatives his written declaration that no inability exists, he shall resume the powers and duties of his office unless the Vice President and a majority of either the principal officers of the executive department or of such other body as Congress may by law provide, transmit within four days to the President pro tempore of the Senate and the Speaker of the House of Representatives their written declaration that the President is unable to discharge the powers and duties of his office. Thereupon Congress shall decide the issue, assembling within forty-eight hours for that purpose if not in session. If the Congress, within twenty-one days after receipt of the latter written declaration, or, if Congress is not in session, within twenty-one days after Congress is required to assemble, determines by two-thirds vote of both Houses that the President is unable to discharge the powers and duties of his office, the Vice President shall continue to discharge the same as Acting President; otherwise, the President shall resume the powers and duties of his office.

AMENDMENT XXVI

(1971)

Section 1. The right of citizens of the United States, who are 18 years of age or older, to vote, shall not be denied or abridged by the United States or any state on account of age.

Section 2. The Congress shall have the power to enforce this article by appropriate legislation.

AMENDMENT XXVII

(1992)

No law varying the compensation for the services of the Senators and Representatives shall take effect until an election of Representatives shall have intervened.

Appendix C

Federalist Number 10

The Union as a Safeguard Against Domestic Faction and Insurrection

Author: James Madison

To the People of the State of New York:

AMONG the numerous advantages promised by a well-constructed Union, none deserves to be more accurately developed than its tendency to break and control the violence of faction. The friend of popular governments never finds himself so much alarmed for their character and fate, as when he contemplates their propensity to this dangerous vice. He will not fail, therefore, to set a due value on any plan which, without violating the principles to which he is attached, provides a proper cure for it. The instability, injustice, and confusion introduced into the public councils, have, in truth, been the mortal diseases under which popular governments have everywhere perished; as they continue to be the favorite and fruitful topics from which the adversaries to liberty derive their most specious declamations. The valuable improvements made by the American constitutions on the popular models, both ancient and modern, cannot certainly be too much admired; but it would be an unwarrantable partiality, to contend that they have as effectually obviated the danger on this side, as was wished and expected. Complaints are everywhere heard from our most considerate and virtuous citizens, equally the friends of public and private faith, and of public and personal liberty, that our governments are too unstable, that the public good is disregarded in the conflicts of rival parties, and that measures are too often decided, not according to the rules of justice and the rights of the minor party, but by the superior force of an interested and overbearing majority. However anxiously we may wish that these complaints had no foundation, the evidence, of known facts will not permit us to deny that

they are in some degree true. It will be found, indeed, on a candid review of our situation, that some of the distresses under which we labor have been erroneously charged on the operation of our governments; but it will be found, at the same time, that other causes will not alone account for many of our heaviest misfortunes; and, particularly, for that prevailing and increasing distrust of public engagements, and alarm for private rights, which are echoed from one end of the continent to the other. These must be chiefly, if not wholly, effects of the unsteadiness and injustice with which a factious spirit has tainted our public administrations.

By a faction, I understand a number of citizens, whether amounting to a majority or a minority of the whole, who are united and actuated by some common impulse of passion, or of interest, adverse to the rights of other citizens, or to the permanent and aggregate interests of the community.

There are two methods of curing the mischiefs of faction: the one, by removing its causes; the other, by controlling its effects.

There are again two methods of removing the causes of faction: the one, by destroying the liberty which is essential to its existence; the other, by giving to every citizen the same opinions, the same passions, and the same interests.

It could never be more truly said than of the first remedy, that it was worse than the disease. Liberty is to faction what air is to fire, an aliment without which it instantly expires. But it could not be less folly to abolish liberty, which is essential to political life, because it nourishes faction, than it would be to wish the annihilation of air, which is essential to animal life, because it imparts to fire its destructive agency.

The second expedient is as impracticable as the first would be unwise. As long as the reason of man -continues fallible, and he is at liberty to exercise it, different opinions will be formed. As long as the connection subsists between his reason and his self-love, his opinions and his passions will have a reciprocal influence on each other; and the former will be objects to which the latter will attach themselves. The diversity in the faculties of men, from which the rights of property originate, is not less an insuperable obstacle to a uniformity of interests. The protection of these faculties is the first object of government. From the protection of different and unequal faculties of acquiring property, the possession of different degrees and kinds of property immediately results; and from the influence of these on the sentiments and views of the respective proprietors, ensues a division of the society into different interests and parties.

The latent causes of faction are thus sown in the nature of man; and we see them everywhere brought into different degrees of activity, according to the different circumstances of civil society. A zeal for different opinions concerning religion, concerning government, and many other points, as well of speculation as of practice; an attachment to different leaders ambitious-ly contending for pre-eminence and power; or to persons of other descriptions whose fortunes have been interesting to the human passions, have, in turn, divided mankind into parties, inflamed them with mutual animosity, and rendered them much more disposed to vex and oppress each other than to co-operate for their common good. So strong is this propensity of mankind to fall into mutual animosities, that where no substantial occasion presents itself, the most frivolous and fanciful distinctions have been sufficient to kindle their unfriendly passions and excite their most violent conflicts. But the most common and durable source of factions has been the various and unequal distribution of property. Those who hold and those who are without property have ever formed distinct interests in society. Those who are creditors, and those who are debtors, fall under a like discrimination. A landed interest, a manufacturing interest, a mercantile interest, a moneyed interest, with many lesser interests, grow up of necessity in civilized nations, and divide them into different classes, actuated by different sentiments and views. The regulation of these various and interfering interests forms the principal task of modern legislation, and involves the spirit of party and faction in the necessary and ordinary operations of the government.

No man is allowed to be a judge in his own cause, because his interest would certainly bias his judgment, and, not improbably, corrupt his integrity. With equal, nay with greater reason, a body of men are unfit to be both judges and parties at the same time; yet what are many of the most important acts of legislation, but so many judicial determinations, not indeed concerning the rights of single persons, but concerning the rights of large bodies of citizens? And what are the different classes of legislators but advocates and parties to the causes which they determine? Is a law proposed concerning private debts? It is a question to which the creditors are parties on one side and the debtors on the other. Justice ought to hold the balance between them. Yet the parties are, and must be, themselves the judges; and the most numerous party, or, in other words, the most powerful faction must be expected to prevail. Shall domestic manufactures be encouraged, and in what degree, by restrictions on foreign manufactures? are questions which would be differently decided by the landed and the manufacturing classes, and probably by neither with a sole regard to justice and the public good. The apportionment of taxes on the various descriptions of property is an act which seems to require the most exact impartiality; yet there is, perhaps, no legislative act in which greater opportunity and temptation are given to a predominant party to trample on the rules of justice. Every shilling with which they overburden the inferior number, is a shilling saved to their own pockets.

It is in vain to say that enlightened statesmen will be able to adjust these clashing interests, and render them all subservient to the public good. Enlightened statesmen will not always be at the helm. Nor, in many cases, can such an adjustment be made at all without taking into view indirect and remote considerations, which will rarely prevail over the immediate interest which one party may find in disregarding the rights of another or the good of the whole.

The inference to which we are brought is, that the CAUSES of faction cannot be removed, and that relief is only to be sought in the means of controlling its EFFECTS.

If a faction consists of less than a majority, relief is supplied by the republican principle, which enables the majority to defeat its sinister views by regular vote. It may clog the administration, it may convulse the society; but it will be unable to execute and mask its violence under the forms of the Constitution. When a majority is included in a faction, the form of popular government, on the other hand, enables it to sacrifice to its ruling passion or interest both the public good and the rights of other citizens. To secure the public good and private rights against the danger of such a faction, and at the same time to preserve the spirit and the form of popular government, is then the great object to which our inquiries are directed. Let me add that it is the great desideratum by which this form of government can be rescued from the opprobrium under which it has so long labored, and be recommended to the esteem and adoption of mankind.

By what means is this object attainable? Evidently by one of two only. Either the existence of the same passion or interest in a majority at the same time must be prevented, or the majority, having such coexistent passion or interest, must be rendered, by their number and local situation, unable to concert and carry into effect schemes of oppression. If the impulse and the opportunity be suffered to coincide, we well know that neither moral nor religious motives can be relied on as an adequate control. They are not found to be such on the injustice and violence of individuals, and lose their efficacy in proportion to the number combined together, that is, in proportion as their efficacy becomes needful.

From this view of the subject it may be concluded that a pure democracy, by which I mean a society consisting of a small number of citizens, who assemble and administer the government in person, can admit of no cure for the mischiefs of faction. A common passion or interest will, in almost every case, be felt by a majority of the whole; a communication and concert result from the form of government itself; and there is nothing to check the inducements to sacrifice the weaker party or an obnoxious individual. Hence it is that such democracies have ever been spectacles of turbulence and contention; have ever been found incompatible with personal security or the rights of property; and have in general been as short in their lives as they have been violent in their deaths. Theoretic politicians, who have patronized this species of government, have erroneously supposed that by reducing mankind to a perfect equality in their political rights, they would, at the same time, be perfectly equalized and assimilated in their possessions, their opinions, and their passions.

A republic, by which I mean a government in which the scheme of representation takes place, opens a different prospect, and promises the cure for which we are seeking. Let us examine the points in which it varies from pure democracy, and we shall comprehend both the nature of the cure and the efficacy which it must derive from the Union.

The two great points of difference between a democracy and a republic are: first, the delegation of the government, in the latter, to a small number of citizens elected by the rest; secondly, the greater number of citizens, and greater sphere of country, over which the latter may be extended.

The effect of the first difference is, on the one hand, to refine and enlarge the public views, by passing them through the medium of a chosen body of citizens, whose wisdom may best discern the true interest of their country, and whose patriotism and love of justice will be least likely to sacrifice it to temporary or partial considerations. Under such a regulation, it may well happen that the public voice, pronounced by the representatives of the people, will be more consonant to the public good than if pronounced by the people themselves, convened for the purpose. On the other hand, the effect may be inverted. Men of factious tempers, of local prejudices, or of sinister designs, may, by intrigue, by corruption, or by other means, first obtain the suffrages, and then betray the interests, of the people. The question resulting is, whether small or extensive republics are more favorable to the election of proper guardians of the public weal; and it is clearly decided in favor of the latter by two obvious considerations:

In the first place, it is to be remarked that, however small the republic may be, the representatives must be raised to a certain number, in order to guard against the cabals of a few; and that, however large it may be, they must be limited to a certain number, in order to guard against the confusion of a multitude. Hence, the number of representatives in the two cases not being in proportion to that of the two constituents, and being proportionally greater in the small republic, it follows that, if the proportion of fit characters be not less in the large than in the small republic, the former will present a greater option, and consequently a greater probability of a fit choice.

In the next place, as each representative will be chosen by a greater number of citizens in the large than in the small republic, it will be more difficult for unworthy candidates to practice with success the vicious arts by which elections are too often carried; and the suffrages of the people being more free, will be more likely to centre in men who possess the most attractive merit and the most diffusive and established characters.

It must be confessed that in this, as in most other cases, there is a mean, on both sides of which inconveniences will be found to lie. By enlarging too much the -number of electors, you render the representatives too little acquainted with all their local circumstances and lesser interests; as by reducing it too much, you render him unduly attached to these, and too little fit to comprehend and pursue great and national objects. The federal Constitution forms a happy combination in this respect; the great and aggregate interests being referred to the national, the local and particular to the State legislatures.

The other point of difference is, the greater number of citizens and extent of territory which may be brought within the compass of republican than of democratic government; and it is this circumstance principally which renders factious combinations less to be dreaded in the former than in the latter. The smaller the society, the fewer probably will be the distinct parties and interests composing it; the fewer the distinct parties and interests, the more frequently will a majority be found of the same party; and the smaller the number of individuals composing a majority, and the smaller the compass within which they are placed, the more easily will they concert and execute their plans of oppression. Extend the sphere, and you take in a greater variety of parties and interests; you make it less probable that a majority of the whole will have a common motive to invade the rights of other citizens; or if such a common motive exists, it will be more difficult for all who feel it to discover their own strength, and to act in unison with each other. Besides other impediments, it may be remarked that, where there is a consciousness of unjust or dishonorable purposes, communication is always checked by distrust in proportion to the number whose concurrence is necessary.

Hence, it clearly appears, that the same advantage which a republic has over a democracy, in controlling the effects of faction, is enjoyed by a large over a small republic,—is enjoyed by the Union over the States - composing it. Does the advantage consist in the substitution of representatives whose enlightened views and virtuous sentiments render them superior to local prejudices and schemes of injustice? It will not be denied that the representation of the Union will be most likely to possess these requisite endowments. Does it consist in the greater security afforded by a greater variety of parties, against the event of any one party being able to outnumber and oppress the rest? In an equal degree does the increased variety of parties comprised within the Union, increase this security. Does it, in fine, consist in the greater obstacles opposed to the concert and accomplishment of the secret wishes of an unjust and interested majority? Here, again, the extent of the Union gives it the most palpable advantage.

The influence of factious leaders may kindle a flame within their particular States, but will be unable to spread a general conflagration through the other States. A religious sect may degenerate into a political faction in a part of the Confederacy; but the variety of sects dispersed over the entire face of it must secure the national councils against any danger from that source. A rage for paper money, for an abolition of debts, for an equal division of property, or for any other improper or wicked project, will be less apt to pervade the whole body of the Union than a particular member of it; in the same proportion as such a malady is more likely to taint a particular county or district, than an entire State.

In the extent and proper structure of the Union, therefore, we behold a republican remedy for the diseases most incident to republican government. And according to the degree of pleasure and pride we feel in being republicans, ought to be our zeal in cherishing the spirit and supporting the character of Federalists.

PUBLIUS.

FEDERALIST NUMBER 51

The Structure of the Government Must Furnish the Proper Checks and Balances Between the Different Departments

Author: James Madison

To the People of the State of New York:

TO WHAT expedient, then, shall we finally resort, for maintaining in practice the necessary partition of power among the several departments, as laid down in the Constitution? The only answer that can be given is, that as all these exterior provisions are found to be inadequate, the defect must be supplied, by so contriving the interior structure of the government as that its several constituent parts may, by their mutual relations, be the means of keeping each other in their proper places. Without presuming to undertake a full development of this important idea, I will hazard a few general observations, which may perhaps place it in a clearer light, and enable us to form a more correct judgment of the principles and structure of the government planned by the convention.

In order to lay a due foundation for that separate and distinct exercise of the different powers of government, which to a certain extent is admitted on all hands to be essential to the preservation of liberty, it is evident that each department should have a will of its own; and consequently should be so constituted that the members of each should have as little agency as possible in the appointment of the members of the others. Were this principle rigorously adhered to, it would require that all the appointments for the supreme executive, legislative, and judiciary magistracies should be drawn from the same fountain of authority, the people, through channels having no communication whatever with one another. Perhaps such a plan of constructing the several departments would be less difficult in practice than it may in contemplation appear. Some difficulties, however, and some additional expense would attend the execution of it. Some deviations, therefore, from the principle must be admitted. In the constitution of the judiciary department in particular, it might be inexpedient to insist rigorously on the principle: first, because peculiar qualifications being essential in the members, the primary consideration ought to be to select that mode of choice which best secures these qualifications; secondly, because the permanent tenure by which the appointments are held in that department, must soon destroy all sense of dependence on the authority conferring them.

It is equally evident, that the members of each department should be as little dependent as possible on those of the others, for the emoluments annexed to their offices. Were the executive magistrate, or the judges, not independent of the legislature in this particular, their independence in every other would be merely nominal.

But the great security against a gradual concentration of the several powers in the same department, consists in giving to those who administer each department the necessary constitutional means and personal motives to resist encroachments of the others. The provision for defense must in this, as in all other cases, be made commensurate to the danger of attack. Ambition must be made to counteract ambition. The interest of the man must be connected with the constitutional rights of the place. It may be a reflection on human nature, that such devices should be necessary to control the abuses of government. But what is government itself, but the greatest of all reflections on human nature? If men were angels, no government would be necessary. If angels were to govern men, neither external nor internal controls on government would be necessary. In framing a government which is to be administered by men over men, the great difficulty lies in this: you must first enable the government to control the governed; and in the next place oblige it to control itself. A dependence on the people is, no doubt, the primary control on the government; but experience has taught mankind the necessity of auxiliary precautions.

This policy of supplying, by opposite and rival interests, the defect of better motives, might be traced through the whole system of human affairs, private as well as public. We see it particularly displayed in all the subordinate distributions of power, where the constant aim is to divide and arrange the several offices in such a manner as that each may be a check on the other that the private interest of every individual may be a sentinel over the public rights. These inventions of prudence cannot be less requisite in the distribution of the supreme powers of the State.

But it is not possible to give to each department an equal power of self-defense. In republican government, the legislative authority necessarily predominates. The remedy for this inconveniency is to divide the legislature into different branches; and to render them, by different modes of election and different principles of action, as little connected with each other as the nature of their common functions and their common dependence on the society will admit. It may even be necessary to guard against dangerous encroachments by still further precautions. As the weight of the legislative authority requires that it should be thus divided, the weakness of the executive may require, on the other hand, that it should be fortified. An absolute negative on the legislature appears, at first view, to be the natural defense with which the executive magistrate should be armed. But perhaps it would be neither altogether safe nor alone sufficient. On ordinary occasions it might not be exerted with the requisite firmness, and on extraordinary occasions it might be perfidiously abused. May not this defect of an absolute negative be supplied by some qualified connection between this weaker department and the weaker branch of the stronger department, by which the latter may be led to support the constitutional rights of the former, without being too much detached from the rights of its own department?

If the principles on which these observations are founded be just, as I persuade myself they are, and they be applied as a criterion to the several State constitutions, and to the federal Constitution it will be found that if the latter does not perfectly correspond with them, the former are infinitely less able to bear such a test. There are, moreover, two considerations particularly applicable to the federal system of America, which place that system in a very interesting point of view.

First. In a single republic, all the power surrendered by the people is submitted to the administration of a single government; and the usurpations are guarded against by a division of the government into distinct and separate departments. In the compound republic of America, the power surrendered by the people is first divided between two distinct governments, and then the portion allotted to each subdivided among distinct and separate departments. Hence a double security arises to the rights of the people. The different governments will control each other, at the same time that each will be controlled by itself.

Second. It is of great importance in a republic not only to guard the society against the oppression of its rulers, but to guard one part of the society against the injustice of the other part. Different interests necessarily exist in different classes of citizens. If a majority be united by a common interest, the rights of the minority will be insecure. There are but two methods of providing against this evil: the one by creating a will in the community independent of the majority that is, of the society itself; the other, by comprehending in the society so many separate descriptions of citizens as will render an unjust combination of a majority of the whole very improbable, if not impracticable. The first method prevails in all governments possessing an hereditary or self-appointed authority. This, at best, is but a precarious security; because a power independent of the society may as well espouse the unjust views of the major, as the rightful interests of the minor party, and may possibly be turned against both parties. The second method will be exemplified in the federal republic of the United States. Whilst all authority in it will be derived from and dependent on the society, the -society itself will be broken into so many parts, interests, and classes of citizens, that the rights of individuals, or of the minority, will be in little danger from interested combinations of the majority. In a free government the security for civil rights must be the same as that for religious rights. It consists in the one case in the multiplicity of interests, and in the other in the multiplicity of sects. The degree of security in both cases will depend on the number of interests and sects; and this may be presumed to depend on the extent of country and number of people comprehended under the same government. This view of the subject must particularly recommend a proper federal system to all the sincere and considerate friends of republican government, since it shows that in exact proportion as the territory of the Union may be formed into more circumscribed Confederacies, or States oppressive combinations of a majority will be facilitated: the best security, under the republican forms, for the rights of every class of citizens, will be diminished: and consequently the stability and independence of some member of the government, the only other security, must be proportionately increased. Justice is the end of government. It is the end of civil society. It ever has been and ever will be pursued until it be obtained, or until liberty be lost in the pursuit. In a society under the forms of which the stronger faction can readily unite and oppress the weaker, anarchy may as truly be said to reign as in a state of nature, where the weaker individual is not secured against the violence of the stronger; and as, in the latter state, even the stronger individuals are prompted, by the uncertainty of their condition, to submit to a government which may protect the weak as well as themselves; so, in the former state, will the more powerful factions or parties be gradually induced, by a like motive, to wish for a government which will protect all parties, the weaker as well as the more powerful. It can be little doubted that if the State of Rhode Island was separated from the Confederacy and left to itself, the insecurity of rights under the popular form of government within such narrow limits would be displayed by such reiterated oppressions of factious majorities that some power altogether independent of the people would soon be called for by the voice of the very factions whose misrule had proved the necessity of it. In the extended republic of the United States, and among the great variety of interests, parties, and sects which it embraces, a coalition of a majority of the whole society could seldom take place on any other principles than those of justice and the general good; whilst there being thus less danger to a minor from the will of a major party, there must be less pretext, also, to provide for the security of the former, by introducing into the government a will not dependent on the latter, or, in other words, a will independent of the society itself. It is no less certain than it is important, -notwithstanding the contrary opinions which have been entertained, that the larger the society, provided it lie within a practical sphere, the more duly capable it will be of self-government. And happily for the REPUBLICAN CAUSE, the practicable sphere may be carried to a very great extent, by a judicious modification and mixture of the FEDERAL PRINCIPLE.

PUBLIUS.

FEDERALIST NUMBER 78

The Judiciary Department

Author: Alexander Hamilton

To the People of the State of New York:

WE PROCEED now to an examination of the judiciary department of the proposed government.

In unfolding the defects of the existing Confederation, the utility and necessity of a federal judicature have been clearly pointed out. It is the less necessary to recapitulate the considerations there urged, as the propriety of the institution in the abstract is not disputed; the only questions which have been raised being relative to the manner of constituting it, and to its extent. To these points, therefore, our observations shall be confined.

The manner of constituting it seems to embrace these several objects: 1st. The mode of appointing the judges. 2d. The tenure by which they are to hold their places. 3d. The partition of the judiciary authority between different courts, and their relations to each other.

First. As to the mode of appointing the judges; this is the same with that of appointing the officers of the Union in general, and has been so fully discussed in the two last numbers, that nothing can be said here which would not be useless repetition.

Second. As to the tenure by which the judges are to hold their places; this chiefly concerns their duration in office; the provisions for their support; the precautions for their responsibility.

According to the plan of the convention, all judges who may be appointed by the United States are to hold their offices DURING GOOD BEHAVIOR; which is conformable to the most approved of the State constitutions and among the rest, to that of this State. Its propriety having been drawn into question by the adversaries of that plan, is no light symptom of the rage for objection, which disorders their imaginations and judgments. The standard of good behavior for the continuance in office of the judicial magistracy, is certainly one of the most valuable of the modern improvements in the practice of government. In a monarchy it is an excellent barrier to the despotism of the prince; in a republic it is a no less excellent barrier to the encroachments and oppressions of the representative body. And it is the best expedient which can be devised in any government, to secure a steady, upright, and impartial administration of the laws.

Whoever attentively considers the different departments of power must perceive, that, in a government in which they are separated from each other, the judiciary, from the nature of its functions, will always be the least dangerous to the political rights of the Constitution; because it will be least in a capacity to annoy or injure them. The Executive not only dispenses the honors, but holds the sword of the community. The legislature not only commands the purse, but prescribes the rules by which the duties and rights of every citizen are to be regulated. The judiciary, on the contrary, has no influence over either the sword or the purse; no direction either of the strength or of the wealth of the society; and can take no active resolution whatever. It may truly be said to have neither FORCE nor WILL, but merely judgment; and must ultimately depend upon the aid of the executive arm even for the efficacy of its judgments.

This simple view of the matter suggests several important consequences. It proves incontestably, that the judiciary is beyond comparison the weakest of the three departments of power [1]; that it can never attack with success either of the other two; and that all possible care is requisite to enable it to defend itself against their attacks. It equally proves, that though individual oppression may now and then proceed from the courts of justice, the general liberty of the people can never be endangered from that quarter; I mean so long as the judiciary remains truly distinct from both the legislature and the Executive. For I agree, that "there is no liberty, if the power of judging be not separated from the legislative and executive powers." [2] And it proves, in the last place, that as liberty can have nothing to fear from the judiciary alone, but would have every thing to fear from its union with either of the other departments; that as all the effects of such a union must ensue from a dependence of the former on the latter, notwithstanding a nominal and apparent separation; that as, from the natural feebleness of the judiciary, it is in continual jeopardy of being overpowered, awed, or influenced by its co-ordinate branches; and that as nothing can contribute so much to its firmness and independence as permanency in office, this quality may therefore be justly regarded as an indispensable ingredient in its constitution, and, in a great measure, as the citadel of the public justice and the public security.

The complete independence of the courts of justice is peculiarly essential in a limited Constitution. By a limited Constitution, I understand one which contains certain specified exceptions to the legislative authority; such, for instance, as that it shall pass no bills of attainder, no ex-post-facto laws, and the like. Limitations of this kind can be preserved in practice no other way than through the medium of courts of justice, whose duty it must be to declare all acts contrary to the manifest tenor of the Constitution void. Without this, all the reservations of particular rights or privileges would amount to nothing.

Some perplexity respecting the rights of the courts to pronounce legislative acts void, because contrary to the Constitution, has arisen from an imagination that the doctrine would imply a superiority of the judiciary to the legislative power. It is urged that the authority which can declare the acts of another void, must necessarily be superior to the one whose acts may be declared void. As this doctrine is of great importance in all the American constitutions, a brief discussion of the ground on which it rests cannot be unacceptable.

There is no position which depends on clearer principles, than that every act of a delegated authority, contrary to the tenor of the commission under which it is exercised, is void. No legislative act, therefore, contrary to the Constitution, can be valid. To deny this, would be to affirm, that the deputy is greater than his principal; that the servant is above his master; that the representatives of the people are superior to the people themselves; that men acting by virtue of powers, may do not only what their powers do not authorize, but what they forbid.

If it be said that the legislative body are themselves the constitutional judges of their own powers, and that the construction they put upon them is conclusive upon the other departments, it may be answered, that this cannot be the natural presumption, where it is not to be collected from any particular provisions in the Constitution. It is not otherwise to be supposed, that the Constitution could intend to enable the representatives of the people to substitute their WILL to that of their constituents. It is far more rational to suppose, that the courts were designed to be an intermediate body between the people and the legislature, in order, among other things, to keep the latter within the limits assigned to their authority. The interpretation of the laws is the proper and peculiar province of the courts. A constitution is, in fact, and must be regarded by the judges, as a fundamental law. It therefore belongs to them to ascertain its meaning, as well as the meaning of any particular act proceeding from the legislative body. If there should happen to be an irreconcilable variance between the two, that which has the superior obligation and validity ought, of course, to be preferred; or, in other words, the Constitution ought to be preferred to the statute, the intention of the people to the intention of their agents.

Nor does this conclusion by any means suppose a superiority of the judicial to the legislative power. It only supposes that the power of the people is superior to both; and that where the will of the legislature, declared in its statutes, stands in opposition to that of the people, declared in the Constitution, the judges ought to be governed by the latter rather than the former. They ought to regulate their decisions by the fundamental laws, rather than by those which are not fundamental.

This exercise of judicial discretion, in determining between two contradictory laws, is exemplified in a familiar instance. It not uncommonly happens, that there are two statutes existing at one time, clashing in whole or in part with each other, and neither of them containing any repealing clause or expression. In such a case, it is the province of the courts to liquidate and fix their meaning and operation. So far as they can, by any fair construction, be reconciled to each other, reason and law conspire to dictate that this should be done; where this is impracticable, it becomes a matter of necessity to give effect to one, in exclusion of the other. The rule which has obtained in the courts for determining their relative validity is, that the last in order of time shall be preferred to the first. But this is a mere rule of construction, not derived from any positive law, but from the nature and reason of the thing. It is a rule not enjoined upon the courts by legislative provision, but adopted by themselves, as consonant to truth and propriety, for the direction of their conduct as interpreters of the law. They thought it reasonable, that between the interfering acts of an EQUAL authority, that which was the last indication of its will should have the preference.

But in regard to the interfering acts of a superior and subordinate authority, of an original and derivative power, the nature and reason of the thing indicate the converse of that rule as proper to be followed. They teach us that the prior act of a superior ought to be preferred to the subsequent act of an inferior and subordinate authority; and that accordingly, whenever a particular statute contravenes the Constitution, it will be the duty of the judicial tribunals to adhere to the latter and disregard the former.

It can be of no weight to say that the courts, on the pretense of a repugnancy, may substitute their own pleasure to the constitutional intentions of the legislature. This might as well happen in the case of two contradictory statutes; or it might as well happen in every adjudication upon any single statute. The courts must declare the sense of the law; and if they should be disposed to exercise WILL instead of JUDGMENT, the consequence would equally be the substitution of their pleasure to that of the legislative body. The observation, if it prove any thing, would prove that there ought to be no judges distinct from that body.

If, then, the courts of justice are to be considered as the bulwarks of a limited Constitution against legislative encroachments, this consideration will afford a strong argument for the permanent tenure of judicial offices, since nothing will contribute so much as this to that independent spirit in the judges which must be essential to the faithful performance of so arduous a duty.

This independence of the judges is equally requisite to guard the Constitution and the rights of individuals from the effects of those ill humors, which the arts of designing men, or the influence of particular conjunctures, sometimes disseminate among the people themselves, and which, though they speedily give place to better information, and more deliberate reflection, have a tendency, in the meantime, to occasion dangerous innovations in the government, and serious oppressions of the minor party in the community. Though I trust the friends of the proposed Constitution will never concur with its enemies, [3] in questioning that fundamental principle of republican government, which admits the right of the people to alter or abolish the established Constitution, whenever they find it inconsistent with their happiness, yet it is not to be inferred from this principle, that the representatives of the people, whenever a momentary inclination happens to lay hold of a majority of their constituents, incompatible with the provisions in the existing Constitution, would, on that account, be justifiable in a violation of those provisions; or that the courts would be under a greater obligation to connive at infractions in this shape, than when they had proceeded wholly from the cabals of the representative body. Until the people have, by some solemn and authoritative act, annulled or changed the established form, it is binding upon themselves collectively, as well as individually; and no presumption, or even knowledge, of their sentiments, can warrant their representatives in a departure from it, prior to such an act. But it is easy to see, that it would require an uncommon portion of fortitude in the judges to do their duty as faithful guardians of the Constitution, where legislative invasions of it had been instigated by the major voice of the community.

But it is not with a view to infractions of the Constitution only, that the independence of the judges may be an essential safeguard against the effects of occasional ill humors in the society. These sometimes extend no farther than to the injury of the private rights of particular classes of citizens, by unjust and partial laws. Here also the firmness of the judicial magistracy is of vast importance in mitigating the severity and confining the operation of such laws. It not only serves to moderate the immediate mischiefs of those which may have been passed, but it operates as a check upon the legislative body in passing them; who, perceiving that obstacles to the success of iniquitous intention are to be expected from the scruples of the courts, are in a manner compelled, by the very motives of the injustice they meditate, to qualify their attempts. This is a circumstance calculated to have more influence upon the character of our governments, than but few may be aware of. The benefits of the integrity and moderation of the judiciary have already been felt in more States than one; and though they may have displeased those whose sinister expectations they may have disappointed, they must have commanded the esteem and applause of all the virtuous and disinterested. Considerate men, of every description, ought to prize whatever will tend to beget or fortify that temper in the courts: as no man can be sure that he may not be to-morrow the victim of a spirit of injustice, by which he may be a gainer to-day. And every man must now feel, that the inevitable tendency of such a spirit is to sap the foundations of public and private confidence, and to introduce in its stead universal distrust and distress.

That inflexible and uniform adherence to the rights of the Constitution, and of individuals, which we perceive to be indispensable in the courts of justice, can certainly not be expected from judges who hold their offices by a temporary commission. Periodical appointments, however regulated, or by whomsoever made, would, in some way or other, be fatal to their necessary independence. If the power of making them was committed either to the Executive or legislature, there would be danger of an improper complaisance to the branch which possessed it; if to both, there would be an unwillingness to hazard the displeasure of either; if to the people, or to persons chosen by them for the special purpose, there would be too great a disposition to consult popularity, to justify a reliance that nothing would be consulted but the Constitution and the laws.

There is yet a further and a weightier reason for the permanency of the judicial offices, which is deducible from the nature of the qualifications they require. It has been frequently remarked, with great propriety, that a voluminous code of laws is one of the inconveniences necessarily connected with the advantages of a free government. To avoid an arbitrary discretion in the courts, it is indispensable that they should be bound down by strict rules and precedents, which serve to define and point out their duty in every particular case that comes before them; and it will readily be conceived from the variety of controversies which grow out of the folly and wickedness of mankind, that the records of those precedents must unavoidably swell to a very considerable bulk, and must demand long and laborious study to acquire a competent knowledge of them. Hence it is, that there can be but few men in the society who will have sufficient skill in the laws to qualify them for the stations of judges. And making the proper deductions for the ordinary depravity of human nature, the number must be still smaller of those who unite the requisite integrity with the requisite knowledge. These considerations apprise us, that the government can have no great option between fit character; and that a temporary duration in office, which would naturally discourage such characters from quitting a lucrative line of practice to accept a seat on the bench, would have a tendency to throw the administration of justice into hands less able, and less well qualified, to conduct it with utility and dignity. In the present circumstances of this country, and in those in which it is likely to be for a long time to come, the disadvantages on this score would be greater than they may at first sight appear; but it must be confessed, that they are far inferior to those which present themselves under the other aspects of the subject.

Upon the whole, there can be no room to doubt that the convention acted wisely in copying from the models of those constitutions which have established GOOD BEHAVIOR as the tenure of their judicial offices, in point of duration; and that so far from being blamable on this account, their plan would have been inexcusably defective, if it had wanted this important feature of good government. The experience of Great Britain affords an illustrious comment on the excellence of the institution.

PUBLIUS.

---

1 The celebrated Montesquieu, speaking of them, says: "Of the three powers above mentioned, the judiciary is next to nothing." "Spirit of Laws." vol. i., page 186.
2 Idem, page 181.
3 Vide "Protest of the Minority of the Convention of Pennsylvania," Martin's Speech, etc.

INDEX

9/11 attacks 74, 82–3, 139, 252

abortion 113–16, 139, 142, 161, 304, 307
Abraham, Henry 287, 290, 308
Adams, Abigail 287
Adams, John 3, 13, 185, 286
Adams, John Quincy 185
Adamson v. California (1947) 68
Addams, Jane 112
adversary process 290
advice and consent 23
affirmative action 106–7; in schools 108–11, 307; in the workplace 107–8
Affordable Care Act (ACA; 2010) 50, 56, 57, 163, 306; reform 236, 246, 266
Afghanistan 139, 252, 261, 280
AFL-CIO 155, 159, 161
age and voter turnout 190
Age of Reason 4
Agricultural Adjustment Act (AAA) 53
Alito, Samuel 64, 109, 210, 298, 302, 305
American Anti-Slavery Society (AASS) 99
American Association of Retired Persons (AARP) 161
American Bar Association (ABA) 160, 161, 268–9, 301
American Civil Liberties Union (ACLU) 71
American Colonization Society (1817) 99
American Creed 124, 125–6
American Federation of Labor (AFL) 159
American Federation of Teachers (AFT) 159
American Medical Association (AMA) 160
American Petroleum Institute 159, 163
American Revolution: background to 8–13; governance during 14–17
The American Voter 168–9
American Woman Suffrage Association (AWSA) 112
amicus curiae briefs 298
Annapolis Convention 17
Anthony, Susan B. 112

Anti-Federalists 26–7, 28, 67, 93
appellate jurisdiction 291, 301
appointment power 256
appropriations committees 233
Arms Control and Disarmament Agency 278
Articles of Confederation 15, 22, 25, 39
Asian-Americans 139, 223
Athens 2–3
Atkins v. Virginia (2002) 84
authorizing committees 232–3
Axelrod, David 277
Azzimonti, Marina 168

Bacon, Francis 4
Baker, James 276
Bakke, Allan 106–7
bankruptcy 294–5
Bannon, Steve 133, 179, 277, 278
Barron v. Baltimore (1833) 67–8
Barrow, Deborah 299
Baum, Lawrence 294
Baumgartner, Frank 157
Baze v. Rees (2008) 84–5
Beer, Samuel 38–9
Beschloss, Michael 179
bicameralism 22
Biden, Joe 96, 198, 277, 279
Bill of Rights 3, 42; debate on need for 28, 93; origins of 27–8, 67–8; text of B7–B8
bills: calendars 237–8; committee deliberation 236–7; conference committees 239–40; floor debate and amendment 238–9; introduction and assignment 236; referral practices 236
Bipartisan Campaign Reform Act (BCRA) *see* McCain-Feingold Act (2002)
birth control 93, 113–14
Black, Hugo 68
Black Lives Matter 110–11, 138
Blackmun, Harry 94, 114
blacks: in Congress 223; and death penalty 84; Democratic Party

identification 173; discrimination against 50, 73, 102, 305; enfranchisement of men 101, 104, 105–6; in federal bureaucracy 271; income 109–10; and political socialization 138–9; prisoners 87; voter turnout 190–1
Blackstone, William 111
block grants 54
Bonham's Case (1610) 289, 312
Boston Marathon bombing 84
Boston Massacre 10, 11
Boston Tea Party 10
Bowdoin, James 17
Bradley, Joseph P. 102
Bradwell v. Illinois (1873) 112
Brady Handgun Violence Protection Act 37
Brandeis, Louis 69–70, 79
Brandenburg v. Ohio (1969) 70, 71
Brearley Committee 21
Breitbart News 133
Brennan, William 73, 85, 107
Breyer, Stephen 116, 298
briefs 298
Broadman, Michelle 268
Brown, Jerry 58
Brown, Michael 110
Brown v. Board of Education (1954) 103, 302, 308
Bryant, Phil 77
Buckley v. Valeo (1976) 206, 210
budgetary process, federal 242–4
Bureau of the Budget 267, 278
bureaucracy 270–1; control of 241, 269–70, 274–5; structure 271–5
Burger, Warren 304
Burke, Edmund 226
Burr, Aaron 185
Bush, George H. W. 114, 175, 205, 279, 300
Bush, George W. 288; 2000 election campaign 186, 198, 296; cabinet 276, 279; civil rights 115; domestic policy 55, 206–7, 266; expanding presidential power 252, 253, 258,

260, 261; on freedom of religion 75; and Guantanamo detainees 262, 264; and Iraq war 261, 262, 280; judicial appointees 300, 301, 305, 311; national security policy 82, 275; signing statements 268; support in Congress 175–6, 195; veto power 268
Bush, Jeb 198, 199, 201
Business Roundtable 158–9
Byrd, Robert 224

cabinet 276
cabinet departments 271–3
Calhoun, John C. 46
campaign funding 194, 197
Canada, colonial 9
candidates: attributes 192–3; Congressional challengers 194–6; incumbency advantage 193–4; issues 192
Card, Andrew 276
Cardozo, Benjamin 79
Carson, Ben 166, 199, 201
Carter, Jimmy 135, 175, 275, 276, 279
cases and the law 290
casework 241
categorical grants 53–4
caucuses 199, 200
census 218–19
Center for Responsive Politics 194
Central Intelligence Agency (CIA) 278
Chafee, Lincoln 198
Chamber of Commerce 155, 158, 159, 166
Charles I, King of England 6
checks and balances 22, 241, 274
Cheney, Dick 253, 276, 277, 279, 280
Chief Diplomat role of president 264, 265
Chief Executive role of president 269–70
Chief Legislator role of president 267–9
Chief Trade Negotiator role of president 264–5
Christie, Chris 198
circuit courts *see* appellate jurisdiction
Citizens United v. Federal Election Commission (2010) 209, 211, 305–6, 309
civil law 289
civil liberties 65–7, 94–5; freedom of expression 68–74, 210–11; freedom of religion 74–8, 307; Patriot Act and restrictions on 82–3; and prisoners 85–7; *see also* Bill of Rights
civil rights 15, 66, 94, 96, 311; and Civil War amendments 99–102; in colonial America 8; and federalism 45–6; gay marriage debate 96–7, 306; modern civil rights movement

102–6; Rehnquist court and 304–5; Warren court and 303–4
Civil Rights Act (1875) 99, 100, 101, 102
Civil Rights Act (1957) 104
Civil Rights Act (1964) 104, 106, 107, 108, 173
Civil Rights Act (1965) 104, 173
Civil Rights Cases (1883) 102
Civil Rights Commission 104
civil rights groups 157
civil rights movement 102–6
civil rights organizations 160–1
Civil War 49, 50, 100; background to 36, 46
Civil War amendments 99–102
class: political socialization 137–8; and voter turnout 188–9
Clay, Henry 46, 99
climate change accords 58
Clinton, Bill: 1992 presidential campaign 205; approval ratings 267; character 192; and civil rights 96, 115, 311; domestic policy 55; on freedom of religion 75; impeachment 257; judicial appointees 300; staffing 276, 279; support in Congress 175, 176
Clinton, Hillary: 2008 nomination 198, 208; 2016 nomination 198, 199, 200, 201; 2016 presidential campaign 133, 138, 171, 188, 192, 194, 207, 209; character 116, 192–3; in Obama administration 276, 277; opinion polls 137
cloture 239
Clyburn, James 221
coercive federalism 54
Cohen, Bernard 132–3
Coke, Sir Edward 289
Colbert, Stephen 131, 219
Cold War 262
colonial America 3, 5–6; economic opportunity and social fluidity 8; equality in 8, 29; European politics in 9–10; first steps to Independence 10–12; political environment 8–10; religious persecution 6; social and economic opportunity 6–7, 9; *see also* Declaration of Independence
Commander in Chief 257, 261–4
commerce clause 15, 20, 21, 48, 49, 55, 56; *see also* interstate commerce
Commission on the Status of Women 113
Committee of the Whole 238
Common Cause 160, 161, 162
common law 288–9
communism 262
Concerned Women of America (CWA) 114
concurrent powers 41
confederation 39

Confederation Congress 15, 18, 39
conference committees 233
confirmation hearings 302–3
Congress 219; challengers and their challenges 194–6; and the Constitution 220–1; decision making 240–1; enumerated powers 23, 40–1, 46, 48, 93; implied powers 40–1; inherent powers 41, 260; judicial review of legislation 292–3; legislative process 235–40; membership and service 219, 221–5; organization 225–35; origins and powers 220–1; party role in 227–30; powers denied 41; presidential support 175; president's program 175; public disapproval 245–6; reform 245–6; representation of constituents 226–7, 240–1; tenure, incumbency, and reelection 224–5; *see also* Congressional committees
Congress of Industrial Organizations (CIO) 159
Congress Watch 160, 161
Congressional Black Caucus 221
Congressional Budget Office (CBO) 235, 243
Congressional committees 230, 235; division of labor 231–2; staff structure 233–5; types of committees 232–3, 234
Congressional Research Service (CRS) 234
Conservative Political Action Conference (CPAC) 166
conservatives 143–5
constituents and Congress 226–7, 240–1
Constitution *see* constitutional amendments; state constitutions; U.S. Constitution
constitutional amendments: 1st 27–8, 67, 68–75, 153–4, 210–11, B7; 2nd 29, 64–5, 305, B7; 3rd B7; 4th 29, 78–80, B7–B8; 5th 29, 81–4, B8; 6th 29, 80–1, B8; 7th B8; 8th 29, 84–5, 123–4, B8; 9th 29, 67, 93–4, B8; 10th 29, 36–7, 42, 48, 50, 55, 56, 57, B8; 11th B8; 12th B8–B9; 13th 100, 102, B9; 14th 68, 69, 71, 78, 81, 94, 101, 102, 103, 107, 114, 153, B9; 15th 101, B10; 16th B10; 17th B10; 18th B10; 19th 112, B10; 20th B10–B11; 21st B11; 22nd B11; 23rd B11; 24th B11–B12; 25th B12; 26th B12; 27th B12; process for making 24–5, 67
Constitutional Convention 2, 17–18, 254; debates 18–22, 185; delegates 25–6, 218; principles 22–5, 40; ratification of Constitution 25–9, 36

constitutional democracy 44
constitutional reform 29–30
Consumer Product Safety Commission (CPSC) 273
consumer safety groups 157
Consumers' Leagues 112
containment 262
Continental Congress 10–13, 14, 18, 46
Controlled Substances Act (CSA) 36
cooperative federalism 49
Corker, Bob 264
Corwin, Edward S. 253
Cotton, John 6, 7
Council of Europe 123
courts of appeals 80, 294, 295, 296
coverture 111
creative federalism 54
crime 87
criminal defendents, rights of 78–87
criminal law 289
Cromwell, Oliver 6
cross burning 71
cruel and unusual punishment 84–5
Cruz, Ted 172, 179, 198, 201
Cuban, Mark 197
Cuccinelli, Ken 56

Dahl, Robert A. 30
Davis, Jefferson 46
Davis, Theodore J. 138
Dean, Howard 192
death penalty 84–5, 123–4, 139
Deaver, Michael 276
Decker, Bernard 154
Declaration of Independence 12–13, 14, 41, 126, 218; text of A1–A3
Declaratory Act (1766) 10
Defense of Marriage Act (DOMA; 1996) 96, 306
defense spending 139
Dejonge v. Oregon (1937) 153–4
Delaware Plan 210–11
DeLay, Tom 246
delegates 227
democracy: constitutional democracy 44; in the early colonies 2–3; growth of 21, 26, 29–30
Democratic National Committee (DNC) 171, 174, 208, 209
Democratic Party 155–6; black commitment to 173; national conventions 201; party identification 169–71
Department of Defense 269, 272
Department of Education 272, 275
Department of Energy 272, 275
Department of Health and Human Services 272, 275
Department of Health, Education, and Welfare 272, 275

Department of Homeland Security 271, 272, 275, 278, 286
Department of Justice 104, 272
Department of the Treasury 272, 278
Department of Veterans Affairs 272, 275
desegregation 103, 141
devolution 54–7
Dickinson, John 2
Dingell, John 224
direct discrimination 106
district courts 294–5, 301
District of Columbia v. Heller (2008) 64
divine right of kings 3, 4
Dole, Robert 239
domestic policy, presidential 265–70
Donahue, Thomas 155, 159, 163
Douglas, Stephen A. 48–9
Douglas, William O. 93
Dred Scott v. Sandford (1857) 48, 99, 292–3
dual federalism 46–9, 101
dual sovereignty 41
due process of law 78, 81, 94, 153

Eagle Forum 114
education: gender in 116; and voter turnout 189–90
Education Act (1972) 116
Eisenhower, Dwight D. 104, 175, 192, 267, 276, 301, 308
"elastic clause" *see* "necessary and proper" clause
Electoral College 21, 30, 171, 185–6, 202–4, 211
electoral process 186–7
electoral rules 178
Elementary and Secondary Education Act (ESEA; 1965) 105
elitism 156
Ellis, Christopher 144
Emancipation Proclamation 100, 173
Emanuel, Rahm 276
Employment Act (1946) 260
Employment Division v. Smith (1990) 76
Encyclopedia of Associations 157
Engel v. Vitale (1962) 77
English civil wars 4, 6, 39
enumerated powers 23, 40–1, 46, 48, 93
environmental groups 157
Environmental Protection Agency (EPA) 274
Equal Rights Amendment (ERA) 113, 114, 115
equality: in colonial America 8, 29; Fourteenth amendment 101, 102, 103
Erikson, Robert 128
establishment clause 74–5
ethnicity: and income 109–10; and political socialization 138–9; and voter turnout 190–1

exclusionary rule 78–80
executive: Article II of Constitution 23, 252–3, 254; Chief Executive role of president 269–70; control of bureaucracy 269–70
executive agreements 256–7
Executive Office of the President (EOP) 259, 276–8
expression, freedom of 68–74, 210–11
extradition 44

factions 156
fake news 133
family and political socialization 127
Federal Bureau of Investigation (FBI) 74
Federal Communications Commission (FCC) 273, 274
Federal Convention *see* Constitutional Convention
federal courts 24, 30, 287–8, 291, 294; structure of 294–9
Federal Election Campaign Act (FECA; 1971) 206, 207
Federal Election Commission v. Wisconsin Right to Life, Inc. (2007) 210–11
federal judges 299; backgrounds 299–300; confirmation process 302–3; disputed role of 307–9; nomination process 301–2
Federal Reserve (Fed) 140, 168, 273, 274
federalism: and American constitutional thought 37–8; coercive federalism 54; in the Constitution 24, 40–6; cooperative federalism 49; creative federalism 54; "devolution" in contemporary federalism 54–7; dual federalism 46–9, 101; fiscal federalism 53–7; fluidity of American federalism 44–6; future of American federalism 57–8; national 46–8, 50; original meaning of 38–40; state-centred 46, 47–9
Federalist Papers 26–7; Number 10 27, C1–C4; Number 14 3; Number 39 42; Number 45 45; Number 48 27; Number 51 27, 44, C5–C7; Number 78 286, 291, 311–12, C7–11
Federalists *vs.* Anti-federalists 26–8, 93, 226
Feingold, Russ 207
Fenno, Richard 225
Filburn, Roscoe 53
filibusters 177, 238–9, 302
Fiorina, Carly 199
Fiorina, Morris 169
fiscal decision making 242–4
fiscal federalism 53–7
Fisher, Abigail 109
Fisher v. Texas (2012) 307

flag burning 70
Flynn, Michael 164, 277
Forbes, Steve 206
Ford, Gerald 175, 279
Foreign Intelligence Surveillance Act
    (FISA) 74
foreign policy: under Confederation
    Congress 15; presidential role
    256–7, 261–5
Fortune 500 159
Founders and the people 2–4
Franken, Al 118
Franklin, Benjamin 2, 4, 12, 13, 39,
    99, 185
free choice 5
Free Congress Foundation 160
free exercise clause 76–7
free-riders 157
free thought 154
freedom of expression 68–74, 210–11
freedom of religion 74–8, 307
freedom of speech 68–72, 154, 210–11
freedom of the press 68–9, 72–4
French and Indian War 9
French Canada 9
Friedan, Betty 113
front-loading 199–200
full faith and credit 24, 43
Furman v. Georgia (1972) 84, 123–4

Gage, Thomas 10, 12
Gaines, Lloyd 103
Gallego, Ruben 43
Gallup 123, 131, 137, 141
Gannett, Richard 305
Garcia, Chris 137
Gardner, John 160
Garrison, William Lloyd 99
Gates, Robert 276
gay marriage 96–7, 306
gay rights 93, 96
gender: in education 116; and income
    112, 116–17; and political
    socialization 139; and voter
    turnout 190
General Accounting Office (GAO) 234
general election campaigns 202–6
General Federation of Women's
    Clubs 112
general revenue sharing (GRS) 54
General Social Survey 144
George III, King of England 12
Gerry, Elbridge 218, 219
Gerrymandering 218–19
Gibbons v. Ogden (1824) 48
Gibson, James 141
Gideon v. Wainwright (1963) 80–1
Gilmore, Jim 198, 200
Gingrich, Newt 134, 198
Ginsburg, Ruth Bader 115, 298

Gitlow v. New York (1925) 69
Glorious Revolution of 1688 5
Goldwater, Barry 170, 192
Gompers, Samuel 159
Gonzales, Alberto 82, 83
Gonzales v. Carhart (2007) 115
Gore, Al 279
Gorsuch, Neil 239, 298, 302, 303
government: spending 41, 53; trust in
    142–3
Government Accountability office
    234–5
Graham, Lindsay 198, 200–1
grants-in-aid 54
Great Depression 36, 51–3, 135,
    259–60
Great Recession 160
Great Society 54, 173, 302
Green, Joshua 133, 265
Greenstein, Fred 126, 128
Gregg v. Georgia (1976) 84, 123–4
Grigg, Charles M. 141
Griswold v. Connecticut (1945) 93
Groseclose, Tim 132
Grutter v. Bollinger (2003) 108–9, 307
Gryski, Gerald 299–300
Guantanamo detainees 252–3, 262, 264
Gulf of Tonkin Resolution 260
gun rights 37, 57, 64–5, 139, 161, 305

Hall, Ralph 224
Hamdan v. Rumsfeld (2006) 252–3
Hamilton, Alexander 2, 46, 99, 255;
    see also Federalist Papers
Handel, Karen 197
Hannity, Sean 125
Harlan, John Marshall, I 102, 103
Harris, Robyn 128
Hayden, Carl 224
health care reform *see* Affordable Care
    Act (ACA; 2010)
health insurance 56
Help America Vote Act (HAVA; 2002) 188
Henry, Patrick 67
Herring v. U.S .(2009) 79
Hillary: The Movie 211
Hispanic Americans 109–10; in
    Congress 223; in federal
    bureaucracy 271; and political
    socialization 138, 139; prisoners
    87; voter turnout 190–1
Hobbes, Thomas 4–5
Holder, Eric 83, 96
Holmes, Oliver Wendell 69, 73, 154
Hoock, Holger 8
Hoover, Herbert 55, 135
House of Representatives 222;
    allocation of seats in 218; ERA
    hearings 113; floor debate and
    amendment 238; majority leader
    228; member characteristics 222–4;

membership 221; minority leader
    228; party unity in 176–7; powers
    and responsibilites of 220–1;
    qualifications for service 221;
    reelection to 193, 194; Speaker
    228; whips 228, 229; *see also*
    Congress
Hrebenar, Ronald 160
Huckabee, Mike 198, 201
Hudson v. Michigan (2006) 79
Huerta, Dolores 43
Huntington, Samuel 126
Hutchinson, Anne 7

immigration 146
immigration reform 43, 57
impeachment 257, 299
implied powers 40–1
income: distribution by race and
    ethnicity 109–10; gender wage gap
    112, 116–17
incorporation 68
Independent voters 127, 139, 169–70
individualism 4–5
industrialization 49, 51
inherent powers 41, 260
intelligent design 75
interest groups 153–4, 156; definitions
    156; goals and strategies 164–6;
    litigation 166; lobbyists 155–6,
    157, 159, 160, 162, 163–6, 241;
    and political parties 179–80;
    reasons for joining 158; resources
    161–4; rise of 157; types of 157–61
Internet: politics, democracy and the
    news 130, 131
interstate commerce 15, 17, 20, 21, 23,
    40, 48, 51, 53, 56
Intolerable Acts 10
Iraq War 139, 195, 246, 252, 261, 262,
    264, 280
Iyengar, Shanto 134

Jackson, Andrew 48, 99, 185, 292, 308
Jacob, Herbert 287
Jagger, Bianca 123
Jarrett, Valerie 277
Jay, John 99; *see also Federalist Papers*
Jefferson, Thomas 3, 4, 10, 13, 14, 18,
    28, 46, 74, 126, 185, 255, 286,
    287, 292
Jim Crow segregation 100, 105
Jindal, Bobby 198, 200–1
Johnson, Andrew 257
Johnson, Gary 179
Johnson, Lyndon B.: civil rights 29,
    104, 173; federalism 54; judicial
    appointees 300; presidency 170,
    258, 275; in the Senate 230; staffing
    276; support in Congress 175
joint committees 233

Jones, Antoine 80
Jones, John E., III 75
judicial activism 308–9, 310–11
judicial branch: in the age of Trump
    311–12; Article III of Constitution
    23–4, 286–7, 290–1, 294, 296,
    B5–B6; cases and the law 290;
    control over bureaucracy 274;
    disputed role of 307–9; reform
    309–12; tenure 310
judicial restraint 303, 310, 311
judicial review 286–7, 291–4
Judiciary Act (1789) 46, 291
justiciability 290

Kagan, Elena 298, 300
Kasich, John 56, 160, 198, 201
Kelly, John 277, 278
Kennedy, Anthony 79, 94, 97, 108, 109,
    115, 211, 298, 306, 307
Kennedy, John F. 54, 104, 113, 173,
    175, 186, 267, 276
Kennedy, Robert 173
Kerry, John 276–7
Kim Jong-un 264
Kimmel, Jimmy 219
Kinder, Donald 134
King, Martin Luther, Jr. 73, 104, 105,
    163, 173
King v. Burwell (2015) 306
Knox, Henry 255
Korean War 53, 260, 280
Kristol, Bill 179
Kushner, Jared 164, 277

laissez faire 51
Lakoff, George 134
Lambda Legal Defense and Education
    Fund 166
Laud, Archbishop William 6
Lauer, Matt 118
law, definitions of 287
Lawrence v. Texas (2003) 94
leadership: of interest groups 163; role
    of president 267
League of United Latin American
    Citizens (LULAC) 160–1
Lee, Richard Henry 13
Lee, Robert E. 71
Leech, Beth 157
legislative branch: Article I of
    Constitution 22–3; common law
    origins of 288–9; control over
    bureaucracy 274; judicial review
    292–4; legislative process in
    Congress 235–40; state *vs.* federal
    laws 36–7
Legislative Reform Act (1970) 245
Legislative Reorganization Act (1946) 245
legislative supremacy 220
LeHaye, Beverly 114

Lemon v. Kurtzman (1971) 75
Levinson, Sanford 30
Lewandowski, Corey 164
Lewis, John L. 159
liberals 143–4, 145
The Liberator 99
Liberia 99
libertarians 145
Light, Paul 266
Lilie, Stuart 145
Limbaugh, Rush 127, 129–30
Lincoln, Abraham 41, 46, 49, 100, 135,
    173, 185, 260
Lindblom, Charles E. 158
Lipset, Seymour Martin 126
litigation, interest groups and 166
Livingston, Robert R. 13
lobbyists 241; inside strategy 164–5;
    interest group spending 157, 159,
    162; litigation 166; outside strategy
    165–6; role of 155–6, 157, 160,
    163–4
local elections 195–6
Locke, John 4, 5, 6, 13, 126, 220, 252
Los Angeles Times 74
Luntz, Frank 134

McCain-Feingold Act (2002) 174,
    207, 210
McCain, John 198, 199, 206–7, 208
McCarthy, Kevin 228
McChesney, Robert W. 132
McCollum, Bill 56
McConnell, Mitch 172, 230, 246, 301,
    302, 312
McConnell v. F.E.C. (2003) 209, 210
McCulloch v. Maryland (1819) 47–8
McDonald v. Chicago (2010) 64, 65
McGovern, George 192
McLaurin v. Oklahoma (1950) 103
McMaster, H.R. 278
Maddox, William 145
Madison, James 2, 3, 17, 18, 19, 27, 28,
    40, 64–5, 67, 93, 99, 154, 218;
    see also Federalist Papers
magazine readership 129
magistrate judges 295
Mansbridge, Jane 114
Mapp v. Ohio (1961) 78
Marbury v. Madison (1803) 46, 286, 291,
    292–3, 311
March for Women's Lives (1992) 114
marijuana 36–7
Marshall, John 46–8, 67–8, 99, 286–7,
    291–2, 308, 311
Marshall, Thurgood 29–30, 103, 104
Martin, Trayvon 110
Mason, George 2, 17
Massachusetts Body of Liberties
    (1641) 66
Mattis, James 277

Mayflower Compact 38
Mayhew, David 225
Meany, George 159
media 129–31; agenda-setting effect
    133; bias in 132–3; educational
    effect 133; fake news 133; framing
    effect 133, 134; news sources
    129–30, 131–5; persuasion effect
    133; political agenda and influence
    of 131–5; political coverage 205;
    and political socialization 129–35
Medicaid 56, 57
Meese, Edwin 276
mental incapacity and the death
    penalty 84
Mexican-American Legal Defense and
    Education Fund (MALDEF) 166
Meyers, Seth 219
Michigan Cases (2003) 108
Michigan v. Jackson (1986) 81, 82
micro targeting 196
Mikulski, Barbara 224
Miller, Samuel F. 101
Miller v. California (1973) 72
Miller v. Texas (1894) 65
minor parties 177–8, 180; obstacles to
    success 178–9
Miranda v. Arizona (1966) 81
Missouri System 309–10
monarchy 3, 4, 5
Mondale, Walter 279
Monroe, James 99
Montejo v. Louisiana (2009) 81–2
Montesquieu, Baron de (Charles
    Secondat) 4, 5
Morse v. Frederick (2007) 71
Motor Voter 187
Mott, Lucretia 112
Muir, David 131

Nader, Ralph 160, 163, 198
National Abortion Rights Action League
    (NARAL) 113, 114
National American Woman Suffrage
    Association (NAWSA) 112
National Association for the
    Advancement of Colored People
    (NAACP) 29, 84, 103, 160–1,
    162, 166
National Association of Manufacturers
    (NAM) 158
National Association of Realtors 159
National Education Association
    (NEA) 159
National Election Study 138
national federalism 46–8, 50
National Institutes of Health (NIH) 274
National Organization for Women
    (NOW) 113, 114, 161, 162, 166
national party conventions 201–2
National Popular Vote Plan (NPV) 186

National Public Radio (NPR) 130
National Rifle Association (NRA) 161, 162, 163
national security 73–4, 82–3
National Security Agency (NSA) 83
National Security Council (NSC) 264, 278
National Socialist Party v. Skokie (1977) 154
National Transportation Safety Board (NTSB) 273, 274
National Voter Registration Act (1993) 187
National Woman Suffrage Association (NWSA) 112
National Women's Political Caucus 114
Native American Rights Fund (NARF) 160–1
Native Americans 223
Near v. Minnesota (1931) 72–3
"necessary and proper" clause 23, 41, 48
Neustadt, Richard E. 270
New Deal 52, 53
New England 6
New England Anti-Slavery Society (1832) 99
New Federalism 54
New Jersey Plan 19–20, 40
New York Charter of Liberties (1683) 66
New York Manumission Society (1785) 99
New York Times 73, 74, 117
New York Times Co. v. Sullivan (1964) 73
news, sources of 129–30, 131–5
newspaper readership and circulation 129, 131
Nichols, John 132
Nix v. Williams (1984) 79
Nixon, Richard M. 54, 170, 175, 186, 258, 263, 276, 304
"No Child Left Behind" Act (2001) 77
no prior restraint *vs.* freedom to publish 72–4
North American Free Trade Agreement (NAFTA) 58, 265
North Korea 261
nuclear arms 264
nullification 36–7, 50

Obama, Barack 56; 2008 nomination 198, 208, 210; 2012 election 138; approval ratings 267; cabinet 276–7, 279; on campaign funding 208, 210, 211; and civil rights 96; on freedom of religion 78; and Guantanamo detainees 264; health care reform 266; judicial appointees 300, 301, 306, 312; national security policy 73, 83; presidential style 253–4; rebuke

to Supreme Court 308–9; signing statements 269; staffing 277; support in Congress 175, 176, 177, 195
Obamacare *see* Affordable Care Act (ACA; 2010)
Obergefell v. Hodges (2015) 97, 306
obscenity 71–2
occupational groups 158
Occupy Wall Street (OWS) 153, 154
O'Connor, Sandra Day 71, 108–9, 210, 305
Office of Management and Budget (OMB) 243, 274, 275, 278
Office of Personnel Management (OPM) 274
Olson, Floyd B. 72–3
Olson, Mancur 157
O'Malley, Martin 198
Open Secrets 162
opinion leaders 140, 146
opinion polls 136–7
oral argument 298

Paine, Thomas 12
Panetta, Leon 276
pardon power 255
Partial Birth Abortion Act (2003) 115
partisan politics 168–9
party identification 169–72, 191
party leaders 228
Pataki, George 198, 200
Patriot Act (2001–present) 82–3
Paul, Alice 112
Paul, Rand 198, 201
Paul, Ron 198
Paul v. Virginia (1869) 44
peak associations 158–60
Pelosi, Nancy 230
Pence, Mike 203, 279
Penn, William 6, 8
Pennsylvania 6, 7
Pennsylvania Charter of Privileges (1701) 66
Pennsylvania Society for the Abolition of Slavery (1784) 99
Pentagon Papers Case (1971) 73
Perot, Ross 198, 206
Perry, Rick 198, 200–1
Pew Hispanic Center 139
Pew Research Center 129, 143
pharmaceutical lobby 157, 162, 163
Philadelphia 7
Pilgrims 6, 7, 38
Planned Parenthood of Southeastern Pennsylvania v. Casey (1992) 114, 116
Plessy v. Ferguson (1896) 102, 103
pluralism 156
"police power" 42
political action committees (PACs) 206

political campaigns 193; incumbency advantage 193–4; organization 196–7; *see also* campaign funding; candidates; presidential election campaigns
political culture 124, 125–6
political ideology 143; and public opinion 143–6; types in U.S. 145–6
political information 124–5, 140–1
political parties 154–5, 168; characteristics of 167–8, 191–2; in the electorate 168–72; in government 168, 174–7; interest groups' relation with 179–80; key roles 167; minor parties 177–9, 180; in opposition 176–7; organization of 168, 172, 174; party identification 169–72, 191; party leader role of president 267; party unity 176–7; role in Congress 227–30
political reform 146
political socialization 125, 126, 135; agents of 126–31; media influence 131–5; variations in 137–40
politicos 227
politics: in colonial America 8–10; roots of American politics 4–8
popular sovereignty 48–9, 220
populism 156
populists 145–6
Powell, Colin 276
Powell, Jerome 274
Powell, Lewis 107
power to propose 255
prayer in schools 77–8
precedent 289
preemption 54
presidency 253–4, 257; 1800–1900 258; 1901–present 258–60; approval ratings 266, 267; Constitutional bases of authority 254–7; control over bureaucracy 241, 274–5; domestic policy 265–70; foreign policy 256–7, 261–5; growth of power 258–60; influence over judiciary 307–8; party leader role of 267; powers of 23, 254–7; reform 279–80; responsibilities 261–70; stewardship theory of 259; war-making 263, 280
presidential election campaigns 197–8; 1992 205; 2000 186, 188, 198, 206–7, 296; 2012 138; 2016 125, 133, 138, 171, 186, 188, 192, 194, 207, 209; election reform 209–12; fundraising 198–9, 206–9, 210–11; nomination campaign 199–202; organization of 204–6
presidential establishment 275–9

presidential oath 23, 255
presidential selection compromise 21–2, 23, 185
president's program 175
press, freedom of the 68–9, 72–4
Presser v. Illinois (1886) 65
Price, Roy 118
primaries 199, 200
Printz v. U.S. (1997) 36, 57
prisons 85–7
privileges and immunities clause 24, 43–4
probability sampling 136
professional associations 160
property rights 111, 112
Protect Act (2003) 72
Prothro, James M. 141
Public Citizen groups 160
public interest groups 160
public opinion 125, 135–6; opinion polling 136–7; and political ideology 143–6; properties of 140–3; variations in 137–40
Puritans 6, 7
push polls 137

Quakers 6, 7

race: discrimination 50, 73, 102, 305; and income 109–10; and political socialization 138–9; and voter turnout 190–1
radio 129–30, 131
railroads 102
Randolph, Edmund 17, 18, 19, 255
ready response teams 205
Reagan, Ronald: approval ratings 135, 170, 267; character 192; civil rights 114; federal bureaucracy reform 55, 275; judicial appointees 107, 300, 301, 304; staffing 276; support in Congress 175
reapportionment 218
reciprocity norm 232
reconciliation 243
redistricting 218–19
Regents of the University of California v. Bakke (1978) 106–7, 304
Regina v. Hicklin (1868) 72
regulatory commissions 273–4
Rehnquist, William 107, 210, 304–5
Reid, Harry 239, 302
religion, freedom of 74–8, 307
Religious Freedom Restoration Act (1993) 76–7
remand by a court 299
Reorganization Act (1939) 259
representation, compromise on 20–1
reprieves 255
republican government 2–3, 24
Republican National Committee 174, 199, 208

Republican Party 155–6; Contract With America 134; election campaigns 206; national conventions 201, 202; party identification 168, 169–71, 172; and race 173
reserved powers 36, 37, 42, 48, 50, 56
reverse discrimination 106–7, 109
Reynolds v. U.S. (1878) 76
Rhode Island 7, 18, 46
Ricci v. De Stefano (2009) 107–8
right to assemble 153–4
right to counsel 80–1
Right to Life movement 161
right to petition 153
Rise and Resist 165
Roane, Spencer 292
Roberts, Jane Sullivan 288
Roberts, John G. 56, 71, 79–80, 109, 210, 211, 288, 298, 301, 302, 305–6, 309
Roe v. Wade (1973) 94, 114, 304
Rome 3
Romney, Mitt 198, 208
Roosevelt, Franklin D.: approval ratings 258, 259, 267; and Great Depression 36, 51, 52, 53, 135, 259–60; judicial appointees 300; staffing 276
Roosevelt, Theodore 51, 53, 259
Roper v. Simmons (2005) 84
Rosenberg, Gerald 105
Roth v. U.S. (1957) 72
Rove, Karl 276
Rubio, Marco 56–7, 198, 201, 209
Rules Committee 237
Rumsfeld, Donald 276
Ryan, Paul 222, 228, 230, 246

Salisbury, Robert 157
Sanchez, G. 137
sanctuary cities 57, 208
Sanders, Bernie: 2016 nomination 171, 190, 198, 200, 201; 2016 presidential campaign 30, 97, 138; partisanship 179
Santorum, Rick 198, 201
Scalia, Antonin 56–7, 64, 79, 82, 93, 301, 305, 306
Schafly, Phyllis 114
Schattschneider, E.E. 167
Schenck v. U.S. (1919) 69
schools: affirmative action 108–11, 307; political socialization in 127–8; reform 146; segregation 102, 103–4, 105, 305
Schumer, Chuck 230, 231
Scott, Rick 56
searches and seizures 78–80
secession 39, 41, 46, 50
segregation 102, 103–4, 105, 305
Seib, Gerald 239

select committees 233
self-incrimination 81–4
Senate: filibustering 177, 238–9, 302; floor debate and amendment 238–9; majority leader 229, 230; member characteristics 222–4; membership 221; minority leader 229–30; party unity in 176–7; powers and responsibilites of 220–1; *president pro tempore* 229; qualifications for service 221; reelection to 193–4; unanimous consent 229; undemocratic nature of 30; vice president duties in 229, 278; *see also* Congress
senatorial courtesy 301
Seneca Falls Convention (1848) 111–12
seniority norm 232
separate but equal 100, 103
separation of church and state 74–5, 77, 307
separation of powers 5, 22, 253, 270, 274, 292
Sessions, Jeff 36, 221
settlement house movement 112
sexual harassment 117–18
sexual privacy 93–4
Shays's Rebellion 16, 17, 24, 95
Shelby County v. Holder (2013) 306
Sherman, Roger 13, 22
Shultz, Howard 197
signing statements 268–9
Silverstein, Mark 302
Simon, Herbert 270
Sinclair, Barbara 235–6
Skowronek, Stephen 253
Slaughterhouse Cases (1873) 101
slavery 48–9; and abolitionism 98–9; emancipation 100; property 48–9; slave trade compromise 21
Smith, Adam 5
Snowden, Edward 83
social contract theory 5, 13
social media 127, 130–1, 205
social movements 95–8
Sojourners 242
Sotomayor, Sonia 298, 300
Souter, David 75, 210–11
Southern Christian Leadership Conference 160–1
sovereignty 39
special courts 295
special revenue sharing (SRS) 54
specialization norm 231–2
speech, freedom of 68–72, 154, 210–11
Stamp Act (1765) 10
Stamp Act Congress 10
standing committees 232, 245, 301
Stanton, Elizabeth Cady 112
stare decisis 289
state constitutions 14–15

State of the Union address 23, 241
states: federal obligations to 42; judicial review of legislation 293; powers denied to 42; powers reserved to 36, 37, 42, 48, 50, 56; relations among 43–4; rights 45–6, 49, 50, 57
Stein, Jill 179
Stevens, John Paul 210, 252–3, 264, 288
Stewart, Malcolm 211
Stimson, James 144
Stone, Lucy 112
STOP ERA 114
Strauder v. West Virginia (1880) 112
students: free speech rights 71
suffrage *see* vote, right to
Sugar Act (1764) 10
supremacy clause 24, 40, 54, 291, 293
Supreme Court 23, 46–7, 56; appellate jurisdiction 24, 296; as arbiter of Constitution 70; as creation of 290–1; and government regulation of economy 52–3; individual rights and 303–7; modern judicial conservatism 304–7; opinions of 64, 65, 67–8, 298–9; original jurisdiction 296; powers of 294, 295–9; rebuked by Obama 308–9
Survey Research Center (SRC) 169
Sweatt v. Painter (1950) 103
symbolic speech 70

"take care" constitutional clause 23, 256
Taney, Roger B. 48, 49, 99–100
Tauzin, Billy 163
taxes 53; in colonial America 9–10; income tax 51; in revolutionary period 17
Tea Party movement 172, 179
Tedin, Kent 128
television: cable and satellite 130, 202; news on 129, 130, 131
terrorism 139
Texas v. Johnson (1989) 70
Thomas, Clarence 108, 298
Thurmond, Strom 224
Tichenor, Dan 157
Tillerson, Rex 277
Tinker v. Des Moines School District (1969) 71
trade: constitutional powers over 44; NAFTA 58, 265; president as chief negotiator of 264–5
trade associations 159
Trans-Pacific Partnership (TPP) 265
treaty-making power of president 256, 262, 265
Trinity Lutheran Church v. Comer (2017) 307
Truman, David B. 156, 157
Truman, Harry S. 258, 260, 275, 276

Trumka, Richard 155, 159
Trump, Donald: 2016 nomination 171, 172, 192, 198, 199, 201, 202; 2016 presidential campaign 30, 116, 125, 140, 186, 188, 193, 197, 203, 209; approval ratings 267; cabinet 277, 279; on climate change 58; conflicts of interest 164; devolution 56–7; domestic policy 266; on education 57; executive role 269, 270; fake news 133; foreign policy 261; on freedom of speech 71; health care program 165, 280; immigration policy 75, 253, 280, 286; impeachment 257; judicial appointees 300, 301, 311–12; on libel laws 69, 73; opinion polls 137; populism 156; presidential style 254, 264; rebuke to Supreme Court 309; and the Republican Party 168; staffing 277–8; support in Congress 175, 195, 246; on trade 265; Twitter 130, 131, 267
Trump, Ivanka 164, 277
Trump, Melania 202
trustees 227
Truth, Sojourner 112
Tsarnaev, Dzhokhar 84
Twain, Mark 219

unitary executive theory 252–3
unitary government 39
United Nations Security Council 262
United States Government Manual 2017-2018 274
United Steelworkers of America v. Weber (1979) 107
unprotected speech 71–2
Urban League 160–1
urbanization 49, 51
U.S. Constitution 3–4, 22; Article I 22–3, 40–1, 53, 56, 218, 220, 241, 256, 257, 263, 295, B1–B4; Article II 23, 39–40, 42, 46, 185–6, 252–3, 254–5, 256–7, 263, B4–B5; Article III 23–4, 286–7, 290–1, 294, 296, B5–B6; Article IV 2, 24, 42, 43–4, B6; Article V 24–5, 42, B6; Article VI 24, 36, 40, 50, 54, B6–B7; Article VII 26, B7; and Congress 220–1; federalism in 24, 40–6; overview of 22–5; Preamble 2, 22; ratification 25–9; reform 29–30; text of B1–B7; *see also* constitutional amendments
U.S. v. Anthony (1873) 112
U.S. v. Cruikshank (1875) 65
U.S. v. E.C. Knight (1895) 51
U.S. v. Lopez (1995) 55
U.S. v. Miller (1939) 65

U.S. v. Morrison (2000) 55
U.S. v. Windsor (2013) 96–7, 306

veto power 256, 268
Vice President 23, 278–9; role in Senate 229, 278
Vietnam War 73, 170, 260, 262, 280
Vinson, Fred M. 103
Violence Against Women Act (1994) 55
Virginia 6, 7, 16, 67
Virginia Plan 19, 20, 40
Virginia v. Black (2003) 71
vote, right to 2, 186–7; black men 101, 104, 105–6; in colonial America 9; compromise on 21; in revolutionary period 14, 15, 16–17; women 112
voter registration 187–8
voter turnout 186, 187; characteristics influencing 188–93; ways to increase 187–8
voters' decision-making 188–93, 194
Voting Rights Act (1965) 105, 173, 306

Walker, David 49
Walker, Jack 157
Walker, Scott 160, 198, 200–1
Wallis, Jim 242
war-making, presidency and 263, 280
War on Terror 252
War Powers Resolution (1973) 262, 263, 280
Warren, Earl 103, 303–4
Washington, George 12, 15, 17, 18, 19, 255, 290
Washington Post 73, 74
Watergate scandal 170
Webster v. Reproductive Health Services (1989) 304
Wechsler, Henry 73
Weeks v. U.S. (1914) 78–9
Weinstein, Harvey 117
Whig Party 179
whips 228, 229
White House Staff 276–8
Whitney v. California (1927) 69–70
Wickard v. Filburn (1942) 53, 55
Wildavsky, Aaron 261
Wilderness Society 160
Willard, Frances 112
Williams, Roger 7
Wilson, Graham 156
Wilson, James 28
Wilson, Woodrow 45, 51, 112, 259
Winthrop, John 6, 7
Wisdom, John Minor 311
women: in colonial America 8, 14, 29; in Congress 223, 224; coverture 111; discrimination against 50, 141; in education 116; equal rights and personal control 113–16; in